Introduction to Electronic Control Engineering

Introduction to Electronic Control Engineering

Friedrich Fröhr Fritz Orttenburger

PUBLISHING FOR ONE WORLD

NEW AGE INTERNATIONAL (P) LIMITED, PUBLISHERS

New Delhi • Bangalore • Chennai • Cochin • Guwahati • Hyderabad
Jalandhar • Kolkata • Lucknow • Mumbai • Ranchi
Visit us at www.newagepublishers.com

Published by New Age International (P) Ltd., Publishers

First Edition: 1982

Reprint: 2010

Branches:

- No. 37/10, 8th Cross (Near Hanuman Temple), Azad Nagar, Chamrajpet, **Bangalore**-560 018 Tel.: (080) 26756823, Telefax: 26756820, E-mail: bangalore@newagepublishers.com
- 26, Damodaran Street, T. Nagar, **Chennai**-600 017. Tel.: (044) 24353401, Telefax: 24351463 E-mail: chennai@newagepublishers.com
- CC-39/1016, Carrier Station Road, Ernakulam South, **Cochin**-682 016. Tel.: (0484) 2377004 Telefax: 4051303. E-mail: cochin@newagepublishers.com
- Hemsen Complex, Mohd. Shah Road, Paltan Bazar, Near Starline Hotel, **Guwahati**-781 008 Tel.: (0361) 2513881. Telefax: 2543669, E-mail: guwahati@newagepublishers.com
- No. 105, 1st Floor, Madhiray Kaveri Tower, 3-2-19, Azam Jahi Road, Nimboliadda **Hyderabad**-500 027. Tel.: (040) 24652456, Telefax: 24652457 E-mail:hyderabad@newagepublishers.com
- RDB Chambers (Formerly Lotus Cinema)106A, 1st Floor, S.N. Banerjee Road **Kolkata**-700 014. Tel.: (033) 22273773, Telefax: 22275247 E-mail:kolkata@newagepublishers.com
- 16-A, Jopling Road, **Lucknow**-226 001. Tel.: (0522) 2209578, 4045297, Telefax: 2204098 E-mail: lucknow@newagepublishers.com
- 142C, Victor House, Ground Floor, N.M. Joshi Marg, Lower Parel, **Mumbai**-400 013 Tel.: (022) 24927869. Telefax: 24915415, E-mail: mumbai@newagepublishers.com
- 22, Golden House, Daryaganj, **New Delhi**-110 002. Tel.: (011) 23262370, 23262368 Telefax: 43551305. E-mail: sales@newagepublishers.com

---

ISBN : 978-81-224-2595-6

Rs. 200.00

C-10-02-4305

Printed in India at Ajit Printers, Delhi.

PUBLISHING FOR ONE WORLD
NEW AGE INTERNATIONAL (P) LIMITED, PUBLISHERS
4835/24, Ansari Road, Daryaganj, New Delhi-110002
Visit us at **www.newagepublishers.com**

Preface

Electronic control is used in almost all applications in the field of automation, whether it is in the largest power station installations, in heavy industry, or in miniature drives with currents of only a few milliamperes.

Concepts and processes in control circuits are explained to the reader as well as the various effects of analogue control equipment which is continuous or quasi continuous in operation. The relationships which exist and the control methods used are clearly indicated. The descriptions are concerned with practical applications, drive control being preferred for the examples.

The advancing development of integrated linear amplifiers, so-called operational amplifiers, is taken into account in this edition. As a result of this, circuits are developed using several amplifiers in one controller, a facility which was not formerly possible owing to economic considerations. These circuits, utilizing the most modern techniques, with inverting, non-inverting and differential amplifiers, and the consequent electronic assemblies are discussed in detail.

Only a little mathematical knowledge is necessary although the reader should be able to deal with simple differentiation and integration. To a large extent, complex number notation is used. The representation of system elements by means of transfer functions and calculation with the simpler algebraic form simplifies the treatment. Mathematical rigour which should be reserved for the specialist, was consciously avoided.

Consideration of stability conditions is superfluous owing to the optimum regulation of control circuits in conformity with the modulus optimum and symmetrical optimum conditions. Moreover, for these mathematically based optimization techniques, no diagrammatic aids are necessary. The relationships obtained mathematically between plant behaviour and the necessary controller are summarized in clearly arranged tables.

A large number of figures, curves, tables and diagrams, as well as a summary of the necessary functions and formulae in use in the field, will be a valuable aid to the reader.

September 1981

SIEMENS AKTIENGESELLSCHAFT

Contents

1. Basic Principles of Control Engineering

Control engineering is still a relatively new science, taken from the time when it was recognized that it was possible to produce a common theory for the solution of physical problems of widely differing kinds. This theory is characterized by the feedback principle and independent of the nature of the individual system, the theory follows the same principles.

Control engineering is the basis of automation which is finding more and more application. A knowledge of control engineering is therefore of considerable importance for anyone involved with automatic control systems.

The terms and symbols used in this book are based mainly on the German Industrial Standard, DIN 19226, May 1968. Draft standards DIN 19229, October 1975, and DIN 19232, November 1975, and the VDI/VDE Guidelines 2185 were also consulted.[1]) The examples are restricted to electronic control systems using transistor amplifiers. Only control system behaviour as seen in propulsion, drive systems and power engineering is dealt with. That is, only continuously and quasi-continuously operating control systems, in which the controller is continuously in operation except when it reaches the control limit. Therefore, we are concerned with control processes which are represented by a continuous function in the time and frequency domains. Hence all the elements of a system are assumed to be linear and non-interactive.

No description is given of control systems with very large idle periods, with sampled data control or with two or three operating states, i.e. those chiefly encountered in process control engineering.

1.1. Terms and Symbols

Several terms and symbols unique to control engineering need explanation. This will follow from a simple example taken from mechanical engineering.

1.1.1. Open loop control

A continuously energized d.c. motor drives the shaft of a machine tool which must be run at a specified rotational speed. This speed is the physical variable

[1]) Some variation in these standards has been made in the present English language edition.

which must be determined by the machine operator. To obtain it, he must set the voltage on the armature of the motor to a specific value using a suitable d.c. regulator, so that with an easily worked material, a speed of, for example, 600 rev/min is obtained. This is the optimum speed for the operation. It should therefore be held constant throughout the operation and should be reset to the same value for each subsequent similar operation.

In the arrangement described there is only one method of controlling the speed of the machine (Fig. 1.1). The operator sets the desired value of the speed (the command variable) by means of the control (1) of the set value controller (2). As a result the control voltage produced by the controller controls the drive unit (3), which in turn controls the mains powered static converter (4). This controls the direct voltage V_A to the armature of the d.c. motor (5) which in turn drives the spindle of the machine tool (6) at the required speed of 600 rev/min.

This arrangement can be represented by a block diagram in which each element acts upon the next. It starts with the speed requirement which is represented by the control voltage, produced by the controller (2). This requirement is transferred along the chain of system elements. The whole chain of system elements is called an open loop control system. It begins with the speed requirement or command variable and ends with the physical quantity controlled (the speed). This is called the task or output value. The output is set in accordance with the command variable or input. In Fig. 1.1 this is achieved by means of the drive unit and static converter. These together comprise the control element. The whole system is called a control system.

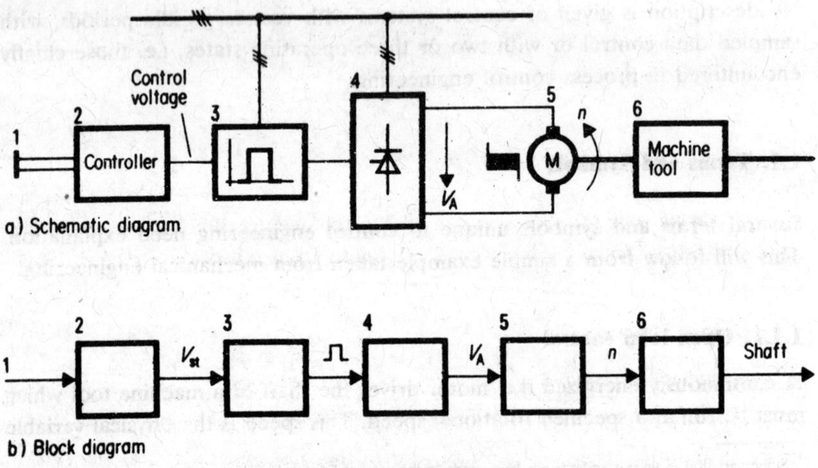

Fig. 1.1 Open loop control system (variable speed drive)

If the easily worked material is replaced by one which is less easily worked, there will be a substantially heavier load on the drive motor. This will cause the machine to run at a lower speed, i.e. the speed departs from the former setting of 600 rev/min. If the variation of load on the machine is sufficiently small that the output speed does not vary more than the tolerance acceptable in the production technique employed, the use of an open loop control system is acceptable.

The term open loop control can be defined, in accordance with DIN 19226, as follows:

An open loop control system acts upon a defined system with external stimuli, the input or command variable, in such a way that the required value of the output variable is to be expected in accordance with prescribed physical laws. The output variable does not influence the input variable. Hence, external factors can cause the output value to deviate considerably from the desired value.

1.1.2. Closed loop control

From consideration of the d.c. drive example above, it was observed that the output value in an open loop system can only follow the input or required value in a very limited manner, as external factors can influence the value of the output quantity. A constant load of any value on the machine of Fig. 1.1 can be taken account of by an appropriate setting of the input controller. However, if external factors cause arbitrary changes of load on the machine, it is desirable to monitor the value of the output variable and during deviations from the required value, and to override the open loop system in order to compensate for this. Therefore, feedback from the output to the input is necessary. This produces what is called a closed loop control system. This is required when arbitrary changes in external factors affecting the output are likely to occur.

Closed loop control requires elements in addition to those of the open loop system already described. The output quantity which is to be kept constant and dependent on the required or input variable, is the controlled variable. In the example of Fig. 1.1 it is the rotational speed, which is measured by means of a tachogenerator.

In many cases, the output variable is not easily accessible. For example, suppose the output variable is the magnetic flux in the air gap of a d.c. machine. It is not possible to accommodate a Hall probe in the air gap to measure the flux. The excitation current in this case must serve as the output variable. It is, of course, a function of the flux and can be measured easily. We see therefore that the output variable and the controlled variable are not always identical, but they must be directly related.

If a direct current is to be measured, as in the latter example, a measurement resistor is necessary, and since the voltage across the resistor will be small, also an amplifier. The resistor is the measurement sensor and the associated highly accurate linear voltage amplifier is the measurement amplifier. The sensor and amplifier together form the measurement converter or transducer, which is able to measure the controlled variable and convert it to a form which can be used in the controller.

The measurement transducer may consist of several components. The tachogenerator in Fig. 1.1 consists of only one component which can convert the rotational speed into a voltage.

The measurement transducer performs the first function of the control equipment. It measures the controlled variable and converts it into a signal which is compatible with the other components of the control system. In the control systems which are being considered here it does this continuously.

The signal representing the physical quantity in drive or power engineering is usually a direct voltage, typically in the range from −10 V to +10 V. In this case, 10 V would be the maximum voltage for the signal and the sign indicates the direction. For example, a torque may be clockwise or anti-clockwise. The value of 10 V would correspond to 100% of the nominal value of the physical quantity. It is sometimes called the unit value.

In some cases, mainly in process control engineering, a direct current, typically in the range 0 to 20 mA is used to represent the physical quantity.

The command or input variable must be compared with the controlled or output variable in order to establish the difference between the actual value of the controlled variable and the required value. Thus the value of the controlled variable obtained from the measurement transducer must be subtracted from the input value set by the controller. A comparison circuit or comparator is necessary, at the output of which appears the error signal.

If the input and output variables are each represented by a voltage, then these voltages must be connected to the comparator circuit in such a manner as to obtain the difference between the two signals. Also a similar argument would apply if the two variables were represented by two currents.

It is necessary to distinguish between the transient condition and the steady-state condition of the control system. A transient error signal is one which occurs only during an external disturbance or a change of input setting and which eventually disappears. If the error signal does not disappear, it is termed an offset error signal and this will lie within a specified range of tolerance. This will be expressed as a percentage of the overall control range or as a percentage of the change of input variable.

The comparator performs the second function of the control system. It compares the output variable with the input variable and produces the error signal, which is given by the expression

(error signal) = (input variable) − (output variable)

If the error signal is positive, the control system must increase the output variable.

If the error signal is given by

(error signal) = (output variable) − (input variable)

then if the error signal is negative, the output variable is too low. If a measuring instrument is used to indicate the error signal, then the direction of the error signal can be observed at any time.

If the error signal is large, the change in the output signal of the controller must be large. If the error signal is small, a small change in the controller output will bring the controlled variable back to the required value. If the error signal is very close to zero, then the system is correctly adjusted.

The control system usually does not react instantly to a change in the value of the control signal but has a time delay. This delay in the control system must be minimized by the control equipment so that the controlled variable follows the desired value as rapidly, accurately and as free from oscillation as possible. This makes it necessary for the controller to produce, in addition to an action proportional to the error signal, an action compensating for the time delay in the system. These two actions together act on the output variable of the system.

The optimum adjustment of the controller parameters, i.e. the amplification or gain, and the time constant, is termed optimization. This optimization is necessary for an effective control system. Thus the controller is the central element of the control system.

The function of the control equipment is thus to produce the signals necessary for the optimum control of the process. They are derived from the behaviour of the system by the best possible adjustment of the controller parameters.

The device which can determine the difference between the input and output variables and produce the necessary control signals is termed the controller.

Mechanical, hydraulic, pneumatic or electrical controllers can be used. These terms only designate the kind of information carrier the controller deals with at the input and output. Among electrical controllers are those using semiconductors, which are of course electronic controllers.

The variable speed drive shown in Fig. 1.1 is an open loop system. In order to maintain the required speed despite changes in external factors, the system must be replaced by a closed loop system.

In Fig. 1.2 components are added to the open loop system which produce the required modification. The significant factor is the feedback loop. The rotational speed, measured and converted by the tachogenerator (7) into the output voltage, is fed back to the comparator (8) and then to the input of the controller. In the comparator, which may be classed as part of the controller, the output voltage is compared to the input voltage obtained from the setting device (2), i.e. the required value voltage.

The measurement of the controlled variable can take place continually as in Fig. 1.2 or periodically. It is thus either continuous control or sampled control. Only continuous control will be considered here.

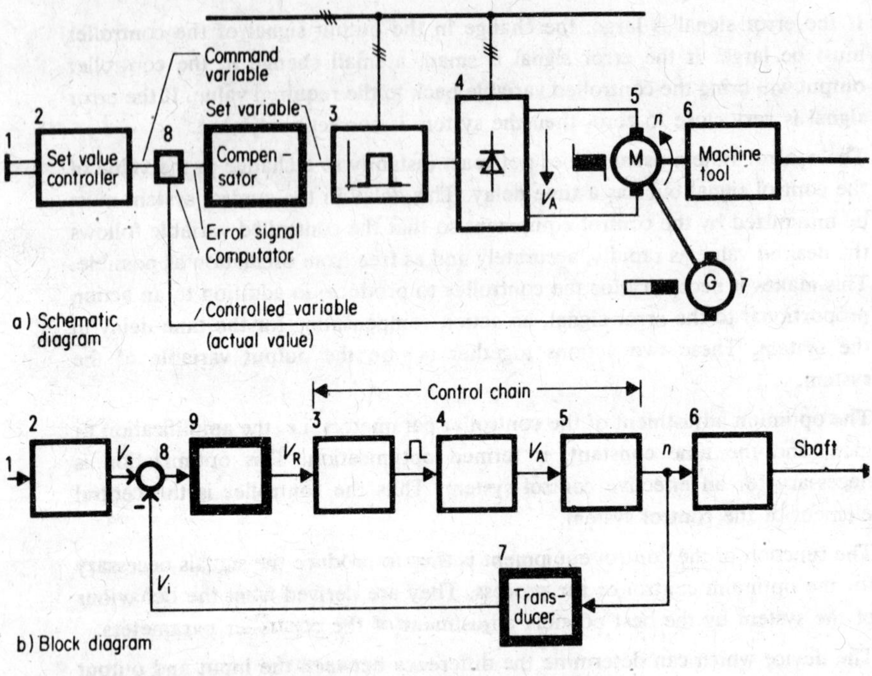

Fig. 1.2 Closed loop control system (speed control system)

The compensator (9) which produces proportional and time response provides the signal to operate the drive unit (3) which controls the static converter (4) which in turn produces the direct voltage V_R which is required for the d.c. drive motor.

Controllers are manufactured with relatively small output signals, such as 10 V or 10 mA maximum, and a single type of controller can be used for various control systems, as the power for controlling the system is produced by the drive unit (4), not by the controller itself. However, the controller controls the power from the static converter (4) to the drive motor.

The above controller can assume any arbitrary voltage value within the range of the controller, say −10 V to +10 V, and can move continuously throughout the range. Such a controller is called a continuous controller.

There are two further kinds of controller, found mainly in process control. One of these can provide only three discrete values at the output. These could signify, for example, motor clockwise, stop, and motor anti-clockwise. This kind of controller may be found where valves, flaps slides etc. are to be actuated. It is termed a three state controller. An even simpler type is the on–off or two state controller, used, for example, in controlling the temperature of ovens. If the controlled variable falls below a specified value, the controller switches on and if it is above another specified value, it switches off. Two state and three state controllers will not be discussed further, but see Fig. 3.42.

From Fig. 1.2, it can be seen that any changes that occur in the control system take place within a loop due to the feedback from the output to the input. This loop is referred to as the control loop.

A useful representation of the control loop is shown in Fig. 1.3. The controlled system and the controller are arranged in a loop. The controlled variable, say x, which is the output variable of the controlled system, is converted by the measurement converter or transducer into the voltage representation of the controlled variable, say x^*, which can be processed in the controller. In order to distinguish between the controller and the controlled system, one could say that everything which is not necessary for the optimum control of the process belongs to the controlled system.

The control system begins where the variable y acts on the power amplifier or drive unit which produces the signal y^*, amplified by the drive unit to the requirements of the installation. It ends with the controlled variable x. For the study of the behaviour of the controller in regard to control engineering, only the inbuilt proportional behaviour and the time behaviour are of significance.

From Fig. 1.3, still more can be seen. The external disturbances $Z1$, $Z2$ etc.

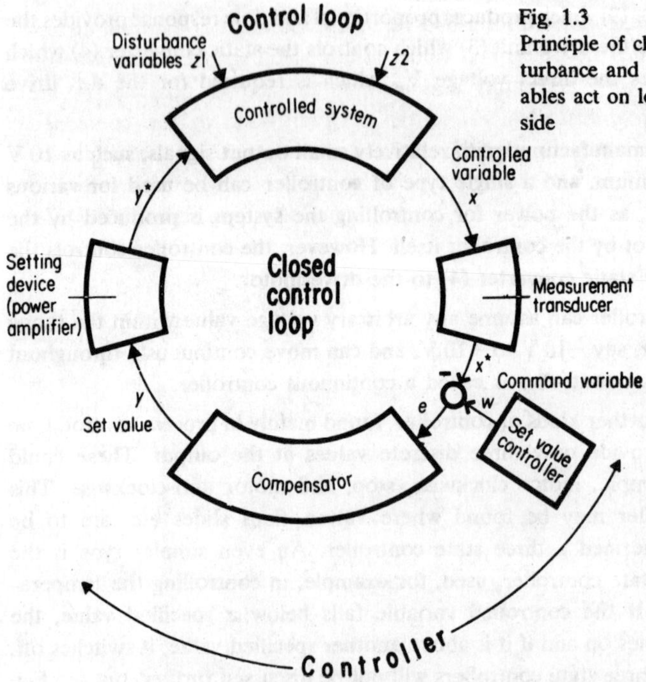

Fig. 1.3
Principle of closed loop. Disturbance and command variables act on loop from outside

act from outside on the closed loop system. Also, the command or input variable *w* which is obtained from the set value control as the required value of the controlled variable, also acts from outside the closed control loop in a similar manner to the disturbances. Therefore all transitional events, whether they are initiated by disturbances or by a change in the input variable, have the same effect. However, as distinct from the disturbances, the input variable acts at the input to the controller, via the comparator or error detector. At this point, the input variable is compared with the output or controlled variable in order to generate the error signal, *e*. Thus the error signals are eliminated from this point in the control loop, that is the controlled variable is made to take up and maintain the desired value as defined by the input variable. On the other hand, disturbances can directly affect the value of the controlled variable but this effect will reach the comparator via the measurement transducer, with a time delay. Then the controller can intervene and correct the controlled variable.

The concept of control can be defined, using the specification DIN 19226 as follows:

By control it is meant that a physical variable is influenced so that it agrees as accurately as possible with a prescribed value, independent of external disturbances. By changing the prescribed value, a new value shall be assumed and maintained as rapidly, accurately and as well damped as possible, in the presence of external disturbances, to the original value of the controlled variable. To achieve this the magnitude of the error signal, i.e. the difference between the prescribed and the actual value, is used to influence the physical variable. This action proceeds in a closed loop in which it has only one direction and is not reversible. The controlled quantity acts in a self-compensating manner via the feedback loop of the control system.

1.2. Analogue and Digital Systems

In the foregoing consideration of controllers, the representation of the physical quantity to be controlled was always a voltage, e.g. in the tachogenerator, for the representation of a rotational speed. This kind of representation is called analogue, because it is similar to the actual quantity (from Greek analogos = similar).

We can therefore make the following definition:

In the analogue representation of a physical quantity, another or the same physical quantity is used as the information carrier in a defined limited range and the value of the representative quantity is proportional to the original quantity over the whole range. Within this range, an infinite number of values can be obtained. There is no limit to the number of discrete values.

However, as in all control equipment, the operation of the controller is not free of error. An essential part of the controller is the control amplifier. Its amplification is not infinitely large and its susceptibility to temperature is not negligible. Also, the output voltage of the control amplifier is not zero when the input voltage is zero, i.e. there is a zero error. Furthermore, not inconsiderable errors arise from the measurement transducers and the input voltage control. These errors are caused by temperature changes and variations of the supply voltage. Thus we see that errors can arise which affect the variables at the controller output and thus the values of the controlled variables. Provided that these errors lie in the region from a few parts per thousand to a few percent, the accuracy of the control system may be sufficient for most purposes. The designer's task is to bring accuracy and constancy to the system as a whole, taking into account the inadequacies of the system components.

If, however, for example, the carriage of a machine tool, with a total track movement of 1m, is to be driven to a given position with an accuracy of one hundredth of a millimetre, such an accuracy (1 in 10^5, referred to the full scale) can only be met with difficulty by analogue techniques because of the large range of values required.

One remedy is to change to a digital system (from the Latin digitus = finger or number). For this purpose it is necessary to represent the physical variable to be controlled by a number. The higher the desired accuracy, the finer must be the resolving power of the measuring transducer. Frequently incremental or digital transducers are used, i.e. transducers which produce a pulse for each unit of the physical quantity to be represented and the sum of the pulses, which is stored in a counter, is the value of the physical quantity. The measurement transducer includes, in this case, a four, five or even six digit counter. Counters of this kind usually store the decimal characters with the aid of a binary coded decimal (BCD) code, which produces four 'bits' (0 or 1 representations) for each decimal symbol. If the numerical values do not have to be displayed, pure binary counters are used.

For digital control, it is therefore necessary to compare the number representing the controlled variable with the required number in an error generator in order to process the error signal (number) in a suitable controller.

It can now be stated that the digital representation of the value of a physical variable is composed of a number, a physical unit and a positive or negative sign. The sign gives the direction and the number the absolute value of the variable. In most cases the physical unit is fixed by the transducer and the kind of application.

Thus digital systems offer the possibility of increased accuracy by virtue of the fineness of the measurement available. However, analogue equipment will still be present in the loop and the controlled system will generally be analogue (e.g. the d.c. drive motor) and thus the designers' task will be all the more complicated because of the mixture of analogue and digital components.

In the subsequent sections, the discussion will be mainly concerned with analogue representation.

1.3. Transient Behaviour

A control system has a transient response. That is to say, if a control system is addressed at its input with a time varying signal, it responds at the output with a signal which bears a defined time relationship with the input signal, but which follows the input signal in a way which differs in form and in time. This output variable from the controlled system is fed back to the input of the controller, which also produces a time delay. Because of the closed loop of a closed loop control system, such an arrangement is fundamentally capable of oscillation. Basically, six different forms of change in the controlled variable can be obtained, induced by a given change in the loop and conditioned by the control process, according to the design of the controlled system and controller.

The first feature to notice (Fig. 1.4) is the oscillatory (periodic) or non-oscillatory (aperiodic) nature of the behaviour. In both cases, stable (a) and unstable (c) behaviour can occur and the limiting condition between the two (b) is the stability limit.

It is obvious that unstable behaviour, whether constantly increasing (IIc) or an increasing oscillation (Ic) are undesirable. The same applies for constant

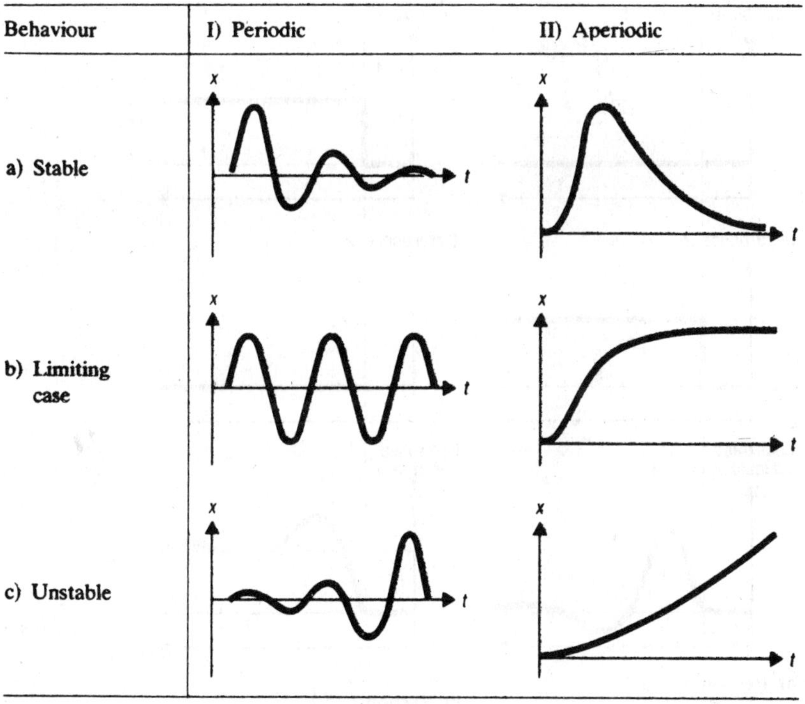

Fig. 1.4
Initial behaviour of controlled variable dependent on characteristics of the closed control loop

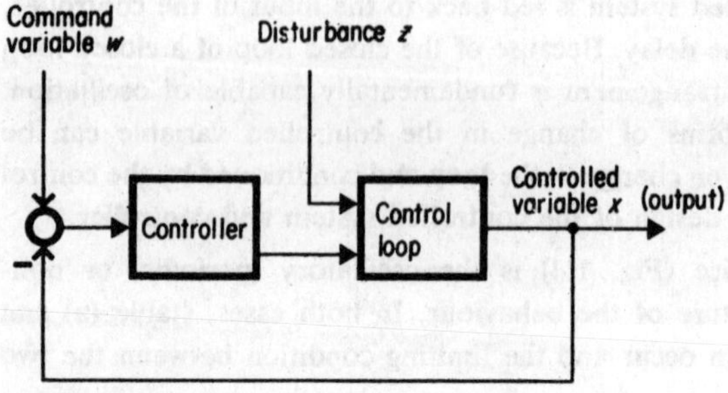

a) Closed control loop

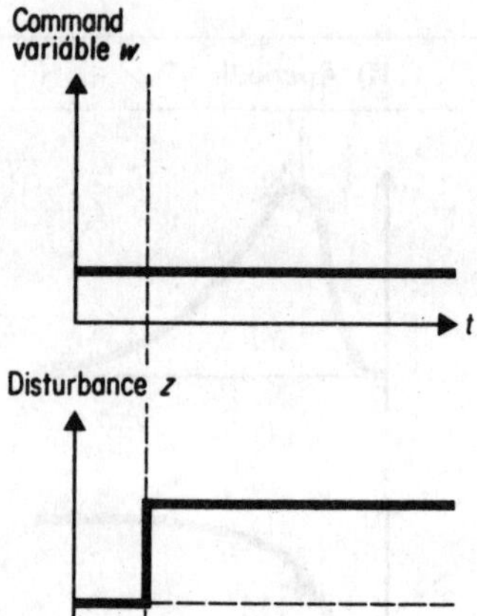

b) Response to a step disturbance

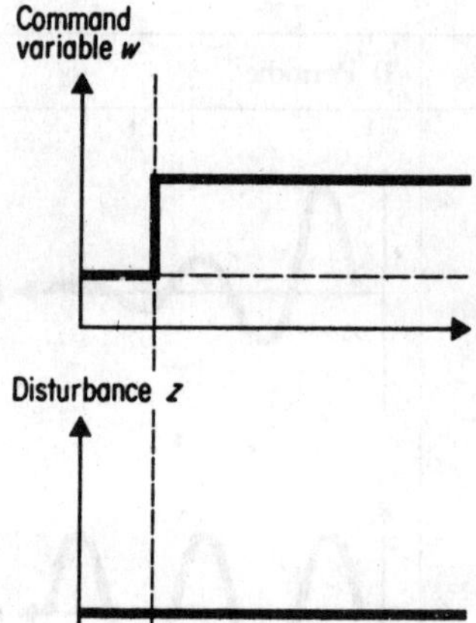

c) Response to a step command variable

Fig. 1.5 Initial behaviour of the controlled variable

oscillation (Ib), the limiting case of periodic behaviour. Stable periodic behaviour (Ia) is of limited use, that is when the number of perceptible oscillations is very small (close to one). The stability limit case for aperiodic behaviour can also be used. In most cases, however, the stable aperiodic condition (IIa) is desired.

If it is desired to compare the behaviour of control loops under different settings of the controller, the action causing the control event must be the same in each case. The most convenient function for this purpose is a step function as this requires only a starting and finishing value for its definition (Fig. 1.5). Since control systems are subject to external disturbances, the reproducible effect should be a step change of disturbance. Figure 1.5(b) shows how a control system tends to respond to such a step disturbance, the input signal being constant. Rarely, however, is it possible to introduce a step form of disturbance into the system. A step function of the input or command variable at the controller, however, can be obtained without difficulty and with consistency. Voltage steps can easily be applied to an electronic controller which uses voltages for the representation of the input and output variables.

The apparatus shown in Fig. 1.6 contains a 12 V battery (1) for a completely ripple free voltage, which is switched on and off by a bounce-free switch (2). A change over switch (3) permits the step polarity to be chosen and a potentiometer (4) sets the step level. The step level is measured at the connectors (6) by a voltmeter (5). If the step is to start from a defined voltage level, a second apparatus of the same kind must be used.

The response of the controlled variable to a step change in the command or input variable is shown in Fig. 1.5(c). In this case there is no external disturbance. From Fig. 1.3 it is possible to deduce the behaviour during an external disturbance from the transitional behaviour of the controlled variable during a step change of input variable. For this reason the optimum controller adjustment can be determined from tests involving input voltage changes.

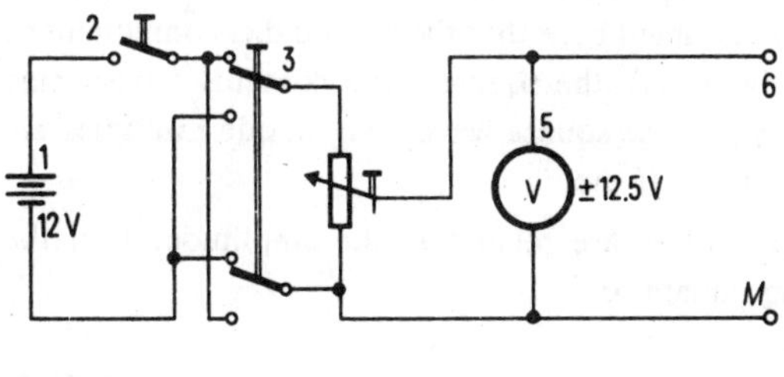

Fig. 1.6
'Battery box' for applying voltage step functions to input of controller

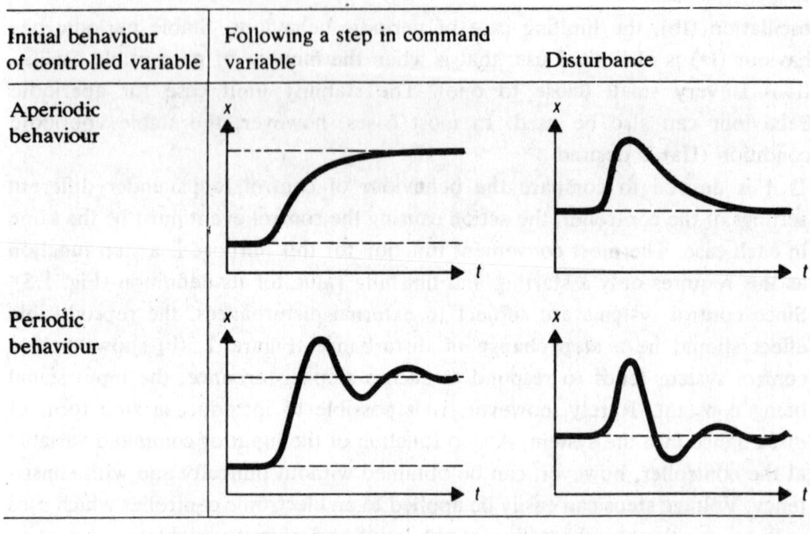

Fig. 1.7 Aperiodic and periodic behaviour

The transient behaviour of the system must always be stable under changes of input signal or disturbances. However, within this constraint, variation of the controller parameters may vary the performance from periodic to aperiodic as shown in Fig. 1.7.

1.4. Step Response and Frequency Response

The behaviour of individual system elements can be described by a step response in the same way as that for the complete control loop. To do this, a step function at the input is necessary. This step function may be regarded as a section of a square wave. A square wave with equal positive and negative values, as in Fig. 1.8(a), can be resolved by means of a Fourier series into a multiplicity of sine waves (it is assumed here that there is no d.c. component or mean value). As shown in Fig. 1.9(a), the square wave contains a basic sine wave with the same frequency f as the square wave, and all odd multiples are contained as harmonics, i.e. $3f$, $5f$, $7f$ etc.

The amplitude A_n of the sine waves are related to the amplitude A of the square wave by the following equation:

$$\frac{A_n}{A} = \frac{4}{n\pi}, \qquad (1.1)$$

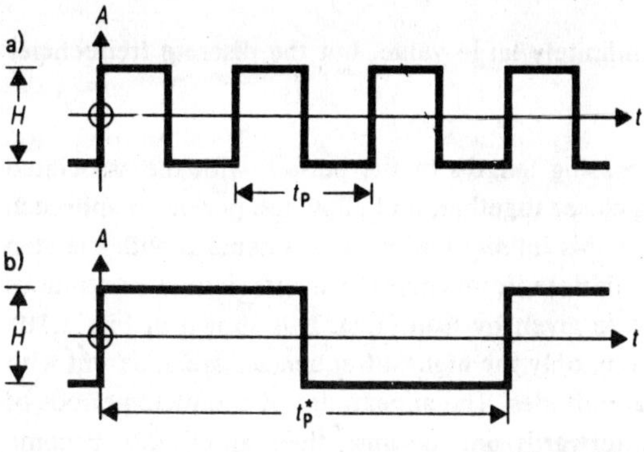

Fig. 1.8
Square waves with amplitude $\pm\frac{1}{2}H$. In a) the frequency is 3 times that in b)

where n is the number of the harmonic. The amplitude decreases with frequency in a hyperbolic manner. The frequency spectrum shows an equally spaced series of discrete frequencies. The fundamental frequency f_1 is defined from the period t_p of the square wave as follows:

$$f_1 = \frac{1}{t_p}.$$

Starting from a second square wave whose period t_p^* is three times that of the first, (Fig. 1.8), then all the sine wave frequencies which comprise the second square wave are one third of those of the first (Fig. 1.9(b)). Even in this case,

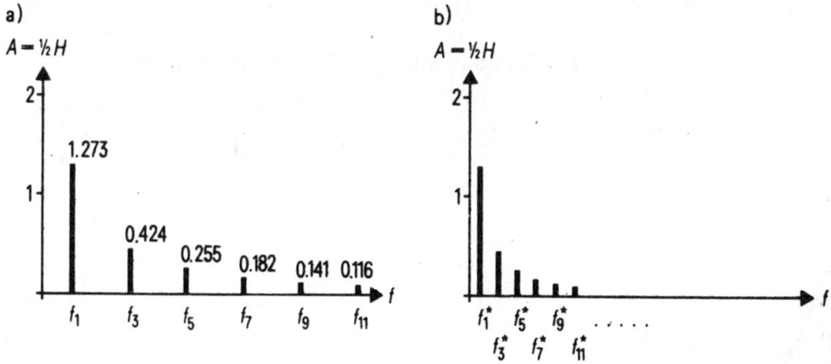

Fig. 1.9
Frequency spectrum of a square wave resolved into individual sine waves according to Fourier's Principle. In a) the fundamental frequency is 3 times as large as in b)

frequencies occur up to an infinitely large value, but the discrete frequencies are crowded closer together.

If we now imagine ever increasing lengths of the period, with the associated discrete sine waves crowding closer together, and allow the period to approach infinity, then the beginning of this infinite period is synonymous with the step function. The spectrum of discrete frequencies converts into a continuous spectrum whose amplitudes are given by Eqn (1.1). It is shown in Fig. 1.10. At the start of the step function, only the highest frequencies are apparent with complete periods and small amplitudes. The appearance of complete periods of lower frequencies follows afterwards and because their amplitudes become greater and greater, they predominate over the effect of the higher frequencies, until finally the zero frequency is reached with the amplitude of the step. Thus, at the moment of the step (time $t = 0$), the highest frequencies arise (frequency $f = \infty$) and at the end, long after the incidence of the step (time $t = \infty$), all frequencies have died away (frequency $f = 0$). At the intermediate times, all frequencies appear. This is termed the frequency band which can be expressed by simple mathematical expressions.

It is therefore meaningful to describe a system element or a complete control loop not just by its behaviour with respect to time in response to a step function, but also by the frequency response in terms of amplitude ratio and phase lag. Thus, with input variable u and output variable v, the following equations can be written.

Behaviour in the time domain when switching a step function:

$$v(t) = u_{step} f(t).$$

Behaviour in the frequency domain with variable input frequency:

$$v(\omega) = u(\omega) F(\omega).$$

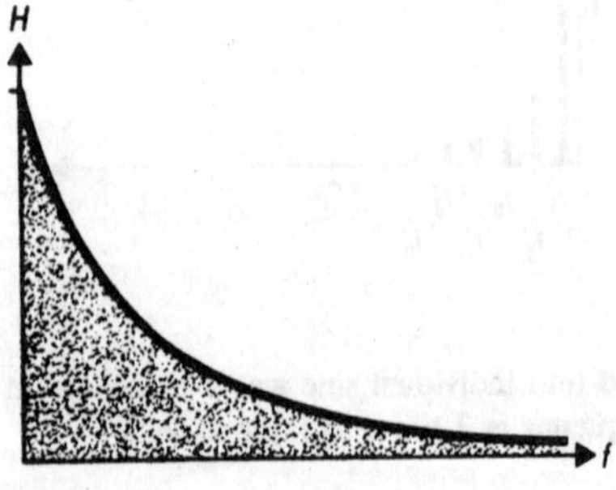

Fig. 1.10
Frequency spectrum of a step function

For two particular conditions, both equations produce identical results for the output variable v:

At the moment of application of the step	$t=0$	$f\to\infty$
In the steady state	$t\to\infty$	$f=0$

For intermediate points, each equation gives its own results. For quick approximate calculations, this information is useful because the frequency response of one system element, or a series of system elements, is usually much easier to define than the time behaviour. Thus, it is possible to determine the time behaviour at the moment of the step and for the steady state from a known frequency response.

2. Behaviour of System Elements Under Dynamic Control

The definition of system elements is necessary for the objective treatment of control systems.

The study of transient behaviour of control systems with direct and alternating currents was originally done with the aid of differential and integral equations in which the primary variable was time. Therefore the time behaviour of control systems will be described, since it is the main interest.

Even simple problems are relatively tedious by this method, which is not very effective in clarity and comprehension. With approximation and recursive formulae, the problems become more manageable, but the accuracy of calculation may then suffer to an unacceptable degree.

The analysis of control systems can be approached in other ways, in which frequency, not time, represents the primary variable. After the frequency equation has been solved, it is transformed back to the time domain, or on the basis of standardized results, the time function may already be known.

The following analysis is not intended to be complete. It is only intended to introduce the most important mathematical relationships and to show in what form the various system elements can be represented. For further study, reference to the mathematical literature is recommended.

2.1. Conversion from the Time Domain to the Frequency Domain

The description of the behaviour of a system element with respect to time is the representation in the time domain.

If a system element is supplied with a sinusoidally varying input, the description of the behaviour with respect to frequency is termed the representation in the frequency domain.

The general expression for the voltage v produced in an inductance carrying a current (see Fig. 2.1) is given as follows:

$$v(t) = L\frac{\mathrm{d}i(t)}{\mathrm{d}t} \tag{2.1}$$

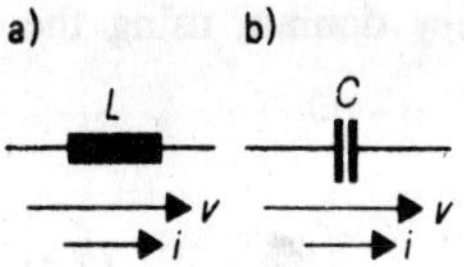

Fig. 2.1
Voltage and current in a) inductance b) capacitance

This can vary with time in any manner. If the current $i(t)$ is a sinusoidally alternating current, say

$$i(t) = \hat{I}e^{j\omega t}$$

then the voltage across the inductance is given by

$$v(t) = j\omega L\hat{I}e^{j\omega t}.$$

which is a sinusoidally alternating voltage.
If the general time representation is now converted from the time domain to the frequency domain with the aid of complex notation,

$$I = \hat{I}e^{j\omega t}.$$

Then

$$V = j\omega LI. \tag{2.2}$$

If Eqns (2.1) and (2.2) are compared, it can be seen that the differential operator d/dt in the time domain corresponds to the term $j\omega$ in the frequency domain.
The same considerations are now applied for a capacitance C (Fig. 2.1). The general time representation is as follows:

$$v(t) = \frac{1}{C}\int_0^t i(t)\,dt. \tag{2.3}$$

If a sinusoidal current is assumed once more, the voltage across the capacitor becomes

$$v(t) = \frac{1}{j\omega C}\hat{I}e^{j\omega t}.$$

The conversion from the time domain to the frequency domain using the complex notation becomes in this case as follows:

$$V = \frac{1}{j\omega C} I. \tag{2.4}$$

Comparison of Eqns (2.3) and (2.4) shows that the integral $\int dt$ in the time domain corresponds to the term $1/j\omega$ in the frequency domain.

Time domain	$\frac{d}{dt}$	$\int_0^t dt$	
Frequency domain	$j\omega$	$\frac{1}{j\omega}$	(2.5)

2.2. First Order Lag System

The relationship between current i and voltage v will be investigated for a series connection of a resistance R and an inductance L (Fig. 2.2). This could be, for example, the exciter winding of a d.c. machine.

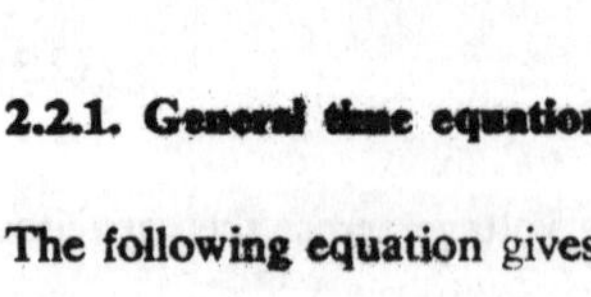

Fig. 2.2
Series connection of resistance R and inductance L

2.2.1. General time equations

The following equation gives the relationship between voltage and current:

$$v(t) = Ri(t) + L\frac{di(t)}{dt}. \tag{2.6}$$

This is a differential equation of the first order. Re-arranging, this becomes

$$\frac{v(t)}{R}=i(t)+\frac{L}{R}\frac{\mathrm{d}i(t)}{\mathrm{d}t}.$$

We can introduce the time constant T given by

$$\frac{L}{R}=T \quad \text{in} \quad \frac{\mathrm{H}}{\Omega}=\frac{\mathrm{VsA}}{\mathrm{AV}}=\mathrm{s}.$$

The time constant of course has the dimensions of time.

The general time equation can now be written as follows:

$$\frac{v(t)}{R}=i(t)+T\frac{\mathrm{d}i(t)}{\mathrm{d}t}. \tag{2.7}$$

2.2.2. Frequency equation

For the series connection of resistance and inductance (Fig. 2.2), let the applied voltage $v(t)$ now be a sinusoidal alternating voltage, whose frequency can take any arbitrary value. Then a sinusoidal current of the same frequency must be obtained, given as follows:

$$i(t)=\hat{I}\mathrm{e}^{\mathrm{j}\omega t}.$$

Putting this current in Eqn (2.7) gives

$$\begin{aligned}\frac{v(t)}{R}&=\hat{I}\mathrm{e}^{\mathrm{j}\omega t}+\mathrm{j}\omega T\hat{I}\mathrm{e}^{\mathrm{j}\omega t}\\&=\hat{I}\mathrm{e}^{\mathrm{j}\omega t}(1+\mathrm{j}\omega T).\end{aligned}$$

In a.c. notation, this becomes

$$V=IR(1+\mathrm{j}\omega T). \tag{2.8}$$

The phase angle between the voltage phasor V and the current phasor I is determined by the tern $(1+\mathrm{j}\omega T)$. The same Eqn (2.8) could have been obtained from the equation

$$V=RI+\mathrm{j}\omega LI.$$

2.2.3. Step response

Consider the differential Eqn (2.7) for the first order lag system and assume that the voltage $v(t)$ makes a step at $t=0$ from zero to V (Fig. 2.3).

$$v(t)=\begin{cases}0 & \text{for} \quad t<0 \\ V & \text{for} \quad t\geqslant 0.\end{cases} \tag{2.9}$$

This step function is the function producing the response of the current which is the output quantity. The solution consists of the particular solution of the differential equation

$$i_{\text{part}} = V/R$$

and the homogeneous solution

$$i_{\text{hom}} = Ke^{-t/T}.$$

Using the initial condition, i.e.

$$\underset{(t=0)}{i} = i_{\text{part}} + i_{\text{hom}} = 0$$

the overall solution is obtained and is given as follows:

$$i(t)=\frac{V}{R}(1-e^{-t/T}). \tag{2.10}$$

A transient variation is observed, which is defined by an exponential function (Fig. 2.4).

$\frac{t}{T}=$	0	1	3	5	∞
$e^{-t/T}=$	1	0.368	0.0498	0.0067	0
$1-e^{-t/T}=$	0	0.632	0.9502	0.9933	1

Fig. 2.3
Voltage step function of magnitude V at time $t=0$

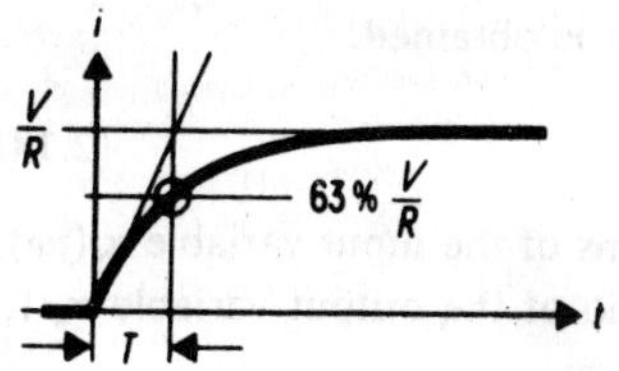

Fig. 2.4

Step response $i(t)=\frac{V}{R}(1-e^{-t/T})$ of first order lag

$$\frac{v(t)}{R}=i(t)+T\frac{di(t)}{dt} \qquad v(t)=\begin{cases}0 & \text{for } t<0\\ V & \text{for } t\geq 0\end{cases}$$

2.2.4. Transient and frequency response

If the circuit of Fig. 2.2 is considered as a system element (Fig. 2.5), in which the applied voltage u is designated as the input variable x_e and the resultant current i as the associated output variable x_a, and in which the factor $1/R$ is termed the proportionality factor, amplification or steady state gain, k_P, the general time equation of the first order lag system can be written as follows:

$$\frac{dx_a(t)}{dt}T+x_a(t)=k_P x_e(t). \tag{2.11}$$

The associated step response is then given by

$$x_a(t)=X_e k_P(1-e^{-t/T}). \tag{2.12}$$

If the output variable is expressed in terms of the input variable, the transient response is then given as follows:

$$f(t)=\frac{x_a(t)}{X_e}=k_P(1-e^{-t/T}). \tag{2.13}$$

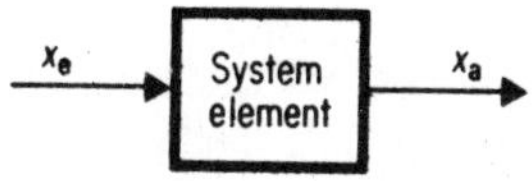

Input variable $x_e=v$
Output variable $x_a=i$
Proportionality factor (steady state gain) $k_P=\frac{1}{R}$

Fig. 2.5 System element with input variable x_e and output variable x_a

From Eqn (2.8) the general frequency equation is obtained:

$$k_P x_e = x_a(1 + j\omega T). \tag{2.14}$$

If the output variable $x_a(j\omega)$ is expressed in terms of the input variable $x_e(j\omega)$, the frequency response is obtained, i.e. the ratio of the output variable x_a to the input variable x_e is defined at each frequency:

$$F(j\omega) = \frac{x_a(j\omega)}{x_e(j\omega)} = \frac{k_P}{1 + j\omega T}. \tag{2.15}$$

It is much simpler to determine the control system behaviour by means of this algebraic frequency response expression than with the equations in the time domain.

2.2.5. Locus curves

By multiplying the numerator and denominator of the frequency response expression by the complex conjugate of the denominator, the real and imaginary parts of the expression can be separated. The real part is

$$\mathrm{Re}\,[F(j\omega)] = k_P \frac{1}{1 + \omega^2 T^2}, \tag{2.16}$$

and the imaginary part is

$$\mathrm{Im}\,[F(j\omega)] = -k_P \frac{\omega T}{1 + \omega^2 T^2}. \tag{2.17}$$

If the amplitude of the sinusoidal input variable $x_e(j\omega)$ is held constant and the frequency ω is varied from zero upwards, the real and imaginary parts of the output variable can be calculated for each frequency and can then be recorded in the complex number plane. The locus curve obtained is called the Nyquist or frequency response diagram.

From the real and imaginary parts, the modulus of the frequency response is given as follows:

$$|F(\omega)| = k_P \sqrt{\left(\frac{1}{1 + \omega^2 T^2}\right)^2 + \left(\frac{\omega T}{1 + \omega^2 T^2}\right)^2}$$

$$= k_P \sqrt{\frac{1}{1 + \omega^2 T^2}}. \tag{2.18}$$

Also, the phase angle is

$$\varphi(\omega) = \arctan \frac{\text{Im}\,[F(j\omega)]}{\text{Re}\,[F(j\omega)]}$$
$$= \arctan(-\omega T) = -\arctan(\omega T). \tag{2.19}$$

Very often, the analysis employs the normalized frequency Ω where

$$T = \frac{1}{\omega_g} \quad \text{and} \quad \omega T = \frac{\omega}{\omega_g} = \Omega.$$

Then

$$F(j\Omega) = k_P\left(\frac{1}{1+\Omega^2} + j\frac{-\Omega}{1+\Omega^2}\right), \tag{2.20}$$

$$|F(\Omega)| = k_P\sqrt{\frac{1}{1+\Omega^2}}, \tag{2.21}$$

$$\varphi(\Omega) = -\arctan \Omega. \tag{2.22}$$

The locus or frequency response curve of the first order lag system in normalized form is shown in Fig. 2.6.

2.2.6. Frequency characteristics

The modulus and phase of a system element can be plotted separately against frequency. Equations (2.18) and (2.21) apply for the modulus and Eqns (2.19) and (2.22) for the phase. It is customary to quote the modulus of the frequency response in decibel units

$$|F(\omega)|_{dB} = 20 \log_{10} |F(\omega)| = 20 \log k_P - \tfrac{20}{2} \log(1+\omega^2 T^2). \tag{2.23}$$

Both traces, modulus and frequency, are plotted separately against frequency, plotted on a logarithmic scale.

The presentation can be simplified by considering the two conditions

$$\omega \ll 1/T \quad \text{and} \quad \omega \gg 1/T.$$

This produces two straight lines (Fig. 2.7) which intersect at the frequency $\omega_9 = 1/T$. At this point, the error relative to the actual curve is -0.293 or 3 dB.

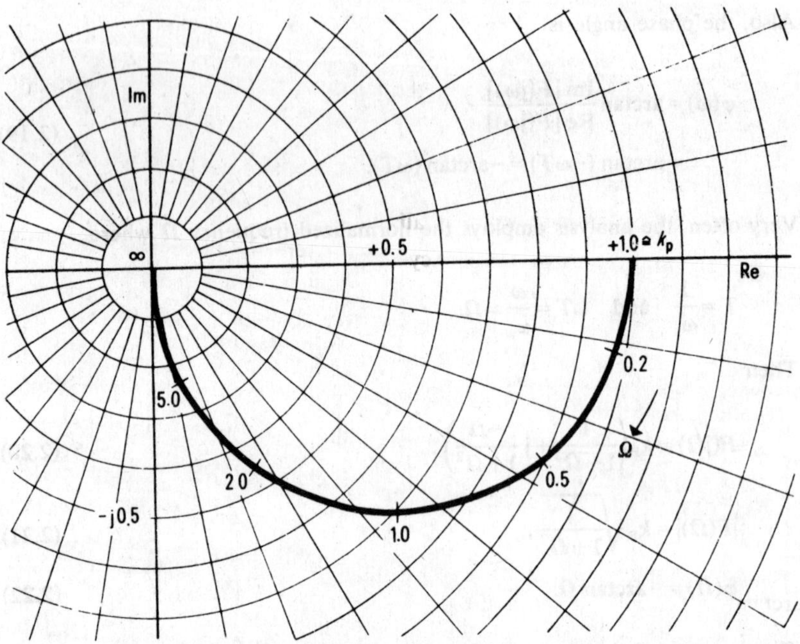

Fig. 2.6
Frequency response curve for first order lag system in normalized form

$$k_p = 1 \quad , \quad \omega T = \frac{\omega}{\omega_g} = \Omega$$

The frequency ω_g is termed the corner frequency because a bend occurs here in the actual trace.
The straight line, falling at 20 dB per decade, cuts the 0 dB line at the crossover frequency

$$\omega_0 = k_P/T$$

i.e. the frequency at which the output variable $x_a(\omega_0)$ is equal to the input variable $x_e(\omega_0)$.
As seen from Fig. 2.7, a phase angle of −45° is obtained at the corner frequency ω_g.
Both frequency characteristics together are termed the Bode diagram. The Bode diagram forms the basis of the study of control systems by the frequency response method.

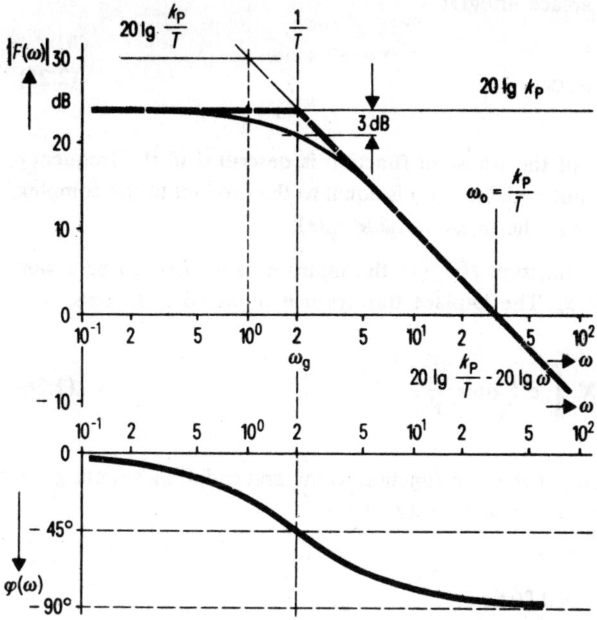

Fig. 2.7 Frequency curves of first order lag system (Bode diagram)

2.2.7. Laplace transformation

There is a close relationship between transient response and frequency response. If a transient function

$$f(t) = \frac{x_a(t)}{x_e}$$

which is a function of time is considered, and we wish to obtain a related function in the frequency domain, the Laplace transformation is applied. For this, we use the complex frequency or Laplace operator

$$s = \delta + j\omega \tag{2.24}$$

in which the decay coefficient δ is made equal to zero for the linear system elements considered here.

With the aid of the Laplace integral

$$L[f(t)] = \int_0^\infty e^{-st} f(t)\,dt \tag{2.25}$$

the Laplace transform of the transient function is described in the frequency domain so that the output variable $x_a(s)$ is equal to the product of the complex transfer function $F(s)$ and the input variable $x_e(s)$.

Consider the transient function $f(t)$, i.e. the input variable $x_e(t)$ to be a step function of magnitude x_e. The Laplace transform is obtained as follows:

$$x_e(s) = L[X_e] = X_e \int_0^\infty e^{-st}\,dt = \frac{X_e}{s}. \tag{2.26}$$

Consider the application of the step function to the first order lag system given by the transient function of Equation (2.13):

$$\begin{aligned} x_a(s) &= \frac{X_e}{s} F(s) = X_e L[f(t)] \\ &= X_e \int_0^\infty e^{-st} k_P (1 - e^{-t/T})\,dt \\ &= X_e k_P \left[\frac{e^{-st}}{-s} - \frac{e^{-(s+1/T)t}}{-\left(s + \frac{1}{T}\right)} \right]_0^\infty \\ &= X_e k_P \left[\frac{1}{s} - \frac{T}{1+sT} \right] \\ &= \frac{X_e}{s} k_P \frac{1}{1+sT}. \end{aligned} \tag{2.27}$$

Thus the transfer function $F(s)$, also referred to as the complex frequency response, for the first order lag system, is given by

$$F(s) = \frac{x_a(s)}{x_e(s)} = \frac{k_P}{1+sT} \tag{2.28}$$

which is also given by Eqn (2.15) with s equal to $j\omega$.

The input variable $x_e(s)$ can assume any arbitrary function of s and thus can also be the product of another input variable $x_e'(s)$ with another transfer function $F'(s)$:

$$x_e(s) = x_e'(s)F'(s).$$

These results are summarized in the following table:

Time domain	$\frac{d}{dt}$	$\int_0^t dt$
Frequency domain	$j\omega$	$\frac{1}{j\omega}$
Transfer function	s	$\frac{1}{s}$.

(2.29)

The validity is restricted, however, in that, in the time domain at $t<0$, all derivatives of the differential equation (general time equation) are zero.

2.3. Second Order Delay Element

A second order delay or lag will be represented in the following analysis by the series connection of a resistance R, an inductance L and a capacitance C. The input variable x_e is the voltage v_1. The output variable x_a is the voltage v_2 across the capacitor C (Fig. 2.8). This circuit is a four terminal or four pole network with two input connections and two output connections.

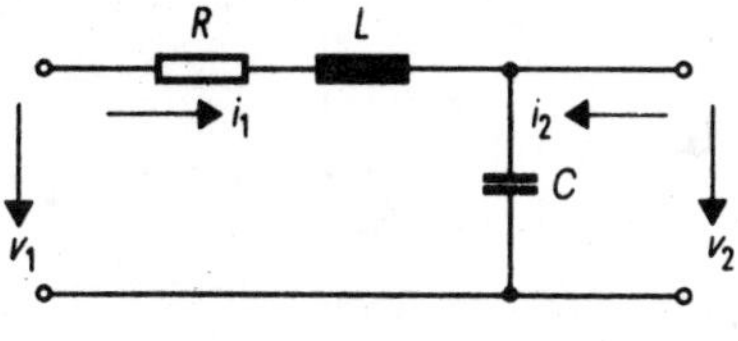

Fig. 2.8
Four terminal second order lag network

2.3.1. Differential equation

Let the circuit shown in Fig. 2.8 be unloaded at the output. The output current is then $i_2 = 0$. The input variable x_e, i.e. voltage v_1, is given as follows:

$$x_e(t) = v_1(t) = Ri_1(t) + L\frac{di_1(t)}{dt} + \frac{1}{C}\int_0^t i_1(t)\,dt. \tag{2.30}$$

The output variable x_a, i.e. the voltage on the capacitor C is

$$x_a(t) = v_2(t) = \frac{1}{C}\int_0^t i_1(t)\,dt. \tag{2.31}$$

Differentiation gives

$$\frac{dx_a(t)}{dt} = \frac{dv_2(t)}{dt} = \frac{i_1(t)}{C}$$

or

$$i_1(t) = C\frac{dv_2(t)}{dt} = C\frac{dx_a(t)}{dt}.$$

putting this in Eqn (2.30) gives the following result:

$$x_e(t) = v_1(t) = RC\frac{dv_2(t)}{dt} + LC\frac{d^2v_2(t)}{dt^2} + v_2(t).$$

The product of inductance L and capacitance C is dimensionally equal to the square of time:

$$LC = \frac{L}{R}RC = T^2.$$

The product of resistance R and capacitance C is also a time constant which can be related to the time constant T as follows:

$$RC = 2\zeta T.$$

where

$$T = \sqrt{LC}$$

and

$$\zeta = \frac{R}{2}\sqrt{\frac{C}{L}}.$$

is called the damping factor.

The general time equation of the second order delay system can thus be written as follows:

$$\frac{d^2x_a(t)}{dt^2}T^2 + \frac{dx_a(t)}{dt}2\zeta T + x_a(t) = x_e(t). \tag{2.32}$$

For the circuit shown in Fig. 2.8, the steady-state condition is given by

$$\underset{t\to\infty}{x_a(t)} = x_e(t).$$

This is a special case, however. In general, for $t \to \infty$, $x_a(t)/x_e(t)$ takes the value k_P:

$$\underset{t\to\infty}{x_a(t)} = x_e(t)k_P.$$

2.3.2. Frequency response and transfer function

If it is assumed that in the general time equation for the second order lag system (Eqn (2.32)), the input variable x_e is sinusoidal, the output variable x_a must also have the same sinusoidal frequency. Thus

$$x_a(t) = \hat{x}_a e^{j\omega t}.$$

From the general time Eqn (2.32)

$$[j\omega]^2T^2\hat{x}_a e^{j\omega t} + j\omega 2\zeta T\hat{x}_a e^{j\omega t} + \hat{x}_a e^{j\omega t} = x_e(t)k_P.$$

In phasor notation, this becomes, the frequency equation:

$$x_a[-\omega^2T^2 + 2j\omega\zeta T + 1] = x_c k_P. \tag{2.33}$$

If the output variable $x_a(j\omega)$ is referred to the input variable $x_e(j\omega)$, the frequency response is obtained:

$$F(j\omega)=\frac{x_a(j\omega)}{x_e(j\omega)}=\frac{k_P}{1+2j\omega\zeta T-\omega^2T^2}. \tag{2.34}$$

Using Eqns (2.29), the transfer function for the second order delay system can be written as follows:

$$F(s)=\frac{x_a(s)}{x_e(s)}=\frac{k_P}{1+s2\zeta T+s^2T^2}. \tag{2.35}$$

In the following sections, the importance of the damping factor ζ will be demonstrated.

2.3.3. Transient response to a step function

Consider a step function of the input variable x_e, i.e.

$$x_e(t)=\begin{cases}0 & \text{at time } t<0\\ x_e & \text{at time } t\geqslant 0.\end{cases}$$

The solution of the differential equation

$$\frac{d^2x_a(t)}{dt^2}T^2+\frac{dx_a(t)}{dt}2\zeta T+x_a(t)=x_e(t)k_P$$

is required for a step function of input variable.

Let the initial conditions be given by

$$\underset{t=0}{x_a(t)}=\frac{dx_a(t)}{dt}=0,$$

and for the final steady state,

$$\underset{t\to\infty}{\frac{dx_a(t)}{dt}}=\frac{d^2x_a(t)}{dt^2}=0.$$

The particular solution of the differential equation is

$$x_{a\,part} = X_e k_P.$$

Assuming the homogeneous solution to be of the form

$$x_{a\,hom} = e^{kt}$$

then we obtain the characteristic equation,

$$k^2T^2 + 2\zeta kT + 1 = 0.$$

The roots for k are as follows:

$$\begin{aligned} k_1 &= -\frac{1}{T}(\zeta - \sqrt{\zeta^2 - 1}), \\ k_2 &= -\frac{1}{T}(\zeta + \sqrt{\zeta^2 - 1}). \end{aligned} \tag{2.36}$$

Three cases can be identified:

(1) $\zeta < 1$. The roots of k are complex numbers.
(2) $\zeta = 1$. The roots of k have only one real value.
(3) $\zeta > 1$. The roots of k are real numbers.

These give three different types of response.

Case 1
Damping factor $\zeta < 1$.
The roots of k are

$$\begin{aligned} k_{11} &= -\frac{1}{T}(\zeta - j\sqrt{1 - \zeta^2}), \\ k_{12} &= -\frac{1}{T}(\zeta + j\sqrt{1 - \zeta^2}). \end{aligned} \tag{2.37}$$

Thus

$$x_{a\,hom} = e^{-(\zeta/T)t}\left[A \cos\left(\frac{t}{T}\sqrt{1-\zeta^2}\right) + B \sin\left(\frac{t}{T}\sqrt{1-\zeta^2}\right)\right]$$

and the complete solution is

$$x_a(t)_a = X_e k_P\left[1 - e^{-(\zeta/T)t}\left(\cos\left(\frac{t}{T}\sqrt{1-\zeta^2}\right) + \frac{\zeta}{\sqrt{1-\zeta^2}}\sin\left(\frac{t}{T}\sqrt{1-\zeta^2}\right)\right)\right]$$

$$= X_e k_P\left[1 - \frac{e^{-(\zeta/T)t}}{\sqrt{1-\zeta^2}}\sin\left(\frac{t}{T}\sqrt{1-\zeta^2} + \arccos\zeta\right)\right]. \tag{2.38}$$

The transient transfer function is

$$f(t)_a = \frac{x_a(t)}{X_e} = k_P\left[1 - e^{-(\zeta/T)t}\left(\cos\omega t + \frac{\zeta}{\omega T}\sin\omega t\right)\right]$$

$$= k_P\left[1 - \frac{e^{-(\zeta/T)t}}{\omega T}\sin(\omega t + \arccos\zeta)\right], \tag{2.39}$$

where

$$\omega = \frac{\sqrt{1-\zeta^2}}{T}.$$

These equations are valid over the range

$$0 < \zeta < 1.$$

A periodic damped oscillation is produced with frequency ω as given above which decays according to the exponential damping term until it assumes the value

$$x_a(t)_a = X_e k_P$$

(See Fig. 2.9, curve 1).

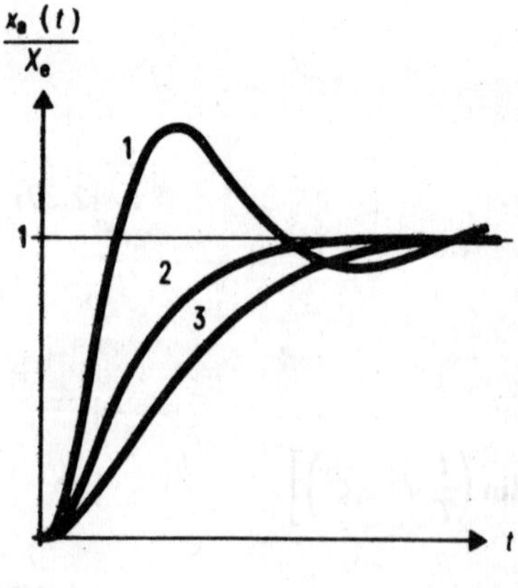

Fig. 2.9
Transient response of second order delay system. Curve 1, periodic $0<\zeta<1$. Curve 2, aperiodic – limiting case, $\zeta=1$. Curve 3, aperiodic – general case, $\zeta>1$

The amount of overshoot for curve 1 is greater the nearer the value of ζ approaches zero.

With the damping factor ζ equal to zero, an undamped sinusoidal oscillation occurs:

$$f(t)=\frac{x_a(t)}{X_e}=k_P\left[1-\cos\frac{t}{T}\right].$$

This corresponds to a differential equation with the first derivative term missing or to the frequency response expression with the $j\omega$ term missing or the transfer function with the s term missing.

If the damping factor is less than zero, i.e. negative, the oscillation starts from zero and increases indefinitely. This is termed forced oscillation.

Case 2

Damping factor $\zeta=1$.

The roots of k are

$$k_{21}=k_{22}=-1/T. \tag{2.40}$$

Thus

$$x_{a\,hom}=A^*e^{-t/T}+B^*te^{-t/T}$$

and consequently, the transient function is

$$f(t)_b=\frac{x_a(t)_b}{X_e}=k_P\left[1-\frac{T+t}{T}e^{-t/T}\right]. \tag{2.41}$$

This is the aperiodic limiting case. The transient curve does not quite oscillate, that is, there is no overshoot but an asymptotic rise to the final value. This is shown in Fig. 2.9, curve 2.

Case 3

Damping factor $\zeta>1$.

The roots of k are

$$\begin{aligned} k_{31}&=-\frac{1}{T_1} \quad \text{where} \quad T_1=\frac{T}{\zeta-\sqrt{\zeta^2-1}},\\ k_{32}&=-\frac{1}{T_2} \quad \text{where} \quad T_2=\frac{T}{\zeta+\sqrt{\zeta^2-1}} \end{aligned} \tag{2.42}$$

and

$$x_{a\,hom} = A^{**}e^{-t/T_1} + B^{**}e^{-t/T_2}.$$

The transfer function is

$$f(t)_c = \frac{x_a(t)_c}{X_e}$$

$$= k_P\left[1 - \frac{T_1}{T_1 - T_2}e^{-t/T_1} - \frac{T_2}{T_2 - T_1}e^{-t/T_2}\right]. \tag{2.43}$$

This is an aperiodic transient. It again represents an asymptotic rise to the final steady-state value. It is shown in Fig. 2.9, curve 3.

It can be seen from Fig. 2.9, that the smaller the damping factor, the smaller is the initial slope of the transfer function.

2.3.4. Locus curves

By multiplying the numerator and denominator of Eqn (2.34) by the complex conjugate of the denominator, the following expression can be obtained:

$$F(j\omega) = \frac{k_P}{1 + 2j\omega\zeta T - \omega^2 T^2}$$

$$= k_P\left[\frac{1 - \omega^2 T^2}{(1 - \omega^2 T^2)^2 + 4\omega^2\zeta^2 T^2} + j\frac{-2\omega\zeta T}{(1 - \omega^2 T^2)^2 + 4\omega^2\zeta^2 T^2}\right]. \tag{2.44}$$

The real part of the expression is

$$\mathrm{Re}\,[F(j\omega)] = k_P \frac{1 - \omega^2 T^2}{1 + 2\omega^2 T^2(2\zeta - 1) + \omega^4 T^4}, \tag{2.45}$$

and the imaginary part is

$$\mathrm{Im}\,[F(j\omega)] = k_P \frac{-2\omega\zeta T}{1 + 2\omega^2 T^2(2\zeta^2 - 1) + \omega^4 T^4}. \tag{2.46}$$

Also the modulus is given by

$$|F(\omega)| = k_P \sqrt{\frac{1}{1 + 2\omega^2 T^2(2\zeta^2 - 1) + \omega^4 T^4}} \tag{2.47}$$

and the phase angle is

$$\varphi(\omega) = -\arctan\frac{2\omega\zeta T}{1-\omega^2T^2}. \tag{2.48}$$

If the locus is to be presented in the rectangular co-ordinate system of the complex number plane, Eqns (2.45) and (2.46) are used. For representation in polar co-ordinates, Eqns (2.47) and (2.48) are used. In both cases, both frequency ω and damping factor ζ are variable parameters. The result is not a single curve but a family of curves.

For a range of damping factor between 0 and $1/\sqrt{2}$ a pronounced resonance is obtained. By differentiation of Eqn (2.47), the resonance frequency of the circuit is obtained as

$$\omega_R = \frac{1}{T}\sqrt{1-2\zeta^2}, \tag{2.49}$$

which produces a significant increase of the output variable x_a.
Using the normalized resonant frequency

$$\omega T\frac{1}{\sqrt{1-2\zeta^2}} = \frac{\omega}{\omega_R} = \Omega_R \tag{2.50}$$

the modulus is found to be

$$|F(\Omega_R)|_{\zeta\leq(1/\sqrt{2})} = k_P\sqrt{\frac{1}{1-(2\Omega_R^2-\Omega_R^4)(1-2\zeta^2)^2}} \tag{2.51}$$

and the phase angle is found to be

$$\varphi(\Omega_R)_{\zeta\leq(1/\sqrt{2})} = \arctan\frac{-2\Omega_R\zeta\sqrt{1-2\zeta^2}}{1-\Omega_R^2(1-2\zeta^2)}. \tag{2.52}$$

Figure 2.10 shows a family of curves in the polar co-ordinate system, in which one parameter is the frequency Ω_R referred to the resonant frequency and the other parameter is the damping factor ζ.

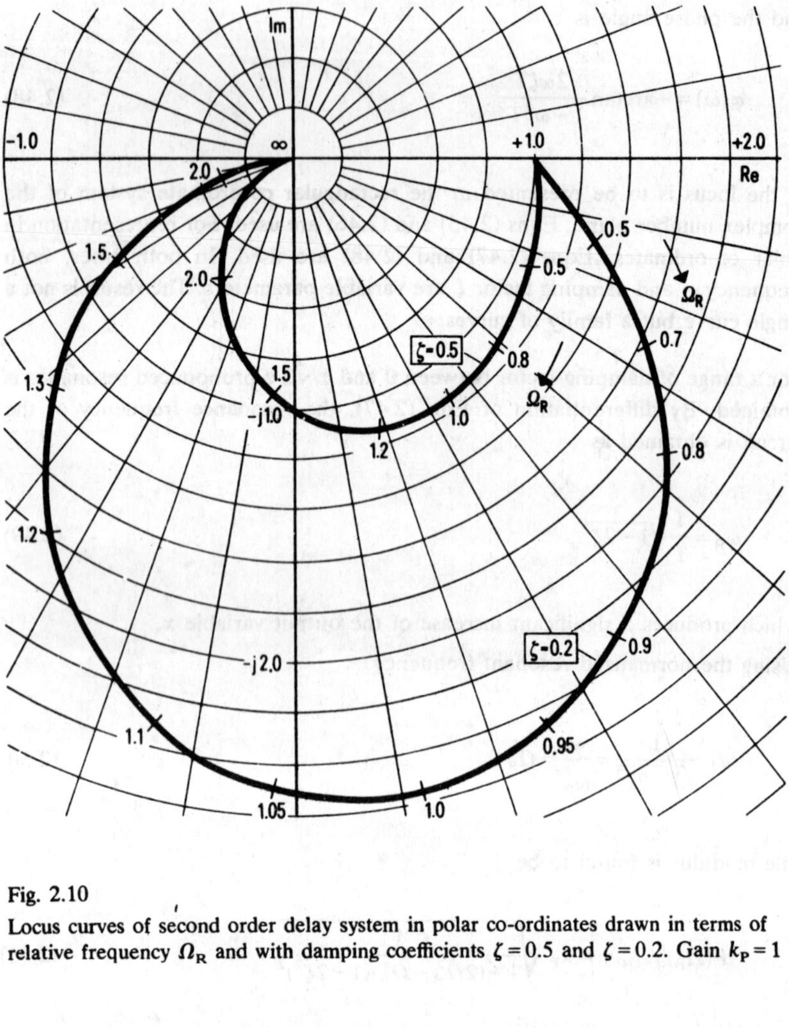

Fig. 2.10
Locus curves of second order delay system in polar co-ordinates drawn in terms of relative frequency Ω_R and with damping coefficients $\zeta = 0.5$ and $\zeta = 0.2$. Gain $k_P = 1$

In accordance with Eqn (2.51), an increase of the amplitude occurs in the case of resonance, which is given as a percentage by the following expression:

$$\left[\frac{1}{2\zeta}\sqrt{\frac{1}{1-\zeta^2}}-1\right]100\%. \tag{2.53}$$

This increase of amplitude is shown in Fig. 2.11.

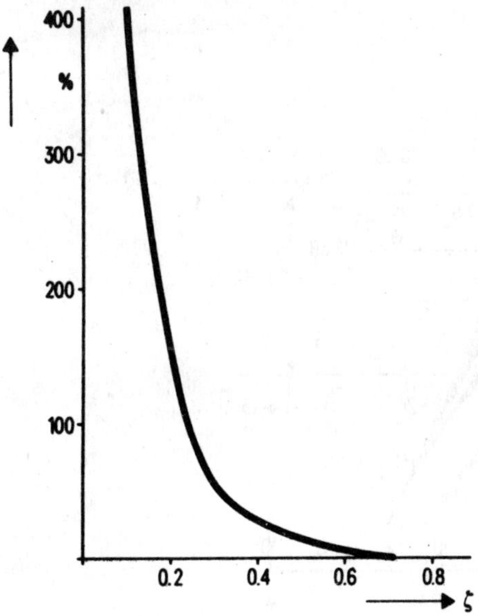

Fig. 2.11
Increase of gain at resonant frequency ω_R dependent on relative damping factor ζ for second order delay system

2.3.5. Frequency characteristics

Figure 2.12 shows the frequency characteristics. The modulus curves may be obtained by considering Eqn (2.47):

$$\begin{aligned}|F(\omega)|_{dB} &= 20 \log |F(\omega)| \\ &= 20 \log k_P - \tfrac{20}{2} \log [1 + \omega^2 T^2 (4\zeta^2 - 2) + \omega^4 T^4],\end{aligned} \tag{2.54a}$$

$$\begin{aligned}|F(\omega)|_{dB} &= 20 \log \frac{k_P}{2\zeta T} - 20 \log \omega \\ &\quad - \tfrac{20}{2} \log \left[\frac{1}{4\omega^2 \zeta^2 T^2} + 1 - \frac{1}{2\zeta^2} + \frac{\omega^2 T^2}{4\zeta^2}\right],\end{aligned} \tag{2.54b}$$

$$\begin{aligned}|F(\omega)|_{dB} &= 20 \log k_P - 20 \log \omega T \\ &\quad - \tfrac{20}{2} \log \left[\frac{1}{\omega^2 T^2} + 4\zeta^2 - 2 + \omega^2 T^2\right].\end{aligned} \tag{2.54c}$$

The evaluation of these equations is best done in stages. Consider first Eqn (2.54a) with the assumption $\omega T \ll 1$

$$|F(\omega)|_{dB\,a)} = 20 \log k_P. \tag{2.55a}$$

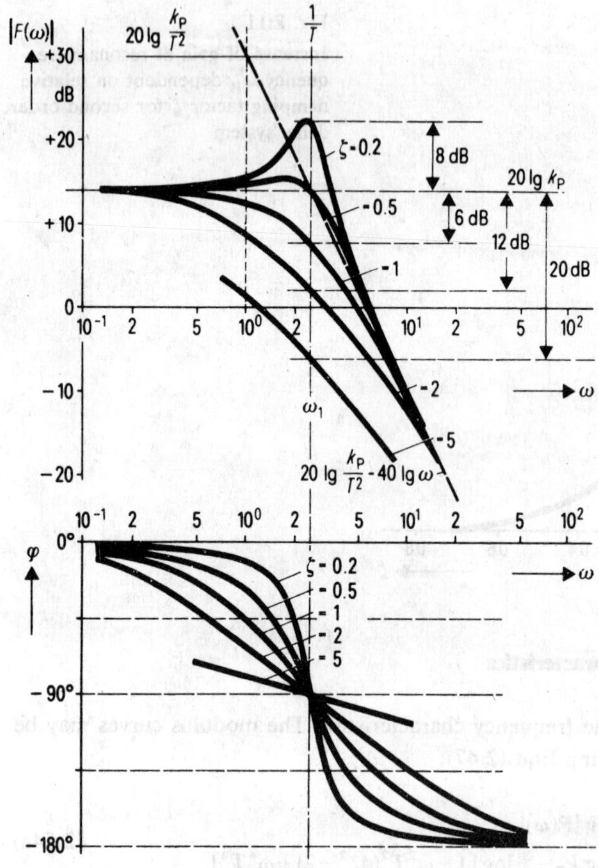

Fig. 2.12
Frequency characteristics of second order lag with arbitrary frequency = 2.5 and arbitrary gain $k_P = 5$. Damping factors $\zeta = 0.2$, 0.5, 1, 2, 5

This is a horizontal straight line parallel to the 0 dB line.

By considering Eqn (2.54b) and the condition $\omega T = 1$, the slope of the frequency characteristic at a frequency $\omega_1 = 1/T$ is obtained:

$$|F(\omega)|_{dB\,b)} = 20 \log \frac{k_P}{2\zeta T} - 20 \log \omega. \tag{2.55b}$$

The slope is -20 dB per decade.

If Eqn (2.54c) is considered again with $\omega T = 1$, we can see how much the frequency characteristic at $\omega = 1/T$ differs from the straight line $20 \log k_P$:

$$|F(\omega)|_{dB\,c)} = 20 \log k_P - 20 \log 2\zeta. \tag{2.55c}$$

Finally, Eqn (2.54c) is used again, but with the condition $\omega T \gg 1$.

The behaviour at very high frequencies is given by

$$|F(\omega)|_{dB\,c)} = 20 \log \frac{k_P}{T^2} - 40 \log \omega. \tag{2.55d}$$

Here the frequency characteristics fall off at -40 dB per decade.

The associated behaviour of the phase angle is given by Eqn (2.48).

2.4. Second Order Delay System Using Two First Order Systems

A second order system can be obtained by connecting together two elements with transfer functions

$$f_1(t) = k_{P1}[1 - e^{-t/T_1}] \tag{2.56a}$$

and

$$f_2(t) = k_{P2}[1 - e^{-t/T_2}] \tag{2.56b}$$

so that the output variable of the first element is the input variable of the second (Fig. 2.13).

Fig. 2.13
Series connection of two first order elements

2.4.1. Differential equation

Equations (2.56a) and (2.56b) characterize at any given time the behaviour with step input variables. The input variable of the second system is not a step function however.

Using the general time equation, the first element (Fig. 2.13) gives

$$k_{P1}x_e(t) = y(t) + T_1\frac{dy(t)}{dt}$$

and the second element gives

$$k_{P2}y(t) = x_a(t) + T_2\frac{dx_a(t)}{dt}.$$

From the last equation, we get

$$\frac{dy(t)}{dt} = \frac{1}{k_{P2}}\left[\frac{dx_a(t)}{dt} + T_2\frac{d^2x_a(t)}{dt^2}\right].$$

Substituting into the first equation, we obtain the following general time equation for the combined system:

$$k_{P1}k_{P2}x_e(t) = x_a(t) + (T_1+T_2)\frac{dx_a(t)}{dt} + T_1T_2\frac{d^2x_a(t)}{dt^2}. \tag{2.57}$$

The second derivative of the output variable x_a appears in the equation, but the derivative of the input variable x_e does not appear. The equation is that of a second order delay system, previously given as follows (Eqn (2.32)):

$$k_Px_e(t) = x_a(t) + 2\zeta T\frac{dx_a(t)}{dt} + T^2\frac{d^2x_a(t)}{dt^2}$$

By comparison of coefficients

$$T_1 + T_2 = 2\zeta T,$$

$$T_1T_2 = T^2$$

we can define the time constant as

$$T = \sqrt{T_1T_2} \tag{2.58a}$$

and the damping factor as

$$\zeta = \frac{1}{2}\sqrt{\frac{T_1}{T_2} + 2 + \frac{T_2}{T_1}}. \tag{2.58b}$$

Although both time constants T_1 and T_2 can assume any arbitrary value, the damping factor ζ is always greater than or equal to 1. This means that in a cascade circuit of first order lag elements, the transient behaviour is always aperiodic. Periodic transient behaviour is not possible.

2.4.2. Transient function

For time constants T_1 and T_2 of equal magnitude, Eqn (2.41) applies, and for unequal time constants Eqn (2.43) applies.

2.4.3. Transfer function

For the two first order elements in series, we have the following transfer functions:

$$y(s) = x_e(s)\frac{k_{P1}}{1+sT_1},$$

$$x_a(s) = y(s)\frac{k_{P2}}{1+sT_2}.$$

If we substitute the first equation into the second, we obtain the transfer function for the composite arrangement of Fig. 2.13 as follows:

$$F(s) = \frac{x_a(s)}{x_e(s)} = \frac{k_{P1}}{1+sT_1}\frac{k_{P2}}{1+sT_2} = k_{P1}k_{P2}\frac{1}{1+s(T_1+T_2)+s^2T_1T_2}. \tag{2.59}$$

The two individual transfer functions are multiplied together.

For the limiting case of aperiodic variation, when $T_1 = T_2 = T$, we get

$$F(s) = \frac{x_a(s)}{x_e(s)} = k_{P1}k_{P2}\frac{1}{(1+sT)^2}. \tag{2.60}$$

2.4.4. Frequency characteristics

The frequency response is obtained from the transfer function, Eqn (2.59):

$$F(j\omega) = \frac{x_a(j\omega)}{x_e(j\omega)} = \frac{k_{P1}k_{P2}}{1-\omega^2T_1T_2+j\omega(T_1+T_2)}. \tag{2.61}$$

The real and imaginary parts can be determined in the usual manner, thus

$$\mathrm{Re}\,[F(j\omega)] = k_{P1}k_{P2}\frac{1-\omega^2 T_1 T_2}{(1-\omega^2 T_1 T_2)^2+\omega^2(T_1+T_2)^2}; \tag{2.62}$$

$$\mathrm{Im}\,[F(j\omega)] = k_{P1}k_{P2}\frac{-\omega(T_1+T_2)}{(1-\omega^2 T_1 T_2)^2+\omega^2(T_1+T_2)^2}. \tag{2.63}$$

Also, the modulus is given as follows:

$$|F(\omega)| = k_{P1}k_{P2}\sqrt{\frac{1}{(1+\omega^2 T_1^2)(1+\omega^2 T_2^2)}} \tag{2.64}$$

and the phase is

$$\varphi(\omega) = \arctan\frac{-\omega(T_1+T_2)}{1-\omega^2 T_1 T_2}. \tag{2.65}$$

The frequency curves can be more easily represented if we convert the time constants T_1 and T_2 into their associated frequencies

$$T_1 = \frac{1}{\omega_1}; \qquad \omega T_1 = \frac{\omega}{\omega_1}$$

$$T_2 = \frac{1}{\omega_2}; \qquad \omega T_2 = \frac{\omega}{\omega_2}.$$

Then the modulus of the frequency response is given as follows:

$$|F(\omega)| = k_{P1}k_{P2}\frac{1}{\sqrt{\left[1+\left(\frac{\omega}{\omega_1}\right)^2\right]\left[1+\left(\frac{\omega}{\omega_2}\right)^2\right]}} \tag{2.66}$$

and the phase is given by

$$\varphi(\omega) = \arctan\frac{-\omega(\omega_1+\omega_2)}{\omega_1\omega_2-\omega^2}. \tag{2.67}$$

The modulus expressed in decibels is

$$|F(\omega)|_{\mathrm{dB}} = 20\lg k_{P1}k_{P2} - 20\lg\sqrt{1+\left(\frac{\omega}{\omega_1}\right)^2} - 20\lg\sqrt{1+\left(\frac{\omega}{\omega_2}\right)^2}. \tag{2.68}$$

The modulus curve can again be approximated by straight lines.

If we first consider $\omega < 1$, we get

$$|F(\omega)|_{\substack{dB\\ \omega \to 0}} = 20 \log k_{P1} k_{P2} \tag{2.68a}$$

which is a straight line parallel to the 0 dB line. Also, if $\omega > 1$, then for

$$T_2 = 0: \; |F(\omega)|_{\substack{dB\\ \omega \to \infty}} = 20 \log k_{P1} k_{P2} - 20 \log \frac{\omega}{\omega_1} \tag{2.68b}$$

and for

$$T_1 = 0: \; |F(\omega)|_{\substack{dB\\ \omega \to \infty}} = 20 \log k_{P1} k_{P2} - 20 \log \frac{\omega}{\omega_2}. \tag{2.68c}$$

This gives two straight lines which cut the straight line given by Eqn (2.68a) at other frequency values ω_1 and ω_2 and fall off at 20 dB per decade with increasing frequency. The points of intersection with the 0 dB line occur at

$$\omega_{01} = \frac{k_{P1} k_{P2}}{T_1} = \omega_1 k_{P1} k_{P2}$$

and

$$\omega_{02} = \frac{k_{P1} k_{P2}}{T_2} = \omega_2 k_{P1} k_{P2}.$$

At very large values of frequency, we obtain approximately another straight line given by

$$|F(\omega)|_{\substack{dB\\ \omega \to \infty}} = 20 \log k_{P1} k_{P2} - 40 \log \frac{\omega}{\sqrt{\omega_1 \omega_2}}. \tag{2.68d}$$

This line cuts the straight line given by Eqn (2.68a) at the circuit resonant frequency $\sqrt{\omega_1 \omega_2}$ and the line given by Eqn (2.68b) at the frequency ω_2. With increasing frequency it falls at 40 dB per decade.

The modulus curve of the second order delay system which was obtained from two first order systems in cascade, can be approximated by the straight lines shown in Fig. 2.14. The three straight line sections intersect at the corner point KI (frequency ω_1) and the corner point KII (frequency ω_2). The straight lines deviate from the actual curve in the range between ω_1 and ω_2 by an amount between 3 dB and 6 dB.

Figure 2.14 also shows the curve of the associated phase angle. The angle 90° is obtained at the circuit frequency $\sqrt{\omega_1\omega_2}$.

At the corner frequencies ω_1 and ω_2 the phase angle values are

$$\varphi(\omega_1) = \arctan \frac{\omega_1+\omega_2}{\omega_1-\omega_2},$$

$$\varphi(\omega_2) = \arctan \frac{\omega_1+\omega_2}{\omega_2-\omega_1}. \tag{2.69}$$

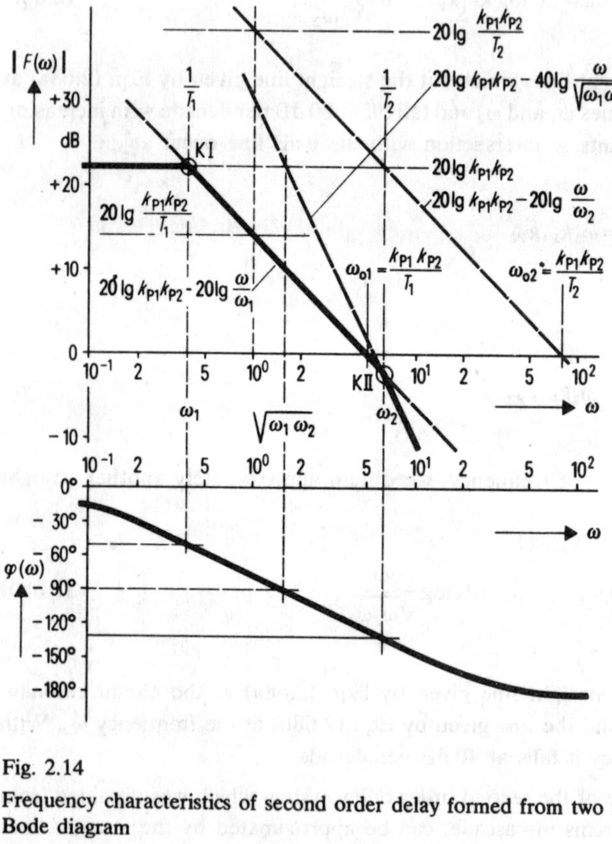

Fig. 2.14
Frequency characteristics of second order delay formed from two first order systems. Bode diagram

The frequency at which the modulus characteristic passes through the 0 dB line is

$$\omega_{0\,\mathrm{dB}} = \sqrt{\omega_1 \omega_2 k_{P1} k_{P2}} = \sqrt{\frac{k_{P1} k_{P2}}{T_1 T_2}} \tag{2.70}$$

and the associated phase angle is

$$\varphi_{0\,\mathrm{dB}} = \arctan\left(\frac{-\sqrt{k_{P1} k_{P2}}}{1 - k_{P1} k_{P2}} \frac{T_1 + T_2}{\sqrt{k_{P1} k_{P2}}}\right). \tag{2.71}$$

3. Behaviour of Control System Elements

Different kinds of system elements are found in a control system and if the variables in the system are to be controlled to achieve the optimum results, a knowledge of the behaviour of the system elements and their correct assessment is necessary for the choice of a suitable controller and for the correct setting of the controller parameters.

First, it must be decided whether the system elements exhibit linear or non-linear behaviour. If the input variable x_e of a system element is proportional to the output x_a in the steady-state condition, then the graphical relationship between the two is a straight line and the element is known as a linear element. If this linear relationship is not universally true so that the characteristic cannot be represented by a straight line, it is termed a non-linear element. In the considerations which follow, linear systems are the primary concern.

Figure 3.1 shows a synopsis of the most important behaviour patterns. In the sphere of drive and power engineering, the most common are: the proportional element, the integrating element and the first order delay or lag. The usual representation of system elements is a rectangle into which an arrow points to indicate the input. An arrow leading away from the rectangle represents the output (see Fig. 3.2). Often a graphical indication of the transfer function is placed in the rectangle to identify the behaviour of the system element.

To determine the behaviour of the system element with respect to time and amplitude, signals which are easily repeatable are applied to the input and the resulting signals at the output are examined. With respect to transient behaviour, the usual input signal is the step function.

In addition to the graphical representation of the behaviour of a system element, we have the important mathematical definition, called the transfer function or frequency response. We also have the transient function or general time equation which is a differential or integral equation. This is not so commonly used.

3.1. Proportional System Element

Characteristic of the proportional element is the fact that the output variable x is unchanged with respect to time in response to a constant variable x_e at the

System element		Step response	Output variable x_a
Behaviour	Symbol		
Proportional	P		Proportional to input variable x_e with no delay.
Integral	I	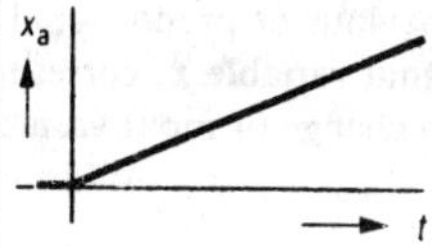	Time integral of the input variable
First order dealy	$P-T_1$	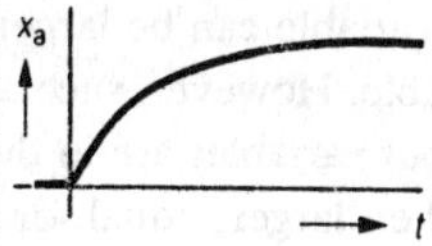	Proportional to input variable but delayed according to exponential function
Second order delay	$P-T_2$	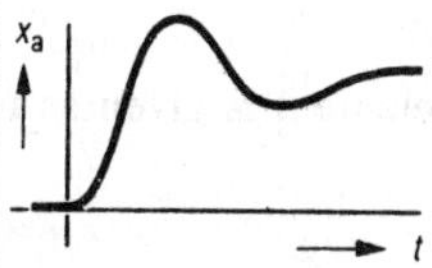	Proportional to input variable but delayed according to transient function
Phase advance proportional plus derivative	PD	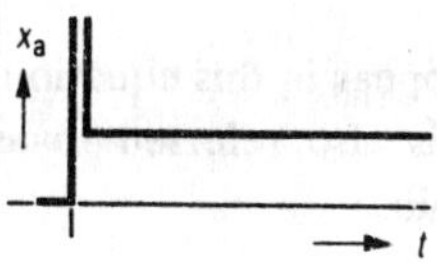	Proportional to input variable with addition of differential of input
Differentiating	$D-T_1$	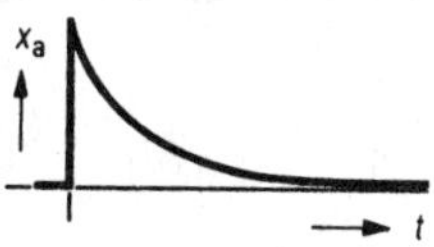	Zero. With input variations, the differential of the input variable appears with a delayed decay
Dead time	$P-T_t$	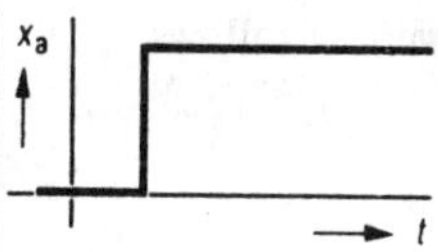	Proportional to input variable but at a fixed time later

Fig. 3.1 Summary of the most important characteristics used in control systems

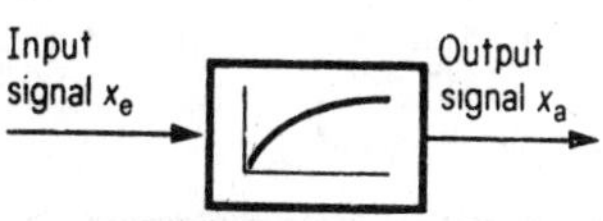

Fig. 3.2 Representation of a system element

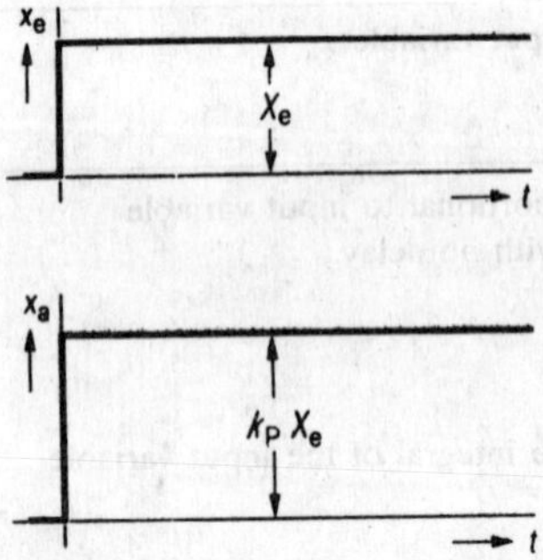

Fig. 3.3
Behaviour of proportional system element. Output variable x_a corresponding to a step change of input variable x_e

input. The amplitude of the output variable can be larger, equal to, or smaller than the amplitude of the input variable. However, such an amplitude ratio can only be defined if the output and input variables are in the same physical units. If the physical units are different, then larger, equal, or smaller ratios cannot be defined.

The behaviour of the proportional element is given as follows:

$$x_a(t) = k_P x_e(t). \tag{3.1}$$

A time varying response does not appear in this equation. It is defined only by the amplification factor k_P which is also referred to as the proportionality factor or system amplification or gain.

For a step function input, X_e, the following transient function is obtained (Fig. 3.3):

$$f(t)_P = \frac{x_a(t)}{X_e} = k_P. \tag{3.2}$$

Similarly, the transfer function is given as follows:

$$F(s)_P = \frac{x_a(s)}{x_e(s)} = k_P.$$

The block diagram representation of the proportional element is shown in Fig. 3.4.

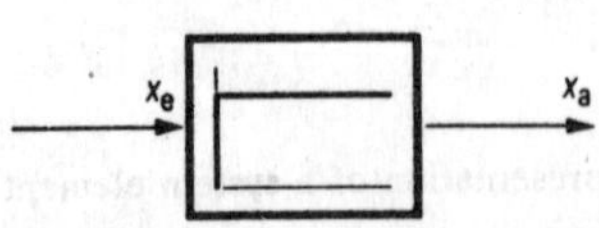

Fig. 3.4
Block diagram of proportional system element

3.1.1. Voltage divider

The voltage divider is used when a signal voltage such as that from a tachogenerator is too high (Fig. 3.5). The input variable is the voltage V_1, and the output variable the voltage V_2. If the voltage divider is unloaded, then

$$\frac{V_2}{V_1}=\frac{R_2}{R_1+R_2}.$$

The proportionality factor k_P is always less than 1 in this case and is dimensionless.

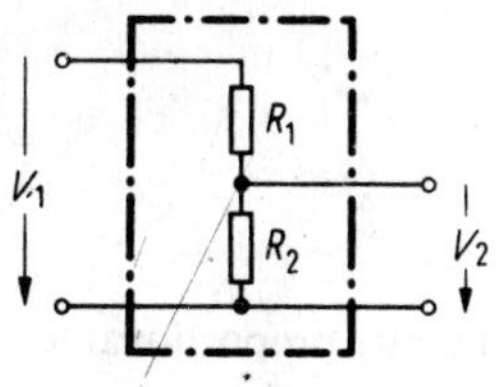

Fig. 3.5
Voltage divider as a proportional system element

3.1.2. Tachogenerator

A permanent magnet tachogenerator (Fig. 3.6) has an input variable x_e which is the speed of the shaft n, which is usually measured in revolutions per minute. The output variable is the generated voltage V_T measured in volts. This is proportional to the speed. The factor k_P in this case has the dimensions volts/revolutions per minute.

If we introduce normalized, i.e. dimensionless, variables as is common in control engineering, we get

$$x_a=\frac{V_T}{V_{Tmax}} \quad \text{and} \quad x_e=\frac{n}{n_{max}}.$$

The amplification factor k_P is then dimensionless.

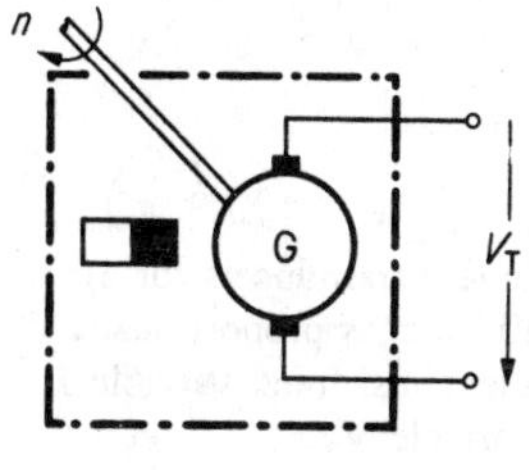

Fig. 3.6
Tachogenerator as a proportional system element. Input variable n, outside variable V_T

3.1.3. A.c. and d.c. measurement converters

The input variable x_e in Fig. 3.7(a) is a three-phase alternating current and in Fig. 3.7(b), a direct current. A voltage appears on the output side. Therefore the gain k_P has the dimensions volts/ampere. It is also possible here to apply normalized variables.

The output variable of a measurement converter, i.e. a voltage, will be the input variable of a controller. The output variable of the controller will be the input variable of the controlled system, again a voltage. Thus the amplification of the whole system is usually a dimensionless quantity.

3.2. Integrating System Element

A system element whose output variable x_a is changed at a rate proportional to the input variable x_e is an integrating element. An input variable of zero causes no change in the output variable. Thus it shows the value that it had reached due to a previous input variable. This can be any value within the overall range. If the input variable x_e of the integrating element is small, the change of the output variable x_a is slow. On the other hand, if the input is large, the output variable changes rapidly. The change of the output variable is, of course, only possible up to the limits of the control range.

We see then that the integrating element produces the integration of the input variable over a given period. For the available control range, the general time equation is given as follows:

$$x_0(t) = \frac{1}{T_i} \int_0^t x_e(t)\,dt. \tag{3.4}$$

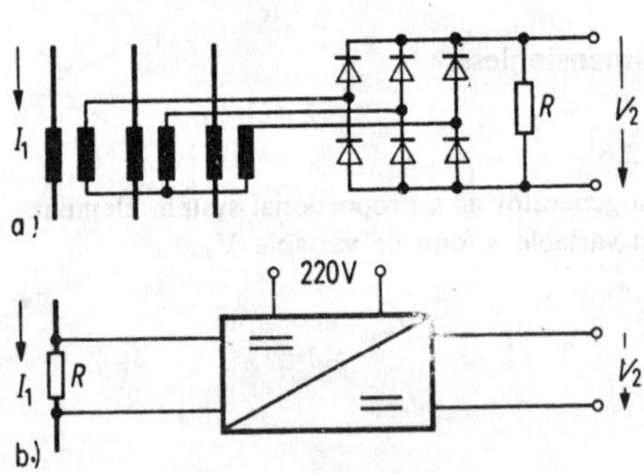

Fig. 3.7
Measurement transducers for a) a.c. and b) d.c. as proportional system elements. Input variable I_1, output variable V_2

The characteristic parameter is the integration time constant T_i, which is measured in seconds. Often the reciprocal of the integration time constant is used in Eqn (3.4) and this is called the integration constant or integration factor K_i:

$$K_i = 1/T_i.$$

The greater the integration time constant, the smaller is the rise in the output variable per unit time for a given input variable.

Equation (3.4) is not complete mathematically. It lacks a term which states the level at which the integration has to begin. The control engineer, however, regards this level as zero level.

The integration time constant T_i can be determined simply if the input and output variables are the same physical quantities. If the input variable changes as a step function at time $t = 0$ from zero value to a value X_e, then the output variable rises linearly with time and the increase of the output variable x_a after a time T_i is equal to the input variable X_e, i.e. the step value (Fig. 3.8).

Thus the transient function can be defined as follows:

$$f(t)_I = \frac{x_a(t)}{X_e} = \frac{t}{T_i}. \tag{3.5}$$

If the input and output variables are different physical quantities, the conversion ratio must also be taken into account in the integration time constant. Figure 3.9 shows the block diagram representation of the integrating element.

In the frequency domain, the operator s in the denominator stands for the integral $\int dt$ in the time equation. Thus, the transfer function can be written as

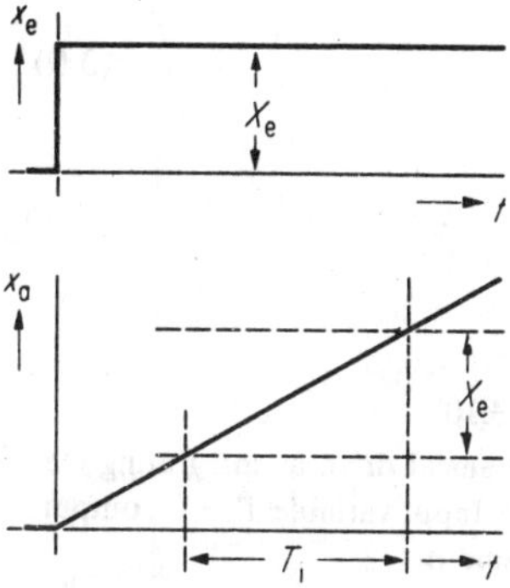

Fig. 3.8

Transient behaviour of an integrating system element. Response of output variable x_a to a step change of input variable x_e

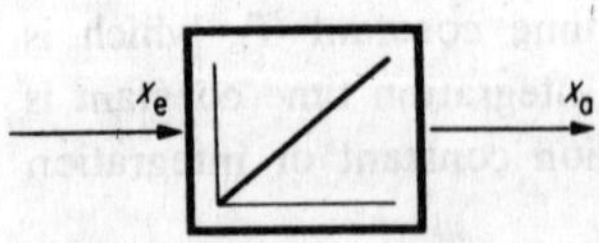

Fig. 3.9
Block diagram of integrating element

follows:

$$F(s)_I = \frac{x_a(s)}{x_e(s)} = \frac{1}{sT_i}. \tag{3.6}$$

An example of integrating behaviour is the mechanical aspect of a d.c. motor drive system (Fig. 3.10). If the field current of the d.c. machine is constant, then the torque produced by the machine T_e is proportional to the armature current I_A:

$$T_e = K_1 \Phi I_A \tag{3.7}$$

If the retarding torque due to friction on the shaft T_f is equal to the torque produced by the machine, the motors runs at a constant speed of n revs/min. If for any reason, the retarding torque becomes smaller so that the machine produces more torque than is required, the extra torque produced by the motor will cause an acceleration of the machine. The accelerating torque is

$$T_a = T_e - T_f. \tag{3.8}$$

The accelerating torque acts on the moment of inertia J of the drive and produces an acceleration given by the equation

$$T_a = J\frac{d\omega}{dt} \tag{3.9}$$

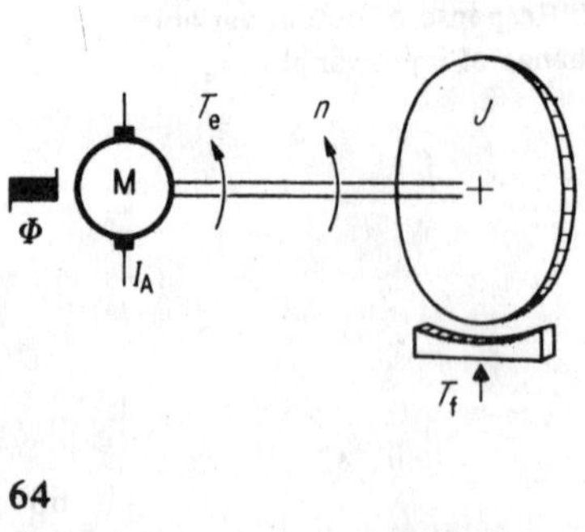

Fig. 3.10
Mechanical drive as integrating element. Input variable $T_e - T_f$, output variable n

where ω is the rotational speed in rad/s. Using normalized units, ω can be written as follows:

$$\omega = \frac{2\pi}{60} n_R \frac{n}{n_R}.$$

The accelerating torque can also be written as follows:

$$T_a = T_R \frac{T_a}{T_R}$$

where n_R is the unloaded or rated speed and T_R is the rated torque. If these values are inserted in Eqn (3.9) and the equation integrated with respect to time, the following result is obtained for the change of speed over the specified time:

$$\Delta n(t) = \frac{n_R}{T_R} \frac{1}{\frac{2\pi}{60} J \frac{n_R}{T_R}} \int_0^t T_a(t)\, dt. \tag{3.10}$$

The run up time of the machine t_R is defined as

$$t_R = \frac{2\pi}{60} J \frac{n_R}{T_R}. \tag{3.11}$$

With a torque equal to the rated torque T_R the machine would run up from standstill to the rated speed n_R in a time t_R.

The moment of inertia J includes all masses involved in the turning motion. Figure 3.11 shows the block diagram of the system.

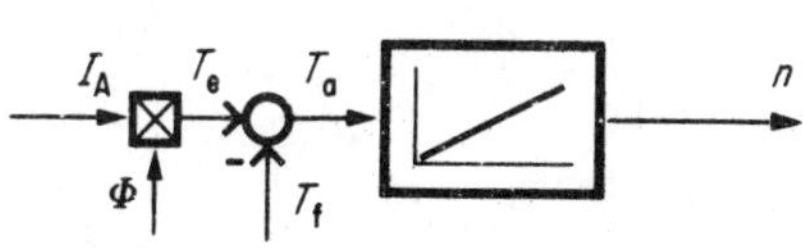

Fig. 3.11
Block diagram of mechanical drive system involving a d.c. motor

3.3. First Order Delay System

The first order delay was discussed in detail in Section 2.2. The differential equation is

$$\frac{dx_a(t)}{dt}T_1+x_a(t)=kx_e(t). \tag{3.12}$$

The transient function is

$$f(t)=\frac{x_a(t)}{X_e}=k(1-e^{-t/T_1}) \tag{3.13}$$

and the transfer function is

$$F(s)=\frac{x_a(s)}{x_e(s)}=\frac{k}{1+sT_1}. \tag{3.14}$$

The block diagram of the system is shown in Fig. 3.13.

By integration of Eqn (3.12), the similarity between the first order delay system and the integrating element is observed:

$$x_a(t)=\frac{k}{T_1}\int_0^t x_e(t)\,dt-\frac{1}{T_1}\int_0^t x_a(t)\,dt.$$

If a short time period is considered, the second integral term will be insignificant and the integration period is T_1/k. This determines the initial slope, i.e. the slope of a tangent to the curve at $t=0$. This tangent cuts the 100% line at a

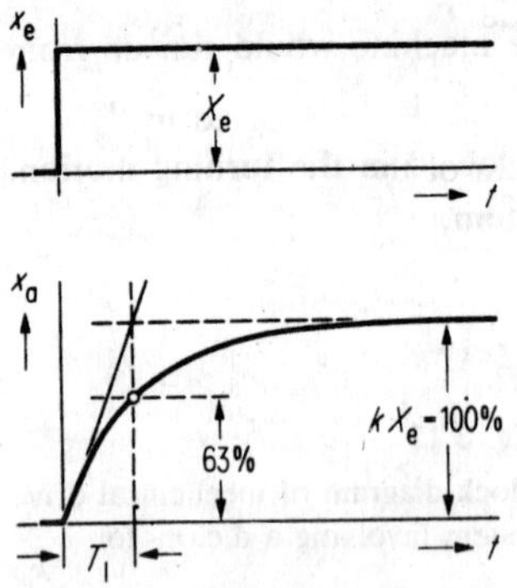

Fig. 3.12
Time behaviour of a first order delay element. Output variable x_a as the response to a step input x_e

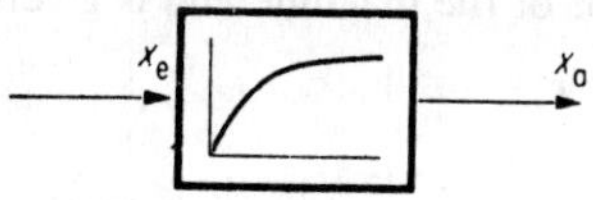

Fig. 3.13
Block diagram of a first order delay element

time T_1. However, it is not easy to obtain T_1 by drawing this tangent. A more satisfactory method of obtaining T_1 is by using the fact that the x_a curve reaches 63% of the final value in a time T_1 (see Fig. 3.12).

An example of behaviour corresponding to a first order delay is the armature circuit of a d.c. machine (Fig. 3.14).

Let R_A and L_A be the resistance and inductance of the armature circuit, respectively. The armature circuit time constant is given as follows:

$$T_A = L_A/R_A. \tag{3.15}$$

The generated e.m.f. E produced by the rotation of the machine is given as follows:

$$E = n\Phi K_2 \tag{3.16}$$

where Φ is the flux produced by the field winding.

The actual input variable is

$$(V_A - E).$$

If the rated armature voltage V_{AR} were applied to a stationary machine, the armature current (short circuit current) I_{SC} would be much greater than the normal current I_{AR}. Let this be expressed as follows:

$$I_{SC} = k_{SC} I_{AR} \tag{3.17a}$$

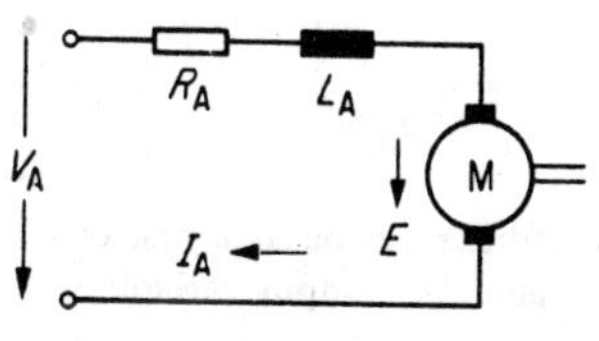

Fig. 3.14
Armature circuit of a d.c. machine as a first order delay. Input variable $(V_A - E)$, output variable I_A

where k_{SC} is called the current amplification factor of the machine and is given as follows:

$$\frac{V_{AR}}{I_{AR}}\frac{1}{R_A}=k_{SC}. \tag{3.17b}$$

The transfer function of this system can be stated as follows (see Fig. 3.14):

$$F(s)_{arm}=\frac{I_A(s)}{(V_E-E)(s)}\frac{V_{AR}}{I_{AR}}=\frac{k_{SC}}{1+sT_A}. \tag{3.18}$$

Figure 3.15 shows the block diagram.

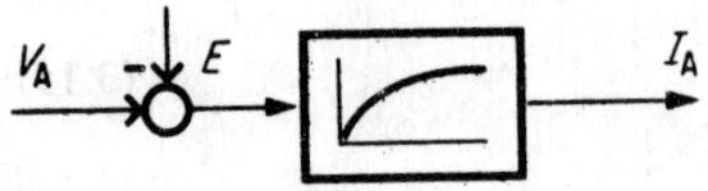

Fig. 3.15
Block diagram of d.c. machine armature circuit performance

3.3.1. Field circuit of d.c. machine

The time constant of the field circuit (Fig. 3.16) is given as follows:

$$T_F=L_F/R_F \tag{3.19}$$

where L_F is the field winding inductance and R_F is the total resistance of the field circuit. The eddy current equivalent resistance, say R_W, can be neglected since flux changes are negligible. However, if rapid changes in field circuit voltage V_F occur, then significant eddy currents may occur because of rapid changes in the field current and the corresponding changes in flux in the laminations of the magnetic circuit. This gives rise to power loss which will be represented by resistance loss in the equivalent resistor R_W.

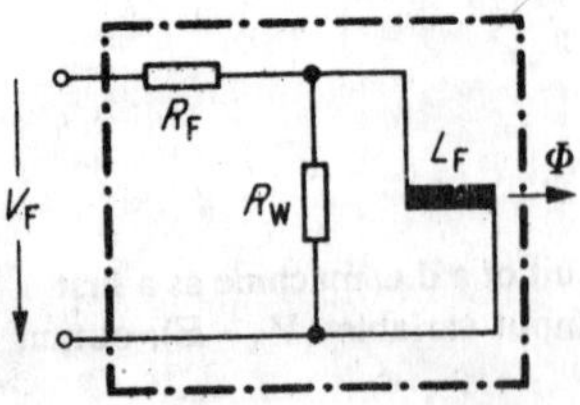

Fig. 3.16
Field circuit of a d.c. machine as a first order delay. Input variable V_F, output variable Φ

In this case, therefore, we have field circuit time constant T_F given by

$$T_F = L_F \frac{R_F + R_W}{R_F R_W}. \tag{3.20}$$

The transfer function involving the flux in the machine is

$$F(s)_F = \frac{\Phi(s)}{V_F(s)} = k_\Phi \frac{1}{1 + sT_F}. \tag{3.21}$$

3.4. Second Order Delay Element

In Section 2.3 the second order delay element was discussed. For completeness the most important equations will be presented again.

The differential equation is

$$\frac{d^2x_a(t)}{dt^2} T^2 + \frac{dx_a(t)}{dt} 2\zeta T + x_a(t) = kx_e(t). \tag{3.22}$$

The transient function is

$$f(t) = \frac{x_a(t)}{X_e} = k\left[1 - e^{-\zeta t/T}\left(\cos \omega t - \frac{\zeta}{\omega T} \sin \omega t\right)\right] \tag{3.23}$$

where

$$\omega = \frac{\sqrt{1-\zeta^2}}{T}.$$

The transfer function is

$$F(s) = \frac{x_a(s)}{x_e(s)} = \frac{k}{1 + 2s\zeta T + s^2 T^2}. \tag{3.24}$$

In Eqn (3.23), it is assumed that the damping factor lies in the range between 0 and 1.

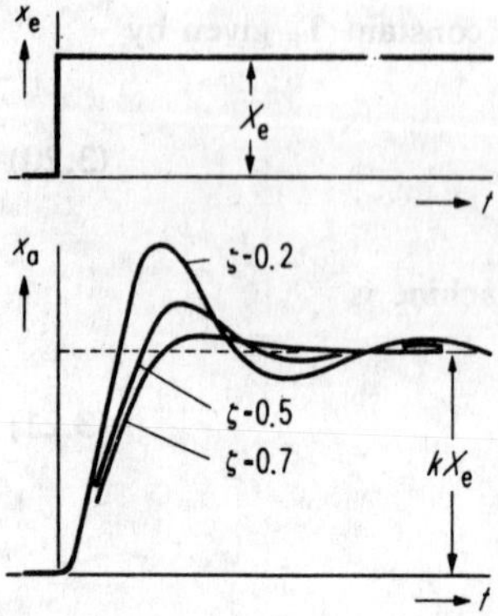

Fig. 3.17

Step response of second order delay element with damping factor between 0 and +1. Output variable x_a, step input variable x_e

Figure 3.17 shows the step response of the output variable for various damping factors. The block diagram is shown in Fig. 3.18.

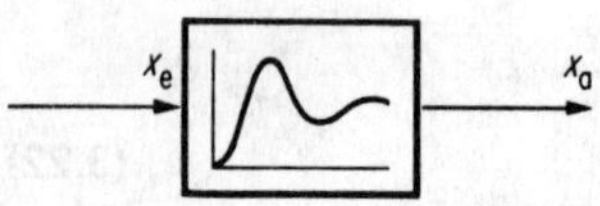

Fig. 3.18

Step response of a second order delay element with damping factor between 0 and +1

The damping factor determines the behaviour:

$\zeta > +1$	aperiodic
$\zeta = +1$	aperiodic, limiting case
$0 < \zeta < +1$	oscillatory
$\zeta = 0$	sinusoidal oscillation
$\zeta < 0$	forced oscillation.

If two first order delay elements with time constants T_1 and T_2 are connected in series, a second order delay is obtained, having a damping factor given as follows (see Eqn (2.58b)):

$$\zeta = \frac{1}{2}\sqrt{2 + \frac{T_1}{T_2} + \frac{T_2}{T_1}}. \tag{3.25}$$

This must be equal to or greater than 1.

We thus obtain the following function, the transfer being given by Eqn (2.43):

$$f(t) = \frac{x_a(t)}{X_e} = k\left[1 - \frac{T_1}{T_1 - T_2}\,e^{-t/T_1} - \frac{T_2}{T_2 - T_1}\,e^{-t/T_2}\right]. \tag{3.26}$$

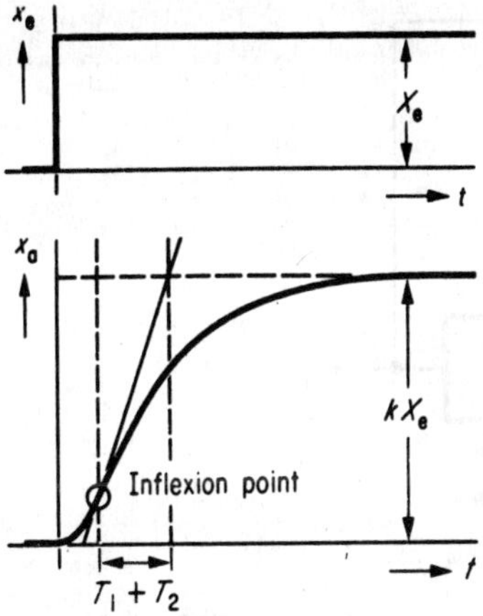

Fig. 3.19
Step response of second order delay with damping factor greater than +1. Response of output variable x_a to a step input variable x_e. The tangent at the point of inflexion of the x_a curve cuts the straight line representing the final steady state and a distance T_1+T_2 from the inflexion point

The response of the output variable x_a to a step change of input is shown in Fig. 3.19. From the figure it can be seen how the sum of the two time constants T_1 and T_2 can be determined from the tangent at the point of inflexion.

3.4.1. D.c. machine

The d.c. machine is the most important example of a second order delay in drive engineering. In order to derive an overall block diagram of the d.c. machine, the diagrams for the mechanical part (Fig. 3.11) and the armature circuit (Fig. 3.15) are combined (Fig. 3.20).

Let us assume that the flux Φ in the machine is constant (Fig. 3.21).

The rotational speed n of the machine may vary for two reasons. The friction or load torque may be constant while the armature voltage is varied or the armature voltage may be constant and the load torque varied.

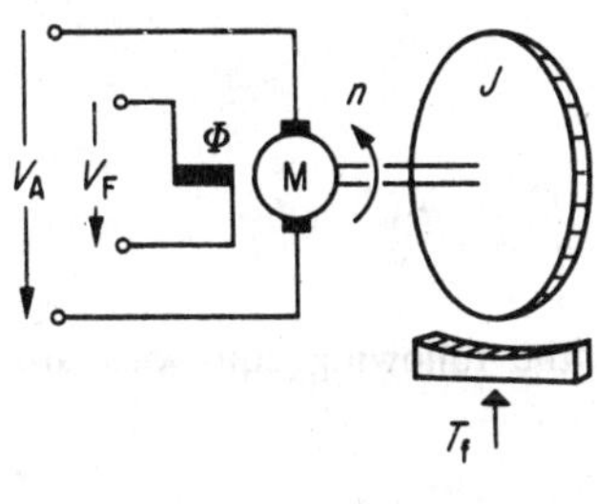

Fig. 3.20
Diagram of a d.c. machine, for determining the dynamic response. The value of V_F and thus Φ is assumed constant. Input variable V_A or T_f, output variable n

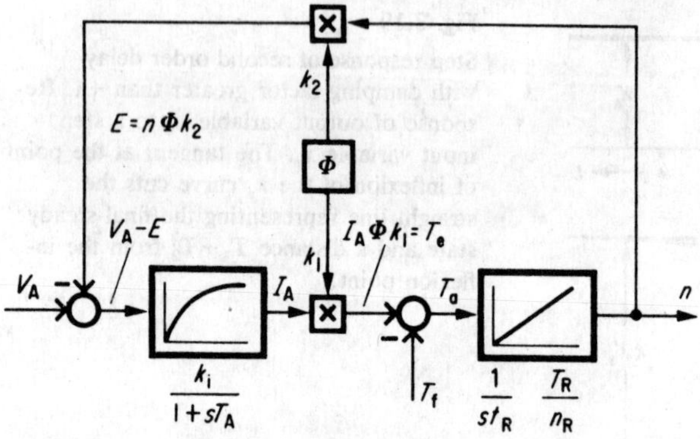

Fig. 3.21
Representation of d.c. machine with constant field current. The controlled variable (speed n) is fed back in the control loop as the generated voltage E_1. The command variable is V_A and T_F is the friction torque which represents the load on the machine

The transfer function involving the speed can be obtained from Eqns (3.7), (3.8) and (3.10):

$$\frac{n(s)}{n_R}=\frac{I_A(s)\Phi k_1-T_f}{st_R T_R} \tag{3.27}$$

The rated torque T_R of the machine is

$$T_R=I_{AR}\Phi_R k_1.$$

With the aid of Eqns (3.16), (3.17) and (3.18) we obtain the transfer function for the armature current:

$$I_A(s)=\frac{k_i}{1+sT_A}\frac{I_{AR}[V_A(s)-n\Phi k_2]}{V_{AR}}. \tag{3.28}$$

The equation

$$E_R=n_R\Phi_R k_2=V_{AR}$$

applies for the induced voltage E_R (rated).

If Eqn (3.28) is now inserted in Eqn (3.27), the following equations are obtained for the normalized speed.

(1) Variable armature voltage V_A

$$\frac{n}{n_R}(s) = \frac{\dfrac{V_A}{V_{AR}}(s)}{\dfrac{\Phi}{\Phi_R}} \frac{1}{1+s\dfrac{t_R}{k_i\left(\dfrac{\Phi}{\Phi_R}\right)^2}(1+sT_A)} - \frac{\dfrac{T_f}{T_R}}{k_i\left(\dfrac{\Phi}{\Phi_R}\right)^2}. \tag{3.29}$$

(2) Variable load

$$\frac{n}{n_R}(s) = -\frac{\dfrac{T_f}{T_R}(s)}{k_i\left(\dfrac{\Phi}{\Phi_R}\right)^2} \frac{1}{1+s\dfrac{t_R}{k_i\left(\dfrac{\Phi}{\Phi_R}\right)^2}(1+sT_A)} + \frac{\dfrac{V_A}{V_{AR}}}{\dfrac{\Phi}{\Phi_R}}. \tag{3.30}$$

The transfer functions exhibit similar behaviour, whether the effect is due to changing armature voltage or changing load torque. Figure 3.21 will indicate that this must be so.

The d.c. machine can exhibit periodic or aperiodic behaviour depending on the magnitude of the damping factor. By comparing the coefficients of Eqns (3.29) and (3.30) with Eqn (3.24) we find that

$$\zeta = \sqrt{\frac{t_R}{4k_i\left(\dfrac{\Phi}{\Phi_R}\right)^2 T_A}}. \tag{3.31}$$

Aperiodic behaviour is to be expected of the machine of course when the damping factor is greater than 1. This is always the case when

$$t_R > 4T_A k_i\left(\frac{\Phi}{\Phi_R}\right)^2. \tag{3.32}$$

As the field weakens, i.e. the factor Φ/Φ_R becomes smaller, the machine behaviour becomes more aperiodic.

If the behaviour is aperiodic, the second order system may be resolved into two first order delays (see Section 2.4). If we define the ratio of the run up time t_R to the armature circuit time constant T_A as follows:

$$t_R = 4k_H T_A k_i\left(\frac{\Phi}{\Phi_R}\right)^2$$

where the factor k_H is equal to or greater than 1, we can calculate the delay times T_1 and T_2 of both first order delays from Eqn (2.42), i.e.

$$T_1 = 2T_A \frac{1}{1-\sqrt{1-1/k_H}}$$

$$T_2 = 2T_A \frac{1}{1+\sqrt{1-1/k_H}}. \tag{3.33}$$

If k_H is large enough a mechanical time constant T_M appears for T_1:

$$T_M = \frac{t_R}{k_i\left(\frac{\Phi}{\Phi_R}\right)^2} \tag{3.34}$$

and the armature circuit time constant T_A appears for T_2.

3.5. System Element Giving Phase Advance

The system element giving phase advance, also called the error rate element, is made up of two components. One component gives the proportional behaviour described in Section 3.1 (P component). The second component involves the error rate. This is derived by differentiating the input variable, and may be called the D component. The general time equation obtained is then as follows:

$$x_a(t) = k_P x_e(t) + T_d \frac{dx_e(t)}{dt}. \tag{3.35}$$

The time constant T_d is called the differentiation time. The larger the value of T_d, the more significant the error rate becomes, i.e. for a given rate of change of input variable x_e, the constant T_d determines the magnitude of the error rate term in the above equation. However, this term only exists when the input variable is changing, and the greater its rate of change, the greater the magnitude of the error rate term.

If the input variable is a step function with a step of X_e, the proportional component can easily be determined. However, the D component presents problems, for at the instant of application of the step ($t=0$), the rate of change

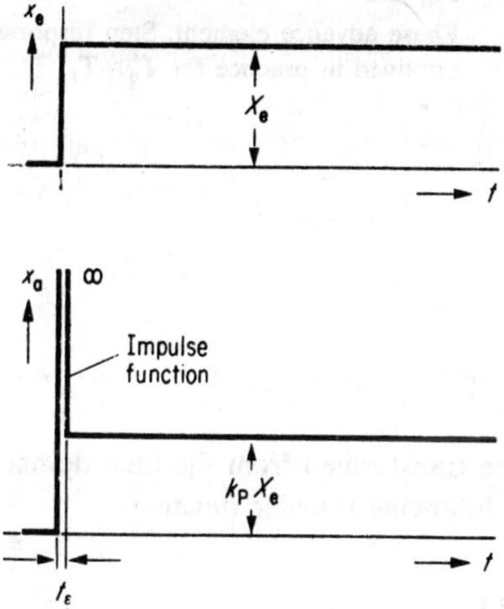

Fig. 3.22
Step response of phase advance element. Output variable x_a is the response to a step change in the input variable x_e. The area of the impulse function is $T_d X_e$

of the input variable is infinite. Theoretically, therefore, the output variable must be infinitely large. However, after an infinitely short time t_ε, the D component must be zero again. This is called an impulse function or Dirac function. This has the property that the product of the amplitude (∞) and the time t_ε is equal to the product of T_d and X_e:

$$\infty t_\varepsilon = T_d X_e. \tag{3.36}$$

The amplitude/time area of the impulse function is finite even though the amplitude is infinite. The step response can be deduced from Fig. 3.22. The following transient function is obtained:

$$f(t) = \frac{x_a(t)}{X_e} = k_P + \text{impulse function.} \tag{3.37}$$

The block diagram of the phase advance element is shown in Fig. 3.23.

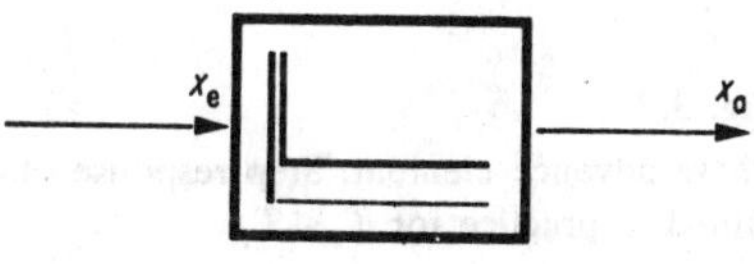

Fig. 3.23
Block diagram of a phase advance element.

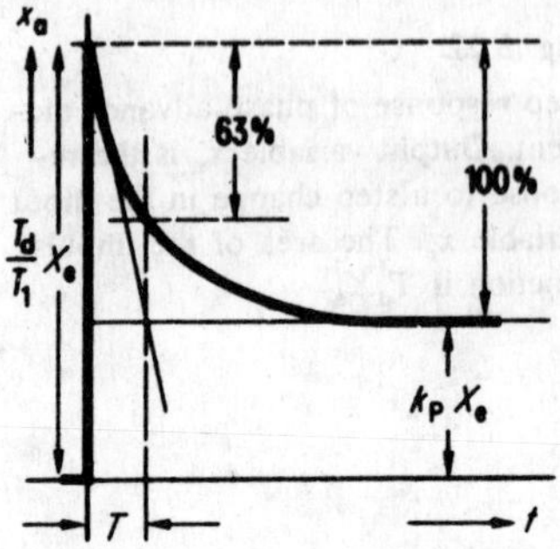

Fig. 3.24
Phase advance element. Step response obtained in practice for $T_d > T_1$

Referring to Eqn (2.29), Eqn 3.35 can be transformed from the time domain to the frequency domain, producing the following transfer function:

$$F(s) = \frac{x_a(s)}{x_e(s)} = k_P + sT_d = k_P\left(1 + s\frac{T_d}{R_P}\right). \tag{3.38}$$

In practice an infinitely large impulse function amplitude cannot occur as it would be limited by the control equipment. Thus the theoretical amplitude/time curve will be distorted. This will be determined by the ratio of the differentiation constant T_d to the delay time T_1. If T_d is larger than T_1, a step response of the form shown in Fig. 3.24 occurs.

If however, T_d is smaller than T_1, a response of the form shown in Fig. 3.25 is obtained.

The transient function including the effect of both time constants is given as follows:

$$f(t) = \frac{x_a(t)}{X_e} = k_P\left(1 - e^{-t/T_1} + \frac{T_d}{k_P T_1} e^{-t/T_1}\right) \tag{3.39}$$

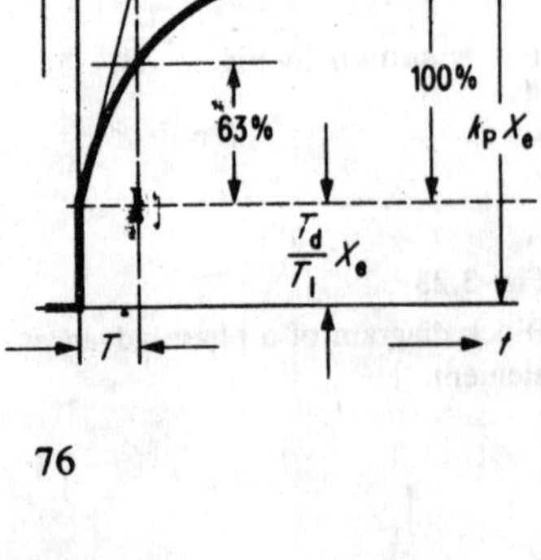

Fig. 3.25
Phase advance element. Step response obtained in practice for $T_d < T_1$

The term $(1-e^{-t/T_1})$ represents a first order delay and the term $\left(\frac{T_d}{k_P T_1}\right)e^{-t/T_1}$ represents the phase advance.

Modifying Eqn (3.35) to take into account the effect of the time constant T_1, we obtain the following equation:

$$\frac{dx_a(t)}{dt}T_1+x_a(t)=k_P x_e(t)+T_d\frac{dx_e(t)}{dt}. \tag{3.40}$$

The corresponding transfer function is

$$F(s)=\frac{x_a(s)}{x_e(s)}=k_P\frac{1+sT_d/k_P}{1+sT_1}. \tag{3.41}$$

3.5.1. Field current circuit of a d.c. machine

The field circuit of a d.c. machine is an example of a phase advance element (Fig. 3.26). In this case we consider the field current I_F, and not, as in Fig. 3.16, the flux Φ in the machine.

For slow variations of the field circuit voltage V_F, the field current I_F will produce only very small rates of change of the flux in the iron and thus eddy currents in the iron can be neglected.

However, if rapid changes of excitation voltage take place, as is necessary in the weak field region when using speed control, then the associated current variations will produce relatively fast changes of flux in the iron. The iron now acts as a secondary winding with a resistive short circuit and eddy currents will appear and produce a power loss. The eddy currents can be kept to a minimum by laminating the iron but cannot be entirely eliminated. The effect of the eddy currents can be accounted for by means of a resistance R_W as shown in Fig. 3.26.

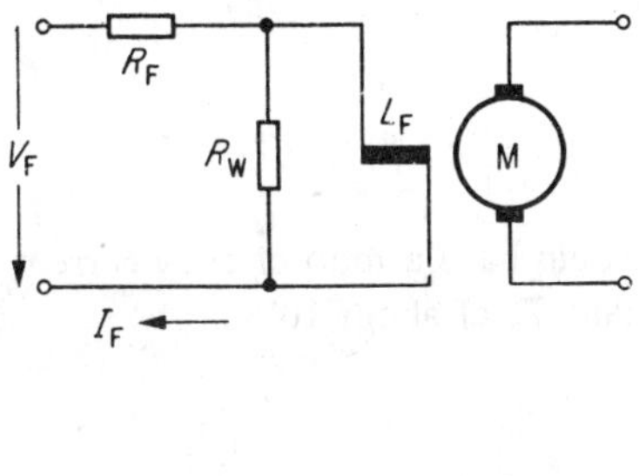

Fig. 3.26
Equivalent circuit of a d.c. machine

The resistance R_F must be considered to exist only during variations of the field current. If the applied voltage V_F is constant or changes only very slowly, then R_W must be considered infinite.

From the equivalent circuit diagram shown in Fig. 3.26, the transfer function can be established as the ratio of field current I_F to field circuit voltage V_F.

$$\frac{I_F(s)}{V_F(s)}=\frac{1}{R_F}\frac{1+s\dfrac{L_F}{R_W}}{1+sL_F\dfrac{R_F+R_W}{R_FR_W}}. \tag{3.42}$$

Comparison with the transfer function, Eqn (3.41), shows that the amplification factor

$$k_P=1/R_F.$$

This is the conductance of the field circuit. The delay time or field circuit time constant is given as follows:

$$T_F=L_F\frac{R_F+R_W}{R_FR_W}. \tag{3.43}$$

The differentiation constant is

$$T_d=\frac{L_F}{R_WR_F}.$$

The eddy current or damping constant, which is the differentiation constant is

$$T_W=\frac{L_F}{R_W}. \tag{3.44}$$

Also the phase advance constant is

$$T_V=\frac{T_d}{R_P}.$$

A d.c. machine suitable for speed control would have a ratio of eddy current time constant T_W to field circuit time constant T_F of about 10%.

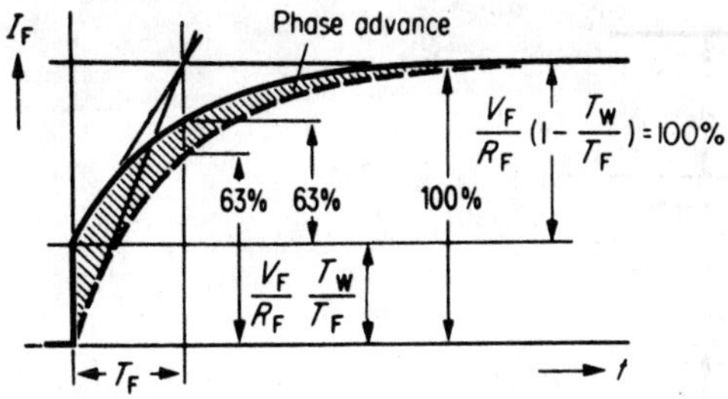

Fig. 3.27
Step response of the field current of a d.c. machine

Referring to Eqn (3.39) and Fig. 3.25, the step response for the field current I_F can be sketched as shown in Fig. 3.27.

The phase advance is represented by the hatched area. This lies between the broken curve representing the first order delay (Eqn (3.21)) and the step response.

3.6. Differentiation Element

In practice, a pure differentiation element cannot be realised and the differential equation obtained in practice is as follows:

$$\frac{dx_a(t)}{dt}T_1+x_a(t)=T_d\frac{dx_e(t)}{dt}. \tag{3.45}$$

If the constant T_1 is small compared to the constant T_d, then the equation represents differentiation to a reasonable approximation.

If a step change of input is considered of amplitude X_e, the output has an initial value of $(T_d/T_1)X_e$ and decays exponentially to zero. This is shown in Fig. 3.28.

The shaded amplitude/time area is equal in value to the product of the step amplitude X_e and the time T_d. The block diagram is shown in Fig. 3.29. The transient function corresponding to Fig. 3.28 is as follows:

$$f(t)=\frac{x_a(t)}{X_e}=\frac{T_d}{T_1}e^{-t/T_1}. \tag{3.46}$$

The transfer function which can be obtained from Eqn (3.45) is

$$F(s)=\frac{x_a(s)}{x_e(s)}=\frac{sT_d}{1+sT_1}. \tag{3.47}$$

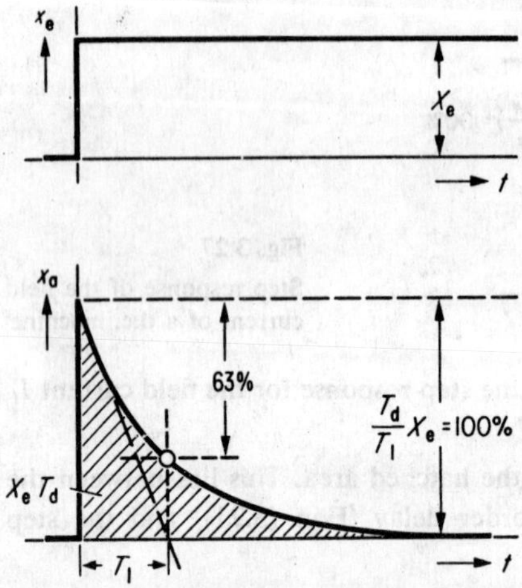

Fig. 3.28
Step response of a differentiating element. Output variable x_a, input variable x_e (step change)

This differentiating element is not normally used in drive controllers. However, it can be used for the measurement of acceleration if speed is measured by a tachogenerator and the tacho voltage is fed into the differentiator unit. This is used for acceleration control in lift and crane installations. Usually a passive differentiating element is used.

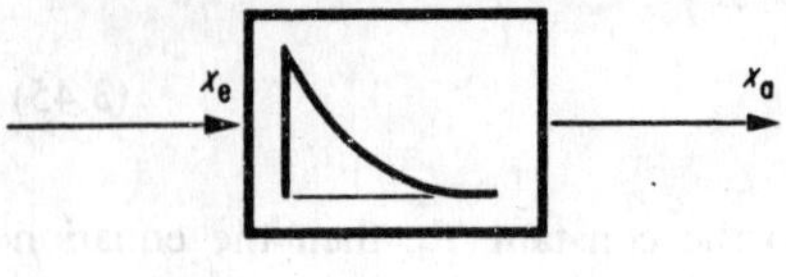

Fig. 3.29
Block diagram of differentiating element

3.6.1. Passive differentiating element

This element is often used for the measurement of acceleration (Fig. 3.30). The transfer function is as follows:

$$F(s) = \frac{V_2(s)}{V_1(s)} = \frac{sR_2C}{1+s(R+R_2)C}. \tag{3.48}$$

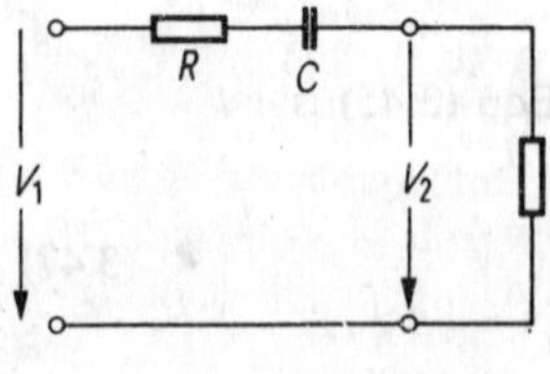

Fig. 3.30
Passive differentiating element for differentiation of a voltage, e.g. a tacho voltage

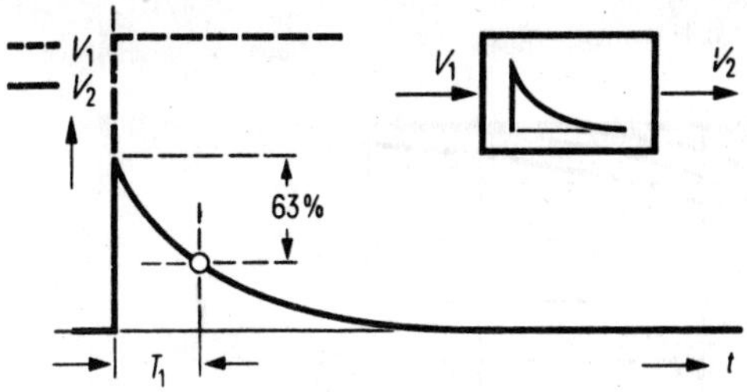

Fig. 3.31
Step response of a passive differentiating element

This includes a delay function and a differentiation function. The differentiation time constant is $R_L C$ and the delay time constant is $(R+R_L)C$ which must be larger than the differentiation time constant. For a step change of input voltage V_1, the initial value of the output voltage V_2 is $V_1 R_L/(R+R_L)$, which is of course smaller than V_1. The output voltage subsequently reduces exponentially to zero (Fig. 3.31).

The passive differentiating element is usually employed in combination with an amplifier. The load resistance is then very small. Considering then the output current I_2 in terms of the maximum current given by $I_m = V_1/R$, the following equation can be written:

$$I_2(s) = I_m \frac{sRC}{1+sRC}. \tag{3.49}$$

The differentiation time constant and the delay time constant are now equal.

3.7. Dead Time or Delay Element

The dead time element gives an output variable which is identical to the input variable but displaced in time by the dead time T_t. There may also be a change in amplitude between the input and output, indicated by the amplification factor k. The general time equation is thus given as follows:

$$x_a(t) = kx_e(t-T_t). \tag{3.50}$$

The dead time behaviour with dead time T_t can be considered as arising from an infinitely large number of first order delay elements arranged in series if the sum of the time constants of these individual non-interacting delays is equal to the dead time T_t. This is illustrated by Fig. 3.32 for which we have

$$T_1 = \sum t_\mu = T_t.$$

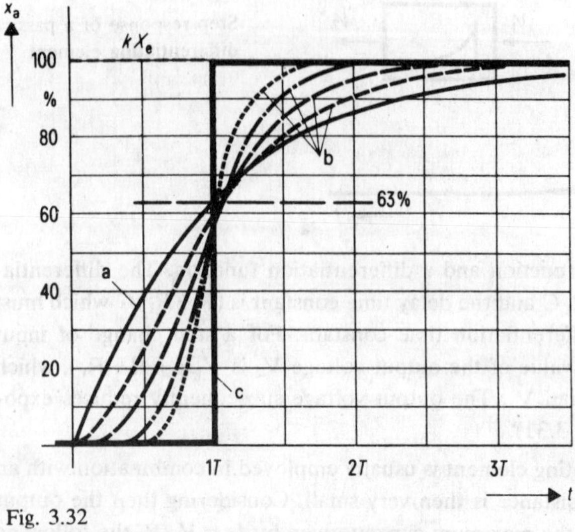

Fig. 3.32
Formation of a dead time element from a series of delay elements with dead time equal to the sum of the delay time constants.
Step responses:
a) One first order delay with time constant T_t
b) Several first order delays with sum of time constants equal to T_t
c) Infinite number of delays with sum of time constants equal to T_t

The step response of the dead time element is another step, displaced in time by the dead time T_t. The dead time element is a system element of an infinitely high order.

The output response to a step input of magnitude X_e is shown in Fig. 3.33. The block diagram is shown in Fig. 3.34.

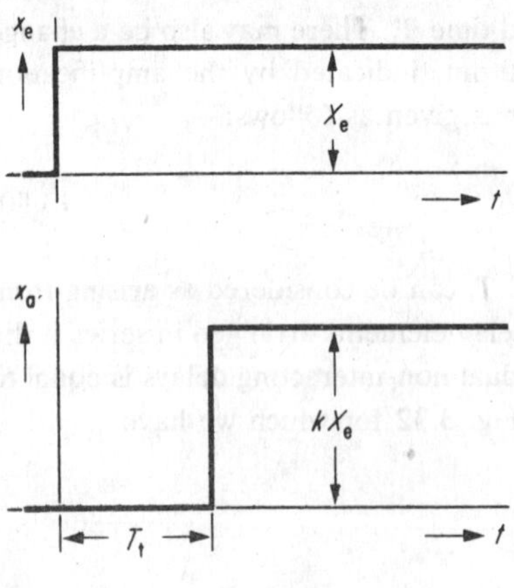

Fig. 3.33
Step response of a dead time element. Output variable x_a, step input x_e

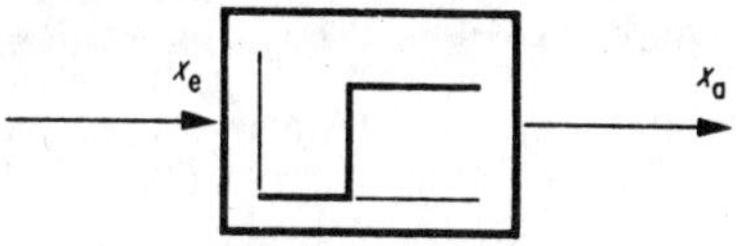

Fig. 3.34
Block diagram of dead time element

The transient function is given as follows:

$$x_a(t) = kX_e(t - T_t). \tag{3.51}$$

It is not possible to define the transient function in the form used in previous sections.

The transient function is given as follows:

$$F(s) = \frac{x_a(s)}{x_e(s)} = ke^{-sT_t}. \tag{3.52}$$

The factor e^{-sT_t} indicates that the output amplitude does not vary with frequency, but the phase angle of the dead time element increases negatively with increasing frequency. At a frequency of $f = 1/T_t$, the phase angle is 360°.

In process engineering, dead times are usually large. An example is a conveyor belt, which issues at the output end the same amount of material delivered to the input end with a dead time of T_t between the two events. In drive engineering, dead times are usually very small.

3.7.1. Controlled rectifiers

An example of a dead time element which is frequently found in drive engineering is the controlled rectifier or thyristor (Fig. 3.35).

Usually, three phase bridge circuits are used, the star connection being illustrated here. Each rectifier is made to conduct by means of triggering pulses from the triggering unit or drive unit.

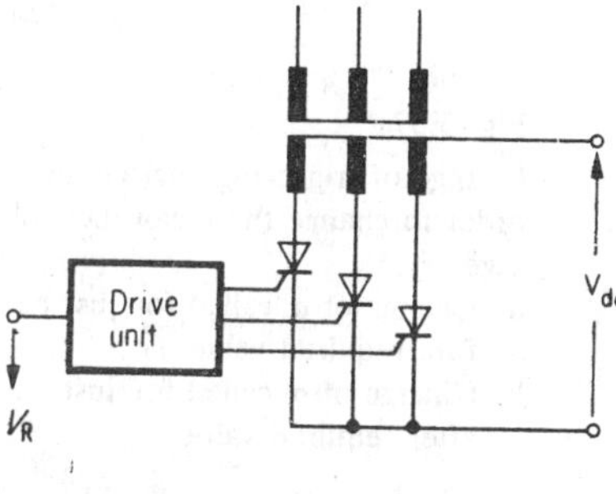

Fig. 3.35
The rectifier as an example of a dead time element. The triggering angle α is proportional to the controlling voltage V_R

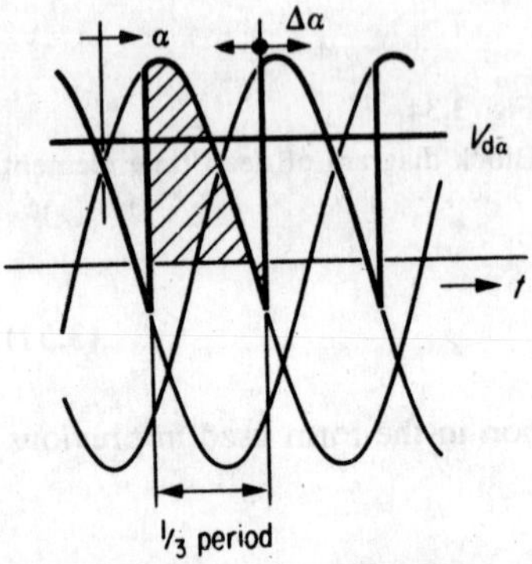

Fig. 3.36
Three triggering points within one period of a three phase rectifier. The natural triggering point is 30° after the rising alternating voltage cuts the zero line

The position of the triggering pulses with respect to the natural conduction point of an untriggered rectifier is called the triggering delay angle. The input voltage V_R to the triggering unit determines the triggering angle α. This voltage is the input variable and the voltage $V_{d\alpha}$ which the rectifier delivers is the output variable of the element.

Each rectifier can be triggered only once in one voltage cycle. In the star connected system shown with three rectifiers, the result is three triggering points within one period (Fig. 3.36). The mean value of the shaded voltage/time area is the mean d.c. output voltage $V_{d\alpha}$ which is dependent on the triggering angle and hence on the input voltage to the triggering unit V_R.

In controlling the d.c. voltage $V_{d\alpha}$ by means of the driving voltage V_R, the following extreme cases can arise (Fig. 3.37):

a) If a change of triggering angle is called for just before the new triggering angle occurs, then the change will take place immediately, without any delay.

b) If a change of triggering angle is called for just after the new triggering angle has passed, then approximately one third of a cycle will elapse before the new value of triggering angle can begin to operate. In this case we have a dead time behaviour.

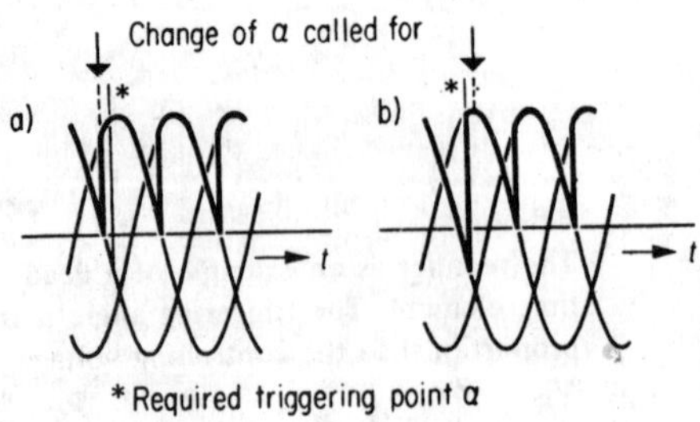

Fig. 3.37
Change of triggering angle α in order to change the mean d.c. voltage $V_{d\alpha}$
a) Change of α called for just before required value
b) Change of α called for just after required value

In general the rectifier dead time will be given by the following statistical mean value:

$$T_{SR} = \frac{1}{2} \frac{\text{Period duration}}{\text{Number of pulses per cycle}} . \tag{3.53}$$

With a 50 Hz mains supply, $T_{SR} = 3.3$ ms for the three pulse star connection and $T_{SR} = 1.7$ ms for a six pulse three-phase bridge connection.

Since these rectifier dead times are particularly small in comparison with the usual time constants, they may be treated as a first order delay.

It may be noted that in many cases the input circuit of the triggering unit also exhibits first order delay or integrator behaviour. However, this time constant is always very small, about 1 to 3 ms.

3.8. Non-Linear System Element

Many system elements do not have a linear relationship for the static behaviour of the output variable with respect to the input variable. This means that a change of input variable of say Δx_e results in a smaller or larger change Δx_a of the output variable, depending on the position of the points on the characteristic curve. This is shown in Fig. 3.38.

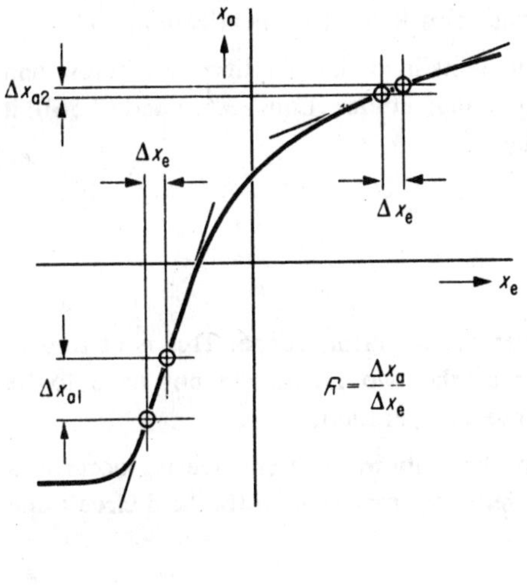

Fig. 3.38
Static characteristic of a non-linear system element. Output amplitude plotted against input amplitude. The slope of the characteristic is the amplification k of the system element

The output variable is some specific function of the input variable, i.e.

$$x_a(t) = f[x_e(t)]. \tag{3.54}$$

This equation includes an amplification factor which depends on the position of the operating point on the characteristic:

$$k = k_0 \Phi_1(x_e). \tag{3.55}$$

It also has a similar time constant behaviour:

$$T = T_0 \Phi_2(x_e). \tag{3.56}$$

The amplification at any point on the characteristic (Fig. 3.38) is defined by the following equation:

$$k = \frac{\Delta x_a}{\Delta x_e}. \tag{3.57}$$

This is the slope of the tangent to the characteristic at the given point, or in other words, the differential of the curve at that point.

Non-linear behaviour can occur with all the previously considered systems. Since a non-linear characteristic can be replaced by its tangent at any working point for small changes Δx_e of the input variable x_e, then any of the previously considered systems, if non-linear, can be represented in the usual way by linear theory, if considering small variations. This is termed linearization.

For a series of non-linear system elements involving amplification factors and time constants dependent on the signal magnitudes (Eqns (3.55) and (3.56)), it is possible to define a ratio given by

$$\frac{\text{Time constant}}{\text{Amplification}}$$

which is approximately constant over the operating range. This is of importance for the associated controller as the two factors do not have to be adjusted independently over the range of operation.

The most important examples of non-linearity in drive engineering occur in a d.c. machine armature circuit when fed from rectifiers, in the field circuit due to iron saturation, and in rectifier systems due to the sinusoidal relationship between rectified output voltage and triggering angle.

3.8.1. Rectifier fed armature circuit of d.c. machine

The voltage which feeds the armature circuit when obtained from a rectifier unit has a waveform as shown in Fig. 3.36. However, the generated voltage produced in the armature is constant. The armature current I_A is driven by the difference between the applied voltage V_A and the generated voltage E (Eqn (3.18) and Fig. 3.15). There may be periods in which the instantaneous value of the armature voltage V_A is less than the generated voltage E. If the mean value of the armature voltage $V_{d\alpha}$ (Fig. 3.36) is only slightly greater than the generated voltage E, then the time intervals with a noticeable negative voltage difference are large. The curent smoothing action due to the inductance of the armature circuit is then insufficient to ensure a continuous armature current and the current becomes discontinuous, i.e. there are periods of zero current. In the discontinuous current range (Fig. 3.39), the mean value of armature current varies much less than above the limit of discontinuous current, for equal change of driving voltage $V_A - E$. The amplification k and the armature circuit time constant T_A are dependent on the voltage and current magnitudes.

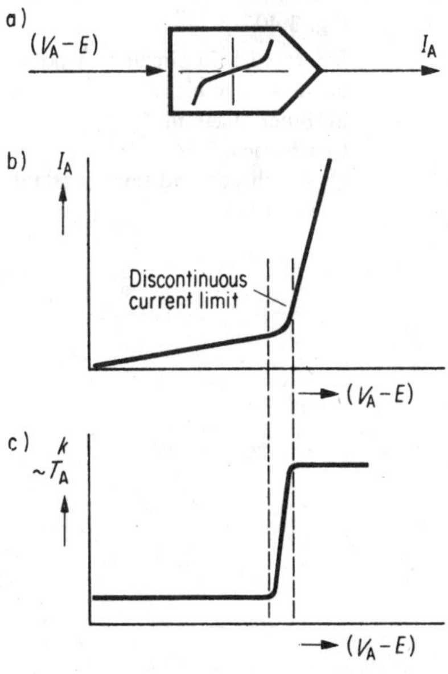

Fig. 3.39
Armature circuit of d.c. machine as a non-linear element.
a) Block diagram
b) Characteristic
c) Amplitude and time constant variation

3.8.2. Iron saturation

The excitation flux of a d.c. machine is produced in the laminated iron field poles. If the field current is very large, the iron becomes saturated and the flux is no longer proportional to the field current. Further increase of the field current produces only a small increase of flux (Fig. 3.40).

At first the flux Φ follows the field voltage V_F linearly. At the onset of saturation, however, the characteristic contains a bend and then increases only slowly.

The slope at each point of the curve is the effective amplification k:

$$k = \frac{\Delta \Phi}{\Delta V_F}. \tag{3.58}$$

This slope is also a measure of the permeability μ of the iron. The inductance L_F of the field winding is proportional to the permeability and since the winding resistance is almost constant, the following relationship is obtained for any point on the characteristic:

$$\frac{T_F}{k} = \text{constant.}$$

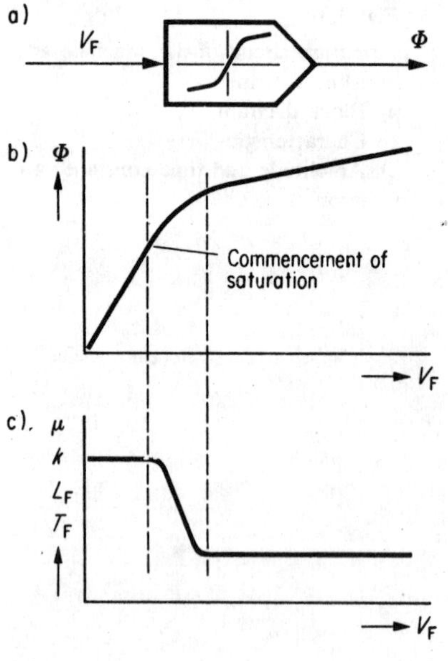

Fig. 3.40
Saturated field circuit as a non-linear system element
a) Block diagram
b) Characteristic
c) Amplitude and time constant variation

3.8.3. Relationship between rectifier voltage and triggering angle

Let us define the mean d.c. voltage of a rectifier with thyristor triggering at the natural triggering point (zero delay) as V_d. If a delay angle is introduced, the rectifier d.c. voltage, now dependent on the triggering angle, is given as follows:

$$V_{d\alpha} = V_d \cos \alpha. \tag{3.59}$$

When α is equal to 90°, the maximum slope of the characteristic occurs and thus the maximum amplification (Fig. 3.41).

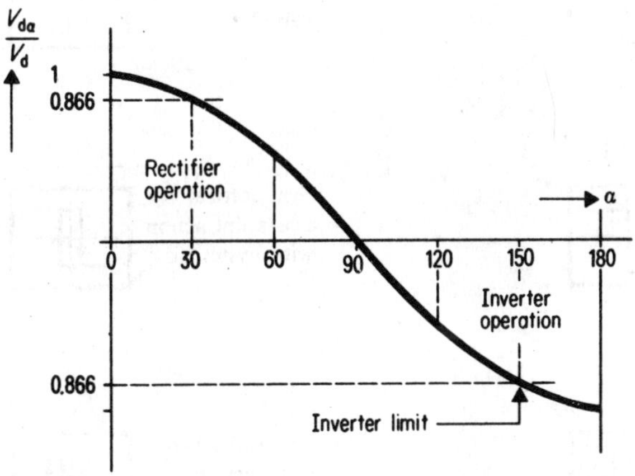

Fig. 3.41
Control characteristic of a controlled rectifier. Mean value of rectifier d.c. output voltage against triggering angle α (commutation time neglected and continuous current flow assumed)

In addition to non-linear system elements with continuous curved characteristics, there are also those whose curves consist of a number of linear sections but with discontinuities. Some of the important cases are illustrated in Fig. 3.42.

One sided limiting

Two sided limiting

One sided zero limiting (diode)

Absolute value generation

One sided zero limiting with threshold value and inversion

Two sided threshold value action

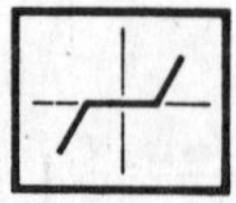

Symmetrical two-point action (e.g. relay)

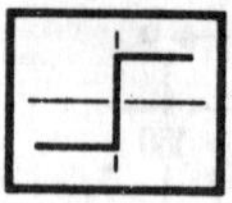

Symmetrical two-point action with hysteresis

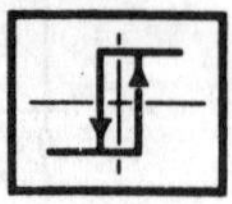

Asymmetrical two-point action

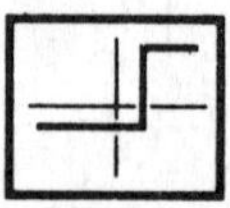

One sided two-point action with hysteresis

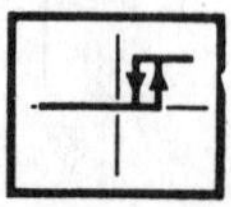

Symmetrical three-point action

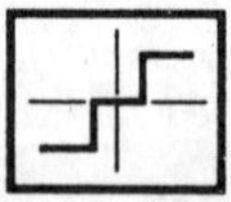

Symmetrical three-point action with hysteresis

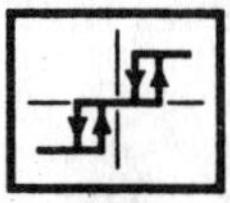

Fig. 3.42 Discontinuous system element characteristics

4. Electronic Controllers

The three tasks of the control equipment have already been discussed in Chapter 1. The first task, measurement of the controlled variable, is performed by the measurement transducer, which is part of the control loop.

The controller performs the remaining two tasks of the control equipment. The main part is the control amplifier or operational amplifier. These are usually multistage d.c. voltage or current amplifiers with a very large value of gain and a very wide frequency range. On the input side, they often have a voltage difference circuit which is balanced or symmetrical (Fig. 4.1).

The potential of the common line M is referred to as the zero or reference potential. The output of the amplifier in contrast to the input is asymmetrical. Within the linear operating range, the output signal of the amplifier is proportional to the input signal. The static characteristic is thus a straight line (Fig. 4.2) and the amplifier is called a linear amplifier.

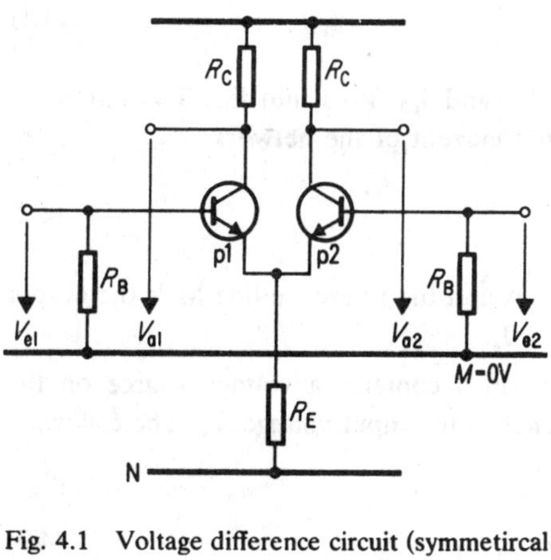

Fig. 4.1 Voltage difference circuit (symmetircal or balanced amplifier input)

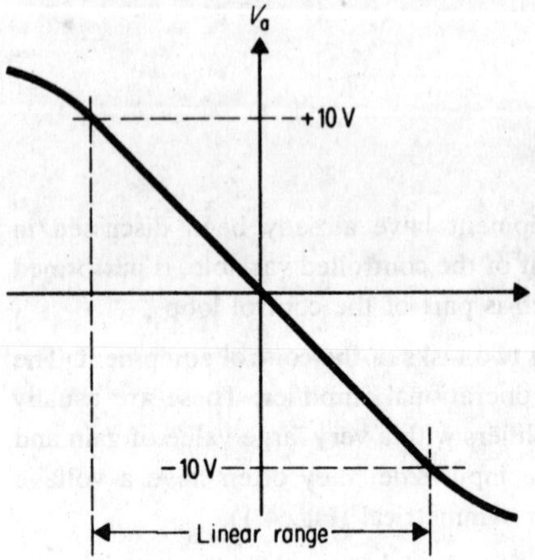

Fig. 4.2
Linear characteristic of the amplifier in the linear operating range

4.1. The Four Terminal Operational Amplifier

The operational amplifier can be regarded as a four terminal network (Fig. 4.3). It has two input connections E_- and E_+ which are isolated from the common line M and a single output connection A, the potential of which is referred to the common line M.

At the inputs E_- and E_+ are the voltages V_{e1} and V_{e2}, which are referred to the potential of M. Their difference is the input voltage V_e:

$$V_e = V_{e1} - V_{e2}. \tag{4.1}$$

A current I_{e1} flows into the input E_- and I_{e2} flows into E_+. The difference between the two currents is the input current of the network:

$$I_e = I_{e1} - I_{e2}. \tag{4.2}$$

The voltage between the connection A and the reference line M is the output voltage $-V_a$. The output current is $-I_a$.

An amplifier is an active network which contains a voltage source on the output side, $-V$, which is proportional to the input voltage V_e. The following equation applies to the output:

$$-V = -V_a - I_a Z_a. \tag{4.3}$$

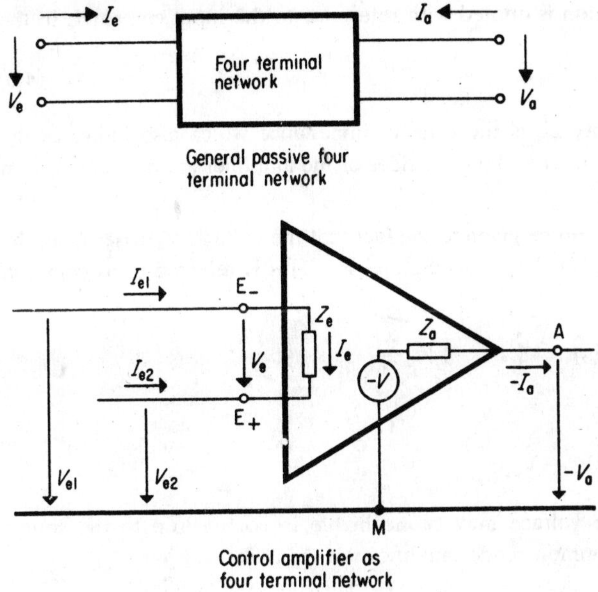

Fig. 4.3 Amplifier as four terminal network

Z_a is the complex output impedance of the amplifier. If the output current is zero, then the source voltage V and the output voltage V_a are identical.

The complex input impedance at the input side is Z_e and the following equation can be written:

$$V_e = I_e Z_e. \tag{4.4}$$

The most important property of the device is the amplification or gain, A_u:

$$-V = V_e A_u. \tag{4.5}$$

The output voltage source supplies a voltage which is greater than the input voltage by the voltage amplification factor A_u. This is often quoted in decibels (dB), i.e.

$$(A_u)_{dB} = 20 \log \left(-\frac{V}{V_e} \right).$$

Often the amplification is quoted with reference to the input current I_e in the form

$$-V = I_e Z_u. \tag{4.6}$$

The complex quantity Z_u is the transfer impedance which also indicates the degree to which the input and output sides of the amplifier are decoupled from each other.

Consideration must also be given to the fact that the voltage V_e arises from the voltages V_{e1} and V_{e2} at the inputs E_- and E_+. This is referred to as common mode input

$$V_g = \tfrac{1}{2}(V_{e1} + V_{e2}).$$

It is important when

$$\tfrac{1}{2}|V_{e1} + V_{e2}| > |V_{e1} - V_{e2}|.$$

This common mode voltage may be negligible in comparison to the source voltage $-V$. The common mode amplification A_g is defined as

$$A_g = -V/V_g$$

and the common mode suppression K_g is defined as

$$K_g = A_u/A_g.$$

4.1.1. Ideal amplifier

The amplification of the ideal amplifier is infinitely large. Thus a large output voltage is obtained with an input voltage and current which are approximately zero. The input power is therefore also approximately zero. The transfer impedance Z_u is very large. Moreover, the phase displacement is zero for all frequencies. The output load has no influence on the output voltage because the output impedance is zero.

The common mode input drive has no effect on the output signal. Thus, for the ideal amplifier, we have

$$A_u \to \infty \quad \text{and} \quad Z_u \to \infty \quad \text{with} \quad P_e \to 0$$

$$Z_a \to 0, \quad A_g \to 0, \quad V_a \text{ as large as required.}$$

No phase displacement.

4.1.2. Real amplifier

The ideal amplifier cannot of course be realised.

Real amplifiers can be constructed with discrete elements or can be produced as integrated circuit linear amplifiers in a single silicon chip. The discrete element amplifier (Fig. 4.4) usually contains relatively few transistors. Its amplification factor A_u is therefore about an order of magnitude smaller ($\geqslant$5000) than that of the integrated circuit amplifier ($\geqslant$50 000) which contains about three times the number of transistors (Fig. 4.5). This is the open loop gain or amplification of the amplifier.

Operational amplifiers usually have three stages:

1. Symmetrical differential input stage,
2. Intermediate voltage amplifier stage,
3. Push–pull output stage with low output impedance.

The ideal amplifier is in fact closely approached. Less than 0.02% of the maximum output value is required at the input to fully control the amplifier.

The input terminal E_- is called the inverting input. This means that if the terminal E_+ is connected directly or via a resistance to the reference line M and the amplifier is driven at the E_- terminal with a positive voltage, the

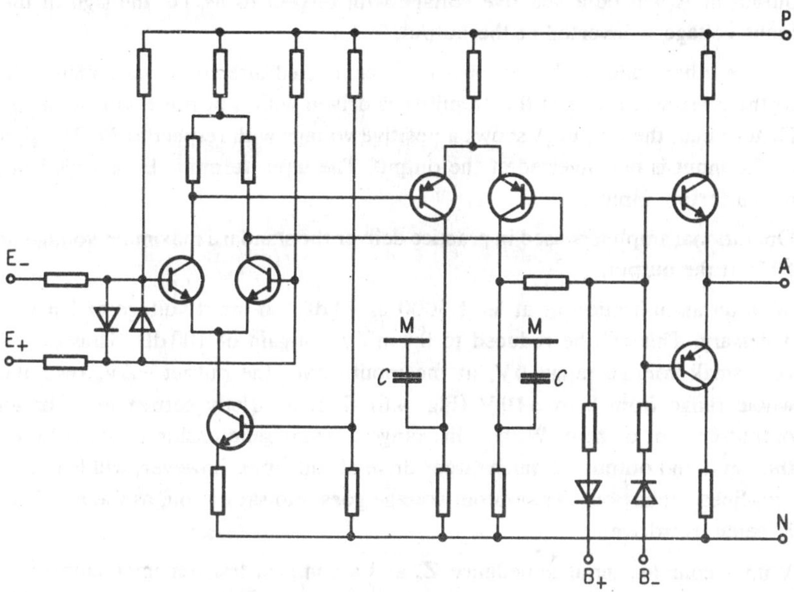

Fig. 4.4 Circuit of a practical operational amplifier using discrete components

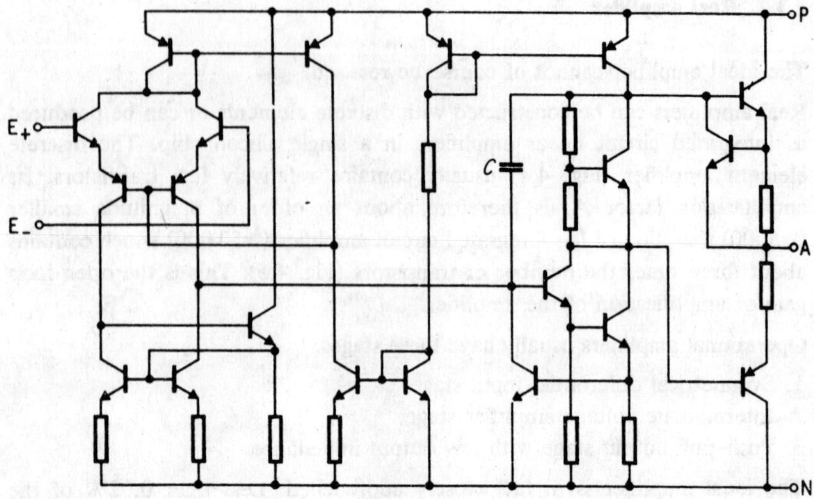

Fig. 4.5 Circuit of a practical integrated circuit operational amplifier

output at A will be a negative voltage with respect to *M*, i.e. the sign of the input voltage is inverted at the output.

On the other hand, if the terminal E_- is connected directly or via a resistance to the reference line and the amplifier is driven with a positive voltage at the E_+ terminal, the output A shows a positive voltage with respect to *M*. The sign of the input is not inverted at the output. The input terminal E_+ is called the non-inverting input.

Operational amplifiers used in practice deliver the standard maximum voltage of 10 V at the output.

With an amplification of at least 5000 or 74 dB, an input voltage of 2 mV is necessary. This will be reduced to 0.1 mV for a gain of 100 dB. Thus only a very small voltage range ΔV_e at the input drives the output $-\Delta V_a$ over the whole range from 0 to ±10 V (Fig. 4.6). This is strictly correct only for an output current of zero. Within this range a linear relationship exists between the input and output. A much larger drive at the input, however, will lead to a non-linear behaviour. The output voltage goes into saturation, as the amplifier is being overdriven.

With a complex input impedance Z_e and a complex transfer impedance Z_u a complex amplification factor A_u results. In the linear control range therefore,

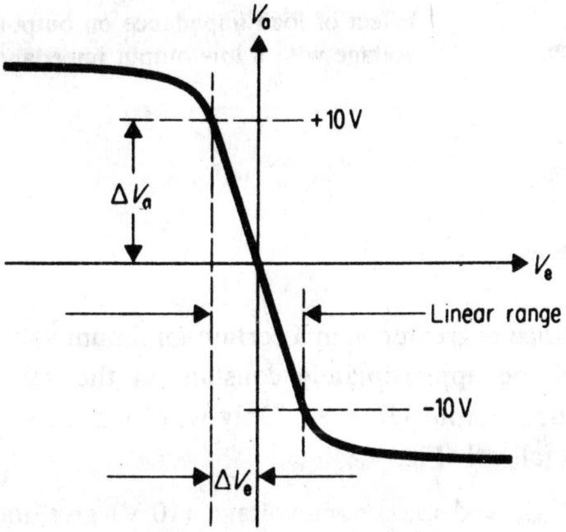

Fig. 4.6
Overall control range at the output of an operational amplifier from −10 V to +10 V

the amplification factor (with output current approximately zero) is

$$\overline{A_u} = -\frac{\Delta V_a}{\Delta V_e} = -\frac{\Delta V_a}{\Delta I_e Z_e} \tag{4.7}$$

and the transfer impedance is

$$Z_u = \overline{A_u} Z_e. \tag{4.8}$$

In practice, the output current I_a of the amplifier cannot be zero as demanded by Eqns (4.7) and (4.8). Thus the output impedance Z_a (Eqn (4.3)) must be kept as small as possible for a limited loading range. This can be achieved by a push–pull output stage as shown in Fig. 4.7.

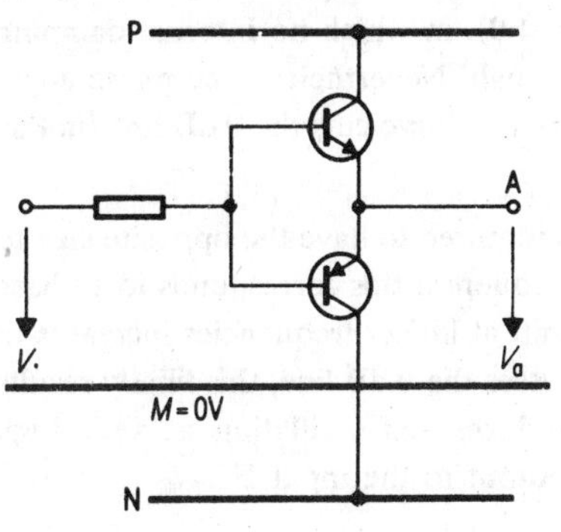

Fig. 4.7
Push–pull output stage with very small output impedance

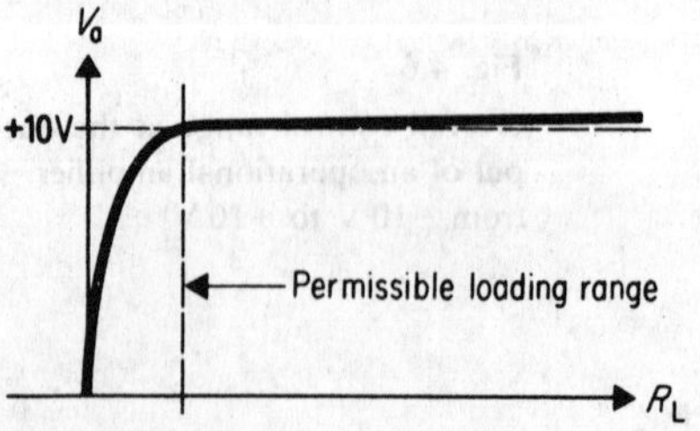

Fig. 4.8
Effect of load impedance on output voltage with a low output impedance

With this circuit, if the load impedance is greater than a certain minimum value R_{Lmin}, the output voltage V_a will be approximately constant at the value obtained with a completely unloaded output ($R_L = \infty$). Only with impedances lower than R_{Lmin} does it begin to fall off (Fig. 4.8).

The minimum load impedance R_{Lmin} and maximum voltage (10 V) give the typical load current for the amplifier. Thus we refer to, for example a 5 mA amplifier with minimum load impedance of 2 kΩ.

Further properties of the real amplifier are concerned with either fast or slow changes of the input voltage V_e, referred to as the dynamic or static behaviour of the amplifier.

4.1.3. Dynamic response of the real amplifier

The dynamic response of amplifiers is very important in the transient analysis of control systems.

The control amplifier is a complex system element. The transistors have self-capacitance, which, together with circuit resistances, results in delays. Thus the general time equation is a higher order differential equation as would also be indicated by the complex amplification and complex impedances. A system element of this kind produces a phase change between input and output, which increases with increase of frequency. The break frequencies in the Bode diagrams of an amplifier (curve $|F_V|$, Fig. 4.9), in which no internal damping precautions have been taken, are all quite high. Nevertheless, the phase angle ϕ_V has exceeded 180° at the point f_T where the curve cuts the 0 dB line (in this case the amplification is 1).

In many applications the output voltage is required to have the opposite sign to the input voltage at terminal E_-. At low frequency, this corresponds to a phase shift of 180°. Since the additional phase shift at higher frequencies increases to 180° before the amplifier characteristic crosses the 0 dB line, this finally results in a total phase shift of 360°. This produces self-oscillation at very high frequency if there is feedback from the output to the input E_-.

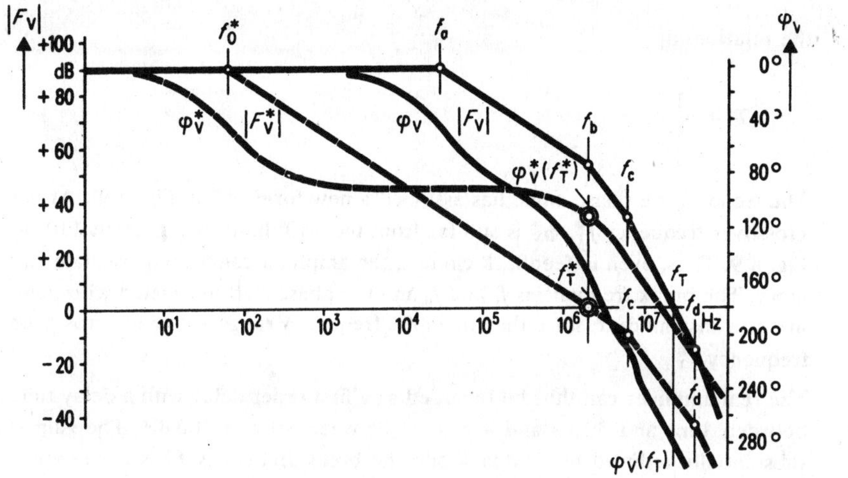

Fig. 4.9 Bode diagram of an operational amplifier

$|F_V|$ Amplification of the undamped amplifier with break frequencies f_a, f_b, f_c, f_d (time constants $T_a = 1/2\pi f_a$ $T_b = 1/2\pi f_b$ etc.)

ϕ_V Phase angle of undamped amplifier

$|F_V^*|$ Amplification of damped amplifier with break frequencies f_0^*, f_c, f_d

ϕ_V^* Phase angle of damped amplifier

Whereas the phase angle $\phi_V(f_T)$ is about 280° at the crossover frequency f_T of the undamped amplifier, the phase angle $\phi_V^*(f_T^*)$ for the damped amplifier is about 110° at the crossover frequency f_T^*.

By means of additional capacitors C (see Figs. 4.4 and 4.5), it is possible to shift the lowest corner frequency (f_a in Fig. 4.9) to a lower frequency (f_0^*) and possibly to eliminate the next highest corner frequency (f_b in Fig. 4.9) by compensation.

In this way, using a feedback circuit, a first order delay behaviour is produced by the control amplifier in the operating range, that is, up to the intercept frequency f_T^*. The transfer function is

$$F_V(s) = \frac{-\Delta V_a}{\Delta V_e} = \frac{A_u}{1 + sT_v} = \overline{A_u} \tag{4.9}$$

(Z_a is assumed to approach zero).

Here A_u is the real voltage amplification for an input frequency close to zero and the delay time T_v is the new or equivalent time constant which results from the relationship

$$T_v = \frac{1}{2\pi f_0}.$$

The trend of the phase angle has assumed a new form (ϕ_V^* in Fig. 4.9). At the crossover frequency f_T^*, ϕ_V^* is still far from the 180° limit, being about 110° in Fig. 4.9. Thus, even in feedback circuits, the amplifier cannot self-oscillate any more. The break frequencies f_c and f_d and the phase shift associated with them are now insignificant, since they lie in the frequency range above the crossover frequency f_T^*.

The real amplifier can thus be regarded as a first order delay with a delay time between 1 ms and 30 ms and a gain of between 80 and 100 dB. The gain is substantially reduced by feedback and the break frequency f_0^* is correspondingly increased. The result is a corresponding reduction of the delay time.

Since the operational amplifier behaves as a first order delay in the operating range and accordingly has no tendency to oscillate, even with feedback, the parameters of the amplifier can be quoted as real values. Thus:

Input impedance $R_e = \frac{\Delta V_e}{\Delta I_e}$,

Output impedance $R_a = \frac{\Delta V_a}{\Delta I_a}$,

Amplification $A_u = \frac{-\Delta V_a}{\Delta V_e}$,

Transfer impedance $R_u = \frac{-\Delta V_a}{\Delta I_e}$.

A relationship between the amplification A_u, transfer impedance R_u, and input impedance R_e is as follows:

$$A_u R_e = R_u.$$

4.1.4. Static response of the real amplifier

The static response of the operational amplifier is significant from the point of view of accuracy of control.

The parameters of semiconductor amplifiers are affected by changes of supply voltage and changes of temperature. The effects would be eliminated by an absolutely symmetrical input circuit (Fig. 4.1) but absolute symmetry is not possible. Integrated circuit amplifiers, however, (Fig. 4.5) are better in this respect than those built from discrete components (Fig. 4.4).

Three properties are important in static response:

the common mode rejection ratio (CMRR);
the input offset voltage;
the offset current.

The common mode rejection ratio K_g is defined as the quotient of the voltage amplification A_u and the common mode amplification A_g.

The voltage amplification A_u is defined according to Eqn (4.7) by

$$A_u = \frac{-\Delta V_a}{\Delta V_e} \quad \text{or} \quad (A_u)_{dB} = 20 \log \frac{-\Delta V_a}{\Delta V_e} \tag{4.10}$$

with an amplification factor of 10 000 to 100 000 or 80 dB to 100 dB.

The common mode amplification A_g, as defined by Fig. 4.10, can be obtained from

$$A_g = \frac{-\Delta V_a}{V_g} \quad \text{or} \quad (A_g)_{dB} = 20 \log \frac{-\Delta V_a}{V_g}. \tag{4.11}$$

The amplification factor A_g lies between 0.05 and 0.5, i.e. between −26 dB and −6 dB. In most amplifiers the common mode drive at the input may even exceed the nominal signal range of ±10 V.

The common mode rejection ratio K_g is given as follows:

$$K_g = \frac{A_u}{A_g} \quad \text{or} \quad (K_g)_{dB} = 20 \log \frac{A_u}{A_g} = (A_u)_{dB} - (A_g)_{dB}. \tag{4.12}$$

It lies between 50 000 and 200 000 or 94 to 106 dB.

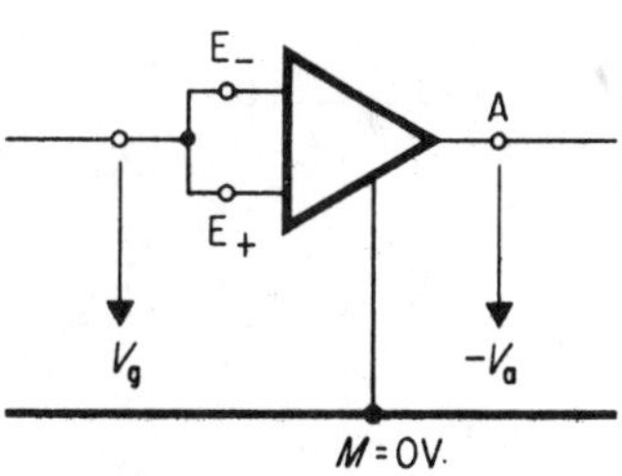

Fig. 4.10
Amplifier with common mode drive

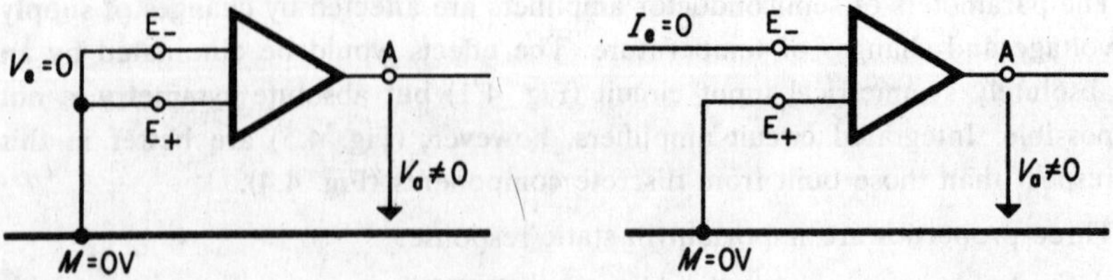

a) Inputs short circuited to M ($V_e = 0$)

b) Input open circulated ($I_e = 0$)

Fig. 4.11 Amplifier with non-zero output voltage

Owing to the amplifier input circuit not being perfectly symmetrical, a non-zero voltage at the amplifier output circuit may appear under the following conditions:

a) when the amplifier inputs are connected together and to the common terminal M (Fig. 4.11a),

b) when input E_- is open circuited with E_+ connected to M (Fig. 4.11b).

The amplifier characteristic $-V_a = f(V_e)$ (Fig. 4.12) indicates how large the input offset voltage V_{e0} must be in order to bring the output voltage to zero.

A simple measuring circuit for determining the offset voltage is shown in Fig. 4.13. In this circuit, we have

$$-V_a = V_{e0} + \Delta V_e = V_{e0} + \frac{-V_a}{A_u}$$

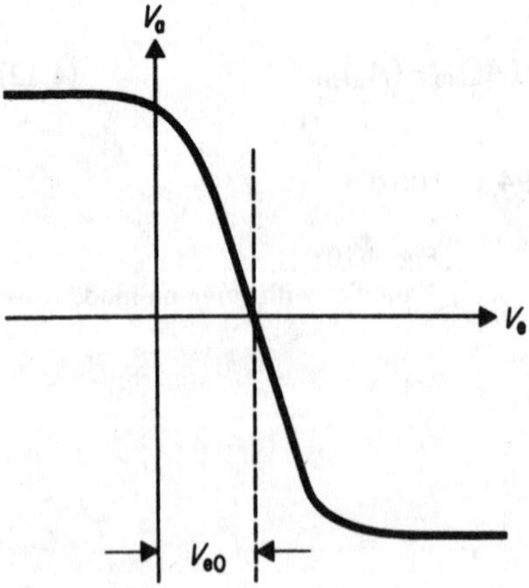

Fig. 4.12
Amplifier characteristic
$-V_a = f(V_e)$

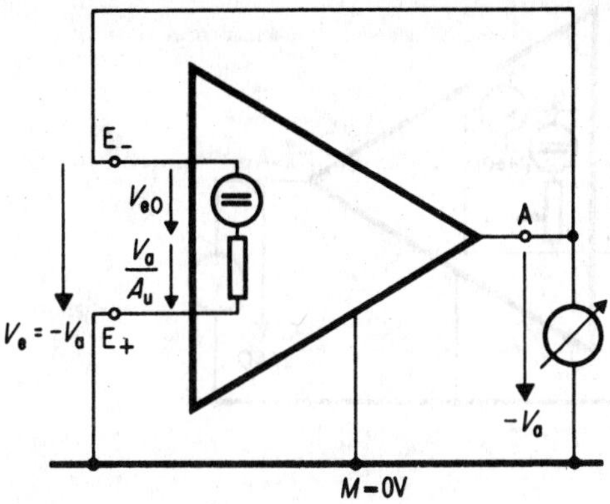

Fig. 4.13
Simple measuring circuit for determination of input offset voltage V_{e0}

and thus

$$V_{e0} = -V_a\left(1 - \frac{1}{A_u}\right). \tag{4.13}$$

The measured voltage $-V_a$ is equal to the input offset voltage. The measurement has an error of approximately $1/A_u \simeq 10^{-4}$. The input offset voltage can be positive or negative. By inserting an additional voltage V_{e0}, the offset voltage can be compensated.

There is also an input bias current which is shown in the amplifier characteristic $-V = f(I_e)$ (Fig. 4.14). This characteristic can be determined using the circuit shown in Fig. 4.15, firstly for input E_ and then for input E+.

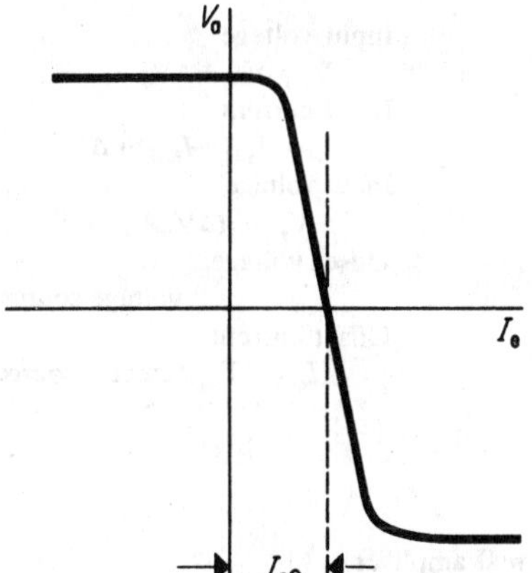

Fig. 4.14
Amplifier characteristic $-V_a = f(I_e)$

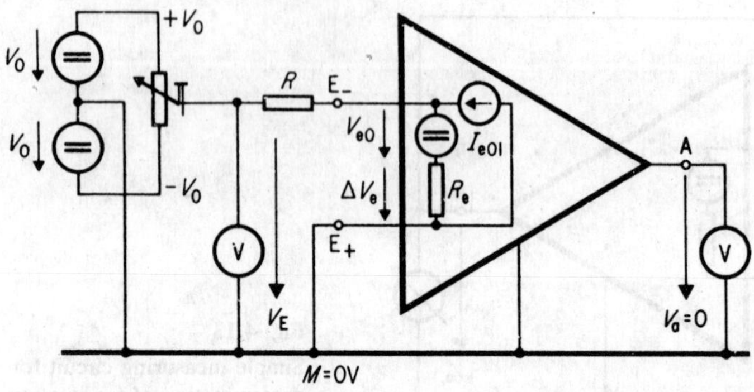

Fig. 4.15
Simple circuit for the determination of input bias current at terminal E_-. If terminals E_- and E_+ are interchanged, the input bias current at input E_+ can be measured. The input offset voltage can be neglected if the voltage drop in resistance R is very large with respect to V_{e0}. I_{e0} is an impressed current.

With the output voltage $V_a = 0$, the input bias current is obtained. The error due to the input offset voltage can be neglected in the measurement if V_{eo} is very small with respect to $I_{eo}R$.
The input bias current is compensated when

$$I_{e01/2} = -V_e/R. \tag{4.14}$$

The input bias currents of both inputs are shown in the complete equivalent circuit diagram (Fig. 4.16).

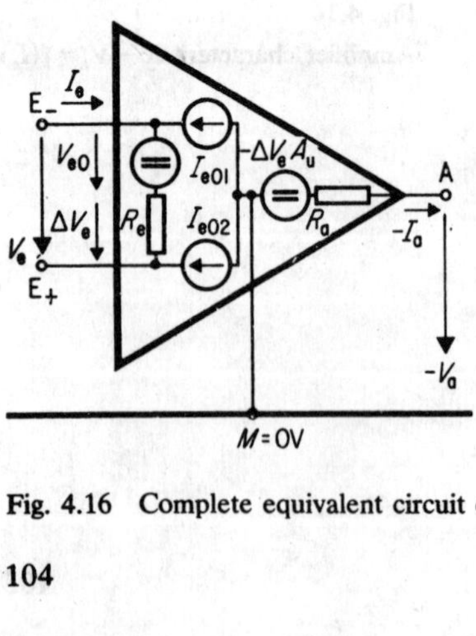

Input voltage
$V_e = V_{e0} + \Delta V_e$
Input current
$I_e = (I_{e01} - I_{e02}) + \Delta T_e$
Input voltage
$-V_a = -(\Delta V_e A_u - I_0 R_a)$
Offset voltage
v_{e0} voltage source
Offset current
$(I_{e01} - T_{e02})$ current source

Fig. 4.16 Complete equivalent circuit of the real amplifier

In general the input bias currents I_{e01} and I_{e02} of the two inputs E_- and E_+ have differents signs so that to a large extent they neutralize each other. This is always the case when the two inputs are connected via resistances. The input offset current

$$I_{e0} = I_{e01} - I_{e02} \tag{4.15}$$

is a minimum when the two resistances are of equal magnitude. Therefore, at the input E_+ a resistance is connected to the common line M of the same value as the overall circuit resistance at the input E_-.

All the parameters introduced in this chapter are dependent on the ambient temperature and the supply voltage and therefore the following equation has to be considered:

$$G = G_N \frac{\delta G}{\delta \theta_u} \Delta\theta_u + \frac{\delta G}{\delta V_v} \Delta V_v \tag{4.16}$$

where

G_N is the nominal value at rated temperature and supply voltage of parameter G

$\delta G/\delta\theta_u$ is the temperature coefficient,

$\Delta\theta_u$ is the temperature difference with respect to the rated temperature,

$\delta G/\delta V_v$ is the voltage coefficient,

ΔV_v is the voltage difference with respect to the rated supply voltage.

Changes in thse variables cannot be suppressed by the controller. It is therefore important tq keep these errors as small as possible.

4.2. Fundamental Circuits of the Control Amplifier

The foremost application of the operational amplifier is its use in controllers. It is used as an inverting or non-inverting amplifier or as a differential amplifier, always with feedback. Further applications arise in analogue computer circuits in which sums, differences, mean values, absolute values, integrals and differentials, products, squares, quotients, roots and reciprocal value circuits are to be found. They also appear in dividing and inverting amplifiers, in impedance changers and function generators, in digital to analogue and analogue to digital converters and as positive feedback amplifiers in flip–flop amplifiers, in limit value alarms and three state switches as required for adjustment controls.

The various functions are obtained by appropriate input and feedback circuits. An important characteristic is whether the feedback is negative so that the amplification is reduced, or positive so that the amplification becomes extremely large.

a) Amplifier with negative feedback

The angle α between the static curve $-V_a = f(I_0)$ of the amplifier (at zero frequency) and the zero line, becomes smaller with increasing conductance of the negative feedback network between the output and inverting input E_- of the amplifier (see Fig. 4.17).

I_0 is the current flowing through R_0 connected to the input E_-.

b) Amplifier with positive feedback

The angle β between the static characteristic $+V_a = f(I_0^*)$ of the amplifier and the zero line becomes increasingly larger with increase of conductance of the positive feedback network between the amplifier output and the non-inverting input E_+ (Fig. 4.18).

I_0^* is the current flowing in the resistance R_0^* connected to the input E_+. At the flipover point with input current I_{0K}^* the feedback current I_f^* is equal to I_{0K}^*, but with opposite sign.

By far the majority of amplifier applications use the amplifier with negative feedback.

It should be remembered that the practical amplifier very nearly approaches the ideal amplifier. This means that the input power for driving the amplifier is

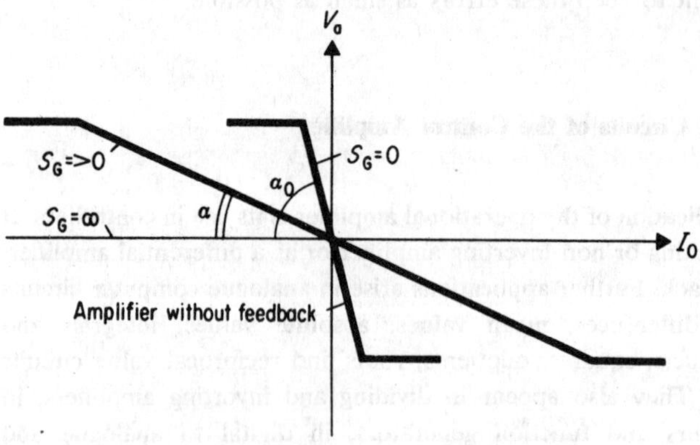

Fig. 4.17
Static characteristic of amplifier with negative feedback. S_G = conductance of the feedback network. Bias current not taken into account

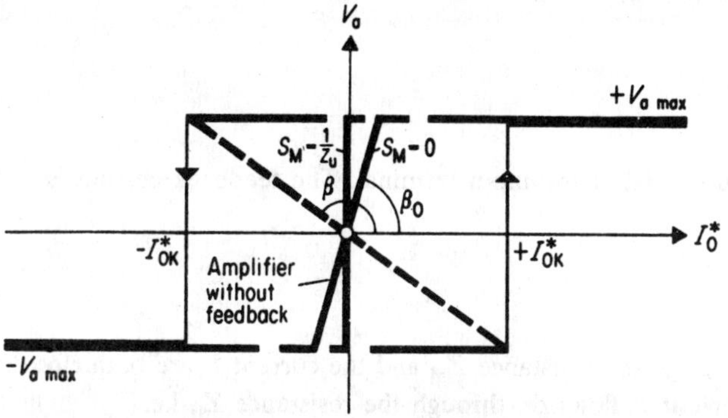

Fig. 4.18
Static characteristic of positive coupled flip–flop amplifier. S_M = conductance of the positive feedback network. Bias current I_{e0} not taken into account

very small as is the input current ΔI_e and the input voltage ΔV_e so that the zero errors should be very small.

4.2.1. Inverting amplifiers

The circuit of Fig. 4.19 allows several input voltages to be fed to the common input terminal E₋ via various input channels. In this way the error signal of a control system may be determined.

In order to minimize the zero difference current, the resistance Z_M should be of magnitude

$$Z_M = \frac{Z_0 Z_f}{Z_0 + Z_f}. \tag{4.17}$$

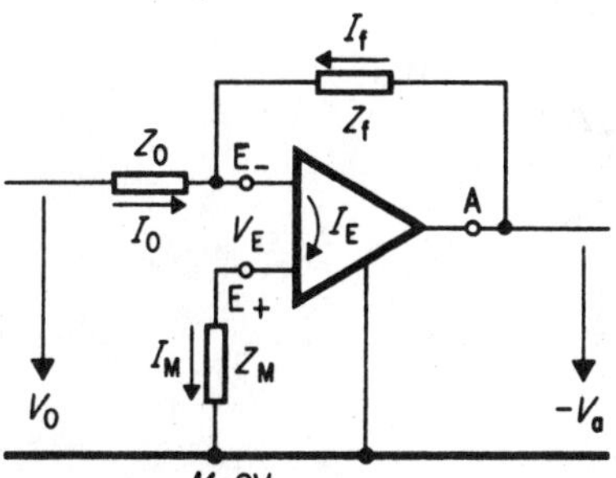

Fig. 4.19 Inverting amplifier

For the input current

$$I_0=\frac{V_0-V_E}{Z_0}$$

where V_E is the potential of the input terminal. The feedback current is

$$-I_f=\frac{V_E-V_a}{Z_f}.$$

The current I_M through the resistance Z_M and the current I_e are both close to zero. Thus the current I_0 flows on through the resistance Z_f, i.e.

$$I_0=-I_f.$$

Also the voltage V_E is close to zero. Thus the output voltage is given by

$$-I_fZ_f=-V_a=\frac{V_0}{Z_0}Z_f. \tag{4.18}$$

This leads to the relationship

$$\frac{-V_a}{V_0}=\frac{Z_f}{Z_0}. \tag{4.19}$$

The accuracy of Eqn (4.19) will be dependent on the assumption that I_e is negligible compared to I_0. The error caused by the current I_e can be thought of as originating from the fact that the amplification A_u is finite. The input resistance of the amplifier R_e is large compared with Z_M (Fig. 4.19). Thus the potential of the terminal E_- is approximately equal to the voltage between the two input terminals E_- and E_+.
From the equations

$$\frac{V_0-V_E}{Z_0}=\frac{V_E-V_a}{Z_f} \quad \text{and} \quad V_e=-V_a/A_u$$

the following equation is obtained:

$$\frac{-V_a}{V_0}=\frac{Z_f}{Z_0}+\frac{1}{1+\left(\frac{1}{A_u}\right)\left(\frac{Z_0+Z_f}{Z_0}\right)}.$$

If the impedances Z_0 and Z_f are purely resistive, we can use the amplification A_R^* of the amplifier. If the amplification were infinitely large, then we would obtain

$$\frac{-V_a^*}{V_0} = A_R^* = R_f/R_0.$$

The voltage ratio with a finite amplification, however, is

$$\frac{-V_a}{V_0} = A_R = A_R^* \frac{1}{1 + \left(\frac{1}{A_u}\right)(1 + A_R^*)}. \tag{4.20}$$

Therefore, the relative error due to the finite value of the real amplifier is

$$\frac{A_R - A_R^*}{A_R^*} = -\frac{1}{1 + \frac{A_u}{1 + A_R^*}}. \tag{4.21}$$

If for example $A_u = 10^4$ and $R_f/R_0 = A_R^* = 3$, then a relative error of -0.04% arises. This would normally be regarded as insignificant.

It is of interest to see how far the amplification of the feedback amplifier deviates from the original value A_{R1} to the value A_{R2} if the amplification A_u of the operational amplifier changes (e.g. by temperature variation) from the value A_u to a new value nA_u.

Referring to Eqn (4.20) we can write

$$\frac{A_{R2} - A_{R1}}{A_R^*} = \frac{\Delta A_R}{A_R^*} = \frac{1}{1 + \left(\frac{1}{nA_u}\right)(1 + A_R^*)}$$

$$-\frac{1}{1 + \left(\frac{1}{A_u}\right)(1 + A_R^*)} \simeq \frac{(n-1)(1 + A_R^*)}{nA_u}. \tag{4.22}$$

This gives a relative change of amplification of -0.02% for a change of amplification of the operational amplifier from 20 000 to 10 000 and a value of A_R^* of 3. This would be considered insignificant for most practical purposes.

Since the impedances Z_f and Z_0 are frequency dependent, so is the voltage ratio of Eqn (4.19). Thus the transfer function is

$$F_R|s| = \frac{-V_a(s)}{V_0(s)} = \frac{Z_f}{Z_0}(s). \quad (4.23)$$

Let us consider the circuit of the inverting amplifier as consisting of three system elements (Fig. 4.20):

Input element,
Feedback element,
Operational amplifier.

The following transfer function is then obtained:

$$F_R(s) = \frac{y(s)}{x_0(s)} = \frac{F_e(s)F_V(s)}{1+F_f(s)F_V(s)} = \frac{F_e(s)}{F_f(s)+[F_V(s)]^{-1}}. \quad (4.24)$$

Let us again consider the circuit of Fig. 4.19, taking into account the very large amplification of the operational amplifier:

$$F_V(s) = \frac{y(s)}{e(s)} = \overline{A}_u \to \infty.$$

Let the voltage at the terminal E₋ with respect to the reference terminal M be V_e. Then the behaviour $F_e(s)$ of the input element (assuming $V_a = 0$) is

$$F_e(s) = \frac{V_e(s)}{V_0(s)}\bigg|_{V_a=0} = \frac{Z_f Z_M}{Z_0 Z_f + Z_0 Z_M + Z_f Z_M}.$$

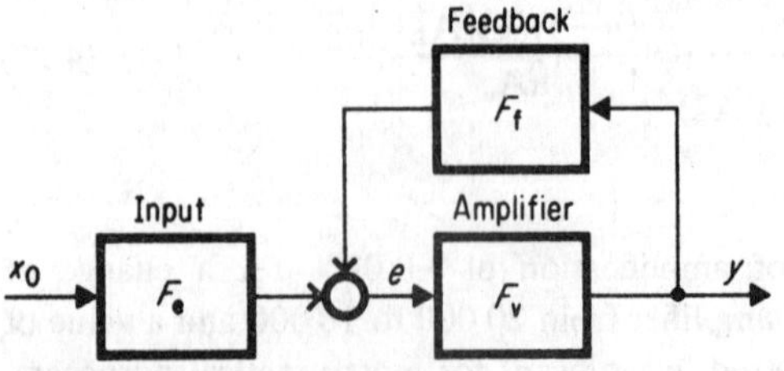

Fig. 4.20
Inverting amplifier comprising input element F_e, feedback element F_f and operational amplifier F_v

The behaviour of the feedback element (with $V_0=0$) is given by

$$F_f(s)=\frac{V_e(s)}{-V_a(s)}\bigg|_{V_0=0}=\frac{Z_0Z_M}{Z_0Z_f+Z_0Z_M+Z_fZ_M}.$$

The overall transfer function of the inverting amplifier then becomes

$$F_R(s)=\frac{-V_a(s)}{V_0(s)}=\frac{Z_f}{Z_0}(s).$$

The same result is obtained even if the resistance between terminal E₋ and the common line M is included in the calculation.

If the impedances Z_0 and Z_f in Fig. 4.19 are purely resistive and of equal magnitude, the output voltage $-V_a$ and the input voltage V_0 are equal but of opposite sign. This is an inverting amplifier with an amplification of 1.

By means of a second input channel it is possible to obtain the difference between two input voltages, for example, to obtain the error signal of a control system. The circuit is shown in Fig. 4.21.

In this case

$$-V_a(s)=\left(\frac{V_s(s)}{Z_s}-\frac{V_i(s)}{Z_i}\right)Z_f. \qquad (4.25).$$

V_s represents the command variable (desired value), V_i the controlled variable (actual value), and Z_s and Z_i are the associated channel impedances.

If a bridge circuit is used for the input circuit of the amplifier (Fig. 4.22), the signals can be represented by voltages and the desired/actual comparison by currents.

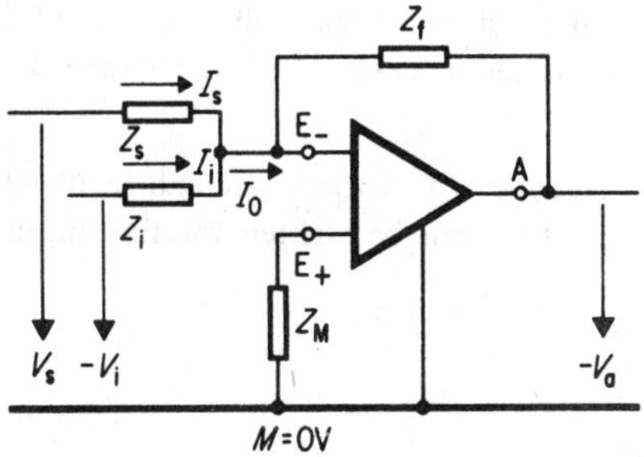

Fig. 4.21
Amplifier with two input channels.

Command variable $V_s/Z_s=I_s$.
Controlled variable $-V_i/Z_i=-I_i$.
Error signal $I_s-I_i=I_0$.

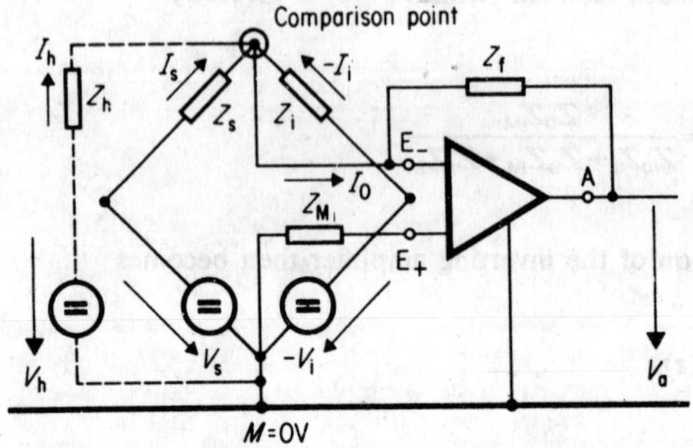

Fig. 4.22
Bridge connection of amplifier input circuit. Command variable channel Z_s, control variable channel Z_i. Bridge can be extended by auxiliary bridge arms V_h, Z_h

All voltages can be referred to the same reference potential M.

In this way a simple series connection of controllers is feasible, as is necessary for a control system with subsidiary control loops (see Section 6.8.2). The desired/actual value comparison at the input of the amplifier also permits other variables such as present signals, auxiliary variables, limiting levels etc., to be brought into the circuit. All branches of the bridge are combined at the comparison point.

The error signal appears as the difference current $I_0 = I_s - I_i$. The current I_0 is of positive sign if it is directed into the amplifier terminal E_. In this case the output voltage V_a (or dV_a/dt) must be negative. If the parameters for command and controlled variables, i.e. voltages V_s and V_i, are now varied in magnitude and sign, then the relationships between input voltages, current I_0 and output voltage V_a are obtained as indicated in Table 4.1. It is assumed that Z_s and Z_i are equal.

The summing amplifier has resistances connected in the input and feedback circuits (Fig. 4.23). The following expression can be written for the output voltage:

$$-V_a = \left(\frac{V_1}{R_1} + \frac{V_2}{R_2} + \frac{V_3}{R_3} + \cdots\right) R_f. \qquad (4.26)$$

Table 4.1: Signs of voltages at input and output of controller (Fig. 4.21).

Comparison $\lvert V_s\rvert > \lvert V_i\rvert$		Desired/actual $\lvert V_s\rvert < \lvert V_i\rvert$		Error signal	Output voltage V_a or rate	Remarks
V_s	V_i	V_s	V_i	I_0	of change $\frac{dV_a}{dt}$	
pos	pos	pos	pos	pos	neg	overdriven
pos	neg			pos	neg	more } direction 1
		pos	neg	neg	pos	less } direction 1
neg	pos			neg	pos	more } direction 2
		neg	pos	pos	neg	less } direction 2
neg	neg	neg	neg	neg	pos	overdriven

The variables to be added V_1, V_2, V_3 etc. may be positive or negative. The respective multipliers for the individual voltages V_n is given by

$$K_n = R_f/R_n.$$

The output of the amplifier is therefore given by

$$\sum_{n=1}^{n} V_v K_n = V_1 K_1 + V_2 K_2 + V_3 K_3 \cdots. \tag{4.27}$$

A special application of the adding circuit is in the calculation of a mean value. If the resistances R_n are all given by the expression

$$R_n = nR_f$$

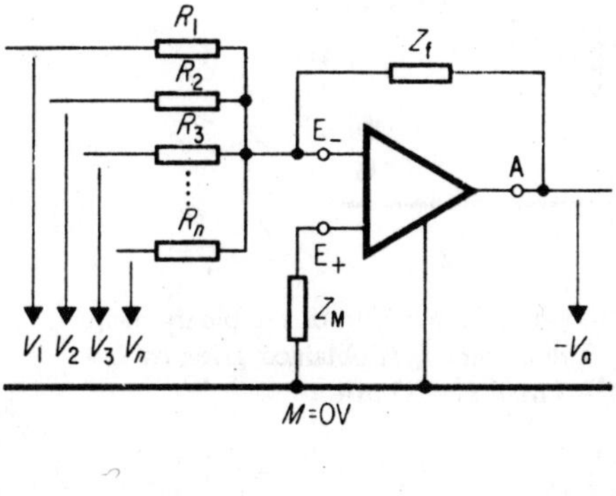

Fig. 4.23
Summing amplifier. Care must be taken not to overdrive the amplifier

where n is the number of inputs, then the output of the amplifier is given by

$$\frac{1}{n}\sum_{n=1}^{n} V_n = \frac{V_1}{n} + \frac{V_2}{n} + \frac{V_3}{n} + \cdots \tag{4.28}$$

which is the mean value of the inputs.

Another application of the summing amplifier is the digital to analogue converter, Fig. 4.24.
Resistance channels are connected to the input of the amplifier by means of electronic switches (e.g. field effect transistors), the number of channels depending on the size of the number to be converted. These channels carry currents which correspond to the respective values of the individual digits. A current I_0 which is the analogue equivalent of the number to be converted flows into the inverting input terminal E_-. This results in an output voltage which is the analogue equivalent of the number:

$$-V_a = V_{ref}\frac{R_f}{R_0} Z. \tag{4.29}$$

Z is the number to be converted into analogue form and V_{ref} is a stabilized reference voltage.

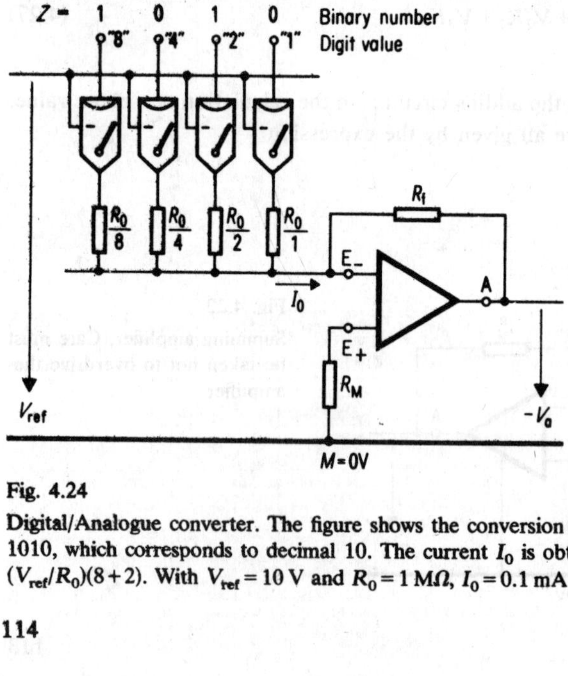

Fig. 4.24
Digital/Analogue converter. The figure shows the conversion of the binary number 1010, which corresponds to decimal 10. The current I_0 is obtained given by $I_0 = (V_{ref}/R_0)(8+2)$. With $V_{ref} = 10$ V and $R_0 = 1\,M\Omega$, $I_0 = 0.1$ mA

If the reference voltage is the analogue of a second variable (the first variable being the digital number), then the digital/analogue converter becomes a hybrid multiplier with an analogue output. It is known as a digital/analogue multiplier.

4.2.2. Non-inverting amplifier

This circuit (Fig. 4.25) has a very input resistance. It scarcely places any load on the driving voltage source V_0. Its behaviour is determined by the impedances Z_M and Z_f. The impedance Z_0 is given by

$$Z_0 = \frac{Z_M Z_f}{Z_M + Z_f}. \tag{4.30}$$

The current I_0 is equal to the amplifier input current I_e which is very small. Also, both input terminals E_- and E_+ are practically at the same potential. Thus

$$V_0 = V_E. \tag{4.31}$$

The current in the feedback channel is given by

$$I_f = \frac{V_a - V_E}{Z_f} = I_M = \frac{V_E}{Z_M}. \tag{4.32}$$

This current I_f cannot flow into the amplifier. It passes through the impedance Z_M. The error due to the amplifier input current is usually less than 0.1%.

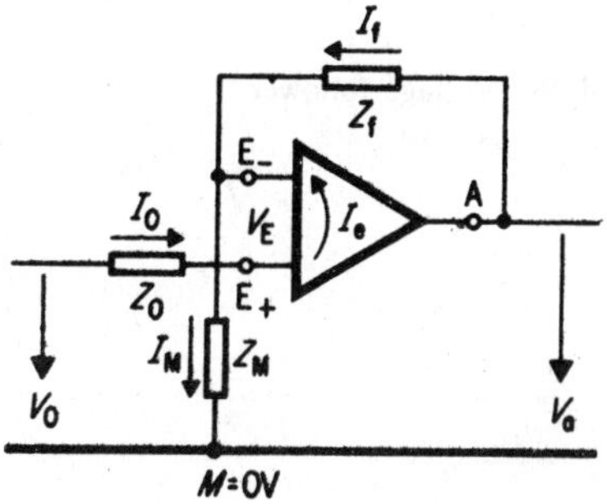

Fig. 4.25 Non-inverting amplifier

From Eqns (4.31) and (4.32), the voltage ratio of the non-inverting amplifier is obtained:

$$\frac{V_a}{V_0} = 1 + \frac{Z_f}{Z_M}. \tag{4.33}$$

This circuit is not suitable for the generation of error signals, if the amplification is to be less than 1.

The impedances Z_M and Z_f are complex and dependent on frequency and the transfer function is therefore

$$F_R(s) = \frac{V_a(s)}{V_0(s)} = 1 + \frac{Z_f}{Z_M}(s). \tag{4.34}$$

The non-inverting amplifier is often connected to the output of an inverting amplifier in order to use the latter with two input channels for the generation of error signals and the non-inverting amplifier for producing the necessary time delay.

A special application is the voltage follower (Fig. 4.26). In this case, the impedance Z_M is infinitely large and the impedance Z_f infinitely small. The input voltage V_0 and the output voltage V_a are virtually the same. This circuit is known as the impedance converter or buffer amplifier.

If a diode is added to the circuit of the voltage follower as shown in Fig. 4.27, the equivalent of a diode with no threshold value, i.e. a perfect diode, is obtained. As long as the output current flows through the diode, the output voltage follows the input voltage. On the other hand, should the output current flow in the diode blocking direction, the diode high impedance decouples the amplifier from the load. Then, since no current flows in the load, the output point A remains at the potential of M and the output voltage V_a is zero.

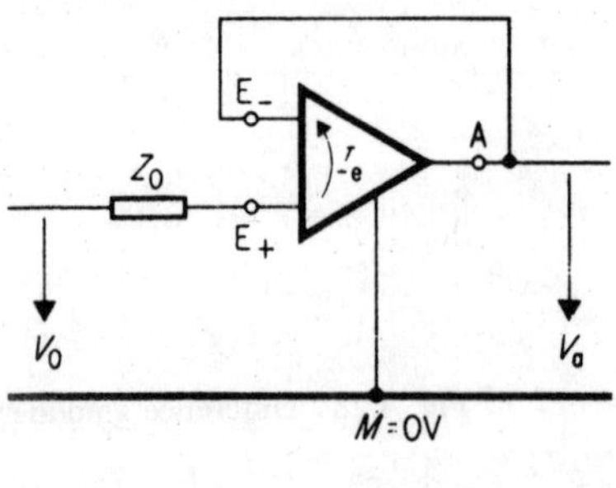

Fig. 4.26 Voltage follower

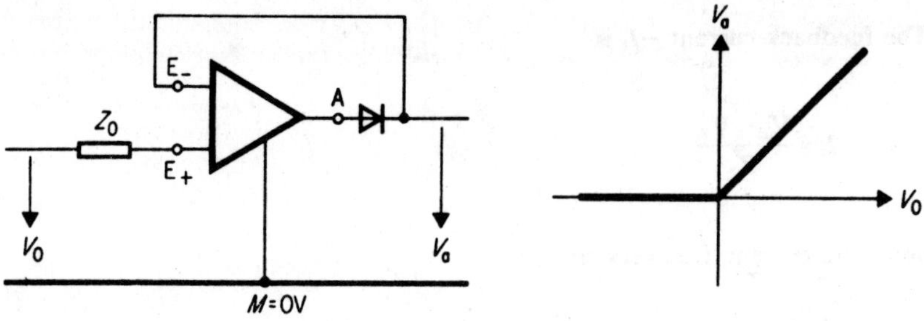

a) Circuit based on voltage follower

b) Characteristic (knee at zero point).

Fig. 4.27 Diode without threshold value

4.2.3. Difference amplifier

The circuit shown in Fig. 4.28 is driven at the input side with two voltages V_1 and V_2 which normally have the same polarity. The output voltage V_a is dependent on the difference between the two input voltages.

The difference amplifier can be regarded as a combination of the inverting and the non-inverting amplifier. The input current I_e and the input voltage V_e of the basic amplifier are very small. Inputs E_- and E_+ are at virtually the same potential V_E.

For the two input currents I_{01} and I_{02}, we have

$$I_{01} = \frac{V_1 - V_E}{Z_{01}} \quad I_{02} = \frac{V_2 - V_E}{Z_{02}}.$$

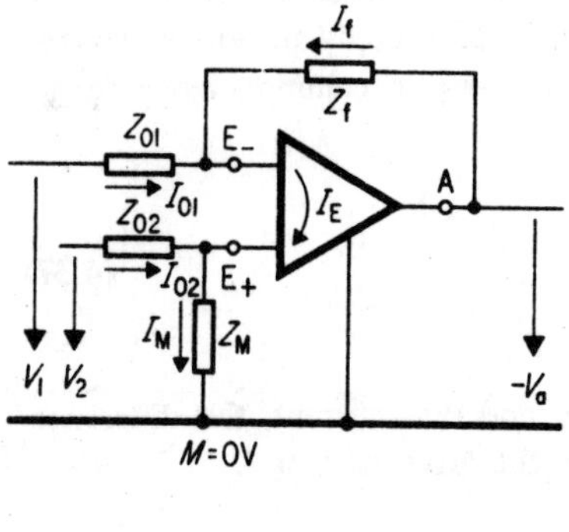

Fig. 4.28 Difference amplifier

The feedback current $-I_f$ is

$$-I_f = \frac{V_E - V_A}{Z_f}.$$

Since the current I_e is very small

$$I_M = I_{02} \quad \text{and} \quad -I_f = I_{01}.$$

Therefore, the output voltage is

$$-V_a = V_1 \frac{Z_f}{Z_{01}} - V_2 \frac{Z_f}{Z_{01}} \left(\frac{Z_{01} Z_M}{(Z_{02} + Z_M) Z_f} + \frac{Z_M}{Z_{02} + Z_M} \right). \tag{4.35}$$

Normally, purely resistive impedances are used for Z_{01}, Z_{02}, Z_f and Z_M and these are given as follows:

$$Z_{01} = Z_{02} = R_0 \qquad Z_f = Z_M = R_f.$$

Then the output voltage is

$$-V_a = (V_1 - V_2) \frac{R_f}{R_0}. \tag{4.36}$$

If V_1 is a command variable and V_2 is a controlled variable, then the value $(V_1 - V_2)$ represents an error signal.

However, instead of the two voltages V_1 and V_2 which are specified with respect to the potential of M, it is also permissible to apply an isolated voltage ΔV_0 between the two inputs, within the permissible common mode range. Then Eqn (4.36) gives

$$-\frac{V_a}{\Delta V_0} = \frac{R_f}{R_0} \tag{4.37}$$

Besides the error due to the offset voltage and bias current, the difference amplifier will also show the error caused by the drive current I_e.

4.2.4. Amplifier with current drive

Occasionally it is necessary to transmit a signal in the form of a voltage to a distant point where it is processed or indicated. In this case, error will occur due to the voltage drop in the transmission path. To avoid this the voltage signal is converted into a current by means of an amplifier. Providing that the resistance of the transmission loop remains within certain limits, the loop resistance has no effect.

The circuit is based on the difference amplifier. It contains purely resistive impedances and is shown in Fig. 4.29. If the output current exceeds 10 mA a current amplifying push–pull output stage is added to the basic circuit.

The potentials at the terminals E_- and E_+ are practically equal to V_E. The factor k in Fig. 4.29 is less than or equal to 1. The current I_e at the amplifier input is virtually zero.

The following equations are obtained:

$$\frac{V_1 - V_E}{R} = \frac{V_E - V_a}{kR},$$

$$\frac{-V_2 + V_E}{R + r} = \frac{-V_E + V_x}{kR},$$

$$\frac{V_a - V_x}{kr} = I_L + \frac{-V_E + V_x}{kR}.$$

From these, the equation for the output current is obtained as follows:

$$I_L = (V_2 - V_1)\frac{1}{r}. \tag{4.38}$$

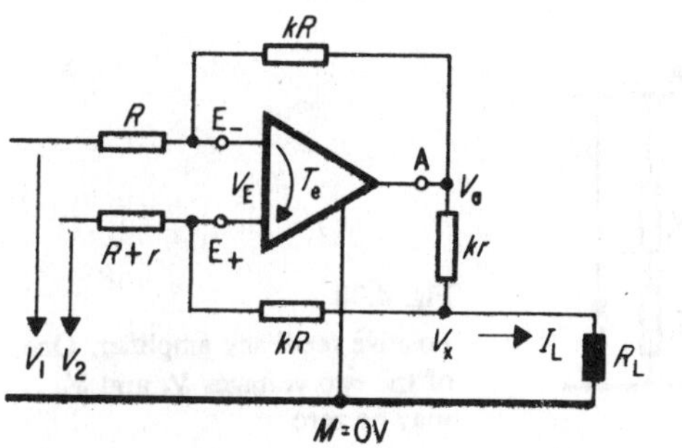

Fig. 4.29
Amplifier using current drive. Circuit using difference amplifier. One of the input voltages may be zero

The factor $1/r$ defines the slope of the amplifier characteristic. For example, if $r = 50\ \Omega$, it is 20 mA/V. If the V_2 input point is connected to the reference potential, then a positive input voltage V_1 gives a negative load current given by

$$-I_L = V_1/r.$$

If, however, the V_1 input point is at reference potential, the load current is given by

$$+I_L = V_2/r.$$

The load resistance R_L may not assume extremely large values if the linear relationship between load current I_L and input voltage $(V_2 - V_1)$ is to be maintained. Therefore, the output voltage V_a may not exceed a specified maximum permissible voltage $V_{a\,max}$. From the equation $V_x = I_L R_L$, the maximum permissible load resistance $R_{L\,max}$ can be determined:

$$R_{L\,max} \leq \left|\frac{V_{a\,max}}{I_{LN}}\right| \frac{R}{R+r} - \left[\frac{r}{2R+r} + \frac{kR}{R+r}\right] r. \tag{4.39}$$

I_{LN} is the rated amplifier output current. It is expedient to choose the factor k not greater than 0.1, otherwise the load resistance becomes too small.

4.2.5. Positive feedback amplifier

The positive feedback amplifier (Fig. 4.30) works as a flip–flop amplifer (Fig. 4.18), which means that the output at A can only take the extreme values $-V_{a\,max}$ or $+V_{a\,max}$. This is also termed on/off behaviour. If the two voltages V_1

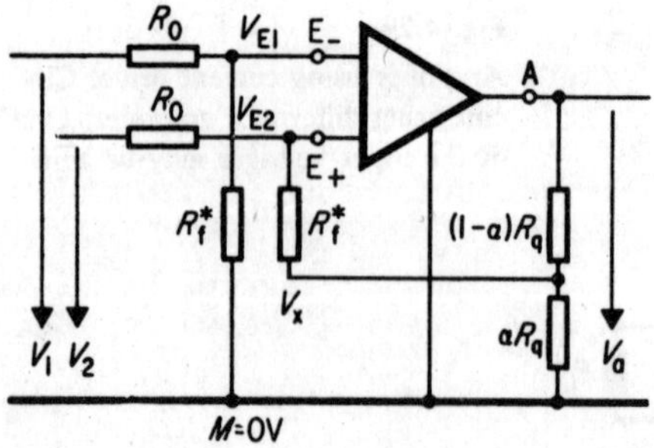

Fig. 4.30
Positive feedback amplifier. One of the two voltages V_1 and V_2 may be zero

and V_2 are the parameters of command variables and controlled variables, the circuit becomes a two state controller. It can also be used as a limit value alarm which changes its output signal if a variable such as V_1 exceeds or falls below a prescribed value such as the voltage V_2.

Let the potential at terminal E_- be V_{E1} and let that at terminal E_+ be V_{E2}. The following equations are obtained:

$$V_{E1} = V_1 \frac{R_f^*}{R_0 + R_f^*},$$

$$V_{E2} = (V_2 - V_x) \frac{R_f^*}{R_0 + R_f^*},$$

$$V_x = \left(\frac{V_2 - V_x}{R_0 + R_f^*} - \frac{V_{amax}}{R_q} \right) \alpha R_q.$$

The amplifier output voltage is negative if V_{E1} is slightly more positive than V_{E2}. If initially this is not the case, the flip over point is reached when $V_{E1} \simeq V_{E2}$. Assuming that the value of αR_q is small with respect to the resistance R_f^* the condition obtained is

$$V_1 = V_2 + \alpha V_{amax}. \tag{4.40}$$

The input voltage V_1 must exceed the voltage V_2 in the positive direction by the value

$$|\varepsilon| = |\alpha V_{amax}|.$$

If so the voltage V_{amax} which was positive now flips over to the maximum negative value (Fig. 4.31a).

For a change of the input voltage V_1 in the reverse direction, i.e. V_1 changes from greater than V_2 to less than V_2, assuming $|+V_{amax}| = |-V_{amax}|$ the same minimum step ε is required, i.e. the magnitude of V_1 must be at least ε less than V_2. The requirement for the difference between V_2 and V_1 to be at least $\pm\varepsilon$ is called hysteresis. The magnitude of the hysteresis effect is dependent on the feedback ratio α (Fig. 4.30), and on the maximum values $+V_{amax}$ and $-V_{amax}$ at the output. The value of α is usually between 0.01 and 0.1.

If the input voltage V_1 is kept fixed and the voltage V_2 is varied, the behaviour of the amplifier is as shown in Fig. 4.31(b). One of the voltages V_1 and V_2 may be zero.

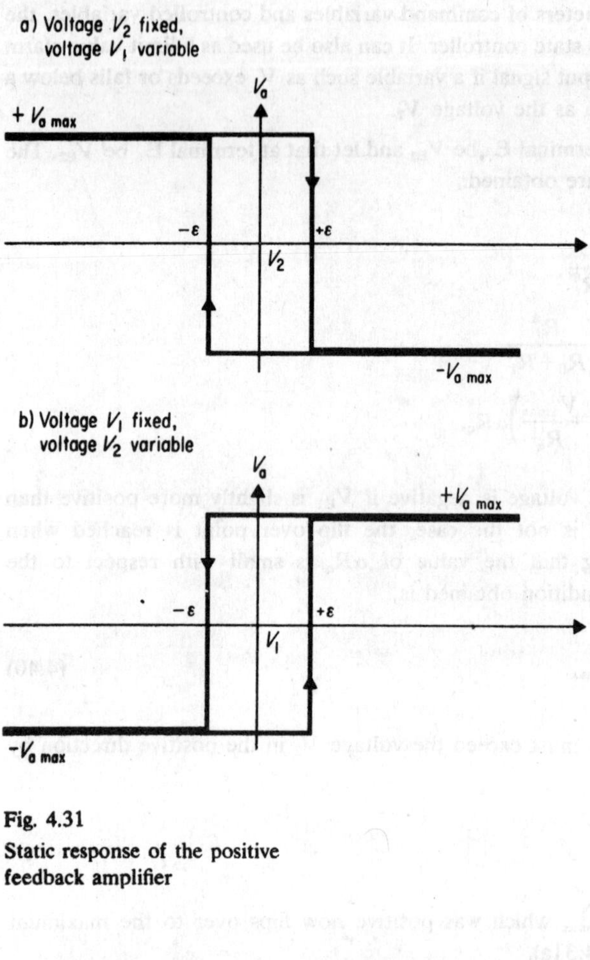

Fig. 4.31
Static response of the positive feedback amplifier

4.3. Transfer Response of Controllers

The difference between command variable and controlled variable, i.e. the error signal, can be proportionally amplified, integrated or differentiated, in order to arrive at the signal to be used as the controlling factor in the control loop. The proportional and the integral components can occur separately in the controller or together and can also be combined with the differential component. Usually the controller takes the form shown in Fig. 4.21, the inverting amplifier having two input channels for command and controlled variables. The actual performance is determined by the feedback loop. In many cases a

non-inverting amplifier also occurs. The impedances in these circuits are, of course, complex impedances.

The types of circuits most frequently used as part of the control circuit are shown in Table 4.2. They usually consist of resistances and capacitors. Inductances are not normally used. The mathematical functions $Z(s)$ of the circuits determines the detailed behaviour as indicated for example by Eqns (4.23), (4.25) and (4.34).

Table 4.2:
Frequently used complex impedances $Z(s)$ for use in operational amplifier circuits.

No.	Title	Circuit	Complex impedance $Z(s)$
1	Two terminal (two pole) network	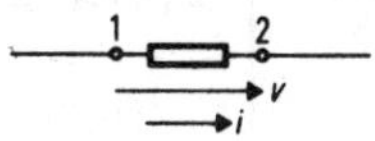	$Z(s)=\frac{v(s)}{i(s)}$
2	Four terminal (four pole) network	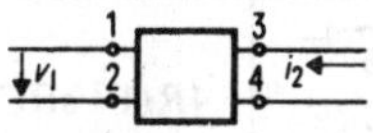	$Z(s)=\frac{v_1(s)}{i_2(s)}$
3	Resistance		R
4	Capacitance	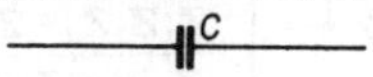	$1/sC$
5	Series circuit		$\frac{1}{sC}(1+sRC)$
6	Parallel circuit	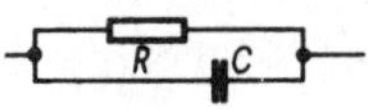	$R/(1+sRC)$
7	Series–parallel	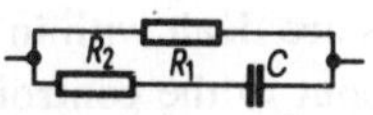	$R_1\frac{1+sR_2C}{1+s(R_1+R_2)C}$
8	T circuit	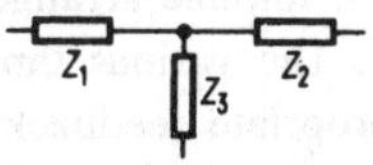	$Z_1+Z_2+\frac{Z_1Z_2}{Z_3}$
9	T circuit 1 (low pass)	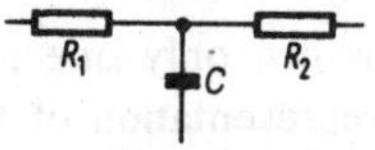	$(R_1+R_2)\left(1+s\frac{R_1R_2}{R_1+R_2}C\right)$
10	T circuit 2	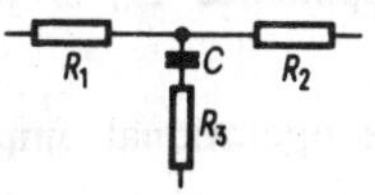	$\frac{(R_1+R_2)\left(1+s\left(\frac{R_1R_2}{R_1+R_2}+R_3\right)C\right)}{(1+sR_3C)}$

Table 4.2:

No.	Title	Circuit	Complex impedance $Z(s)$
11	T circuit 3	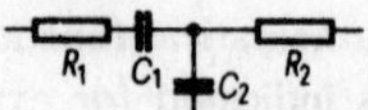	$\frac{1}{sC_1}\left[(1+s(R_1+R_2)C_1)\times \left(1+s\frac{R_1R_2}{R_1+R_2}C_2\right)\right]$
12	T circuit 4	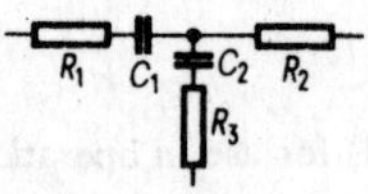	$(1+s(R_1+R_2)C_1)\times \frac{\left(1+s\left(\frac{R_1R_2}{R_1+R_2}+R_3\right)C_2\right)}{sC_1\cdot(1+sR_3C_2)}$
13	Double T circuit	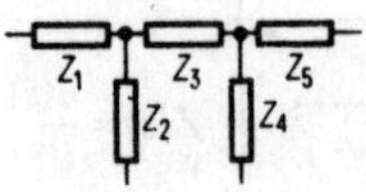	$Z_1+Z_3+Z_5+\frac{Z_1Z_3}{Z_2}+\frac{Z_1Z_5}{Z_2}+\frac{Z_1Z_5}{Z_4}+\frac{Z_3Z_5}{Z_4}+\frac{Z_1Z_3Z_5}{Z_2Z_4}$
14	Double T circuit (low pass)	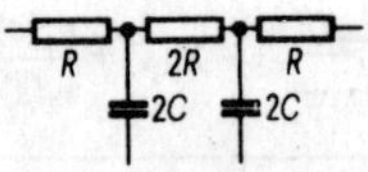	$4R(1+sRC)(1+s2RC)$
15	Bridged T circuit	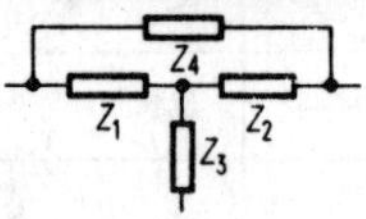	$\frac{Z_1Z_2Z_4+Z_1Z_3Z_4+Z_2Z_3Z_4}{Z_1Z_2+Z_1Z_3+Z_2Z_3+Z_3Z_4}$

The most important controller circuits are dealt with in the following sections. The error signal is produced at the input to the controller. The circuit of Fig. 4.21 using the inverting amplifier is a suitable arrangement, as proportional amplification is usually also required. The various time constant parameters required are obtained either by appropriate feedback or by adding a non-inverting amplifier to the circuit.

For the discussion of the various circuits, only one input channel need be considered. The voltage ΔV_0 is the representation of the error signal at the input of the controller and the impedance Z_0 is the impedance of the corresponding input channel.

It will be initially assumed that the operational amplifier very nearly approaches the ideal amplifier.

4.3.1. Proportional response

If the complex impedances Z_0, Z_M and Z_f in the inverting amplifier (Fig. 4.19), the non-inverting amplifier (Fig. 4.25) or the difference amplifier (Fig. 4.28) are replaced by purely resistive components as in Figs. 4.32a, b and c, respectively, then proportional response is obtained.

The proportional amplification is given by

$$A_{R(a)} = R_f/R_0 \qquad \text{(see Eqn (4.23))}$$

$$A_{R(b)} = 1 + R_f/R_M \qquad \text{(see Eqn (4.34))}$$

$$A_{R(c)} = R_f/R_0 \qquad \text{(see Eqn (4.36)).}$$

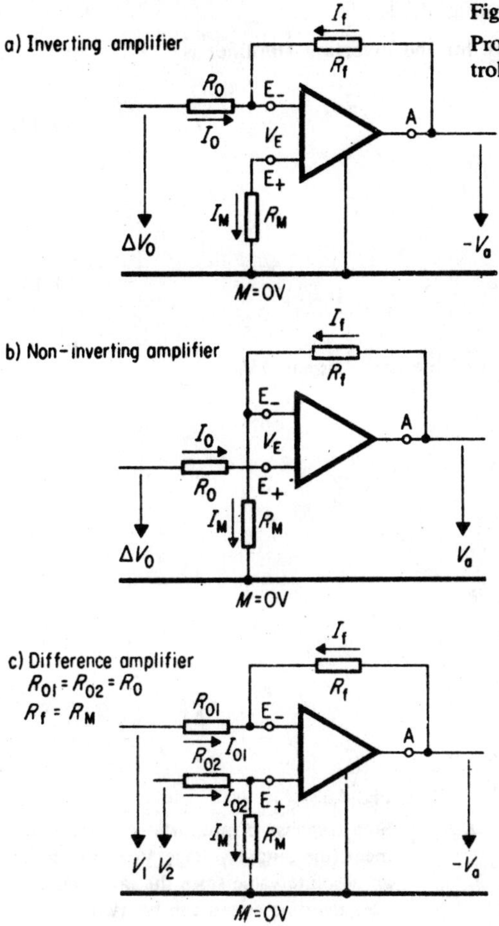

Fig. 4.32
Proportional system element (P controller)

The transfer function of the proportional system element contains no time dependent factor. As indicated by the dimensionless expressions for A_R it is merely a number. The transfer function for the inverting amplifier is thus:

$$F(s)=\frac{-V_a(s)}{\Delta V_0(s)}=\frac{R_f}{R_0}=A_{R(a)}. \tag{4.41}$$

The amplification of the inverting and difference amplifiers A_R can be greater than, equal to or less than 1, depending on the values of R_f and R_0. However, the amplification A_R of the non-inverting amplifier is always greater than 1.

There is no time delay between the input signal ΔV_0 (error signal) and the output signal V_a (set variable) (Fig. 4.33).

Thus the general time equation for the inverting amplifier is

$$-V_a(t)=A_{R(a)}\Delta V_0(t) \tag{4.42}$$

and the step response is

$$f(t)=\frac{-V_a(t)}{\Delta V_{0step}}=A_R \tag{4.43}$$

where ΔV_{0step} is a step function of the error signal ΔV_0.

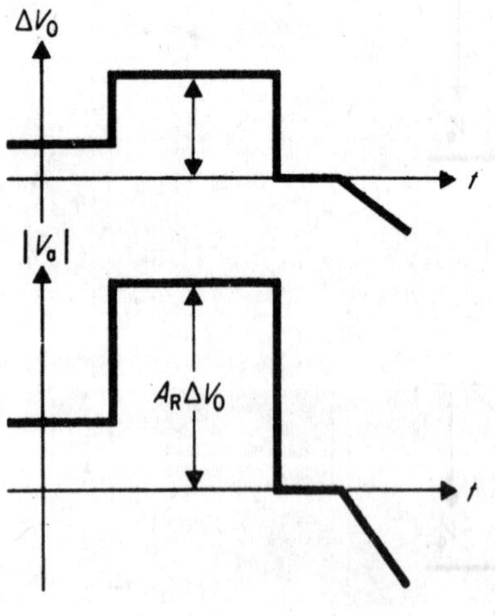

Fig. 4.33
Step response of proportional system element (the output voltage V_a is quoted as an absolute value since the inverting or non-inverting circuit can be used)

The proportional or P controller is a very fast controller which responds immediately with a proportional change of the set variable for every change of the error signal. If, of course, the error signal is zero, which will be approximately so for good control in the steady state, then a zero set variable will be obtained. However, a zero set variable is not normally desirable. For example, suppose that a d.c. motor is to have the armature current controlled with a proportional controller. The command variable and the controlled variable (armature current) are compared at the input of the controller. The controller output voltage produces the set variable which determines the armature voltage. If the required armature current is obtained, the error signal will be zero, but this would produce an armature voltage of zero, which is not what is required. In order that the required current shall flow in the steady state, a specified armature voltage must exist. Thus a specified non-zero value of the output voltage of the controller must exist, and, therefore, also a specific non-zero value of the error signal.

Thus in most proportional controller applications the controlled variable in the steady state has an error with respect to the command variable so that the set variable will have the required value. This is called the offset error or steady-state error of the proportional controller. The larger the proportional amplification, the smaller this error becomes.

Normally, a controller should only be operated within its specified range, from $-V_{a\,max}$ (usually -10 V) to $+V_{a\,max}$ (usually $+10$ V). In order to keep within this range, the voltage ΔV_0, which represents the error signal, must not exceed the value $\left|\frac{V_{a\,max}}{A_R}\right|$:

$$|\Delta V_0| \leq \left|\frac{V_{a\,max}}{A_R}\right| \qquad (4.44)$$

If the input voltage ΔV_0 is larger than allowed by Eqn (4.44), the output voltage V_a can no longer follow it. It remains at $V_{a\,max}$ and the operational amplifier is said to be overdriven.

If it is intended to make the proportional amplification variable, it is possible to provide an adjustable resistance as the feedback resistance R_f. Thus the amplification can be varied in the range

$$0 \leq A_R \leq R_{f\,max}/R_0$$

for the inverting and difference amplifiers, and in the range

$$1 \leq A_R \leq \left(1+\frac{R_{f\max}}{R_0}\right)$$

for the non-inverting amplifier.

A second possibility can be applied to the circuit of the inverting amplifier. In this case, a potentiometer is connected between the output of the amplifier and the reference point M and the feedback resistance R_f is connected to the tapping point (see Fig. 4.34). At the tapping point of the potentiometer, a specific fraction of the output voltage appears

$$-\alpha V_a = \Delta V_0 \frac{R_f}{R_0}.$$

If R_f/R_0 is defined as A_{R0}, then the amplification is given by

$$A_{R\alpha} = \frac{-V_a}{\Delta V_0} = \frac{A_{R0}}{\alpha} \tag{4.45}$$

The amplification $A_{R\alpha}$ thus increases as α decreases. To limit the value of the amplification, a fixed resistance r_q is normally connected between the potentiometer and the reference point.

The potentiometer R_q is not always of low resistance compared to the feedback impedance R_f. Therefore, Eqn (4.45) must be modified by means of a correction factor as follows:

$$A_{R\alpha} = \frac{1}{\alpha} A_{R0}\left[1+(\alpha-\alpha^2)\frac{R_q}{R_f}\right]. \tag{4.46}$$

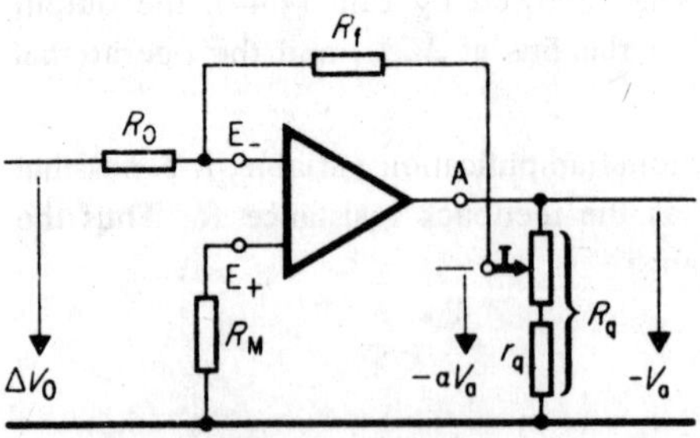

Fig. 4.34
Proportional system element with variable amplification

Table 4.3: Correction factor K for proportional amplification

$\frac{R_q}{R_f}=$	0.1	0.2	0.5	1	2	5	10
			$K_\alpha = 1+(\alpha-\alpha^2)\frac{R_q}{R_f}$				
$\alpha = 0.1$	1.009	1.018	1.045	1.09	1.18	1.45	1.9
0.2	1.016	1.032	1.080	1.16	1.32	1.80	2.6
0.3	1.021	1.042	1.105	1.21	1.42	2.05	3.1
0.4	1.024	1.048	1.120	1.24	1.48	2.20	3.4
0.5	1.025	1.050	1.125	1.25	1.50	2.25	3.5
0.6	1.024	1.048	1.120	1.24	1.48	2.20	3.4
0.7	1.021	1.042	1.105	1.21	1.42	2.05	3.1
0.8	1.016	1.032	1.080	1.16	1.32	1.80	2.6
0.9	1.009	1.018	1.045	1.09	1.18	1.45	1.9

The correction factor is a maximum when $\alpha = 0.5$. It becomes smaller for larger values of α. However, it is only of significance when the feedback impedance is equal to or smaller than the potentiometer resistance R_q. The magnitude of the correction factor can be obtained from Table 4.3.

The output potentiometer for the adjustment of the amplification can always be used if the series section of the feedback circuit is a pure resistance.

4.3.2. Integrating behaviour

If the impedance Z_f in the inverting amplifier (Fig. 4.19) is replaced by a capacitor C_f and the impedance Z_0 by a resistor R_0 (Fig. 4.35), i.e.

$$Z_f = \frac{1}{sC_f} \qquad Z_0 = R_0$$

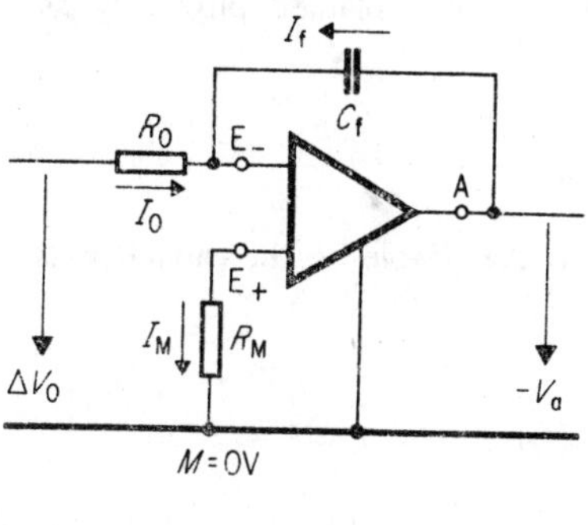

Fig. 4.35
Integrating system element (I controller) (only inverting circuit may be used)

then the transfer function becomes

$$F_R(s)_I = \frac{-V_a(s)}{\Delta V_0(s)} = \frac{1}{sR_0C_f} = \frac{1}{sT_I} \quad (4.47)$$

with the integrating time constant given by $T_I = R_0C_f$.

Since the resistance R_0 is already determined by the conditions at the controller input, the choice of the feedback capacitance C_f determines the integration time constant T_I. It is called the integration capacitance. The operator s appears in the denominator of the transfer function, Eqn (4.47). Referring to Eqn (2.29) therefore, we see that the general time equation is

$$-V_a(t) = \frac{1}{T_I}\int_0^t \Delta V_0(t)\,dt + V_{a0} \quad (4.48)$$

where V_{a0} is the initial value of the output voltage V_a at time $t = 0$. The output voltage of the integrating system element is the addition of the products of momentary values of the error signal (ΔV_0) and the time unit dt, multiplied by the factor K_I which is the reciprocal of the integration time constant T_I:

$$K_I = 1/T_I.$$

If the error signal ΔV_0 is a step function (ΔV_{0step}), the associated step response is as follows:

$$f(t)_I = -\frac{V_a(t)}{\Delta V_{0step}} = \frac{t}{T_I}. \quad (4.49)$$

Thus we see that the integration time constant is the time taken for the output voltage V_a to change by an amount equal to the input step function (Fig. 4.36).

The behaviour of the integrating element can be explained physically as follows. Referring to Fig. 4.35 we obtain

$$I_0 = \Delta V_0/R_0 = -I_f.$$

The current I_f charges the capacitor and thus the charge on the capacitor at any instant is given by

$$Q(t) = \int_0^t I_0\,dt = \frac{1}{R_0}\int_0^t \Delta V_0\,dt = C_f[-V_a(t)].$$

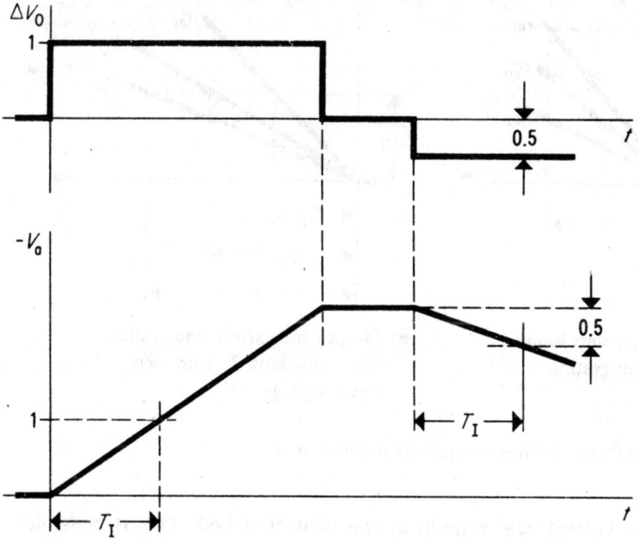

Fig. 4.36 Step response of the integrating circuit element

Thus

$$-V_a(t) = \frac{1}{R_0 C_f} \int_0^t \Delta V_0(t)\, dt$$

which is the general time equation already obtained (Eqn (4.48)).

The rate of change of the output voltage of the integrating element is dependent on the magnitude of the input voltage (error signal) and the integrating time constant $T_I = R_0 C_f$ (Fig. 4.37).

The integrating controller is a relatively slow controller. It changes its output voltage at a rate which is dependent on the integrating time constant, until the input (error signal) is cancelled. In contrast to the proportional controller, which acts in the control chain immediately in proportion to the error signal, the integrating controller requires time to build up an appreciable output voltage. However, it continues to act until the error signal disappears.

Let us assume that the controller for controlling the armature current of a d.c. machine has an integrating characteristic and assume that the required current is 1000 A. As long as the armature current is less than 1000 A, the armature voltage, controlled by the controller, will increase and will continue to do so until the error signal is zero, i.e. until the current reaches a value of 1000 A.

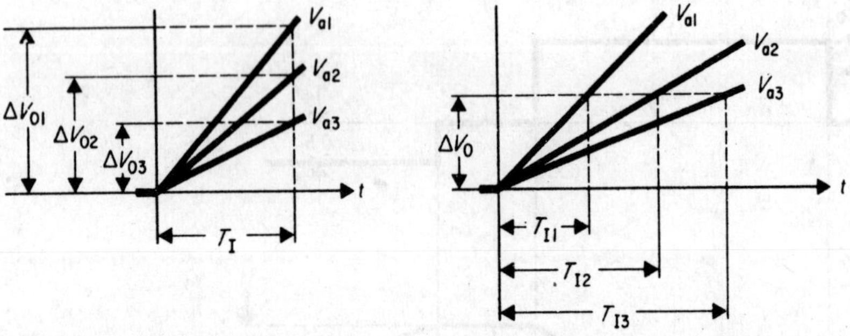

a) Output for various step inputs ΔV_0 with fixed integrating time constant T_I

b) Output for various integrating time constants T_I with step input voltage ΔV_0

Fig. 4.37 Output voltage of integrating system element V_a

Then the armature voltage will remain at the value reached. This is possible because the output voltage of the integrating controller can remain at any value within its range if the input is zero.

If the zero error of the control amplifier is neglected, the controlled variable has the steady-state value prescribed by the command variable. The integrating amplifier does not exhibit a steady-state error.

The controller must not be overdriven as it will not then be effective. Therefore both the magnitude and the duration of the error signal are of importance in the integrating controller.

If the output voltage at a given instant is V_{a0}, and a step function ΔV_{0step} of the error signal takes place, then the maximum permissible duration of the error signal to avoid overdriving the amplifier if the integration time constant is T_I is given by

$$t_{perm} = T_I \left| \frac{V_{a\,max} - V_{a0}}{\Delta V_{0step}} \right| . \tag{4.50}$$

It has been assumed that the integrator has been based on the ideal amplifier. If the real amplifier has a finite amplification of A_u and a finite input impedance of R_e, the transfer function becomes

$$F_R(s) = \frac{-V_a(s)}{\Delta V_0(s)} = \frac{A_u}{1+R_0/R_e} \frac{1}{1+sT_I \dfrac{1+A_u}{1+R_0/R_e}} . \tag{4.51}$$

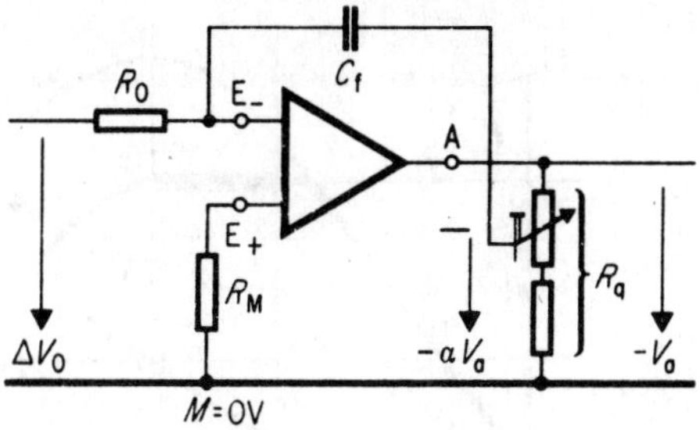

Fig. 4.38
Integrating circuit element with variable integration time constant

This is the characteristic of a first order delay system. If R_e is large compared with R_0, the amplification approaches the value A_u and the delay time constant approaches the value $A_u T_1$. These values are large and could only be observed outside the range of the amplifier.

The integrating time constant of the integrating element can be varied in the same manner as the amplification of the proportional element (Fig. 4.34), by means of a potentiometer (Fig. 4.38). However, in this case, the correction factor cannot be dealt with so easily. The transfer function becomes

$$F_R(s) = \frac{-V_a(s)}{\Delta V_0(s)} = \frac{1}{s\alpha R_0 C_f}[1+(\alpha-\alpha^2)sR_q C_f]. \tag{4.52}$$

The correction factor, in the square brackets, is the characteristic of a phase advance with time constant $[(\alpha-\alpha^2)R_q C_f]$. The following conditions must be fulfilled if this phase advance is to be negligible:

1. Resistance R_q must be small compared to the input resistance R_0.
2. In order to make the phase advance negligible, the input voltage is damped by the phase advance time constant.

The simple integrating controller, with or without variable time constant, is not very commonly used as an individual controller.

4.3.3. Comparison of the properties of proportional and integrating controllers

Let us consider the behaviour of the controller when overdriven. The proportional controller goes into the overdriven state when the product of the input and the amplification factor ($\Delta V_0 A_R$) is greater than the maximum possible output voltage $V_{a\,max}$ (Fig. 4.39a). The integrating controller goes into the overdriven state when the input is present for too long so that the controller

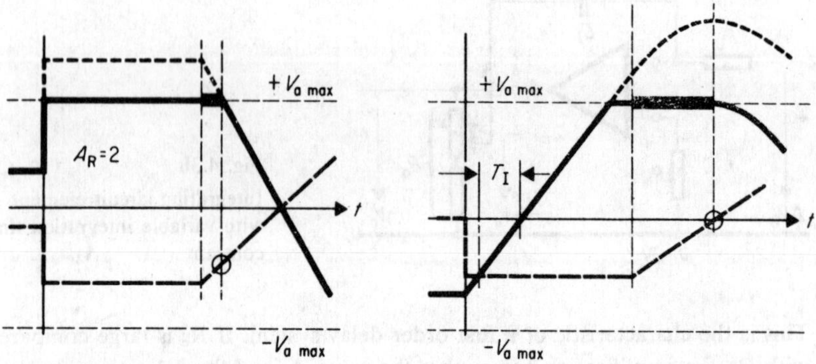

Fig. 4.39

a) Behaviour of proportional controller

b) Behaviour of integrating controller

——— Error signal ΔV_0
▬▬▬ Output voltage V_a
------- Voltage which controller would reach without $V_{a\max}$ limit
▬▬▬ Delay period until controller leaves overdriven state

attempts to integrate beyond the maximum possible output voltage $V_{a\max}$ (Fig. 4.39b).

Now suppose that the input voltage ΔV_0 (error signal) which led to the overdriven state, becomes smaller:

1. The proportional controller goes out of the overdriven state at the point where the product of the input voltage and the amplification becomes less than the maximum output voltage. The time taken to go out of the overdriven state is relatively short.
2. The integrating controller only goes out of the overdriven state if the input voltage changes its polarity. The delay before the controller leaves the overdriven state is relatively long. The controlled variable attains the value prescribed by the command variable (error signal zero) with the set variable at maximum and it thus swings above the limit demanded by the command variable.

We see then that the proportional controller leaves the overdriven state faster than the integrating controller. An overshoot of the controlled variable due to overdriving the controller is not to be expected.

Table 4.4 shows the behaviour of proportional controllers and integrating controllers during the occurrence of an error signal.

Table 4.4:
Behaviour of proportional and integrating controllers during the occurrence of an error signal

Controller	Initial behaviour	Steady-state behaviour
P	Acts immediately – action according to amplification	Offset error always remains – the larger the amplification, the smaller the error signal
I	Acts slowly – time integral of error signal	Error signal always becomes zero – when zero, integration stops

The proportional controller reacts very rapidly to a change of command variable or disturbance, in order to reach a steady state. However, there is always an offset error. Thus the controlled variable in the steady state never assumes the value required by the command variable except when the command variable is zero.

The integrating controller however, on the occurrence of a change in the command variable or disturbance, only ceases changing its output voltage when the error signal has attained the value required by the command variable. Thus the error signal is zero in the steady state (ignoring the offset error of the amplifier). However, it cannot be reduced as rapidly as the proportional controller due to the time behaviour of the integration.

The proportional controller is more favourable for the initial response and the integrating controller is better for the steady-state response.

By combining the two controllers, properties which include the advantages of both are obtained and the disadvantages can be ignored. A proportional plus integral controller can be thought of as arising from the parallel connection of a proportional controller and an integrating controller. (Fig. 4.40).

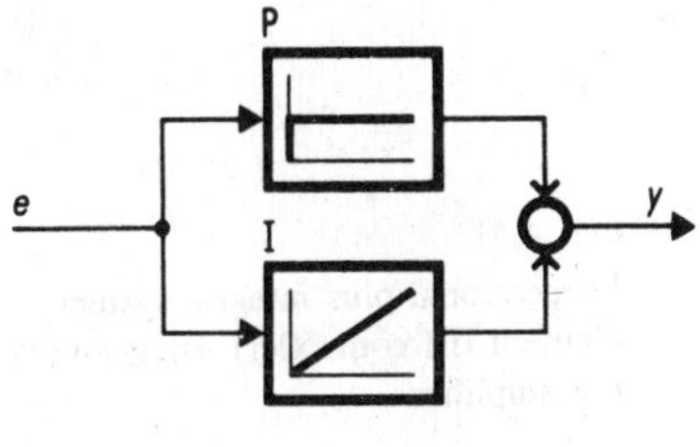

Fig. 4.40
Proportional plus integral system element formed from the parallel connection of proportional and integrating elements with the subsequent summing of the two outputs

4.3.4. Proportional plus integral response

A controller with proportional plus integral response, the PI controller, is the most frequently used controller in drive and power engineering.

The resistance in the feedback circuit of the inverting amplifier produces the proportional action (Fig. 4.32a) and the capacitance brings about the integrating action (Fig. 4.35). Both circuit elements together in the feedback must cause proportional plus integral response (Fig. 4.41).

With the complex feedback impedance as in Table 4.2 (number 5),

$$Z_f = R_f + \frac{1}{sC_f} = \frac{1 + sR_fC_f}{sC_f}.$$

The transfer function becomes

$$F_R(s)_{PI} = \frac{-V_a(s)}{\Delta V_0(s)} = \frac{R_f}{R_0} + \frac{1}{sR_0C_f} = A_R + \frac{1}{sT_I} \tag{4.53}$$

$$= \frac{R_f}{R_0}\frac{1+sR_fC_f}{sR_fC_f} = A_R\frac{1+sT_n}{sT_n}. \tag{4.54}$$

In Eqn (4.54) the reset time appears; it arises from the feedback connection:

$$T_n = R_fC_f = \frac{R_f}{R_0}R_0C_f = A_RT_I. \tag{4.55}$$

Equation (4.53) clearly shows both components of the PI action: the proportional part with amplification

$$A_R = R_f/R_0$$

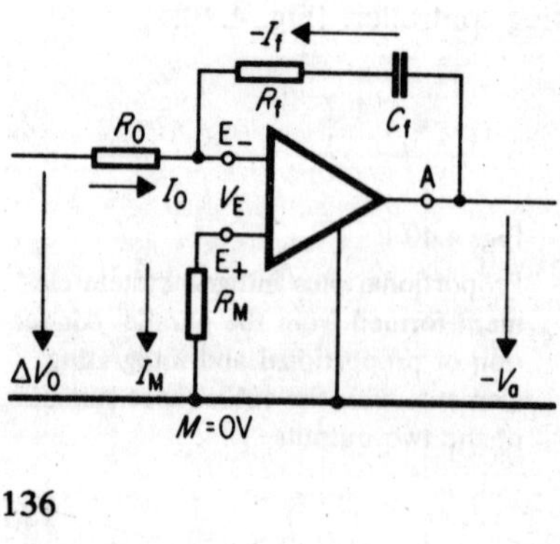

Fig. 4.41
Proportional plus integral system element (PI controller) using inverting amplifier

and the integrating part with the integrating time constant T_I where

$$\frac{1}{sT_I} = \frac{1}{sR_0C_t}.$$

Thus the general time equation can be defined:

$$-V_a(t) = A_R \Delta V_0(t) + \frac{1}{T_I}\int_0^t \Delta V_0(t)\,dt + V_{a0}. \tag{4.56}$$

V_{a0} is the initial output voltage before the advent of the input voltage.

If the voltage ΔV_0 is assumed to be a step function, the step response shown in Fig. 4.42 is obtained.

If the step response is related to the step input, the step response is obtained:

$$f(t) = \frac{-V_a(t)}{\Delta V_{0step}} = A_R + \frac{t}{T_I} \tag{4.57}$$

(V_{a0} is omitted here).

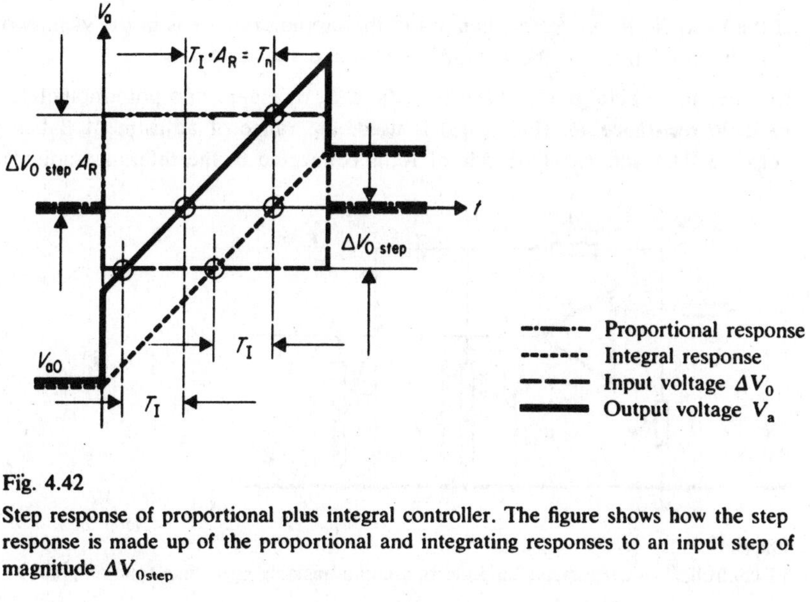

Fig. 4.42
Step response of proportional plus integral controller. The figure shows how the step response is made up of the proportional and integrating responses to an input step of magnitude ΔV_{0step}

From Fig. 4.42, showing the step response, it is seen that after the disappearance of the input voltage ΔV_0, the output voltage of the controller V_a indicates the value which would be obtained by an integrating controller without a proportional part. The excess output voltage, which occurs only during the presence of an error signal, is the result of the proportional function. As long as the error signal is not zero, the PI controller produces a greater output than the pure integrating controller. This is termed phase advance.

The phase advance is shown by the numerator $(1+sT_n)$ in Eqn (4.54). In contrast to the proportional controller and the integrating controller, in which only the amplification A_R and the integrating time constant T_I, respectively, can be varied by the choice of the feedback elements, the PI controller has two parameters. Both the amplification A_R and the reset time T_n can be selected.

By comparison of the command variable with the controlled variable, the input resistance R_0 is fixed. Then the amplification is determined by the resistance R_f. The required reset time is then obtained by means of the capacitor C_f.

If the amplification of the PI controller is to be varied by means of a potentiometer, the circuit of Fig. 4.34 is used. The correction factor K_α introduced in Table 4.3 influences both the amplification and the reset time:

$$T_{n\alpha} = R_f C_f \left[1 + (\alpha - \alpha^2) \frac{R_q}{R_f} \right]. \tag{4.58}$$

If the ratio R_q/R_f is greater than 1 and the tapping ratio α is in the vicinity of 0.5, the adjustment of the amplification affects the reset time.

In order to be able to adjust the reset time T_n by means of a potentiometer, a variable resistance R_p (Fig. 4.43) is used, the range of adjustment β being between 0.01 and 1.0. One side of R_p is connected to the reference point M

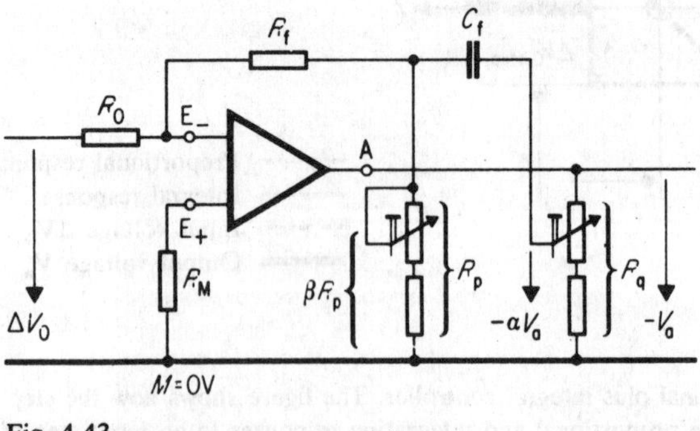

Fig. 4.43
PI controller with adjustable amplification and adjustable reset time (one amplifier)

and the other side between R_f and C_f. The resistance R_f which defines the reset time has one side connected to the amplifier input E_- and is therefore virtually at the potential of the reference point M.

If the fixed part of R_p is about 0.1 R_f and the whole of R_p is about 10 R_f, the reset time $T_{n\beta}$ can be adjusted over a range of 1–10. The adjustment of the amplification $V_{R\alpha}$ and the reset time $T_{n\beta}$ are then independent of each other:

$$A_{R\alpha} = \frac{R_f}{R_0}\frac{1}{\alpha}K_\alpha \tag{4.59}$$

$$T_{n\beta} = \frac{R_f \beta R_p}{R_f + \beta R_p} C_f K_\alpha. \tag{4.60}$$

Thus the amplification is determined by the tapping point α and the reset time is determined by the tapping point β.

If the influence of the finite amplification factor A_u of the amplifier and the finite input impedance Z_e are taken into account, the transfer function of Eqn (4.54) becomes

$$F_R(s) = \frac{A_u}{1 + R_0/R_e} \frac{1 + sT_n}{1 + sT_n\left[1 + \dfrac{1 + \bar{A}_u}{A_R}\dfrac{R_e}{R_0 + R_e}\right]}.$$

This is a first order delay with a very large amplification and a very large delay time as well as a phase advance with time constant T_n. Owing to the phase advance, a proportional output step results at the instant of an input step:

$$-V_{\substack{a\\ t\to 0}} = A_R\, \Delta V_{0\,\mathrm{step}} \frac{1}{1 + \dfrac{1}{\bar{A}_u}\left[1 + A_R\left(1 + \dfrac{R_0}{R_e}\right)\right]}.$$

Within the linear range of the amplifier, only the start of the delay action can be observed after the proportional step, for in the steady state the output voltage $V_{a\infty}$ must reach the value

$$-V_{a\infty} = A_u \Delta V_{0\,\mathrm{step}} \frac{R_e}{R_0 + R_e}.$$

This value, however, lies well outside the range of the amplifier. Therefore, integrating behaviour prevails in the linear range.

The system element of Fig. 4.41 goes into the overdriven state due to the proportional action if there is an input voltage step of magnitude given by

$$|\Delta V_{0\text{step}}| \geqslant \left| \frac{V_{a\max} - V_{a0}}{A_R} \right|. \tag{4.61}$$

The additional integrating action leads to the overdriven state during the input voltage step if the input signal remains longer than

$$t \geqslant \left| \frac{V_{a\max} - V_{a0} - \Delta V_{0\text{step}} A_R}{\Delta V_{0\text{step}}} T_I \right|. \tag{4.62}$$

This time is, of course, only of importance if the proportional action alone has not led to the overdriven state.

Proportional plus integral response can also be achieved with the non-inverting amplifier circuit. This may be done with a capacitance as the feedback impedance as shown in Fig. 4.25, i.e.

$$Z_f = \frac{1}{sC_f}$$

while all other impedances are purely resistive (Fig. 4.44). According to Eqn (4.34), the transfer function is

$$F_R(s) = \frac{V_a(s)}{\Delta V_0(s)} = 1 + \frac{1}{sR_M C_f} = \frac{1 + sT_n}{sT_n} \tag{4.63}$$

in which the amplification $A_R = 1$ and the reset time $T_n = R_M C_f$.

Since at the input to this circuit no comparison can be made between the command variable and the controlled variable and the amplification is always

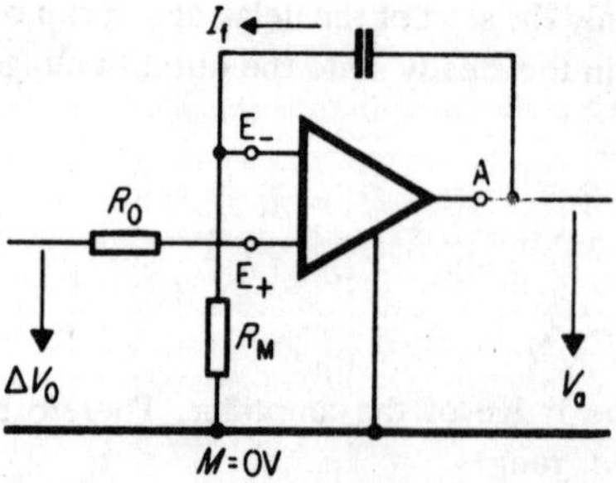

Fig. 4.44
Proportional plus integral system element obtained with the non-inverting amplifier. In this case, the amplification is always 1

1, this circuit is combined with the amplifier of Fig. 4.34. The proportional amplifier at the input can now generate the error signal and an adjustable resistance R_M in the circuit of Fig. 4.44 enables the reset time T_n to be matched to the given circumstances.

The complete circuit of this proportional integrating controller is shown in Fig. 4.45. It is preferable that each controller parameter has its own amplifier, which ensures good decoupling during adjustment of the parameters. However, the variable resistance βR_M may be extremely large or extremely small (β is a factor $\leqslant 1$, which represents the effective part of the total resistance R_M).

The current I_M (Fig. 4.25) must be appreciably larger than the input bias current but the current available at the output of the amplifier y^2 is limited. Therefore the reset time is adjustable over an approximate range of 1–10.

The transfer function of this circuit is obtained from Eqns (4.46) and (4.63). From Eqn (4.46),

$$-V_2(s) = \Delta V_0(s)\frac{R_f}{R_0}\frac{1}{\alpha}\left[1+(\alpha-\alpha^2)\frac{R_q}{R_f}\right]$$

and from Eqn (4.63),

$$-V_a(s) = -V_2(s)\frac{1+s\beta R_M C_f}{s\beta R_M C_f}.$$

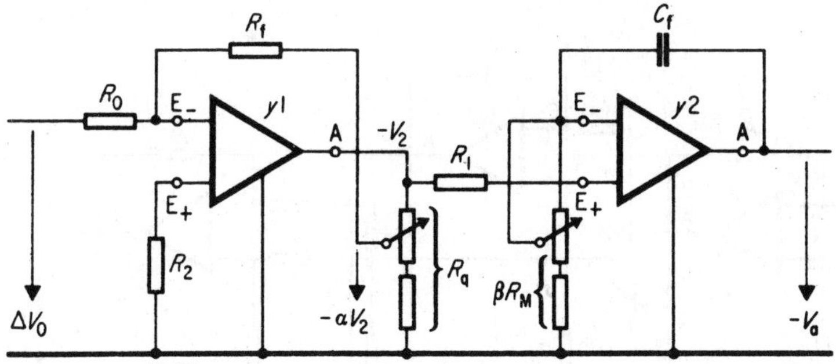

Fig. 4.45

PI controller with variable amplification and variable reset time (proportional element as an inverting amplifier and proportional/integrating element as a back coupled non-inverting amplifier)

Therefore the transfer function of the PI controller is

$$F_R(s)=\frac{-V_a(s)}{\Delta V_0(s)}=\frac{R_f}{R_0}\frac{1}{\alpha}\frac{1+s\beta R_M C_f}{s\beta R_M C_f}K_\alpha$$

$$=\frac{A_{R0}}{\alpha}\frac{1+s\beta T_n}{s\beta T_n}K_\alpha. \tag{4.64}$$

We have the adjustable amplification factor

$$A_{R\alpha}=A_{R0}/\alpha=R_f/R_0\alpha$$

the independently adjustable reset time

$$T_{n\beta}=\beta T_n=\beta R_M C_f$$

and the correction factor

$$K_\alpha=1+(\alpha-\alpha^2)R_q/R_f$$

from Eqn (4.46).

A controller independently adjustable for each controller parameter can also be produced by means of the circuit shown in Fig. 4.46. This also has the advantage that the reset time can be varied over a wide range. However, this advantage is obtained at the cost of a third amplifier connected as a differential amplifier.

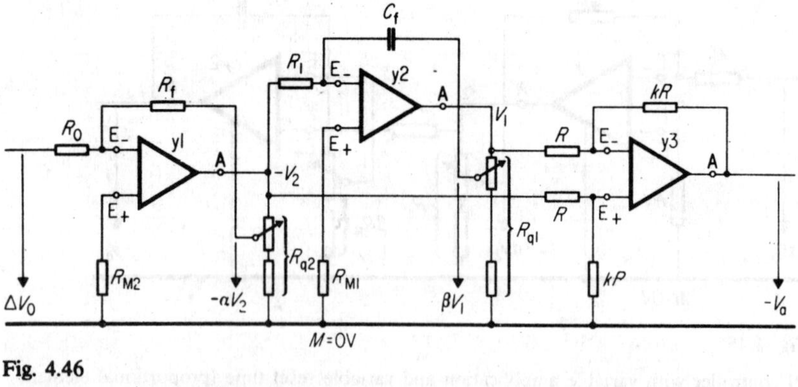

Fig. 4.46

PI controller with adjustable amplification ($0.1<A_R<100$) and adjustable reset time (10 ms $<T_n<$ 2000 ms)

The first amplifier y1 which produces the error signal is designed according to Fig. 4.34. It also provides the adjustable amplification. Its output is fed to both the non-inverting input of the differential amplifier y3 and the adjustable integrator y2 (Fig. 4.38). By applying the integrating channel to the inverting input of the differential amplifier, the addition of a proportional and integrating channel results, as shown in Fig. 4.40.

Equations for the transfer functions of each amplifier can be obtained. For amplifier y1 we have the following equation:

$$-V_2(s) = \Delta V_0(s)\frac{R_f}{R_0}\frac{1}{\alpha}\left[1+(\alpha-\alpha^2)\frac{R_{q2}}{R_f}\right].$$

For amplifier y2 we have

$$V_1(s) = -V_2(s)\frac{1}{s\beta R_1 C_f}[1+(\beta-\beta^2)sR_{q1}C_f].$$

For amplifier y3 we have

$$-V_a(s) = (V_1(s)-V_2(s))\frac{kR}{R}.$$

If the first and second equations are entered in the third, the result is as follows:

$$-V_a(s) = \Delta V_0(s)\frac{R_f}{R_0}\frac{R}{\alpha}\left[1+\frac{1+s(\beta-\beta^2)R_{q1}C_f}{s\beta R_1 C_f}\right]\left(1+(\alpha-\alpha^2)\frac{R_{q2}}{R_f}\right). \tag{4.65}$$

To ensure that the two correction terms in this equation, one of which is a parasitic phase advance, are practically equal to 1, resistances R_{q1} and R_{q2} must be of very low value, i.e.

$$R_{q1} \ll R_1, \qquad R_{q2} \ll R_f,$$

Usually the resistances R_q are smaller than the resistances R_1 or R_f by a factor of 10–100.

Using the adjustable amplification

$$A_{R\alpha} = A_{R0}/\alpha = (R_f k)/(R_0 \alpha)$$

and the adjustable reset time

$$T_{n\beta} = \beta T_n = \beta R_1 C_f$$

the transfer function of the PI controller of Fig. 4.46 is obtained as follows:

$$F_R(s) = \frac{-V_a(s)}{\Delta V_0(s)} = \frac{A_{R0}}{\alpha} \frac{1 + s\beta T_n}{s\beta T_n}. \tag{4.66}$$

The considerations applied to Fig. 4.39 for the integrating controller in the overdriven state also apply in a modified form for the proportional plus integral controller. It is also necessary here for the error signal to change its sign, so that the controlled variable exceeds the command variable, in order to bring the PI controller out of the overdriven state.

4.3.5. Differentiating response

Integrating behaviour is obtained by means of capacitance in the feedback circuit of an amplifier (Fig. 4.35). Differentiation may be obtained by the dual circuit, i.e. an inductance in the series feedback branch or a capacitance in the parallel feedback circuit or alternatively by capacitance in series with the input branch. The latter (Fig. 4.47) is preferred for a simple differentiation circuit. The transfer function for this circuit is

$$F_R(s) = \frac{-V_a(s)}{V_0(s)} = sR_f C_0 = sT_D \tag{4.67}$$

in which the differentiating time constant is $T_D = R_f C_0$.

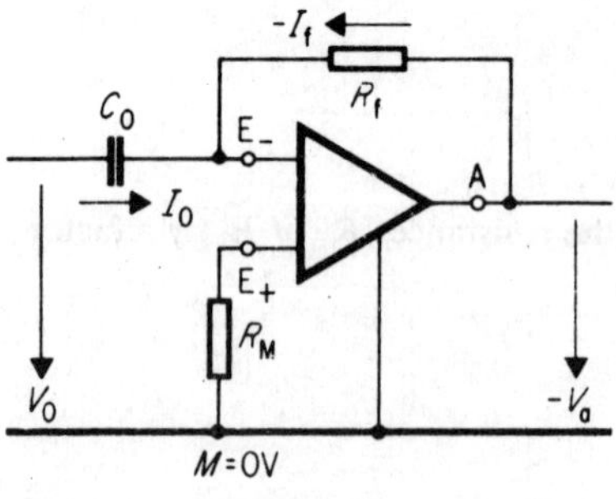

Fig. 4.47
Differentiating system element

Since the operator s appears in the numerator, the general time equation is

$$-V_a(t) = T_D \frac{dV_0(t)}{dt}. \tag{4.68}$$

The greater the rate of change of V_0, the greater is the output voltage. At a constant input voltage the output voltage is zero.

For a step change of the input voltage, the output voltage is very large. In the ideal amplifier it is infinite. The voltage/time area, however, would be finite and equal to the product of the input voltage V_{0step} and the differentiating time constant T_D (compare with Section 3.5, especially Eqn (3.36)).

If account is taken of the internal impedance of the input voltage source Z_i, the finite voltage amplification of the real amplifier and its finite input resistance, the transfer function becomes

$$F_R(s) = \frac{sR_fC_0}{1+\frac{1}{\bar{A}_u}\left(1+\frac{R_f}{R_e}\right)+sR_fC_0\left[\frac{Z_i}{R_f}+\frac{1}{\bar{A}_u}\left(1+\frac{Z_i}{R_f}+\frac{Z_i}{R_e}\right)\right]}.$$

If $\bar{A}_u \gg 1$ and $Z_i = R_i$ then

$$F_R(s) = \frac{-V_a(s)}{V_0(s)} = \frac{sR_fC_0}{1+sR_iC_0}.$$

A parasitic time constant occurs in the denominator of the transfer function. Thus the element is not a pure differentiating element (see Section 3.6).

In order to make the performance independent of the impedance Z_i of the source, a resistance R_0 is placed in series with the differentiating capacitor C_0, having a value much greater than any expected value of the impedance Z_i (Fig. 4.48). The transfer function then becomes

$$F_R(s) = \frac{-V_a(s)}{V_0(s)} = \frac{sR_fC_0}{1+sR_0C_0} = \frac{sT_D}{1+sT_g}. \tag{4.69}$$

If the voltage V_0 is a step function input signal, then from Eqn (3.46) the step response is obtained:

$$f(t) = \frac{-V_a(t)}{V_{0step}} = \frac{R_f}{R_0}e^{-t/T_g}. \tag{4.70}$$

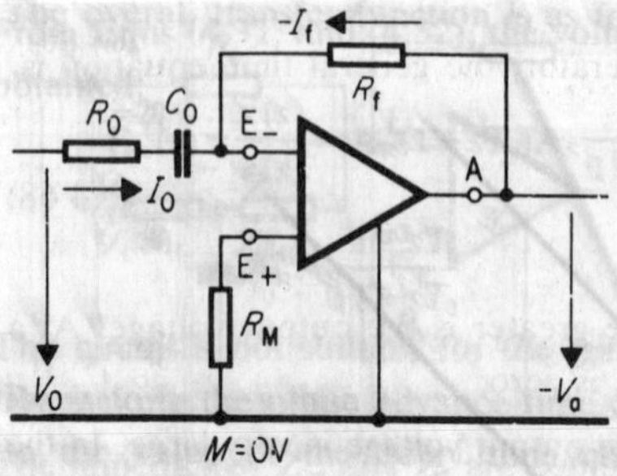

Fig. 4.48
Differentiating system element with delay (practical differentiating element)

The effective voltage/time area at the output is the product $V_{0\text{step}} T_D$ assuming of course that the output voltage does not fall outside the range of the amplifier. Thus for a given differentiation time constant T_D, the resistance R_0 is chosen to be as large as possible. However, R_0 should be as small as possible if the decay time constant T_g is to be kept as small as possible. Of course, if the output voltage V_a should happen to exceed the maximum attainable voltage $V_{a\max}$, part of the effective voltage/time area is lost (Fig. 4.49)

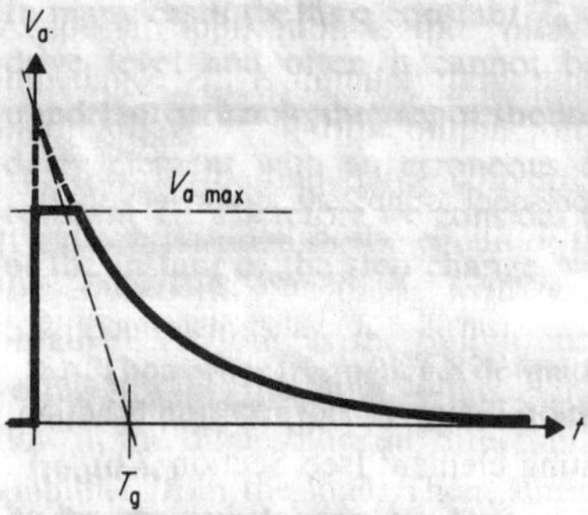

Fig. 4.49
Step response of differentiating element which has been overdriven. The dashed line peak of the curve is lost.

4.3.6. Proportional/differential response

The proportional/differential (PD) controller uses an inverting amplifier. To avoid the loss of part of the voltage/time area, the differentiation is achieved by a capacitor placed in the parallel branch of the feedback circuit. A resistance for decoupling must be placed in the series branch of the feedback at the input side of the amplifier as well as at the output (Fig. 4.50). In this case, the capacitor C_q can only charge or discharge according to the level of the output voltage V_a and whether it lies at the voltage limit $V_{a\max}$.

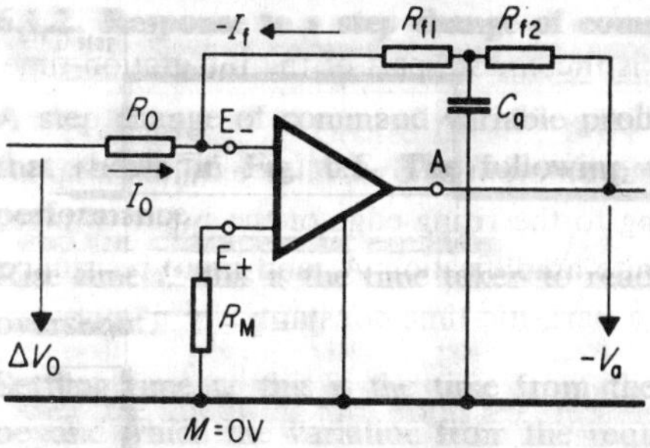

Fig. 4.50
Proportional/differential system element using inverting amplifier

Therefore the voltage across the parallel capacitor C_q and the output voltage V_a always move in conformity with each other and even in the overdriven state, nothing can be lost from the desired voltage/time area.
The feedback circuit of this system is a T circuit (Table 4.2, number 9). Consequently the transfer function is

$$F_R(s) = \frac{-V_a(s)}{\Delta V_0(s)} = \frac{R_{f1}+R_{f2}}{R_0}\left(1+s\frac{R_{f1}R_{f2}}{R_{f1}+R_{f2}}C_q\right)$$

$$= A_R(1+sT_v) \tag{4.71}$$

where A_R is the proportional amplification given by

$$A_R + \frac{R_{f1}+R_{f2}}{R_0}$$

and T_v is the phase advance or present time constant, given by

$$T_v = \frac{R_{f1}R_{f2}}{R_{f1}+R_{f2}}C_q.$$

Corresponding to the transfer function, the general time equation is

$$-V_a(t) = A_R\Delta V_0(t) + A_R T_v \frac{d\Delta V_0(t)}{dt} \tag{4.72}$$

Both components, the proportional part and the differential part, can be recognized. The differentiating time constant T_D appears in the differential part as

$$A_R T_v = \frac{R_{f1}+R_{f2}}{R_0}\frac{R_{f1}R_{f2}}{R_{f1}+R_{f2}}C_q = \frac{R_{f1}R_{f2}}{R_0}C_q = T_D. \tag{4.73}$$

The differentiation time constant T_D is the counterpart of the integration time constant T_I in the integrating controller.

The step response of the proportional/differential controller exhibits a spike tending towards infinity corresponding to the rising edge of the input voltage, but the non-ideal amplifier with a finite amplification A_u and input resistance R_e produces a correction term with a parasitic time constant

$$F_R(s) = \frac{-V_a(s)}{\Delta V_0(s)}$$

$$= A_R(1+sT_v)\frac{1}{1+\frac{1}{A_u}\left[1+A_R\left(1+\frac{R_0}{R_e}\right)\right]+s\frac{A_R}{A_u}\left[1+\frac{R_0}{R_{f1}}+\frac{R_0}{R_e}\right]T_v}.$$

The differentiating phase advance $(1+sT_v)$ leads quite rapidly to self-oscillation, for the damping effect of the delay with the parasitic time constant is not sufficiently large. It is necessary to increase this time constant by means of a resistance R_d placed in series with the parallel capacitance C_q (Fig. 4.51). This, from Table 4.2, number 10, gives the following transfer function:

$$F_R(s) = \frac{-V_a(s)}{\Delta V_0(s)} = \frac{R_{f1}+R_{f2}}{R_0}\,\frac{1+s\left(\frac{R_{f1}R_{f2}}{R_{f1}+R_{f2}}+R_d\right)C_q}{1+sR_dC_q}$$

$$= A_R\frac{1+s(T_v+t_d)}{1+st_d} \tag{4.74}$$

where the new decay time constant $t_d = R_dC_q$ should provide sufficient damping.

The following method is used to determine the minimum value of the damping resistance R_d.

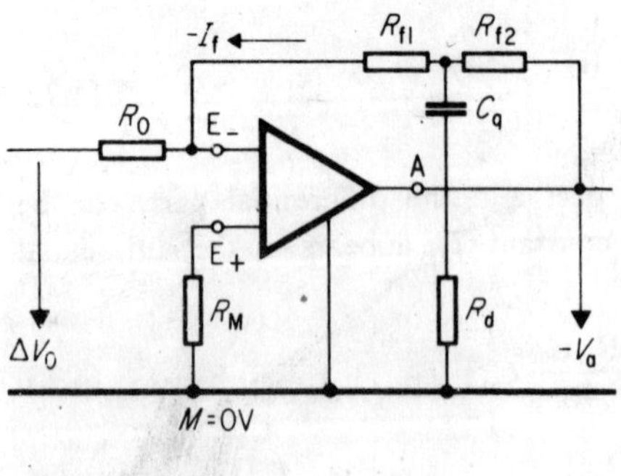

Fig. 4.51
Proportional/differential system element with inverting amplifier prevented from oscillation by the damping resistance R_d

Let us assume that the input resistance is very large, and therefore $1/R_e$ is very small. Let us assume that the amplifier has a characteristic corresponding to a first order delay, as given by Eqn (4.9)

$$\bar{A}_u = A_u \frac{1}{1+s\sigma_V}.$$

Then the transfer function becomes as follows:

$$F_R(s) = A_R \frac{1+s(T_v+t_d)}{1+st_d} \times$$

$$\times \frac{1}{1+\dfrac{1+s\sigma_V}{A_u}\left[1+\dfrac{A_R+s\left(\dfrac{R_{f1}R_{f2}}{R_0}+R_d A_R+R_{f2}\right)C_q}{1+st_d}\right]}$$

Ignoring insignificant terms, the following expression is obtained:

$$F_R(s) = \frac{A_R[1+s(T_v+t_d)]}{1+s\left[\dfrac{T_v}{A_u}\left(A_R+\dfrac{R_{f1}+R_{f2}}{R_{f1}}\right)+t_d\right]+s^2\dfrac{T_v}{A_u}\sigma_v\left(A_R+\dfrac{R_{f1}+R_{f2}}{R_{f1}}\right)} \tag{4.75}$$

Comparing coefficients with Eqn (2.35) for a second order delay, we see that the following damping factor is obtained:

$$\zeta = \frac{C_q\left[R_d+\dfrac{(1+R_{f1}/R_0)R_{f2}}{A_u}\right]}{2\sqrt{\dfrac{\sigma_V}{A_u}C_q(1+R_{f1}/R_0)R_{f2}}}. \tag{4.76}$$

The term σ_V/A_u corresponds to the crossover frequency f_T^* of the internally damped controller amplifier of Fig. 4.9.

$$\frac{\sigma_V}{A_u} = \frac{1}{2\pi f_T^*}.$$

If a periodic but very strongly damped transient condition is required, the damping factor is chosen to be

$$\zeta \geqslant 1/\sqrt{2}.$$

From Eqn (4.76), the minimum necessary damping resistance R_d is now defined:

$$R_d \geq \sqrt{\frac{(1+R_{f1}/R_0)R_{f2}}{\pi f_T^* C_q} - \left(1+\frac{R_{f1}}{R_0}\right)\frac{R_{f2}}{A_u}}. \tag{4.77}$$

A numerical example will illustrate the value of the resistance R_d and the parasitic time constant t_d.

With

$R_{f1} = 50\ \text{k}\Omega \qquad A_u = 10\,000$

$R_{f2} = 50\ \text{k}\Omega \qquad f_T^* = 1\ \text{MHz}$

$C_q = 10\ \mu\text{F} \qquad R_0 = 20\ \text{k}\Omega$

the damping resistance becomes $R_d \geq 38\ \Omega$ and the parasitic time constant $t_d \geq 0.4$ ms. In contrast, the phase advance time constant $T_v = 250$ ms.

The proportional/differential element, adequately damped in accordance with the transfer function, Eqn (4.74), has the general time equation

$$t_d \frac{d[-V_a(t)]}{dt} - V_a(t) = A_R \Delta V_0(t) + A_R T_v \frac{d[\Delta V_0(t)]}{dt} \tag{4.78}$$

and this leads to the step response

$$f(t) = \frac{-V_a(t)}{\Delta V_{0\text{step}}} = A_R\left(1 - e^{-t/t_d} + \frac{T_v}{t_d} e^{-t/t_d}\right). \tag{4.79}$$

The step response is shown in Fig. 4.52. Here the phase advance area f_D is the product of the time constant t_d and the difference between the initial and the final values of output voltage:

$$-V_a\big|_{t\to 0} = \Delta V_{0\text{step}} A_R \left(\frac{T_v}{t_d} + 1\right).$$

$$-V_a\big|_{t\to\infty} = \Delta V_{0\text{step}} A_R$$

Thus

$$f_D = \Delta V_{0\text{step}} A_R T_v. \tag{4.80}$$

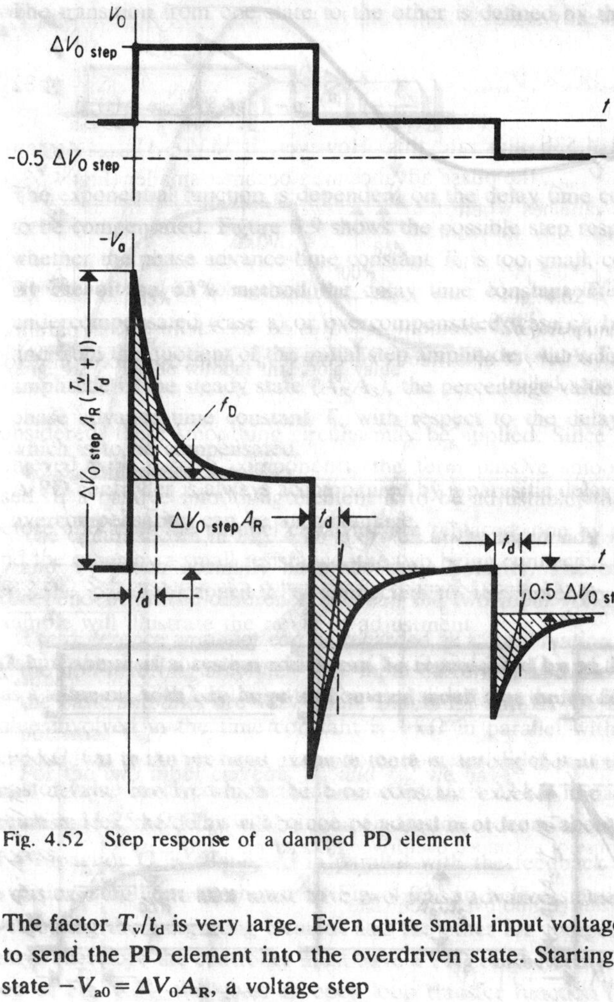

Fig. 4.52 Step response of a damped PD element

The factor T_v/t_d is very large. Even quite small input voltage steps are enough to send the PD element into the overdriven state. Starting with the previous state $-V_{a0}=\Delta V_0 A_R$, a voltage step

$$|\Delta V_{0step}| \geq |V_{a\,max} - V_{a0}| \frac{t_d}{A_R(T_v+t_d)} \tag{4.81}$$

is sufficient to do so.

However, nothing is lost from the phase advance area, since the capacitor C_q is only charged via the voltage divider R_{f1}, R_{f2}, and when overdriven this lies between $V_{a\,max}$ and practically zero potential. Only the amplifier output remains correspondingly longer at the limit $V_{a\,max}$. Thereby nothing is lost, if of course it is assumed that the amplifier is sufficiently clear of the overdriven state when in the steady state:

$$|\Delta V_0 + \Delta V_{0\,step}| A_R \ll |V_{a\,max}|. \tag{4.82}$$

Figures 4.53a and 4.53b illustrate this. However, if $|\Delta V_0 + \Delta V_{0step}|\, A_R$ approaches the value $V_{a\,max}$, the phase advance area becomes smaller (Fig. 4.53c) until it completely vanishes when

$$|\Delta V_0 + \Delta V_{0\,step}|\, A_R \geqslant |V_{a\,max}|.$$

The amplification of the PD element is adjusted by means of a parallel potentiometer (Fig. 4.54). It also needs of course a correction according to

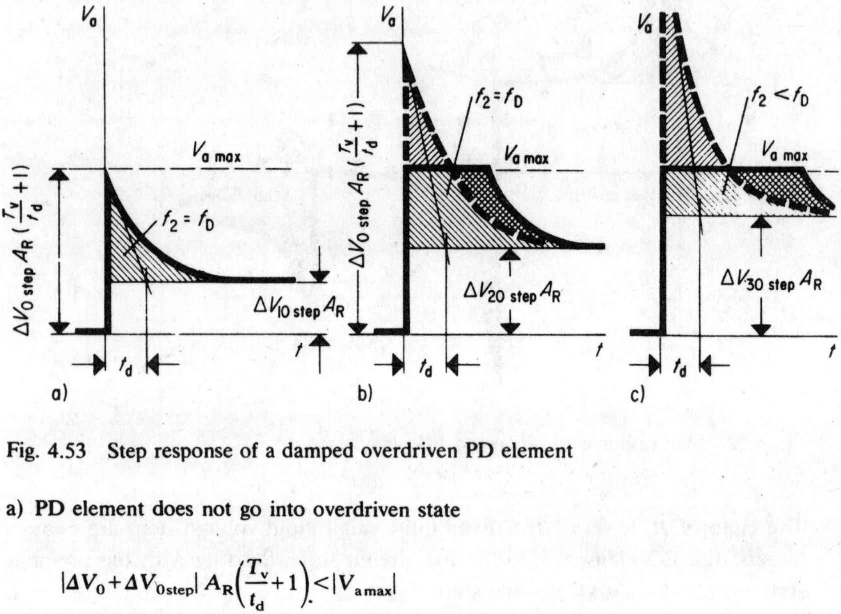

Fig. 4.53 Step response of a damped overdriven PD element

a) PD element does not go into overdriven state

$$|\Delta V_0 + \Delta V_{0\,step}|\, A_R \left(\frac{T_v}{t_d} + 1\right) < |V_{a\,max}|$$

b) PD element enters overdriven state briefly

$$|\Delta V_0 + \Delta V_{0\,step}|\, A_R \left(\frac{T_v}{t_d} + 1\right) > |V_{a\,max}| > |\Delta V_0 + \Delta V_{0\,step}|\, A_R$$

c) PD element remains for a considerable time in the overdriven state

$$|\Delta V_0 + \Delta V_{0\,step}|\, A_R \approx V_{a\,max}$$

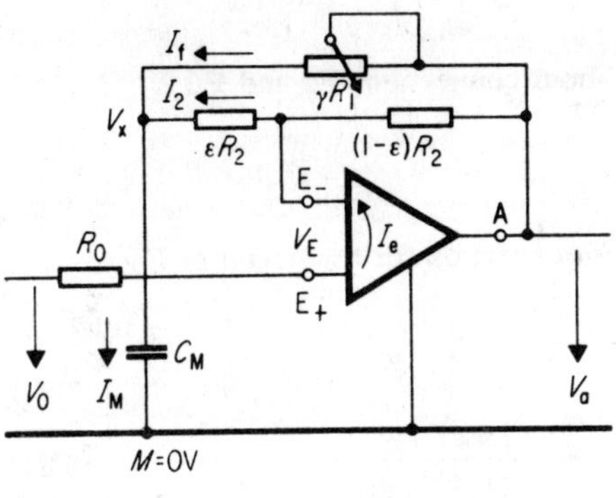

Fig. 4.54
Proportional/differential system element, using the non-inverting amplifier, which is damped by voltage divider εR_2 and $(1-\varepsilon)R_2$

Table 4.3. However, the effect of the take off point α is without significance on the phase advance time

$$T_{v\alpha} = \frac{R_{f1}R_{f2}}{R_{f1}+R_{f2}} C_q \frac{1+(\alpha-\alpha^2)\dfrac{R_q}{R_{f2}}}{1+(\alpha-\alpha^2)\dfrac{R_q}{R_{f1}+R_{f2}}}$$

The non-inverting amplifier circuit (Fig. 4.25) can also be used as a PD element. In this case, the feedback path contains a resistance R_f, while the impedance Z_M is a capacitance. The transfer function, according to Eqn (4.34), is as follows:

$$F_R(s) = \frac{V_a(s)}{V_0(s)} = 1 + sR_fC_M \tag{4.83}$$

with the phase advance $T_v = R_fC_M$. A variable resistance R_f can be used to control the phase advance time.

In this circuit a damping delay must be used to prevent self-oscillation. Therefore resistances εR_2 and $(1-\varepsilon)R_2$ are added to the circuit (Fig. 4.54) α being small with respect to unity.

The input current I_0 which is equal to I_e is practically zero, and the currents I_f, I_2 and I_M (Fig. 4.54) are as follows:

$$I_f = \frac{V_a - V_x}{\gamma R_f}$$

$$I_2 = \frac{V_a - V_x}{R_2}$$

$$I_M = I_f + I_2 = V_x sC_M.$$

The potential V_E common to both input connections E_- and E_+ is

$$V_E = V_x + \varepsilon R_2 I_2.$$

From the above equations, the transfer function for the circuit of Fig. 4.54 is given by

$$F_R(s) = \frac{V_a(s)}{V_0(s)} = \frac{1 + s\dfrac{\gamma R_f R_2}{\gamma R_f + R_2} C_M}{1 + s\varepsilon \dfrac{\gamma R_f R_2}{\gamma R_f + R_2} C_M} = \frac{1 + sT_v(\gamma)}{1 + s\varepsilon T_v(\gamma)} \tag{4.84}$$

in which the adjustable phase advance time constant is

$$T_v(\gamma) = \gamma \frac{R_f R_2 C_M}{\gamma R_f + R_2}. \tag{4.85}$$

The tapping point γ on the resistance R_f cannot of course be made arbitrarily small, because its decoupling effect would then be lost. For this reason and because the factor γ also appears in the denominator in Eqn (4.85), the range of adjustment of the phase advance time is limited.

The capacitance C_M is charged by the currents I_f and I_2 which are obtained from the amplifier output. Thus overdriving the amplifier does not lead to a loss of the phase advance area f_D. This is because the output voltage, once it has reached the overdriven state, can only go out of this state if the capacitance C_M has reached the corresponding state of charge. However, the considerations relating to Fig. 4.53 also apply.

The factor ε, which sets the ratio of the decay time constant t_d' to the phase advance time constant T_v, is usually chosen as less than 2% in order not to make the response of the PD element unnecessarily large

A P element as shown in Fig. 4.34 has to be connected in front of the PD element of Fig. 4.54 if a variable amplification A_R is required and if an error signal has to be obtained at the input.

If the range of adjustment for the phase advance time constant T_v in the PD controller of Fig. 4.54 is insufficient, the circuit shown in Fig. 4.55 is used.

In this circuit, an integrator y3 is positively coupled into the feedback path of an inverting amplifier y2. Its input voltage is tapped off the parallel potentiometer R_q. This is effectively an integration in the reverse direction but a differentiation in the forward direction of y2. An adjustable proportional

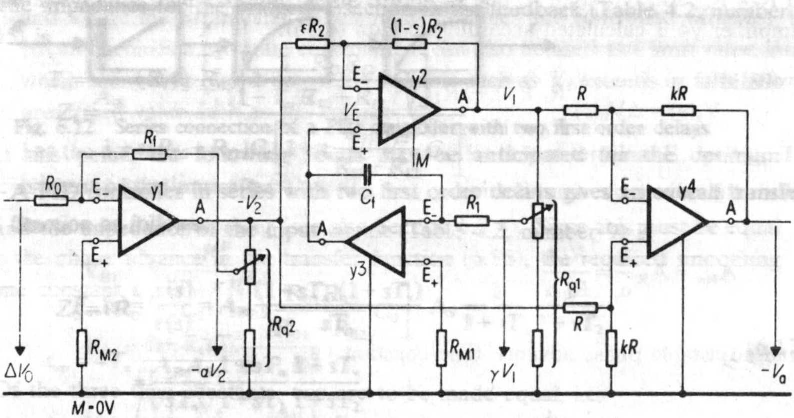

Fig. 4.55
PD controller with variable amplification ($0.1 < A_R < 100$), variable phase advance time constant ($10\ \text{ms} < T_v < 2000\ \text{ms}$) and selectable damping time constant t_d

element y1 at the input end and a differential amplifier y4 at the output end complete the circuit.

The behaviour can be derived from Fig. 4.55. The proportional response for the amplifier y1 is given by

$$-V_2(s) = \Delta V_0(s)\frac{R_f}{R_0}\frac{1}{\alpha}k_\alpha.$$

For the integrator y3, the equation is

$$-V_E(s) = V_1(s)\frac{1}{sR_1C_f}\gamma k_\gamma.$$

V_E is the approximately common potential at the terminals E_- and E_+ of the amplifier y2. Thus

$$\frac{V_1 - V_E}{(1-\varepsilon)R_2} = \frac{V_E - V_2}{\varepsilon R_2}$$

and thus

$$V_E = \varepsilon V_1 + (1-\varepsilon)V_2.$$

If $R_f \gg R_{q2}$ and $R_1 \gg R_{q1}$, k_α and k_γ approach the value 1. The equation for the amplifier y4 is calculated according to Eqn (4.36):

$$-V_a(s) = \Delta V_0(s) \frac{R_f}{R_0} \frac{k}{\alpha} \frac{1 + sR_1C_f/\gamma}{1 + s\varepsilon R_1C_1/\gamma}.$$

With the adjustable amplification

$$A_{R\alpha} = A_R \frac{k}{\alpha} = \frac{R_f}{R_0} \frac{k}{\alpha}$$

and adjustable phase advance time constant

$$T_{v\gamma} = T_v/\gamma = R_1 C_f \frac{1}{\gamma}$$

and the selectable damping time constant

$$t_d = \varepsilon T_v/\gamma = \varepsilon R_1 C_f \frac{1}{\gamma}$$

the transfer function is

$$F_R(s) = \frac{-V_a(s)}{\Delta V_0(s)} = A_R \frac{k}{\alpha} \frac{1 + sT_v/\gamma}{1 + s\varepsilon T_v/\gamma}. \tag{4.86}$$

The factor $\varepsilon = t_d/T_v$ is chosen to be below 5%.

When this system element is overdriven, the source of the charging current for the capacitor C_f is once more the output voltage V_a or more specifically, V_1. V_1 must be less than V_a, since the factor k is selected as equal to or less than 1.

4.3.7. Proportional/integral/differential response

The combination of the proportional/integrating element and the proportional/differentiating element produces the proportional/integrating/differentiating element (PID element). It contains the three separate components. With the inverting amplifier and the feedback network shown in Table 4.2, number 12, the circuit of Fig. 4.56 is obtained. By neglecting the very small

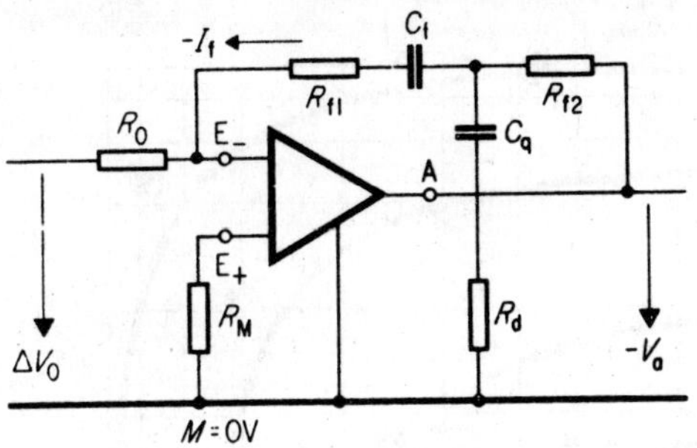

Fig. 4.56
Proportional/integral/differential system element using an inverting amplifier

damping resistance R_d, the equation for the feedback network is

$$Z_f(s) = \frac{1 + s(R_{f1}C_f + R_{f2}C_q) + s^2 R_{f1}R_{f2}C_fC_q + sR_{f2}C_f}{sC_f}.$$

The numerator should have the form $(1+sT_1)(1+sT_2)$, but the numerator also contains the term $sR_{f2}C_f$. This will be negligible if

$$\frac{R_{f1}}{R_{f2}} + \frac{C_q}{C_f} \gg 1. \tag{4.87}$$

Figure 4.57 shows the effect of the extra term on the required time constants. The percentage remains below 5% if the expression

$$\frac{R_{f1}}{R_{f2}} + \frac{C_q}{C_f}$$

is greater than 20. The resistance R_{f1} and capacitance C_q are therefore chosen to be as large as possible. Then

$$\frac{R_{f1}}{R_{f1}+R_{f2}} \approx 1$$

and we obtain

$$Z_f = \frac{-V_a(s)}{-I_f} = \frac{1}{sC_f}[1 + s(R_{f1}+R_{f2})C_f]\left[1 + s\frac{R_{f1}R_{f2}}{R_{f1}+R_{f2}}C_q\right].$$

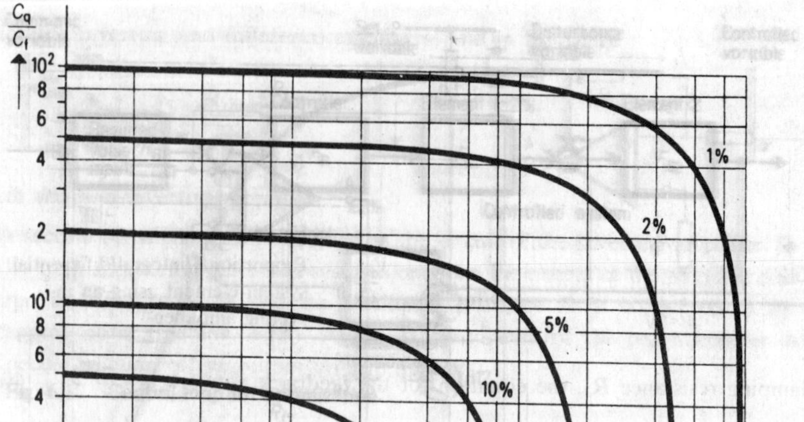

Fig. 4.57
Ratio of the undesired time constant $R_{f2}C_f$ to the sum of time constants $(R_{f1}C_f + R_{f2}C_q)$ as a percentage. Parameter: $\dfrac{100\%}{R_{f1}/R_{f2} + C_g/C_f}$

Including the damping resistance R_d the transfer function is as follows:

$$F_R(s) = \frac{-V_a(s)}{\Delta V_0(s)} = \frac{[1 + s(R_{f1} + R_{f2})C_f]\left[1 + s\dfrac{R_{f1}R_{f2}}{R_{f1} + R_{f2}}C_q\right]}{sR_0C_f(1 + sR_dC_q)}$$

$$= \frac{(1 + sT_n)(1 + sT_v)}{sT_1(1 + st_d)} \tag{4.88}$$

with the following constants:

Integrating time constant	$T_I = R_0C_f$,
Reset time constant	$T_n = (R_{f1} + R_{f2})C_f$,
Phase advance (preset) time constant	$T_v = \dfrac{R_{f1}R_{f2}}{R_{f1} + R_{f2}} C_q$,
Decay time constant	$t_d = R_dC_q$.

The damping resistance R_d can be defined using Eqn (4.77).

Similarly to Eqn (4.71), the amplification A_R is

$$A_R = \frac{T_n}{T_I} = \frac{(R_{f1} + R_{f2})C_f}{R_0C_f} = \frac{R_{f1} + R_{f2}}{R_0'}.$$

Then the transfer function is

$$F_R(s) = \frac{-V_a(s)}{\Delta V_0(s)} = A_R \frac{(1 + sT_n)(1 + sT_v)}{sT_n(1 + st_d)}. \tag{4.89}$$

The individual components here are easy to separate:

$$-V_a(s)(1 + st_d) = \Delta V_0(s)\left[\frac{A_R}{sT_n} + A_R \frac{T_n + T_v}{T_n} + sA_RT_v\right].$$

This resuls in the following general time equation:

$$t_d \frac{d[-V_a(t)]}{dt} - V_a(t) = \frac{1}{T_I}\int_0^t \Delta V_0(t)\,dt + A_R\left(1 + \frac{T_v}{T_n}\right)\Delta V_0(t)$$

$$+ T_D \frac{d[\Delta V_0(t)]}{dt} + V_{ao} \tag{4.90}$$

in which the proportional part is

$$A_R\left(1 + \frac{T_v}{T_n}\right)\Delta V_0(t)$$

the integral part is

$$\frac{1}{T_I}\int_0^t \Delta V_0(t)\,dt$$

and the differential part is

$$T_D \frac{d[\Delta V_0(t)]}{dt}.$$

If the decay time constant is taken into account, the following step response is obtained:

$$f(t) = \frac{-V_a(t)}{\Delta V_{0step}} = \frac{t}{T_1} + A_R\left(1 + \frac{T_v}{T_n}\right) + \frac{T_D}{t_d} e^{-t/t_d} + \frac{V_{a0}}{\Delta V_{0step}} \tag{4.91}$$

(the damping only applies to the differential part).

The step response is shown in Fig. 4.58.

The initial amplitude is

$$\left[A_R\left(1 + \frac{T_v}{T_n}\right) + \frac{T_D}{t_d}\right] \Delta V_{0step}.$$

Normally this peak lies outside the range of the amplifier. However, since the charge on the differentiating capacitor C_q can only vary in accordance with the output voltage V_a, nothing is lost from the voltage–time area (phase advance area) f_D of the differentiating phase advance.

A buffer amplifier is connected as an impedance converter between the two energy stores C_f and C_q as in Fig. 4.59. In the simplest case the impedance converter can be a transistor in the collector circuit

The resistance R_{f2} goes to zero for the capacitor C_f and resistance R_{f1} goes to infinity for the capacitor C_q. Therefore

Amplification	$A_R = R_{f1}/R_0$,
Integration time constant	$T_I = R_0 C_f$,
Reset time constant	$T_n = R_{f1} C_f$,
Phase advance (preset) time constant	$T_v = R_{f2} C_q$,
Decay time constant	$t_d = R_d C_q$.

If it is required to design a PID system element with integrated circuit linear amplifiers, following present day practice, at least one amplifier for each parameter will be used. This means for example that a proportional/integrating action using the circuit of Fig. 4.45 arranged in series with a

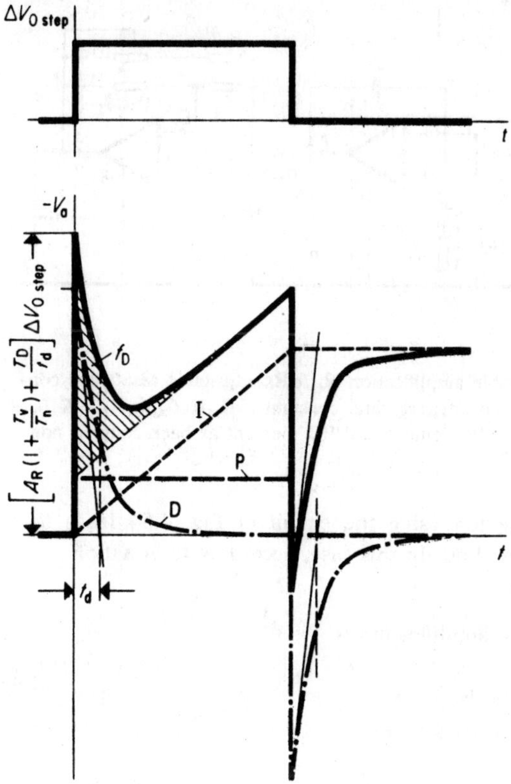

Fig. 4.58

Response of the PID system element to a step

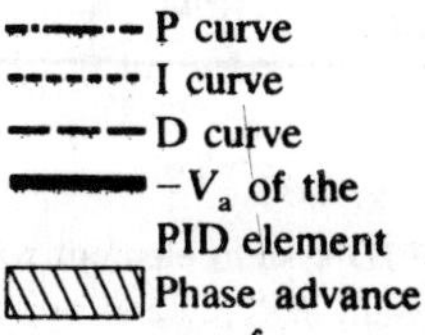

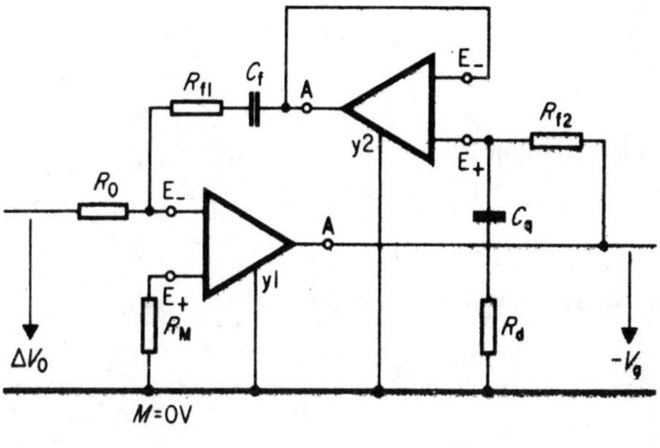

Fig. 4.59

PID system element using an inverting amplifier with an impedance converter in the feedback for isolation of the two capacitors

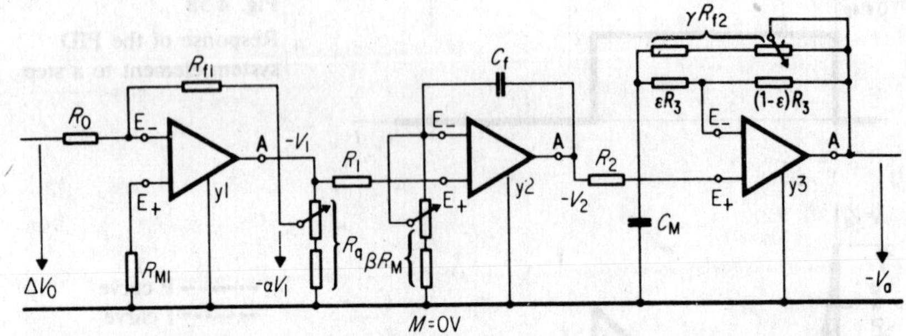

Fig. 4.60
PID system element with adjustable amplification $R_{f1}/\alpha R_0$ adjustable reset time constant $\beta R_M C_f$ and adjustable phase advance time constant $(\gamma R_{f2} R_3 C_M/[\gamma R_{f2}+R_3])$. (P element as inverting amplifier, PI element and PD element as back coupled non-inverting amplifiers)

proportional/differentiating action using the circuit of Fig. 4.54 leads to a variable PID action as in Fig. 4.60. In this case, according to equation

(4.46), the proportional amplification is

$$A_{R\alpha} = \frac{R_{f1}}{R_0}\frac{1}{\alpha}\left[1+(\alpha-\alpha^2)\frac{R_q}{R_{f1}}\right]$$

(4.55), the integration time constant is

$$T_{I\alpha\beta} = \alpha\beta\frac{R_0}{R_{f1}}R_M C_f$$

(4.64), the reset time constant is

$$T_{n\beta} = \beta R_M C_f$$

(4.85), the phase advance (preset) time constant is

$$T_{v\gamma} = \frac{\gamma R_{f2} R_3}{\gamma R_{f2} + R_3} C_M$$

(4.84), the decay time constant is

$$t_d = \varepsilon T_{v\gamma}$$

and hence the transfer function is

$$F_R(s) = \frac{-V_a(s)}{\Delta V_0(s)} = A_{Rd} \frac{(1+sT_{n\beta})(1+sT_{v\gamma})}{sT_{n\beta}(1+st_d)} . \tag{4.92}$$

The suffixes α, β and γ signify that all parameters are variable.

Corresponding to the many forms of representation for the one and two parameter system elements in the previous sections (see Figs. 4.45, 4.46, 4.54 and 4.55), there are many possible combinations for the PID element. However, since there are few applications of the PID controller in the field of drive and power engineering, no further combinations will be discussed in detail.

4.4. Controller Auxiliary Circuits

The three types of behaviour discussed in Section 4.3, that is, proportional, integrating and differentiating and their combinations, are not sufficient on their own for a complete control system. Additional equipment is necessary. This is dealt with in the following sections.

4.4.1. Smoothing

Almost without exception, the voltages which represent the measured values of the controlled variables in drive and power engineering are subject to ripple. Such a ripple can arise in the measurement transducer, e.g. in the demodulation of an actual value voltage when the variable to be measured is modulated, amplified in an a.c. amplifier and afterwards passed through a transformer to the demodulator for evaluation. It can also be a fundamental part of the control quantity such as the direct current produced from a rectifier. This ripple which is not part of the control signal would interfere with the control function and must therefore be smoothed.

Smoothing circuits of the simplest form (Table 4.2, number 9) are used in the input channels of the controller.

The smoothing action will be illustrated by the example of the controlled variable channel of a proportional controller (Fig. 4.61).

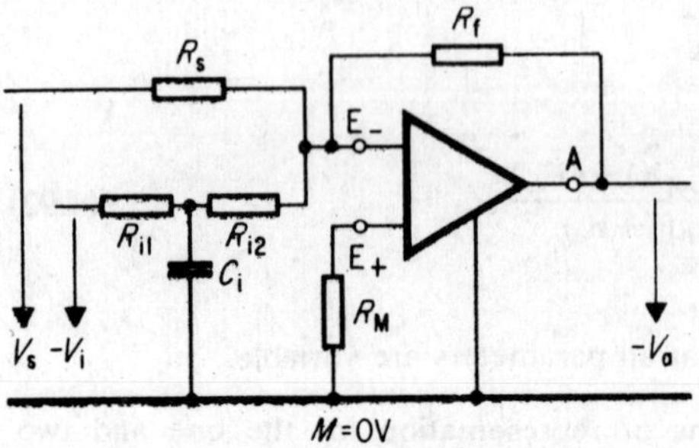

Fig. 4.61
P controller with a passive smoothing element in the controlled variable channel

The complex impedance of the channel is

$$Z_i = (R_{i1} + R_{i2})\left(1 + s\frac{R_{i1}R_{i2}}{R_{i1} + R_{i2}}C_i\right)$$

in which the smoothing time constant is

$$t_{sm} = \frac{R_{i1}R_{i2}}{R_{i1} + R_{i2}}C_i \tag{4.93}$$

and the corner frequency of the low pass element is

$$f_{sm} = \frac{1}{2\pi t_{sm}}$$

n.b. The corner frequency is defined as the frequency where the output voltage or current falls to the -3 dB level with a constant sinusoidal input of increasing frequency.

The transfer function is

$$F(s) = \frac{-V_a(s)}{V_i(s)} = \frac{R_f}{R_{i1} + R_{i2}} \frac{1}{1 + s\dfrac{R_{i1}R_{i2}}{R_{i1} + R_{i2}}C_i}$$

$$= A_R \frac{1}{1 + st_{sm}} \tag{4.94}$$

The step response of this system element is described by Eqns (3.12) and (3.14). Figure 4.62 shows the step response.

The same type of circuit may also appear in the command variable channel with smoothing time constant t_{sm}. In each of the control circuits previously

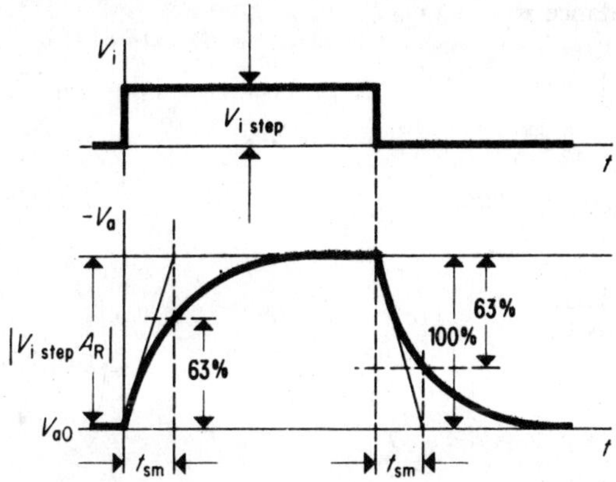

Fig. 4.62
Step response of the P controller with smoothing in the controlled variable channel

considered, these smoothing circuits may be applied. Since the smoothing is achieved with passive components, the term passive smoothing element is used. If a passive smoothing element is to be adjustable, the two resistances before and after the parallel capacitor are replaced, one by a large resistance and the other by a small resistance, the two being connected by a potentiometer. The parallel capacitor is connected to the potentiometer slider. An example will illustrate the range of adjustment.

Assume the resistances have values of 1 kΩ and 22 kΩ, and the potentiometer has a value of 22 kΩ. If the potentiometer slider is at the 1 kΩ end, the resistor value involved in the time constant is 1 kΩ in parallel with 44 kΩ which is 0.98 kΩ. On the other hand, if the potentiometer slider is at the other end, the resistor value involved in the time constant t_{sm} is 22 kΩ in parallel with 23 kΩ which is 11.25 kΩ. This is a range of adjustment from about 1 to 11.

If a capacitor C_f is connected in parallel with the feedback resistor R_f in an inverting amplifier, as shown in Fig. 4.63, an active smoothing element is produced.

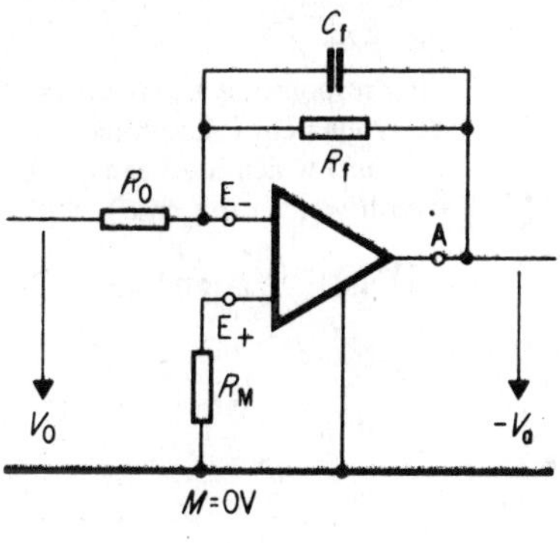

Fig. 4.63 Active smoothing element

The complex feedback impedance is

$$Z_f = \frac{R_f}{1 + sR_fC_f}.$$

This gives the following transfer function:

$$F(s) = \frac{-V_a(s)}{V_0(s)} = \frac{R_f}{R_0} \frac{1}{1 + sR_fC_f}$$
$$= A_R \frac{1}{1 + st_{sm}}. \tag{4.95}$$

In this case the smoothing time constant is

$$t_{sm} = R_fC_f.$$

Thus the transfer functions (4.94) and (4.95) are the same.

Figure 4.64 shows the step response of such a first order delay system when overdriven. In the region of the rising curve, only the steep part up to $V_{a\,max}$ is involved. On the other hand, the complete exponential curve is involved in the falling curve.

Active smoothing (Fig. 4.63) can also be used, according to Eqn (4.34), with adjustable proportional amplification. However, with a step input variable, the output variable makes a proportional step from the level

$$-\Delta V_a|_{t=0} = V_{0\,step} \frac{R_f}{R_0}(1-\alpha)\frac{R_q}{R_f}. \tag{4.96}$$

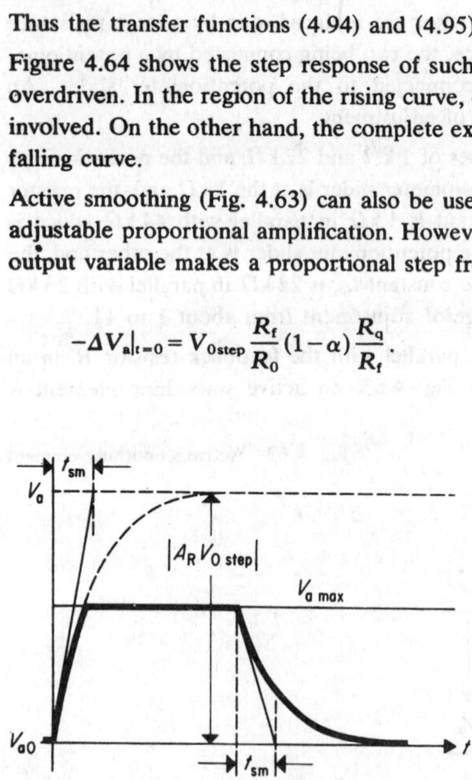

Fig. 4.64
Step response of a first order delay element (smoothing element) which has been overdriven. In this case

$$|V_{0step}| > |V_{a\,max} - V_{a0}|/A_R$$

For better smoothing, a smoothing element of the second order can be produced by driving an active smoothing element (Fig. 4.63) through a passive smoothing circuit (Fig. 4.61). The transient performance is, of course, aperiodic, as it involves two delays of the first order, separated by the amplifier

This behaviour was discussed in Section 2.7. For optimum smoothing, the two time constants

$$t_{sm1} = \frac{R_{01}R_{02}}{R_{01}+R_{02}} C_0$$

and

$$t_{sm2} = R_f C_f$$

should be equal in magnitude.

The frequency characteristics (Fig. 4.65) make it clear that the second order

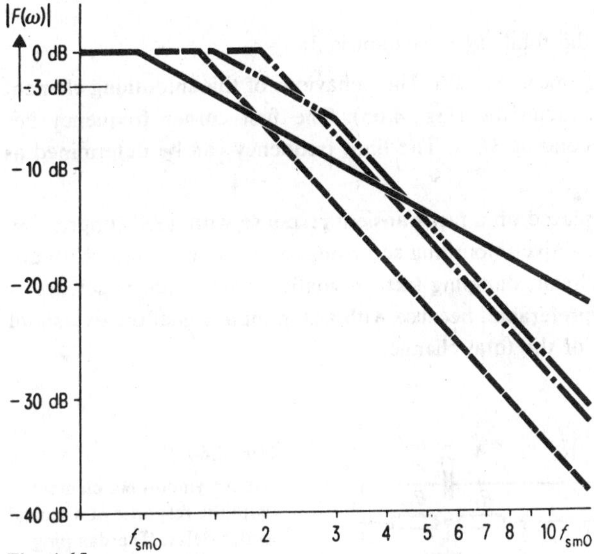

Fig. 4.65

Frequency characteristics of various smoothing elements. Amplification = 1 (0 dB) at zero frequency. Sum of time constants t_{sm} invariant

▬▬▬ passive or active smoothing as in Fig. 4.61 or 4.63

–·—·– second order smoothing with passive (Fig. 4.61) or active (Fig. 4.63) circuit ($t_{sm1} = t_{sm2}$)

—··— passive second order smoothing (Table 4.2, number 14)

------- active second order smoothing as in Fig. 4.66 ($\zeta = 1/\sqrt{2}$)

delay with smoothing time constants t_{sm1} and t_{sm2} gives better smoothing or filtering action than a first order delay with time constant $t_{sm} = t_{sm1} + t_{sm2}$. If the corner point of the first order delay characteristic is denoted by the frequency f_{sm0}, then the corner frequency of the second order delay which comprises two equal first order delays ($\zeta = 1$), occurs at $2f_{sm0}$, but the limit frequency is about $1.3f_{sm0}$.

However, a circuit as shown in Fig. 4.61, with a passive smoothing element according to Table 4.2, number 14, has a less effective smoothing action. This follows from the transfer function:

$$F(s) = \frac{-V_a(s)}{V_0(s)} = \frac{R_f}{4R} \frac{1}{(1+sRc)(1+s2Rc)}$$
$$= A_R \frac{1}{1+s3t_{13}+s^2 2t_{13}^2} \tag{4.97}$$

where $t_{13} = RC$ and the total time constant is $3t_{13} = t_{sm}$.

The damping factor ζ becomes 1.06. The behaviour of this smoothing element is clear from its characteristic (Fig. 4.65). The first corner frequency lies at $1.5f_{sm0}$ and the second at $3f_{sm0}$. The limit frequency can be determined as $1.256f_{sm0}$.

If particular value is placed on a fast transient response with good suppression of higher frequencies, active smoothing according to Fig. 4.66 is used. With this second order delay circuit, damping factors smaller than 1 can be set up. A value of ζ of $1/\sqrt{2}$ is preferable, because with a step input signal the overshoot amounts to only 4% of the total change.

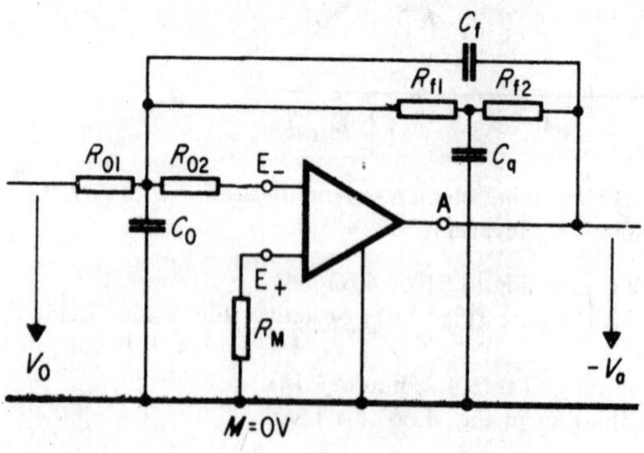

Fig. 4.66
Active smoothing element with the response of a second order delay. The damping factor is adjustable by means of the time constants

The impedance for the bridged T section in the feedback (Table 4.2, number 15) is

$$Z_f=\frac{(R_{f1}+R_{f2})\left[1+s\frac{R_{f1}R_{f2}}{R_{f1}+R_{f2}}C_q\right]}{1+s(R_{f1}+R_{f2})C_f\left[1+s\frac{R_{f1}R_{f2}}{R_{f1}+R_{f2}}C_q\right]}$$

and the impedance of the input circuit (Table 4.2, number 9) is

$$Z_0=(R_{01}+R_{02})\left[1+s\frac{R_{01}R_{02}}{R_{01}+R_{02}}C_0\right]$$

Of the three time constants, two are to be made equal, i.e.

$$\frac{R_{01}R_{02}}{R_{01}+R_{02}}C_0=\frac{R_{f1}R_{f2}}{R_{f1}+R_{f2}}C_q=t_4$$

$$(R_{f1}+R_{f2})C_f=t_5.$$

With the amplification given by

$$A_R=\frac{R_{f1}+R_{f2}}{R_{01}+R_{02}}$$

the transfer function becomes

$$\begin{aligned}F(s)&=\frac{-V_a(s)}{V_0(s)}=A_R\frac{1+st_4}{(1+st_4)(1+st_5+s^2t_4t_5)}\\&=A_R\frac{1}{1+st_5+s^2t_4t_5}\end{aligned}\tag{4.98}$$

and the damping factor is shown to be

$$\zeta=\frac{1}{2}\sqrt{\frac{t_5}{t_4}}.$$

If ζ is to be $1/\sqrt{2}$, the ratio of the time constants must be given by $t_5=2t_4$ and the transfer function assumes the form

$$F(s)=A_R\frac{1}{1+s2t_4+s^2 2t_4}\tag{4.99}$$

and consequently the total time constant is

$$2t_4 = t_{sm}.$$

From Fig. 2.12, the frequency characteristic for a damping factor $\zeta = 1/\sqrt{2}$ can be well represented by a simple straight line approximation with the corner frequency $f_{smo}\sqrt{2}$ (Fig. 4.65) beyond which the slope is 20 dB per decade. The limit frequency lies at the same point.

In many cases, usually in the command variable channel, a first order smoothing is insufficient. In order to achieve special effects, special behaviour is necessary (see Figs. 6.38 and 6.39). For this purpose, a bridged T circuit is used (Table 4.2, number 15). This is connected at the input to the amplifier. The remaining action of the controller can then assume the usual form.

Figure 4.67 shows the circuit with proportional behaviour in the feedback. The input impedance is

$$Z_0 = (R_{01}+R_{02}) \frac{\left(1+s\dfrac{R_{01}R_{02}}{R_{01}+R_{02}}C_0\right)(1+sR_pC_p)}{1+sR_pC_p\left(1+\dfrac{R_{01}+R_{02}}{R_p}\right)+s^2R_pC_p\dfrac{R_{01}R_{02}}{R_{01}+R_{02}}C_0\dfrac{R_{01}+R_{02}}{R_p}}$$

This contains the time constants

$$\frac{R_{01}R_{02}}{R_{01}+R_{02}} = C_0 = t_{sm1}$$

$$R_pC_p = t_{sm2}$$

and the impedance ratio

$$\frac{R_{01}+R_{02}}{R_p} = v.$$

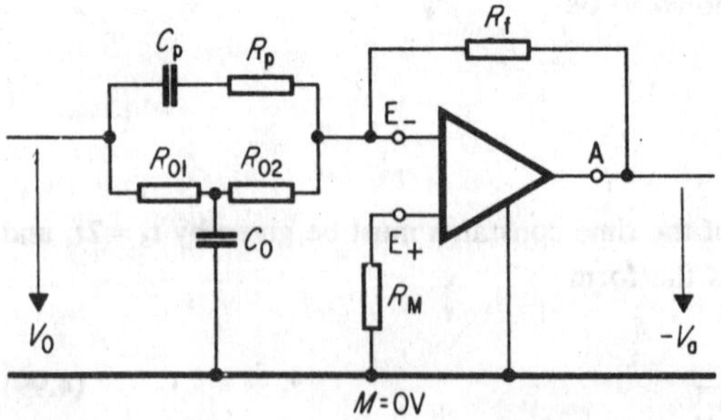

Fig. 4.67
Passive smoothing with phase advance (bridged T element) in the input of the amplifier

The transfer function is

$$F(s)=\frac{-V_a(s)}{V_0(s)}=\frac{R_f}{R_{01}+R_{02}}\,\frac{1+st_{sm2}(1+v)+s^2t_{sm1}t_{sm2}v}{(1+st_{sm1})(1+st_{sm2})} \tag{4.100}$$

It should be pointed out that all smoothing circuits in the amplifier input can be used in combination with all feedback circuits.

It will be recalled that smoothing is always included in the practical differentiator element (see Figs. 3.28 and 4.48). A minor change of the circuit of Fig. 4.48 permits a new application.

For the control of the acceleration of a drive (see Fig. 6.60), the actual acceleration must be determined. This is obtained from the actual value of the rotational speed which is represented by the output voltage of the tachometer which contains ripple. This is first smoothed and differentiated by the circuit of Fig. 3.30 and then integrated to produce the necessary torque demand (see Fig. 4.68, which shows only the actual value channel). The overall transfer function is

$$F(s)=\frac{-V_a(s)}{\Delta V_0(s)}=\frac{C_0}{C_f}\,\frac{1}{1+sR_0C_0}. \tag{4.101}$$

Seen from the voltage ΔV_0 which represents the rotational speed, this system element has the effect of a proportional element with amplification

$$A_R=C_0/C_f.$$

The current I_0 through the capacitor is the parameter for acceleration. The parasitic smoothing action of the controller, with time constant $t_{sm}=R_0C_0$ is very necessary because of the differentiation of the tacho voltage which includes ripple.

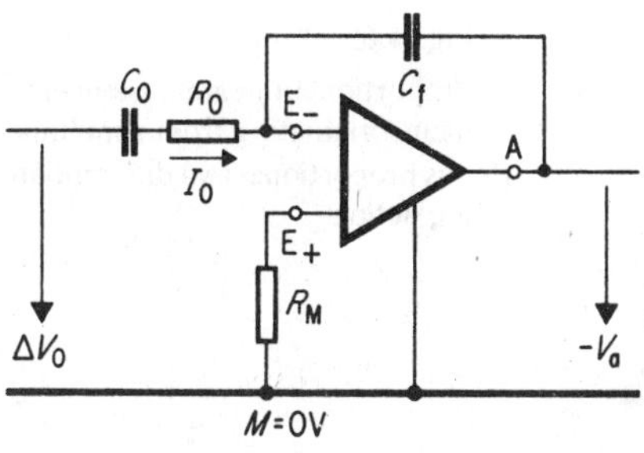

Fig. 4.68
Acceleration control circuit. Passive differentiating circuit combined with integration

An associated speed controller must have a proportional characteristic so that at its output the demand for a possible positive or negative acceleration arises.

If the differentiating input circuit of Fig. 4.68 in the controlled variable channel is modified by the inclusion of a parallel resistor giving proportional action (Fig. 4.69), then fast changes of controlled variable produce a larger response than slow ones. In this way, an overshoot of the controlled variable can be avoided because the fact that the actual value has reached the required value is presented to the controller much sooner (see Figs. 6.61 and 6.62).

In the parallel branches of the input circuit

$$\frac{1}{Z_0}=\frac{sC_0}{1+sR_0C_0}$$

and

$$\frac{1}{Z_1}=\frac{1}{R_1}.$$

Thus the overall transfer function is

$$F(s)=\frac{-V_a(s)}{\Delta V_0(s)}=\frac{1}{sR_1C_f}\,\frac{1+s(R_0+R_1)C_0}{1+sR_0C_0}. \tag{4.102}$$

The controlled variable channel contains the integration time constant $T_1=R_1C_f$ and the reset time constant $T_n=(R_0+R_1)C_0$.

The proportional amplification is

$$A_R=\frac{T_n}{T_1}=\frac{(R_0+R_1)C_0}{R_1C_f}$$

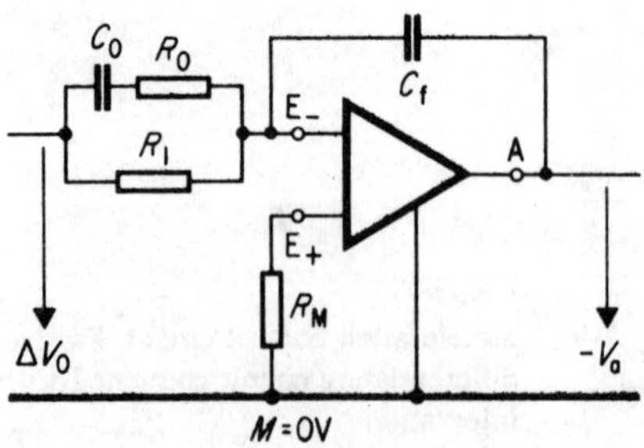

Fig. 4.69
Proportional/integral system element originating from simultaneous proportional and differentiating action

and the smoothing time constant is

$$t_{sm} = R_0 C_0.$$

This is the transfer function of a PI element

$$F(s) = \frac{1}{1 + st_{sm}} A_R \frac{1 + sT_n}{sT_n}$$

$$= \frac{1}{1 + sR_0C_0} \frac{(R_0 + R_1)C_0}{R_1C_f} \frac{1 + s(R_0 + R_1)C_0}{s(R_0 + R_1)C_0}. \tag{4.103}$$

However, in the feedback of the amplifier there is only the capacitor C_f. If the command variable channel has no series capacitor, then this is an integrating action for the command variable.

4.4.2. Limiting

Various possible limiting methods in the output of a controller are shown in Fig. 4.70.

Three applications of limiting can be distinguished:

a) Fixed limiting to the standard values −10 V and +10 V, which is always provided if no other conditions set narrower limits.
b) Adjustable limiting, with a potentiometer, for example, so that other lower values limit the overall control range.
c) Controllable limiting which only comes into effect by intervening in the output signal of the controller when disturbances originating outside the control loop exceed their permissible limits.

Fixed and adjustable limiting are generally carried out with the same circuits. Two kinds are recognized – limiting in direct operation and limiting in feedback parallel operation.

Controllable limiting can act in the controller either by multiplication or by addition.

In passive, direct limiting (Figs. 4.71 and 4.72), the limiting voltages V_{B+} and V_{B-} act via diodes (passive) on the bases of the push–pull final stage of an amplifier in such a manner that the output voltage V_a can never go beyond the potential V_{B+} in the positive direction and never beyond V_{B-} in the negative direction, even if the voltage V^* which drives the final stage of the amplifier exceeds these limits. The limits are modified by a parametric error caused by

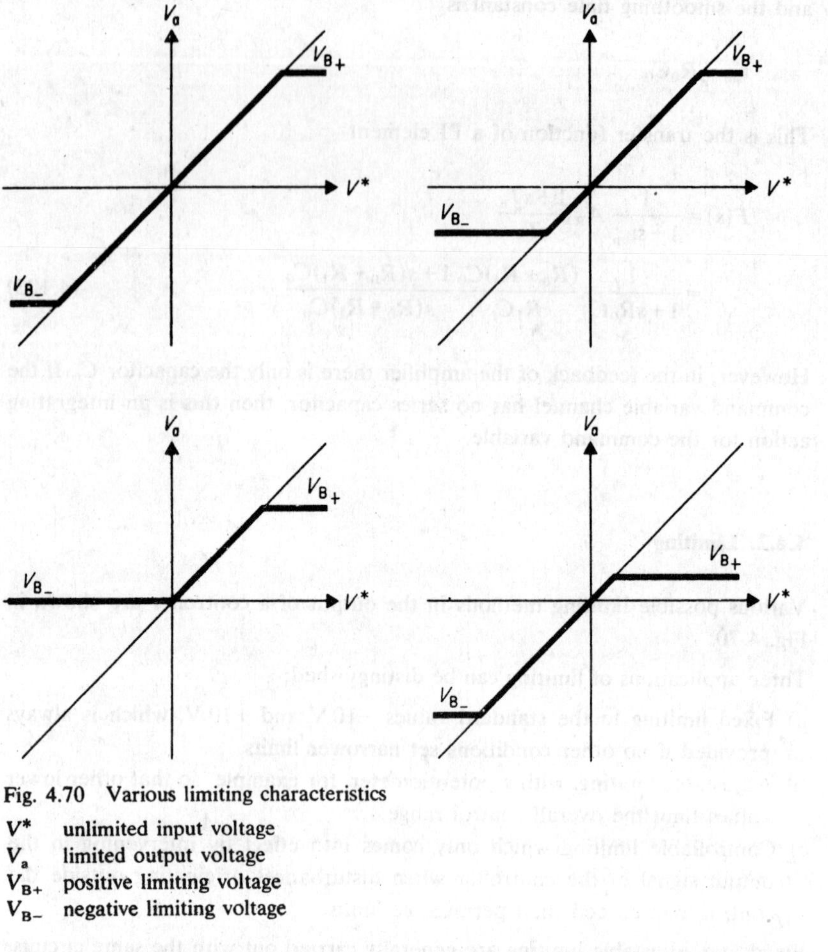

Fig. 4.70 Various limiting characteristics

V^* unlimited input voltage
V_a limited output voltage
V_{B+} positive limiting voltage
V_{B-} negative limiting voltage

the differences in the characteristics of the limiting diodes (n1 and n2) and the base-emitter diodes as well as the voltage drop in the input resistance R_v.

The parametric error between the limiting voltage V_{B+} or V_{B-} and the limited controller output voltage V_a is eliminated by active direct limiting as shown in Fig. 4.73, in which the base-emitter diodes of the push–pull output stage include an active amplifier in the feedback. The inputs to the amplifies y1 and y2 are the inverted limiting potentials.

If no limiting connections are available in the amplifier, active limiting in direct operation as shown in Fig. 4.74 is connected to the output. The limiting potentials V_{B+} and V_{B-} are introduced via two 'perfect diodes' in the form of

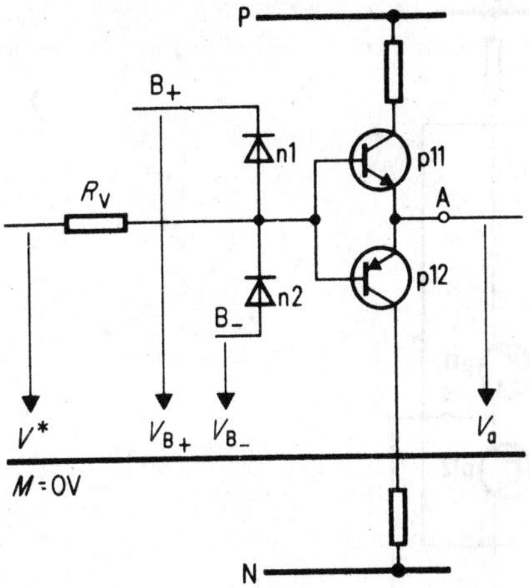

Fig. 4.71
Simple direct limiting in amplifier final stage

y1 and y2. The input resistance R_v does not interfere within the overall control range since the impedance converter y0 takes virtually no current.

It is common to all direct operating limiters that at the limiting point the input of the amplifier goes into the overdriven state. The difference current I_0 can no longer flow via the feedback impedance Z_f but must flow via the amplifier input. This is particularly disturbing if the amplifier input is protected against overvoltages by two inverse-parallel connected diodes. There is a threshold voltage drop in the conducting diode so that the integrating capacitance C_f in the feedback receives an incorrect charge. A resistance R_M from the amplifier terminal E_+ to the reference point M will cause a similar problem.

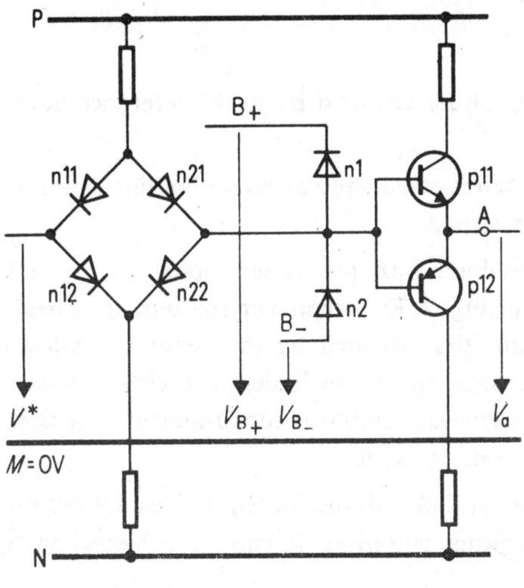

Fig. 4.72
Passive direct limiting with rectifier bridge in the input of the amplifier final stage. When limiting only the diodes n_{12} and n_{21} for positive limiting and diodes n_{11} and n_{22} for negative limiting are conducting

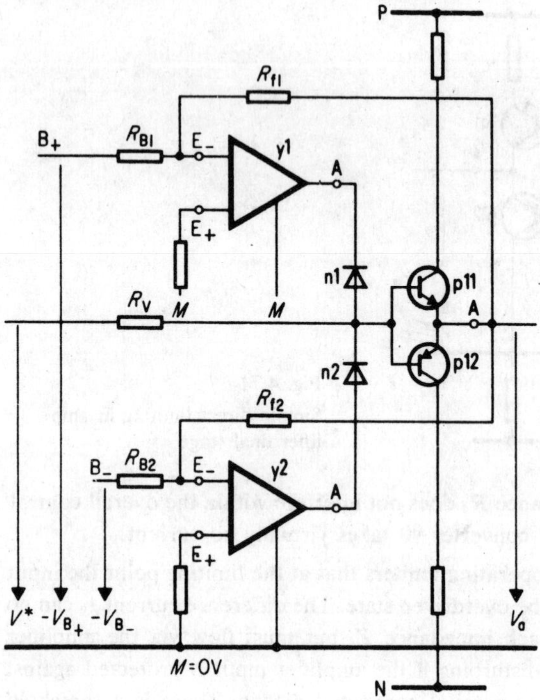

Fig. 4.73
Active direct limiting in the amplifier output stage. The limiting potentials have opposite signs ($R_{B1} = R_{f1} = R_{B2} = R_{f2}$) e.g. in limiting at $-V_{a\,max} = -8$ V, the potential at the terminal B− must be $-V_{B+} = +8$ V

charge. A resistance R_M from the amplifier terminal E_+ to the reference point M will cause a similar problem.

Limiting in parallel feedback operation is considered as direct limiting as far as overdriving on the input side is concerned.

The simplest passive limiting is obtained with two zener diodes n1 and n2 connected back to back as shown in Fig. 4.75. Whenever the output voltage $-V_a$ tries to assume a value greater than defined by the zener breakdown voltage, one of the zener diodes breaks down and limits. The circuit is very readily applied to controllers with a separate amplifier for proportional action, especially to limit it to the overall control range.

Passive limiting with zener diodes in parallel with the feedback does not permit any optional adjustment of the limiting potential. It can be achieved with

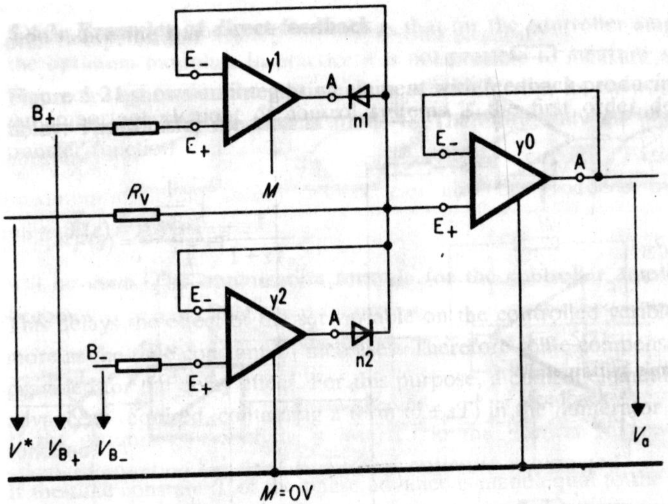

Fig. 4.74
Active direct limiting with 'perfect diodes' and with an impedance converter at the output side

active limiting as shown in Figs. 4.76 and 4.77. However, for each limit a separate control amplifier is required.

If signal inversion exists between the output to be limited and the point of action of the limiting feedback at the controller input (that is, using the inverting amplifier), then the circuit of Fig. 4.76 is used. The limiting potentials V_{B+} and V_{B-} are applied to the inverting inputs E_- of the limiter amplifiers y1 and y2 and compared with the potential $-V_a$ of the controller y0 which is connected to the non-inverting input E_+ of the limiter amplifiers. The limiter amplifiers consequently act as difference amplifiers

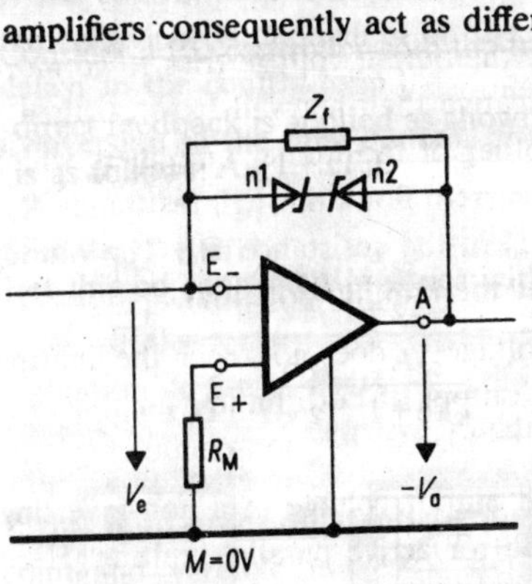

Fig. 4.75
Passive limiting in parallel operation with zener diodes

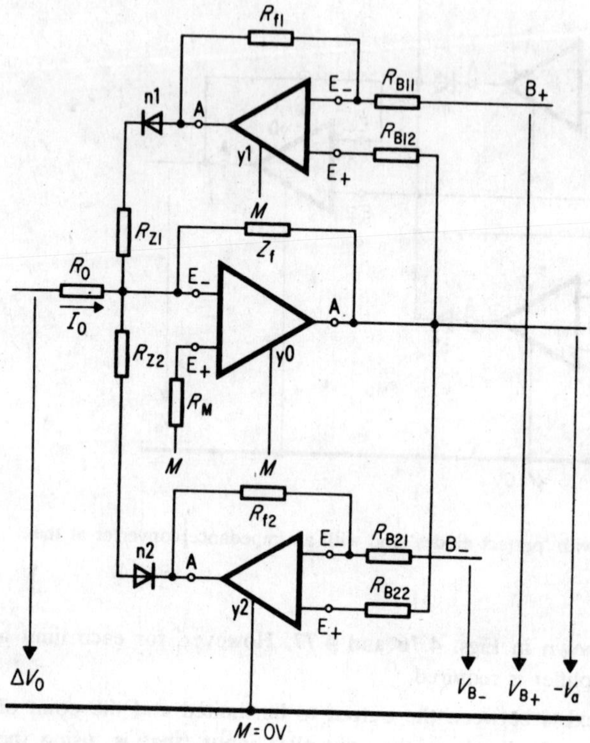

Fig. 4.76

Active limiting in parallel operation with two limiting amplifiers acting as difference amplifiers. Between the output to be limited and the point of action in the controller input, signal inversion takes place

In the limiting condition, that is whenever the output voltage tries to go more positive than defined by V_{B+} or more negative than allowed by V_{B-}, then a potential arises at the output of one or other of the limiter amplifiers which causes diode n1 or n2 to conduct. Then a current flows through resistance R_{Z1} or R_{Z2} which is opposite to the current I_0 in the resistance R_0. The output voltage $-V_a$ is then reduced until it lies at the limiting potential.

In the unlimited region, when the output voltage V_a does not reach the limiting potentials V_{B+} or V_{B-}, the voltage at the output of both limiter amplifiers is such that both diodes n1 and n2 are reverse biased, i.e. non-conducting.

If the problem involves the limiting of the output voltage of a non-inverting amplifier y0, the circuit of Fig. 4.77 is used for active parallel limiting. Here again, both amplifiers y1 and y2 are difference amplifiers. In this case,

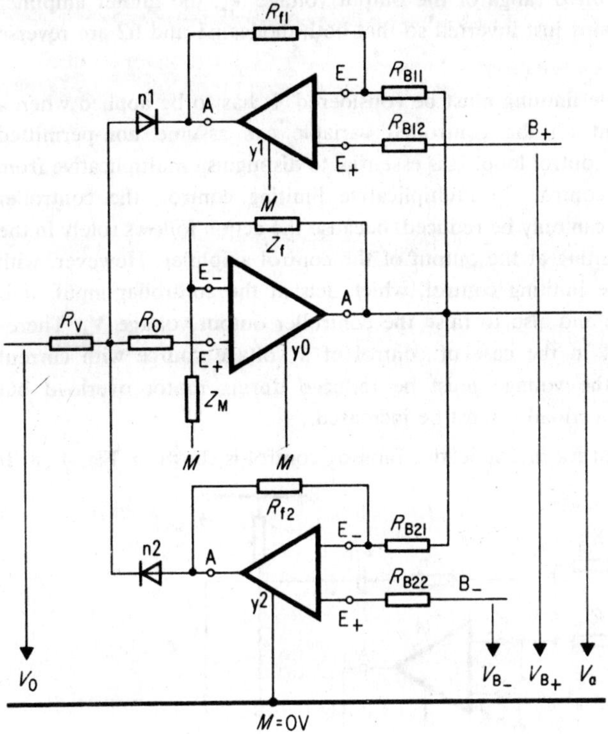

Fig. 4.77

Active limiting in parallel operation with two limiter amplifiers acting as difference amplifiers. The output signal of a non-inverting amplifier y0 is limited

however, the output voltage V_a is connected to the inverting input terminals E_- of the two limiter amplifiers and the limiting potentials V_{B+} and V_{B-} are applied to the non-inverting terminals E_+. This circuit draws a little current from the limited output, since the feedback resistances R_{f1} and R_{f2} require a feedback current, but this current is virtually insignificant with a high amplification factor, which ensures a sharp limiting action.

Whenever the output voltage V_a tries to exceed the limiting potentials V_{B+} and V_{B-} in a positive or negative direction, the input voltage reverses between the terminals E_- and E_+ of one or other of the limiter amplifiers. Then a voltage arises at the output of amplifiers y1 and y2 which causes diode n1 or n2 to conduct. Terminal E_+ of the non-inverting amplifier is held at the limiter voltage. The input resistance R_v serves to decouple the input voltage V_0 from the limiter amplifier output voltage.

Within the non-limited range of the output voltage V_a, the limiter amplifier input voltage remains just inverted so that both diodes n1 and n2 are reverse biased.

Finally, controllable limiting must be considered. It has to be applied when a variable dependent on the controlled variable can assume non-permitted values outside the control loop. It is essential to distinguish multiplicative from additive limiting control. In multiplicative limiting control, the controller output voltage V_a can only be reduced, because the action follows solely in the sense of direct limiting at the output of the control amplifier. However, with the aid of additive limiting control, which acts at the controller input, it is possible to reduce and also to raise the controller output voltage V_a. Therefore, for example, in the case of control of a voltage source with current limiting control, the voltage must be reduced during motor overload but during generator overload it must be increased.

One possible circuit for multiplicative limiting control is shown in Fig. 4.78. It

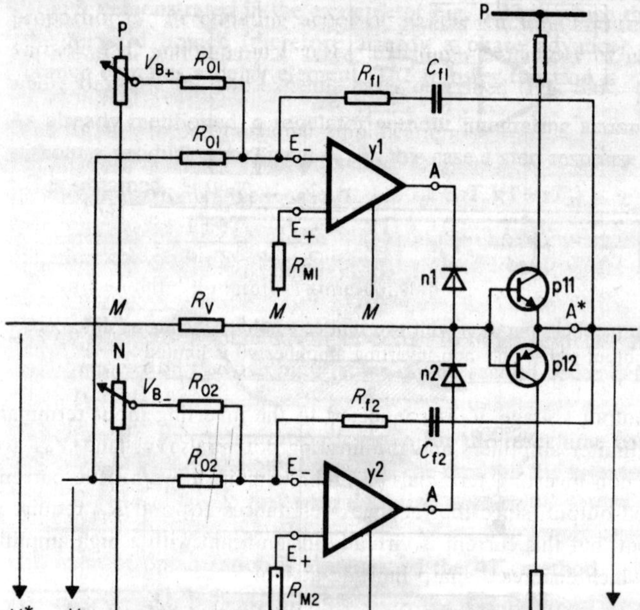

Fig. 4.78
Multiplicative limiting control in the output of an operational amplifier with push–pull output transistors p11 and p12. The positive measured value has the negative actual value $-V_m$ as a result.

is similar to the circuit of Fig. 4.73. Whenever the measured value $\mp V_m$ of the auxiliary controlled variable, which arises outside the control loop, tries to exceed the limit value V_B,

$$|-V_m|>|V_B|$$

then the current I_1 which represents the error signal for the limiting control, reverses its sign and the amplifier y1 provides a voltage at its output A which causes diode n1 to conduct. Then the positive output voltage at the output of amplifier y1 is limited or reduced. In the case of a negative output voltage V_a, the control amplifier y2 takes over the limiting control. It is assumed that on the reversal of the output voltage V_a, the measured value $-V_m$ also changes sign and therefore becomes positive.

An additive limiting control which acts at the input of the control amplifier y0 is shown in Fig. 4.79. An amplifier with a diode characteristic similar to that of Fig. 4.82 is used as one of the possible circuits. Within the permissible overall control range of the auxiliary controlled variable, the output voltage V_a can also assume any arbitrary value within its permitted range. At the input of the limiter amplifiers y1 and y2 the currents I_1 and I_2 are such that both diodes n11 and n21 are conducting and the outputs of the two amplifiers y1 and y2 have zero voltage. The current I_0 which represents the error signal between the desired value and the actual value, has no current added or subtracted.

With a negative controller output voltage $-V_a$, the current I_0 must be positive. If the negative measured value $(-V_m)$ tries to exceed its limit value $(+V_{B+})$, the limiting control must act through the output diode n12. The positive current I_0 is added to the positive current I_{Z1} because the limiting controller output goes positive. This results in a displacement of the voltage $-V_a$ in the negative direction. By raising the negative voltage $|-V_a|$ the measured value $|-V_m|$ of the auxiliary controlled variable is reduced.

If the auxiliary controlled variable has inverted its polarity, i.e. V_m the measured value is positive and now exceeds the permitted value $(-V_{B-})$ while the controlled output voltage $-V_a$ is still negative, then the limiting controller acts through the diode n22. The negative current I_{Z2} is drawn from the positive current of the error signal I_0. This causes a reduction of the negative output voltage $-V_a$.

Let us consider a controlled voltage source E_Q feeding a d.c. machine which is excited separately (Fig. 4.80a). This machine should be able to operate as a motor or a generator and in extreme cases to absorb or give out abnormally high current. The source voltage E_Q which is the main controlled variable, opposes the induced machine voltage E_{GM} which is the disturbance variable.

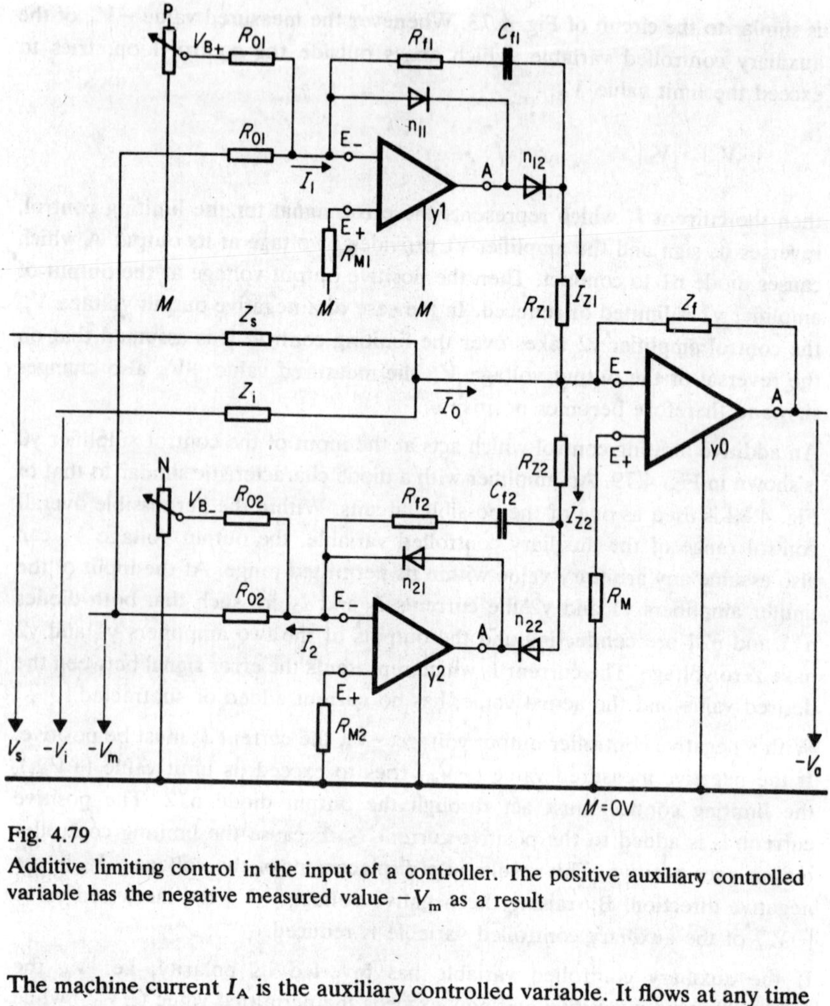

Fig. 4.79

Additive limiting control in the input of a controller. The positive auxiliary controlled variable has the negative measured value $-V_m$ as a result

The machine current I_A is the auxiliary controlled variable. It flows at any time from the higher voltage source to the lower. Whenever the current I_A attempts to become too large, then due to the limiter control, the absolute value of the source voltage E_Q is reduced in the first and third quadrants of the current/voltage diagram (Fig. 4.80b) for motor operation, or raised in the second and fourth quadrants for generator operation.

In Figs. 4.78 and 4.79, a feedback capacitor C_f, which acts as an integrator, is shown in series with the resistance R_f in the feedback of the limiting controller. It is used when the auxiliary controlled variable, with the measured value $-V_m$, is to be held very accurately to the desired limiting value, even if, for other

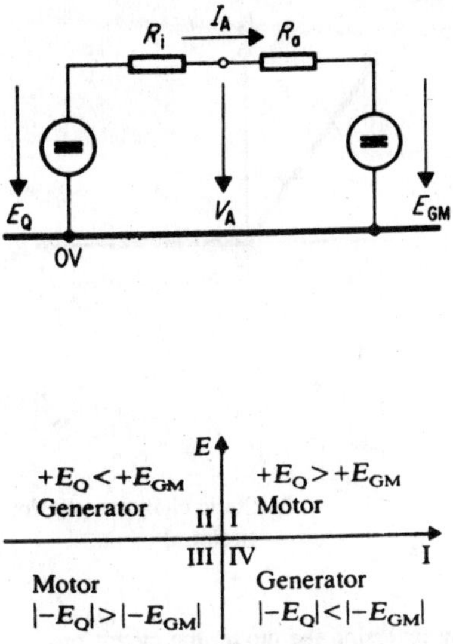

a) Controlled voltage source E_Q with internal impedance R_i feeds the armature circuit of an externally excited d.c. machine with induced voltage E_{GM}

b) Four quadrant representation of current direction (I) in relation to the voltages E_Q and E_{GM}

Fig. 4.80 Example of additive limiting control

reasons, the proportional amplification in the limiting controller is not very high. However, in most cases, the controller amplification is large and then the capacitor C_f can be omitted.

4.4.3. Amplifiers and controllers with diode characteristics

An arrangement in which only one voltage direction is effective at the amplifier output, while the other responds with a voltage very close to zero, can be achieved by placing a diode in parallel with the feedback impedance Z_f as shown in Fig. 4.81. At the output, only a positive voltage can appear. If a negative voltage tends to arise, the diode in the feedback circuit conducts and prevents the output voltage from going more negative than the diode threshold voltage. If negative output voltages only are required, the diode in the feedback must be reversed.

For special applications an improved form of single sided limiting can be used. This has the property of a diode without a threshold and can be obtained by adding an isolating diode n2 and using a resistive feedback impedance R_f (Fig. 4.82). If the output voltage (point A) is positive (V_0 inverted and amplified), the output current flows through the diode n2. The diode n1 is reverse biased and the amplification is determined by R_f. If the output voltage at point A is

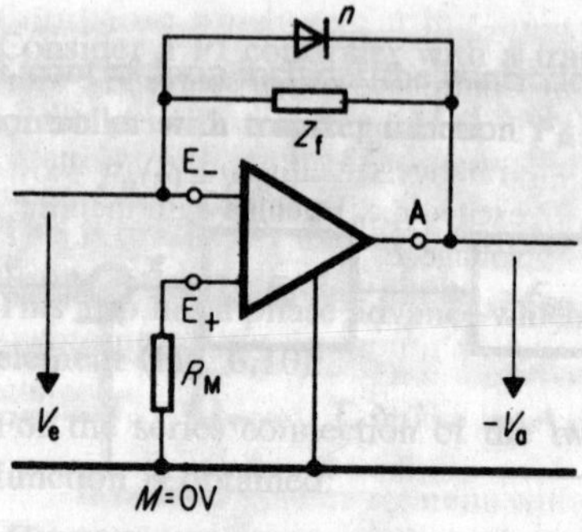

a) Circuit with positive output voltage only

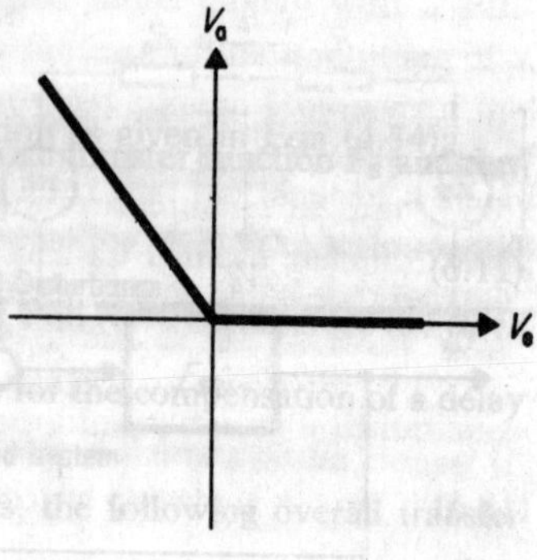

b) Static characteristic for circuit a)

Fig. 4.81

Single sided parallel limiting using a diode. By reversing the diode, the circuit produces only negative output voltage for positive input. If the input voltage is inverted by the amplifier, the characteristic has a reversed slope

negative, the diode n2 is reverse biased and thus isolates the voltage at point A from the output terminals. Thus there is no output current or voltage. The current I_0 flows through diode n1 which is forward biased and the amplification is thus virtually zero. The threshold value disappears because of the isolating diode n2. The behaviour can be written as follows:

$$-V_a = \tfrac{1}{2}[V_0 - |V_0|]\frac{R_f}{R_0}. \tag{4.104}$$

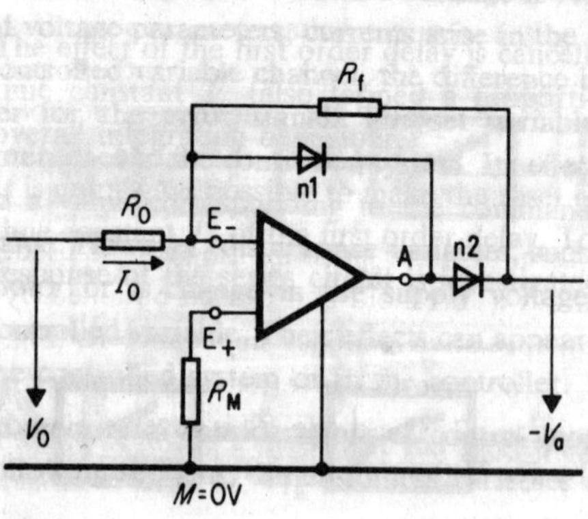

Fig. 4.82

Passive single sided limiting using diode (no threshold value)

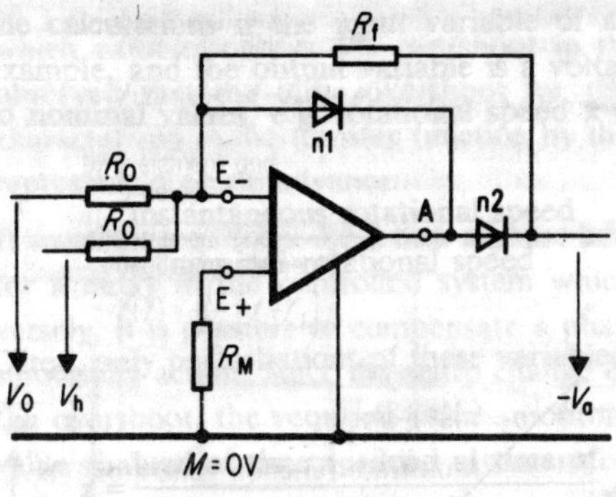

Fig. 4.83
Circuit giving an ideal diode characteristic with adjustable knee point and adjustable slope of characteristic. Knee point is given by $V_{0inf} = -V_h$. Slope is given by R_f/R_0

By changing the directions of diodes n1 and n2, a negative going output voltage can be obtained.

If the circuit has two inputs (Fig. 4.83) and a positive or negative auxiliary voltage V_h is applied, the auxiliary voltage determines whether the knee characteristic lies in the positive or negative region of voltage V_0.

The resistance R_f determined the steepness of the characteristic in the conducting region (Fig. 4.84).

For the circuit shown, we have

$$-V_a = \frac{1}{2}[(V_0 + V_h) - (V_0 + V_h)]\frac{R_f}{R_0}. \tag{4.105}$$

If several such circuits are combined with the aid of a summing amplifier as in Fig. 4.23, a function generator can be obtained in which an arbitrary relationship between input and output variables can be obtained to a close approximation (Fig. 4.85). Thus, for example, the non-linear relationship between excitation current and magnetic flux in a d.c. machine could be represented.

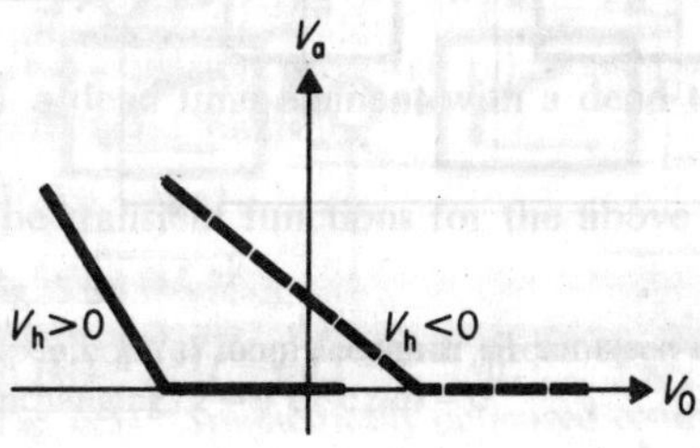

Fig. 4.84
Characteristics of circuit of Fig. 4.83. Output voltage V_a is positive only. Positive voltage V_h displaces the knee point negatively and negative voltage V_h displaces it positively. If diodes n1 and n2 are reversed, the output voltage V_a is negative only, the slope being the same. For an inverse voltage $-V_0$ the slope is also reversed

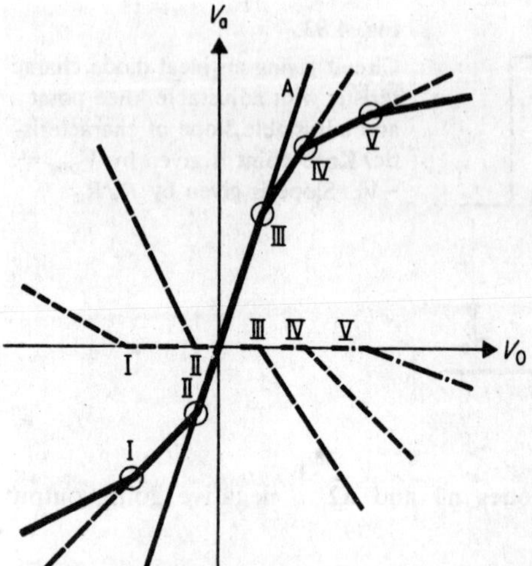

Fig. 4.85
Multitrace function generator. The relationship between the output and input variables (V_a and V_0) is linear in the zero region (A). With the aid of five ideal diodes obtained as in Fig. 4.83, the knee points I, II, III, IV and V are obtained. By using a summing amplifier an approximately continuous curve is obtained

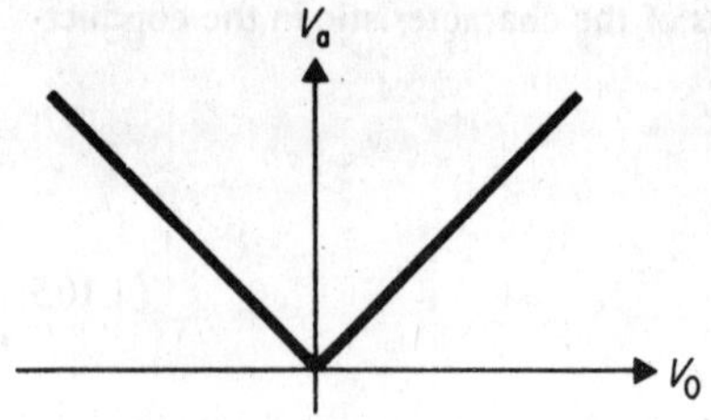

Fig. 4.86
Absolute value of input voltage V_0 represented by a positive output voltage V_a

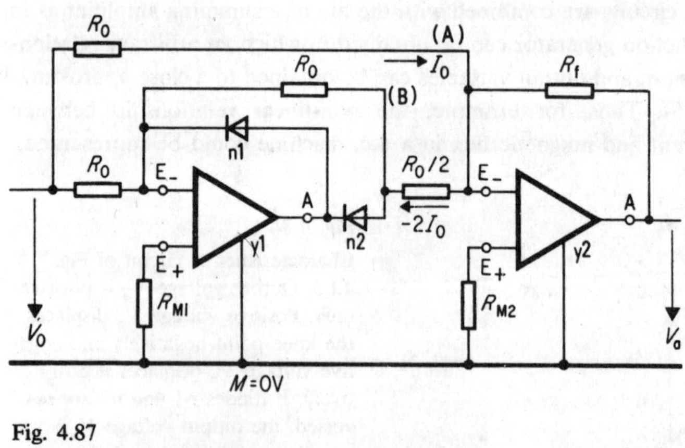

Fig. 4.87
Absolute value circuits using 'ideal diode'. If resistance R_f is made equal to R_0 the parametric ratio is defined by the ratio R_f/R_0

Absolute value determination is another application of this type of circuit (Fig. 4.86):

$$V_a = |V_0|. \qquad (4.106)$$

If the diode direction shown in the circuit of Fig. 4.87 is used, a negative input voltage V_0 only reaches the amplifier y2 via the upper channel (A), while no current flows in the lower channel (B). However, a positive voltage V_0 is inverted by the amplifier y1 and the input E_- of the amplifier y2 receives not only the positive input current I_0 via the upper channel (A) but also the negative current $-2I_0$ via the lower channel (B). The output voltage is always positive. If the diodes are reversed, the sign of the absolute voltage obtained is negative.

4.5. Analogue Computer Circuits

The above sections deal with various computer circuits.

It is possible to perform additions and subtractions using an inverter amplifier as shown in Fig. 4.23. The voltages which represent the mathematical terms can have either positive or negative polarity. Moreover, the terms are multiplied by a fixed constant (Eqn (4.27)) in accordance with the resistance ratio $K_v = R_f/R_v$

$$V_1K_1 + V_2K_2 + V_3K_3 + \cdots = -V_a \qquad (4.27)$$

A hybrid multiplication circuit, that is a multiplication with a factor represented in analogue form and a digital factor, produces the circuit of the digital/analogue converter as shown in Fig. 4.24. In this case the analogue factor is the reference voltage V_{ref} which may have positive or negative polarity. The digital factor is the switched numerical value Z, weighted and in bit form. The analogue product of both variable factors is multiplied by the constants $K_p = R_f/R_0$ (Eqn (4.29))

$$V_{ref}ZK_p = -V_a$$

A simple integrator for a variable which is represented as a voltage V_0 (positive or negative) is shown in Fig. 4.35. Providing the analogue output is kept within the linear range of the variable-gain amplifier the following relationship is valid:

$$K_I \int_0^t V_0(t)\,dt + V_{a0} = -V_a(t) \tag{4.48}$$

In this case the multiplier $K_I = 1/T_I$ is the constant of integration.

With regard to the operating range the above is also valid for the differentiation of a value which is represented by a voltage V_0. The simplest form of differentiating circuit is shown in Fig. 4.47. However, this is not only represented by Eqn (4.68) where the constant of differentiation $K_D = T_D$ occurs as a multiplier but an additional parasitic time lag occurs. The smaller the internal resistance R_i of the analogue input voltage source V_0 can be kept, the less will be the effect of the time constant of this delay T_g:

$$K_d \frac{dV_0(t)}{dt} = -\left[V_a(t) + T_g \frac{dV_a(t)}{dt}\right]$$

Differential equations up to the 3rd or 4th order may be solved by means of time delay components. For this purpose the circuits shown in Fig. 4.63 or Fig. 4.66 may be used or the circuits of the control loops described in Chapter 6, e.g., the circuits shown in Fig. 6.22 or Fig. 6.28.

The circuits described do not permit the multiplication of two analogue values. If multiplication is made possible, then one would also be able to deal with analogue powers and integer exponents. Moreover a multiplier which is fed into a variable-gain amplifier enables two analogue values to be divided. With some minor modifications to the divider we obtain an analogue reciprocal device or even the means for taking analogue roots. The prerequisite for all these mathematical operations is therefore the availability of an analogue multiplier which is capable of solving the voltage equation:

$$V_x V_y = V_a \tag{4.107}$$

The above principle indicates that a Hall effect could be used as a multiplier. One of the values would produce a 'load-independent' current proportional to its magnitude, which would be the so-called control current I_{st} whilst the other value would provide a proportional field current which produces the necessary magnetic flux density B for the Hall effect generator. The Hall effect voltage V_H generated by the deflection of the charge carrier is, however, very small and even with a favourable design of the Hall effect generator, i.e., an optimum Hall effect factor K_H, the amplification will be subject to the following relationship:

$$K_H I_{st} B = V_H \tag{4.108}$$

The production of the necessary flux density involves further complications and the changes required for zero adjustment and linearity are not simple.

Another method of obtaining multiplication is to represent a value by a voltage which produces a frequency in the kHz range in a pulse generator. The mark/space relationship of the rectangular wave form will be governed by the second value. The method, however, requires an adequate smoothing at the output as well as a complicated and costly provision for zero adjustment and linearity. As it is increasingly preferable today to use integrated circuits, the use of the voltage differentiating circuit shown in Fig. 4.1 with suitable modification for the multiplication of two values is common.

Figure 4.88 shows the principle of a 'linear multiplier' in which the emitter current i_E is a representation of the input value V_x. The greater this emitter current, the greater will be the amplification of the voltage differentiator circuit with both transistors p1 and p2, i.e., the slope of the amplifier curve becomes steeper. If the effect of the input value V_y is zero then the collector currents i_1 and i_2 are equal to each other and equal to half the emitter current i_E. If the input value V_y is other than zero then the gain of both transistors p1 and p2 will be different and hence also the currents i_1 and i_2. Thus we obtain the

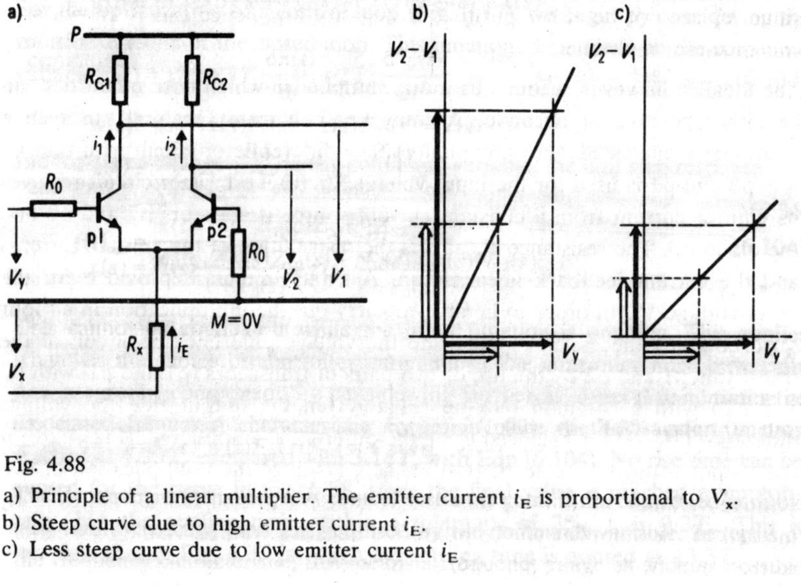

Fig. 4.88

a) Principle of a linear multiplier. The emitter current i_E is proportional to V_x.

b) Steep curve due to high emitter current i_E.

c) Less steep curve due to low emitter current i_E

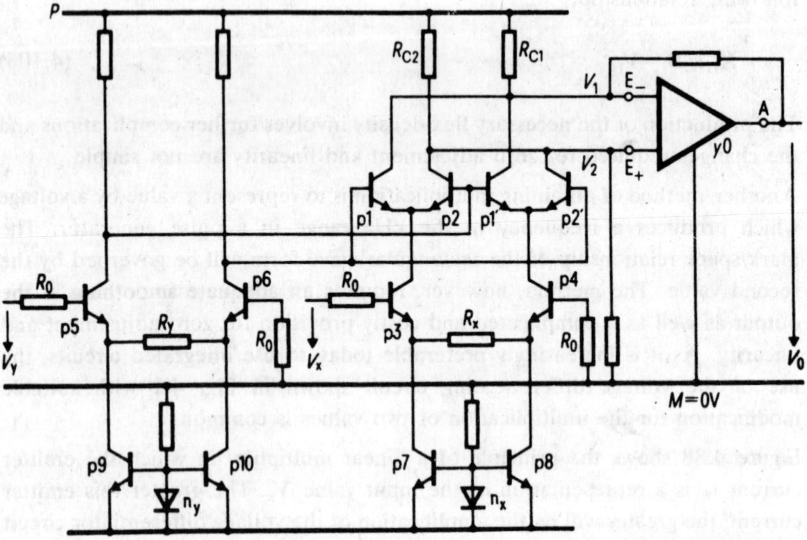

Fig. 4.89

Circuit diagram of a four-quadrant multiplier. This design produces a positive output voltage for a positive product

output voltage $(V_2 - V_1)$ which is proportional to the negative input value V_x as well as to the positive or negative input value V_y. This indicates that the input value V_x can not be either positive or negative and hence this is known as a two-quadrant multiplier.

The ideal is, however, a four-quadrant multiplier in which both quantities can be either positive or negative. As may be seen from Fig. 4.89, in such a multiplier a one sided, zero potential voltage differentiator circuit with transistors p3 and p4 is used for the input voltage V_x. This transistor circuit receives its emitter current from a constant current source (transistors p7 and p8 and the diode n_x). The resistance R_x affects the distribution of the emitter currents and the current feedback linearization. A similar circuit is provided for the input voltage V_y. In order to be able to carry out the multiplication in all four quadrants, it is necessary to duplicate the voltage differentiator circuit of the transistors p1 and p2 by the use of two pairs of transistors (p1 and p1′ with p2 and p2′) with a common pick-up resistor. On the output side the voltage difference $(V_2 - V_1)$ is balanced using the differential amplifier y0 (Fig. 4.28). If the output voltage V_0 is to be positive as a result of the multiplication of two positive voltages V_x and V_y, then the voltage V_1 will be fed to the inverting input E of the amplifier y0. To produce a negative voltage V_0 the connections to the input of the amplifier y0 must be reversed.

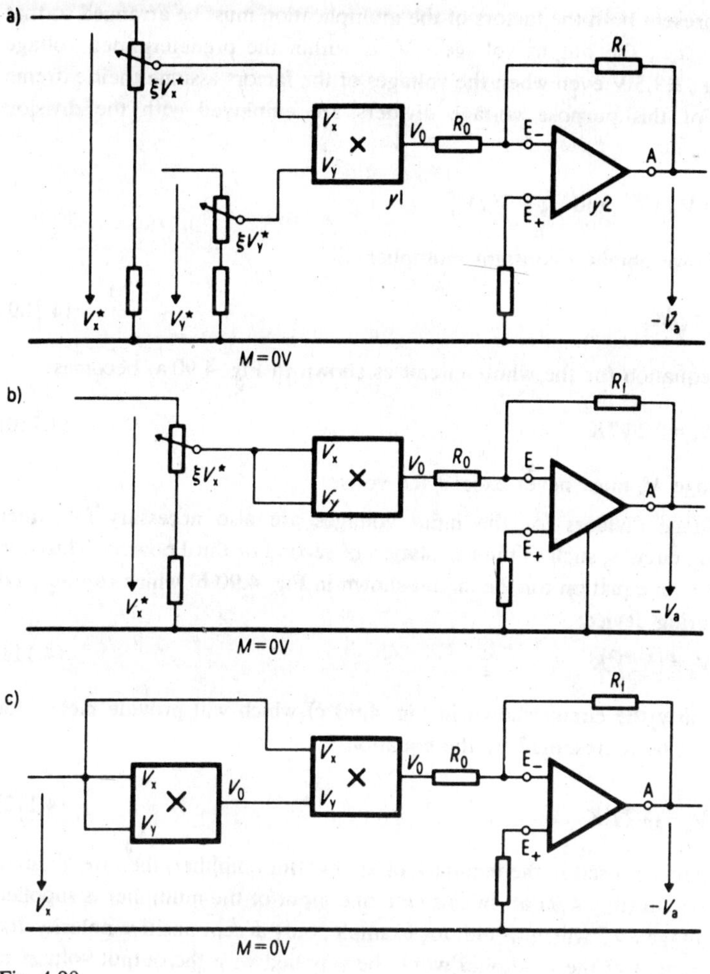

Fig. 4.90

a) Four-quadrant multiplier with an inverter amplifier and variable input values of V_x and V_y.

b) Circuit enabling a quantity, which is represented by a voltage V_x^* to be squared.

c) Circuit enabling a quantity, which is represented by a voltage V_x to be cubed

The basic circuit of the four-quadrant multiplier can be varied in several ways. In all cases however, the individual components must be matched in order to obtain good linearity and to minimize the zero error. Figure 4.90 shows the application of the multiplier unit. In the first instance a simple four-quadrant multiplier with an inverter amplifier on its output side is shown, which produces a proportional amplification $K_p = R_f/R_0$. In most cases the voltages, which represent both the factors of the multiplication must be arranged so that the result, i.e., the output voltage $-V_a$ is within the predetermined voltage range, e.g., ±9.5 V even when the voltages of the factors assume their extreme values. For this purpose voltage dividers are employed with the division factors:

$$\xi = V_x/V_x^* \quad \text{and} \quad \zeta = V_y/V_y^*$$

From this we obtain a constant multiplier

$$K = \xi\zeta K_p \tag{4.109}$$

and the equation for the whole circuit as shown in Fig. 4.90 a) becomes:

$$-V_a = V_x^* V_y^* K \tag{4.110}$$

The voltage V_a must never exceed ten volts.

Such voltage dividers for the input voltages are also necessary for other computing circuits, such as the calculation of second or third powers. Thus one can obtain an equation for the circuit shown in Fig. 4.90 b) which can be used as a squaring device:

$$-V_a = (V_x^*)^2 K \tag{4.111}$$

and similarly the circuit shown in Fig. 4.90 c) which will provide means for cubing will be represented by the equation:

$$-V_a = (V_x^*)^3 K \tag{4.112}$$

If a multiplier is used in the feedback of an inverter amplifier, then we obtain a division circuit (Fig. 4.91 a). In this case one input of the multiplier is supplied with a voltage ξV_x^* which would, for example, only accept positive polarity and the other input of the multiplier would be supplied with the output voltage of the inverter amplifier, $-V_a$. The magnitude of the divisor V_x^* can be varied by the factor ξ by means of a potentiometer. Thus we obtain the following equation for the multiplier:

$$-V_a\xi + V_x^* = -V_0 \tag{4.113}$$

and for the inverter amplifier we have the equation:

$$\zeta + V_z^* \frac{R_f}{R_0} = -V_0 \tag{4.114}$$

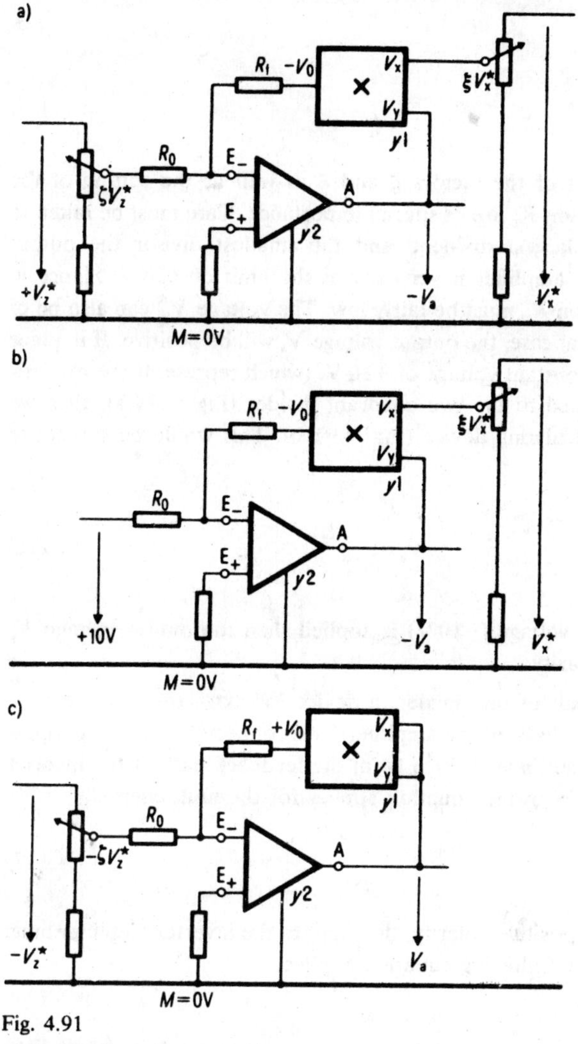

Fig. 4.91

a) Application of a multiplier in the feedback of an inverter amplifier for a division circuit.

b) Reciprocal calculation circuit.

c) Square root calculation circuit

The magnitude of the dividend V_z^* must also be changed by the factor ζ and the amplifier will be subject to the factor of amplification $K_p = R_f/R_0$. In contrast to the divisor V_x^*, the dividend V_z^* can be of either polarity. By applying the Eqns (4.113) and (4.114) we obtain a two-quadrant divider with the equation:

$$-V_a = \frac{+V_z^* \zeta}{+V_x^* \xi} V_p$$

In this case the setting of the factors ζ and ξ as well as the setting of the proportional amplification K_p are of special importance. Care must be taken to ensure that with the largest dividend and the smallest divisor the output voltage of the inverter amplifier never exceeds the limit of ±10 V. Hence in general the amplification K_p must be fairly low. The voltage V_z^* can also be of negative polarity. In that case, the output voltage V_a will be positive. If in place of the dividend V_z^* a constant voltage of +10 V. (which represents the numerical value of 1) is applied to the two-quadrant divider (Fig. 4.91 a), then we obtain a reciprocal calculating device (Fig. 4.91 b). This would be subject to the equation:

$$-V_a = \frac{1}{V_x^*} \frac{K_p}{\xi} \tag{4.116}$$

If a negative constant voltage (−10 V) is applied then the output voltage V_a will be of positive polarity.

By modifying the circuit of the divider, a device for extracting roots can be obtained. The output voltage of the amplifier V_a is connected to the two inputs of the four-quadrant multiplier (which lie in the feedback path of the inverter amplifier) so that the following equation applies for the multiplier:

$$(V_a)^2 = +V_0 \tag{4.117}$$

In order that V_0 be of positive polarity, the input to the inverter amplifier must be negative. Hence the following equation applies:

$$-V_z^* \zeta \frac{R_f}{R_0} = +V_0 \tag{4.118}$$

From the above two equations, it is apparent that the number from which the square root is to be obtained must be represented by a negative voltage. In addition, it must be ensured by means of the factor $K = \zeta(R_f/R_0)$ that the output voltage V_a of the amplifier also never exceeds +10 V. By applying Eqns (4.117) and (4.118) we obtain the following equation for the root calculating device:

$$V_a = \sqrt{K|-V_z^*|} \tag{4.119}$$

Figure 4.91 c) shows the corresponding circuit. Extreme value (maximum/minimum value) devices can also be produced by means of analogue computing circuits.

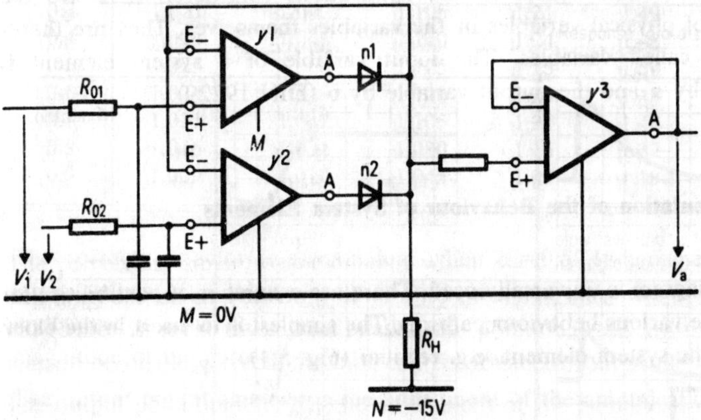

Fig. 4.92
Circuit for maximum value evaluation of two input voltages

Figure 4.92 shows the circuit diagram for a maximum value evaluation device. A 'diode circuit without a threshold value' as shown in Fig. 4.27 is used for each input voltage and a voltage sequence switching circuit as shown in Fig. 4.26 is used for the common output. With such a maximum value evaluation unit, the input voltage which exhibits the highest voltage in the positive direction can be switched to the output. It should be noted that the maximum voltage can have a negative polarity, e.g., a voltage of −3 V is 'more positive' than a voltage of −5 V.

If, in the circuit shown in Fig. 4.92, the direction of current flow of the diodes n1 and n2 is reversed and if the positive supply voltage of +15 V is switched in to the common resistance R_H as an auxiliary voltage, then a minimum value evaluation device is obtained. This means that only that input voltage which exhibits the highest negative value is switched into the output. Thus from a series of voltages such as +9 V, +2 V and +5 V the voltage +2 V. would be obtained as the 'most negative' voltage.

5. Combinations of System Elements

Control systems are obtained by the combination of system elements. These characterize the transfer behaviour along the operational path on which signals are transmitted. The signals in the applications considered here are the parameters of physical variables or the variables themselves. They are therefore simply called variables. The input variable of a system element is represented by u and the output variable by v (DIN 19229).

5.1. Representation of the Behaviour of System Elements

The block diagram is universally used. There are a number of possibilities for indicating the various behaviour patterns. The simplest is to insert in the block the title of the system element, e.g. rectifier (Fig. 5.1).

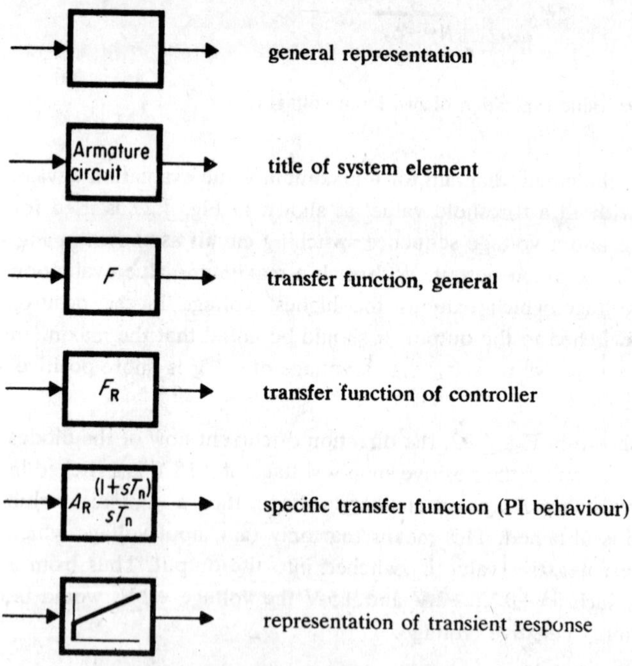

Fig. 5.1 Representation of the behaviour of system elements (block diagram)

However, this is not common. First, it is necessary to distinguish between linear and non-linear system elements (see Section 3.8). For non-linear system elements, the steady-state behaviour is indicated. A system of co-ordinates, the input variable horizontally and the associated output variable vertically, is entered in the block. Only linear system elements will be described further.

Linear system elements are represented by the entry of the system function (in general or specific form) or by a co-ordinate system in the lower left hand corner (Fig. 5.1). The abscissa is the time axis and the ordinate represents the step response. In Fig. 5.2, the transients and the associated transfer functions are shown.

Symbol	Block	Transfer function	Symbol	Block	Transfer function
P		A_S, A_R	$P-T_1$		$A_S\frac{1}{1+sT_1}$
I		$\frac{1}{sT_i}, \frac{1}{sT_1}$	$P-T_2$		$\frac{A_S}{1+s2\zeta T+s^2T^2}$ $\zeta<1$
PI		$A_R\frac{1+sT_n}{sT_n}$	$P-T_2$		$\frac{A_S}{(1+sT_1)(1+sT_2)}$ $\zeta>1$
PID		$A_R\frac{(1+sT_n)(1+sT_v)}{sT_n}$	$D-T_1$		$\frac{sT_d}{1+sT_1}$
PD		$A_S\left(1+\frac{T_d}{A_S}\right), A_R(1+sT_v)$	$PD-T_1$		$A_S\frac{1+sT_d/A_S}{1+sT_1}$ $\frac{T_d}{A_S}>T_1$
$P-T_t$		$A_S\cdot e^{-sT_t}$	$PD-T_1$	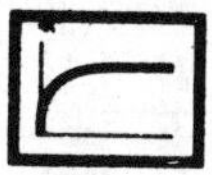	$A_S\frac{1+sT_v}{1+sT_1}$ $T_v<T_1$

Fig. 5.2 Block diagrams with transient response and transfer function

5.2. Lines of Action and Their Combinations

The lines of action between the individual blocks are represented by lines on which arrows indicate the direction. It is assumed that the input of a system element exerts no reaction on the driven output (Fig. 5.3). The term reaction free links is used.

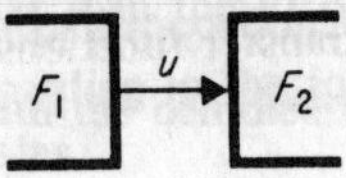

Fig. 5.3
Lines of action. Action of the output of a system element (F_1) on the input of a second system element (F_2)

Lines of action can be branched (Fig. 5.4) in order to apply the same input signal to different system elements. Conversely, the effect of two or more signals can be brought together at a common point. It is therefore possible to add or subtract:

$$v = u_1 + u_2 \tag{5.1}$$

or

$$v = u_1 - u_2. \tag{5.2}$$

Also, we have the combination resulting from multiplication:

$$v = u_1 u_2 \tag{5.3}$$

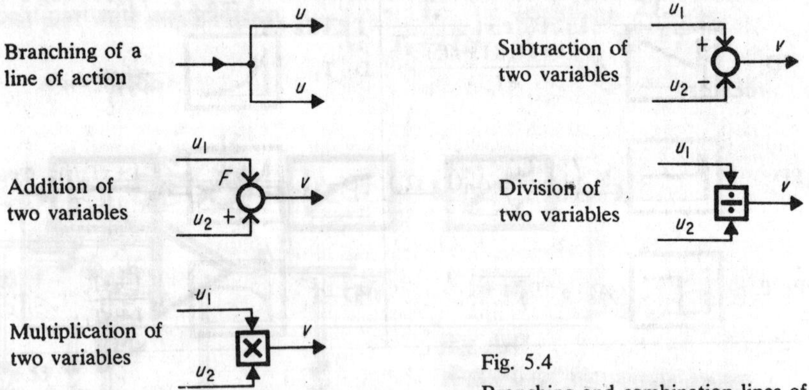

Fig. 5.4
Branching and combination lines of action

and by the use of a multiplier in the feedback branch of an amplifier, we have division

$$v = u_1/u_2. \tag{5.4}$$

These combinations appear in the time domain. Branching, addition and subtraction can be transformed directly into the frequency domain.

5.3. Basic Combinations of System Elements

The behaviour of the sinusoidal output variable of a system element is defined for all frequencies by multiplying the sinusoidal input variable by the transfer function of the system:

$$u(j\omega)F(j\omega) = v(j\omega) \tag{5.5}$$

or

$$u(s)F(s) = v(s). \tag{5.6}$$

The latter form will be used from now on. The basic combinations of system elements are summarized in Fig. 5.5. These circuits occur in practice in various combinations.

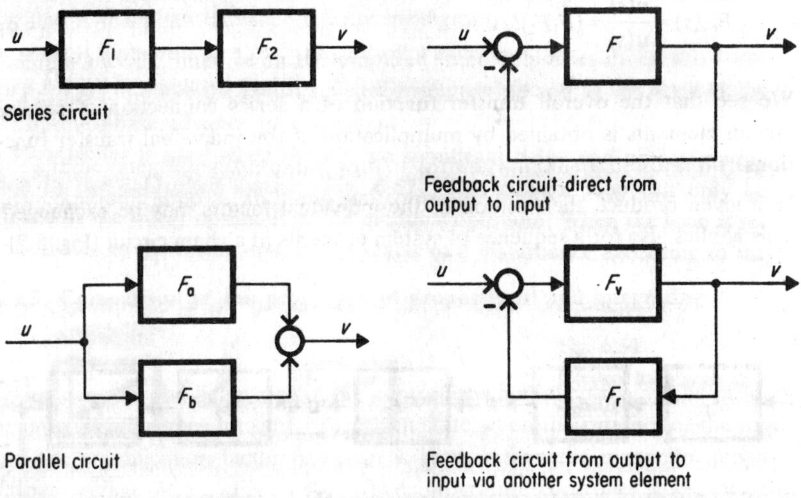

Fig. 5.5 Basic combinations

5.3.1. Series connection of system elements

The most common coupling of two system elements is the series or chain connection (Fig. 5.6).

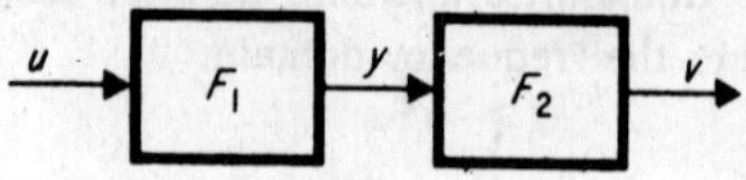

Fig. 5.6
Series connection of two system elements

The output variable v of the second system element is given by

$$v(s) = y(s)F_2(s). \tag{5.7}$$

The output variable of the first system element is

$$y(s) = u(s)F_1(s). \tag{5.8}$$

Putting this in Eqn (5.7) gives

$$v(s) = u(s)F_1(s)F_2(s) = u(s)(F_1F_2)(s).$$

Therefore the overall transfer function is

$$F_{ov}(s) = \frac{v(s)}{u(s)} = (F_1F_2)(s). \tag{5.9}$$

We see that the overall transfer function of a series connection of several system elements is obtained by multiplication of the individual transfer functions.

In a given product, the position of the individual factors may be exchanged. This applies also for a sequence of system elements in a chain circuit (Fig. 5.7).

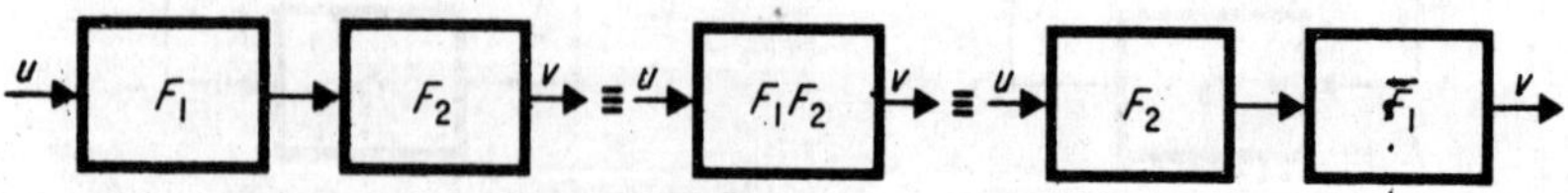

Fig. 5.7 Interchange of the elements of a series circuit

5.3.2. Parallel connection of system elements

Frequently, two system elements are connected in parallel at their inputs, producing an addition at their output (Fig. 5.8). Note that when + or − signs are omitted from the arrow heads at the summing junction or comparison point, then a + is assumed.

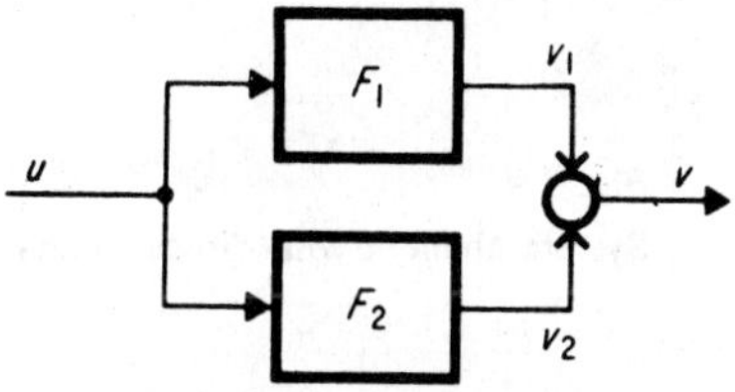

Fig. 5.8
Parallel connection of two system elements

Two output variables then occur for the same input variable:

$$u(s)F_1(s)=v_1(s) \tag{5.10}$$

$$u(s)F_2(s)=v_2(s). \tag{5.11}$$

They are added and produce the common output variable

$$V(s)=v_1(s)+v_2(s)$$

or

$$\begin{aligned} V(s) &= u(s)F_1(s)+u(s)F_2(s) \\ &= u(s)(F_1+F_2)(s). \end{aligned}$$

The overall transfer function is then

$$F_{ov}(s)=\frac{V(s)}{u(s)}=(F_1+F_2)(s). \tag{5.12}$$

Thus we see that the overall transfer function of a parallel connection of several system elements is obtained by the addition of the individual transfer functions.

In this case, the output variables of the individual system elements may be added, not only in the frequency domain, but also in the time domain:

$$v(t)=v_1(t)+v_2(t). \tag{5.13}$$

5.3.3. Direct feedback, output to input

Feedback circuits are of fundamental importance in control engineering as they determine the control system behaviour. The input variable u is compared to the output variable v by subtraction at the input of the system. Between the comparison point or summing junction and the output is the system element with transfer function F (Fig. 5.9).

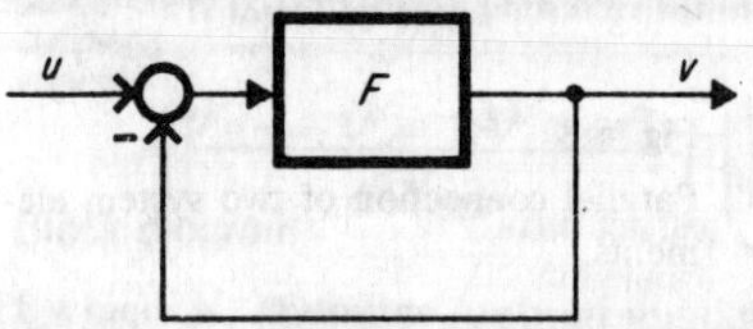

Fig. 5.9
System element with direct feedback

The system is described by the following equation:

$$[u(s)-v(s)]F(s)=v(s). \tag{5.14}$$

From Eqn (5.14), the following equation is obtained:

$$v(s)[1+F(s)]=u(s)F(s)$$

or

$$v(s)=u(s)\frac{F(s)}{1+F(s)}.$$

Thus the overall transfer function is

$$F_{ov}(s)=\frac{v(s)}{u(s)}=\frac{F(s)}{1+F(s)}=\frac{1}{1+[F(s)]^{-1}}. \tag{5.15}$$

This equation is used in considering the relationship of the controlled variable to the command variable. The transfer function can be written as follows:

$$F(s)=\frac{Z(s)}{N(s)}. \tag{5.16}$$

Equation (5.15) can then be written

$$F_{ov}(s)=\frac{v(s)}{u(s)}=\frac{Z(s)}{Z(s)+N(s)} \tag{5.17}$$

5.3.4. Feedback circuit using a second system element

In this case a second system element is connected in the feedback channel from the output of the first system element (F_v) to its input (Fig. 5.10).

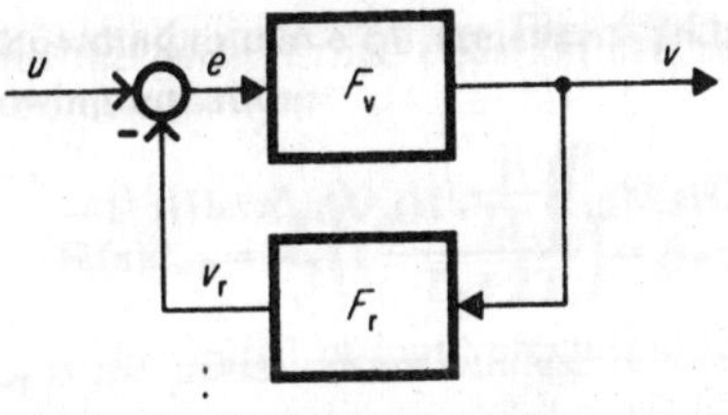

Fig. 5.10

Feedback circuit with a second system element in the feedback circuit

The equations are as follows:

$$u(s) - v_r(s) = e(s)$$
$$e(s)F_v(s) = v(s).$$
$$v(s)F_r(s) = v_r(s).$$

From these the following can be obtained:

$$[u(s) - v(s)F_r(s)]F_v(s) = v(s) \tag{5.18}$$

and thus, we obtain

$$v(s)[1 + F_r(s)F_v(s)] = u(s)F_v(s).$$

The overall transfer function is therefore as follows:

$$F_{ov}(s) = \frac{v(s)}{u(s)} = \frac{F_v(s)}{1 + [F_vF_r](s)} = \frac{1}{[F_v(s)]^{-1} + F_r(s)}. \tag{5.19}$$

This equation gives the relationship between the controlled variable and the command variable.

If we write

$$F_v(s) = \frac{Z_v(s)}{N_v(s)} \quad \text{and} \quad F_r(s) = \frac{Z_r(s)}{N_r(s)}$$

then Eqn (5.19) can be written as follows:

$$F_{ov}(s) = \frac{v(s)}{u(s)} = \frac{[Z_v N_r](s)}{[Z_v Z_r](s) + [N_v N_r](s)}. \tag{5.20}$$

If we write

$$F_v(s) F_r(s) = F_0(s) = \frac{Z_0(s)}{N_0(s)}$$

then Eqn (5.19) can be written as follows:

$$F_{ov}(s) = \frac{v(s)}{u(s)} = \frac{Z_0(s)}{Z_0(s) + N_0(s)} \frac{1}{F_r(s)}. \tag{5.21}$$

5.4. Examples of Basic Combinations of System Elements

The results of various basic types of combination will be discussed and it will be seen that new functions arise from them.

5.4.1. Series connection

Consider an integrating element and a proportional element connected in series (Fig. 5.11).

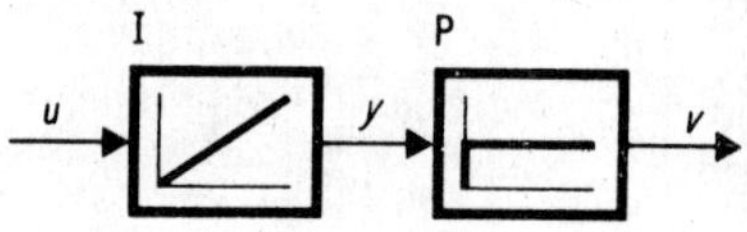

Fig. 5.11
Integrating and proportional element in series

The transfer function for this arrangement is:

$$F(s) = \frac{1}{sT_i} A_S = \frac{1}{sT_i / A_S} \tag{5.22}$$

If the proportional amplification is changed the slope of the step response of the integrating element (y in Fig. 5.12) is changed. The new overall integrating

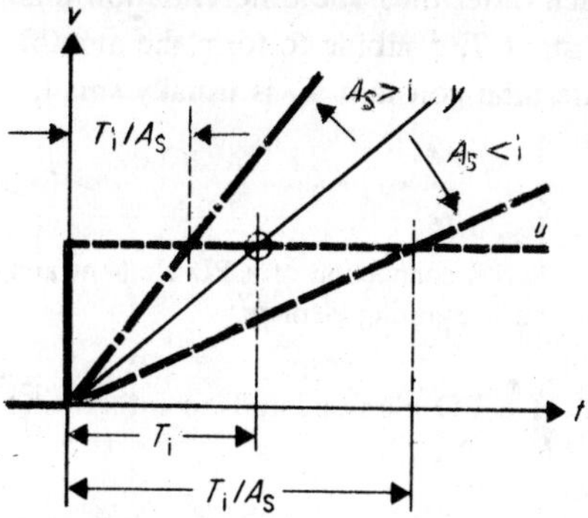

Fig. 5.12
Effect of the P element on the I element in a series connection

time constant is T_i/A_S and is larger if A_S is less than 1 and smaller if the amplification A_S is larger than 1. However, the integrator characteristic is maintained.

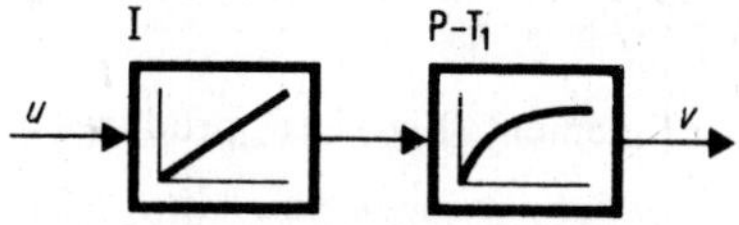

Fig. 5.13
Series connection of integrator element and delay element

The series connection of an integrating element and a first order delay element (Fig. 5.13) has the following transfer function:

$$F(s) = \frac{1}{sT_i}\frac{A_S}{1+sT_i} = \frac{1}{sT_i/A_S}\frac{1}{1+sT_1}. \tag{5.23}$$

This is equivalent to a delay with time constant T_1 and a pure integral with integration time constant T_i/A_S which is adjustable by means of the proportional amplification A_S.

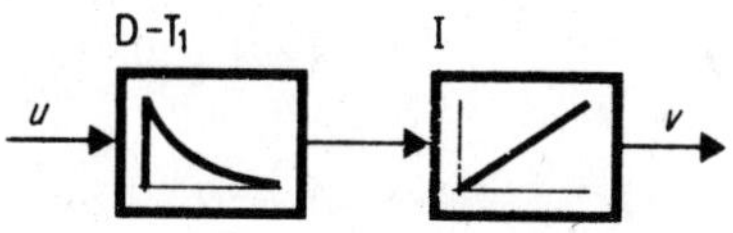

Fig. 5.14
Series connection of a differentiating element and an integrating element

Figure 5.14 shows a differentiating element in series with an integrating element. The transfer function is

$$F(s) = \frac{sT_d}{1+sT_1}\frac{1}{sT_i} = \frac{T_d}{T_1}\frac{1}{1+sT_1}. \tag{5.24}$$

Differentiation and integration cancel each other out. The differentiation time constant T_d and the integrating time constant T_i combine to form the amplification T_d/T_i. The delay with the parasitic time constant T_1 is usually small.

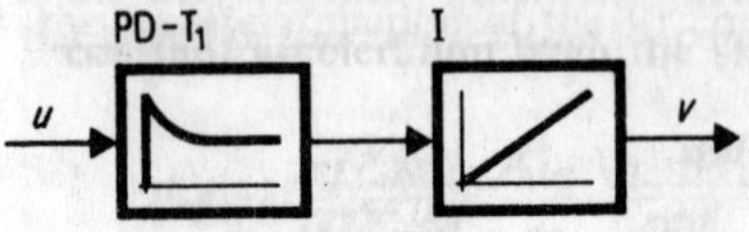

Fig. 5.15
Series connection of a PD element and an integrating element

Figure 5.15 shows the series connection of a PD element and an integrating element with the transfer function:

$$F(s) = A_R \frac{1+sT_v}{1+sT_1} \frac{1}{sT_i} = \frac{1+sT_v}{sT_i/A_S} \frac{1}{1+sT_1} \tag{5.25}$$

This shows a PI response with reset time constant $T_n = T_v$, integration time constant $T_I = T_i/A_S$, and amplification $A_R = A_S T_v/T_i$. The constant T_1 is the decay time constant.

A series connection of a PD element and a PI element (Fig. 5.16) produces a PID behaviour.

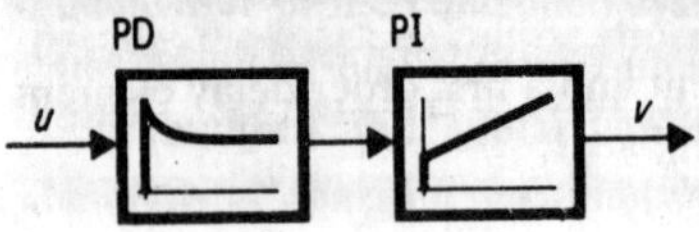

Fig. 5.16
Series connection of a PD element and a PI element

The transfer function is

$$F(s) = A_R \frac{1+sT_v}{1+sT_1} \frac{1+sT_n}{sT_i} = A_R \frac{T_n}{T_i} \frac{(1+sT_n)(1+sT_v)}{sT_n} \frac{1}{1+sT_1}. \tag{5.26}$$

We observe

the integrating part $1/(sT_i/A_R)$,

the proportional part $A_R \dfrac{T_n+T_v}{T_i}$,

and the differentiating part $sA_R \dfrac{T_n T_v}{T_i}$.

T_1 is the decay time constant.

5.4.2. Examples of parallel connection

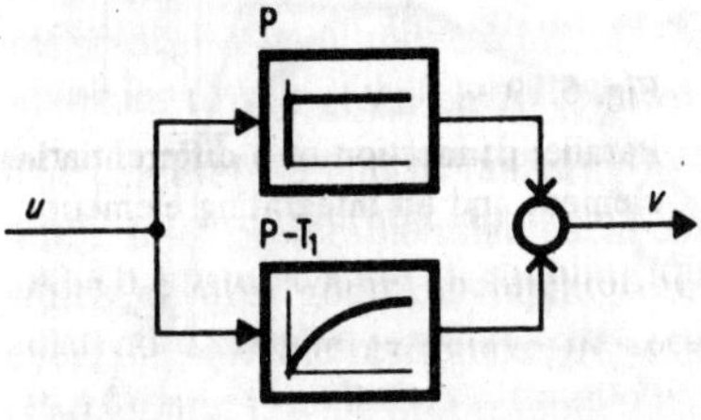

Fig. 5.17
Parallel connection of proportional element and delay element

Parallel connection of a proportional element and a delay element (Fig. 5.17) results in a phase advance. The greater the amplification of the P element, the more the phase advance counteracts the delay behaviour. The transfer function is

$$F(s) = A_S + \frac{1}{1+sT_2} = \frac{1+A_S}{1+sT_2}\left(1+s\frac{A_S}{1+A_S}T_2\right). \tag{5.27}$$

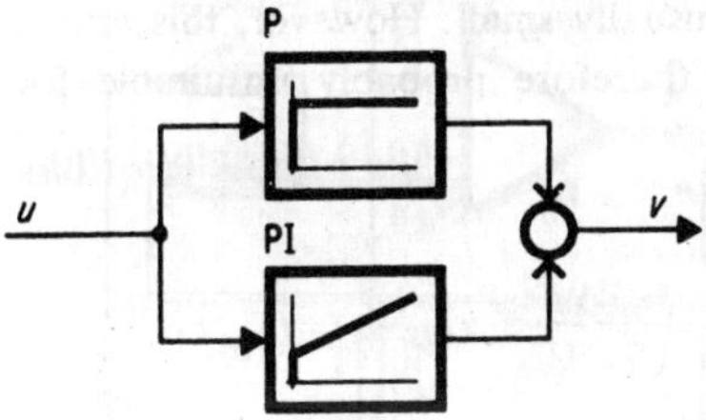

Fig. 5.18
Parallel connection of a proportional element and a PI element

By connecting a proportional element and a PI element in parallel (Fig. 5.18), a PI action is again obtained. The transfer function is

$$F(s) = A_R + \frac{1+sT_n}{sT_i} = \frac{1+s(A_R T_i + T_n)}{sT_i} \tag{5.28}$$

The reset time constant can be varied by variation of the amplification A_R of the P element.

Differentiation and integration do not cancel each other in a parallel connection of D and I elements (Fig. 5.19). The transfer function obtained is

$$F(s) = \frac{sT_d}{1+sT_1} + \frac{1}{sT_i} = \frac{1+sT_1+s^2T_iT_d}{sT_i(1+sT_1)}$$

$$= \left[\frac{1}{sT_i} + \frac{T_1}{T_i} + sT_d\right]\frac{1}{1+sT_1}. \tag{5.29}$$

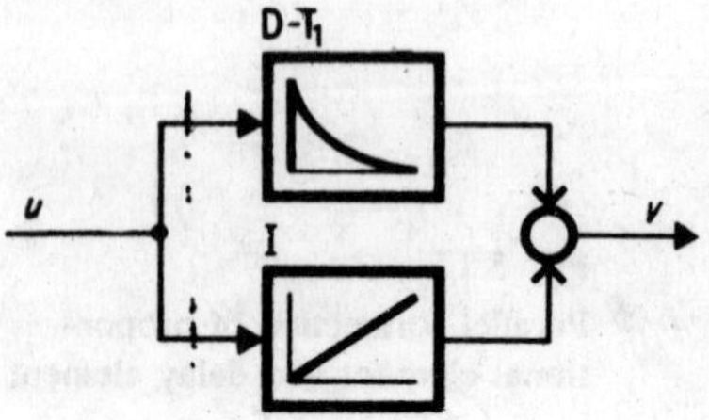

Fig. 5.19
Parallel connection of a differentiating element and an integrating element

The transfer function exhibits a PID characteristic with

I part $1/sT_i$

P part T_1/T_i

D part sT_d

and with a decay time constant which is usually small. However, this circuit has a small amplification (T_1/T_i) and is therefore probably unsuitable for control purposes.

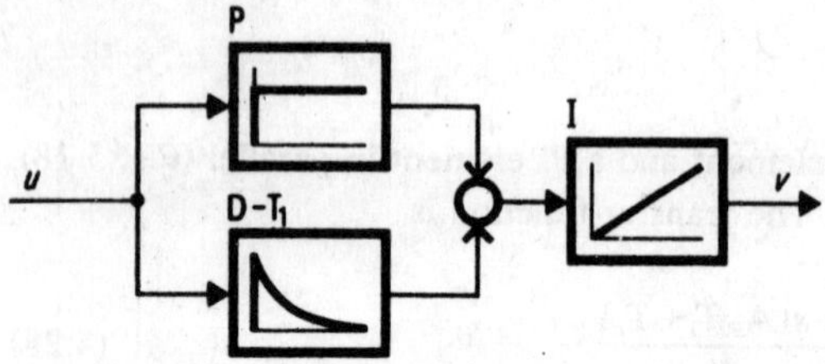

Fig. 5.20
Series parallel connection of P, D, and I elements

A series parallel circuit of D, P and I elements as shown in Fig. 5.20 gives the following transfer function:

$$F(s) = \left[A_S + \frac{sT_d}{1+sT_1}\right]\frac{1}{sT_i} = \frac{1+s(T_1+T_d/A_S)}{sT_i/A_S}\,\frac{1}{1+sT_1}\,. \tag{5.30}$$

A PI action is described by this transfer function. It shows the reset time constant (T_1+T_d/A_S) and proportional amplification $(A_S T_1 + T_d)/T_i$. There is also a first order delay with decay time constant T_1.

5.4.3. Examples of direct feedback

Figure 5.21 shows an integrating element with feedback producing a first order delay. The transfer function is

$$F(s)=\frac{\frac{1}{sT_i}}{1+\frac{1}{sT_i}}=\frac{1}{1+sT_i}. \tag{5.31}$$

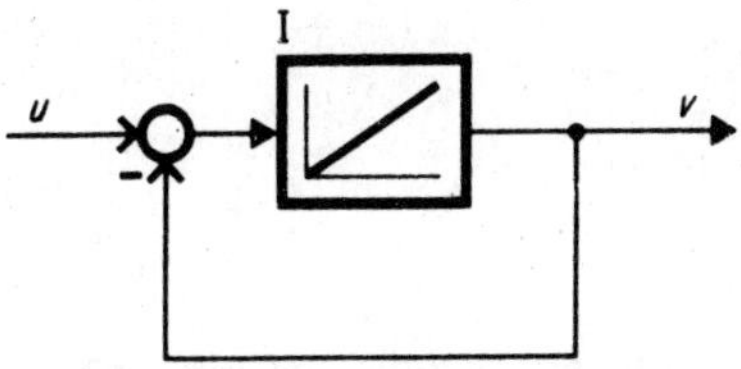

Fig. 5.21
Integrating element with direct feedback

The proportional amplification is 1 and the decay time constant is equal to the integration time constant. First order delays in analogue computers are produced by this circuit.

The connection of two first order delay elements in series produces a second order delay, always with aperiodic response (see Section 2.4). However, if

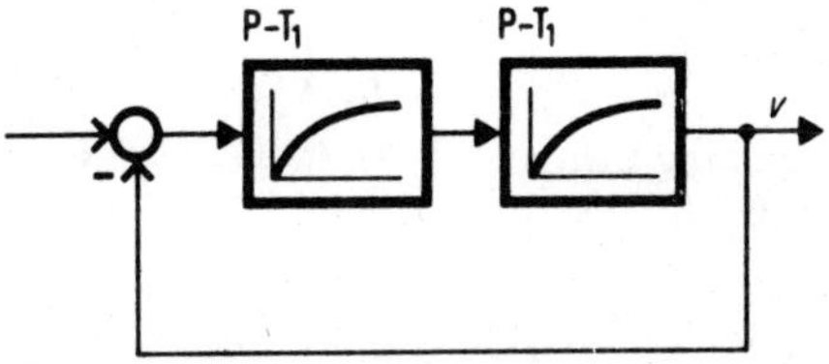

Fig. 5.22
Two series delay elements with direct feedback

direct feedback is applied as shown in Fig. 5.22, the transfer function obtained is as follows:

$$F(s)=\frac{\frac{A_{S1}}{1+sT_1}\frac{A_{S2}}{1+sT_2}}{1+\frac{A_{S1}}{1+sT_1}\frac{A_{S2}}{1+sT_2}}=\frac{A_{S1}A_{S2}}{A_{S1}A_{S2}+1}$$

$$\times\frac{1}{\left[1+s(T_1+T_2)\frac{A_{S1}A_{S2}}{A_{S1}A_{S2}+1}+s^2T_1T_2\frac{A_{S1}A_{S2}}{A_{S1}A_{S2}+1}\right]} \tag{5.32}$$

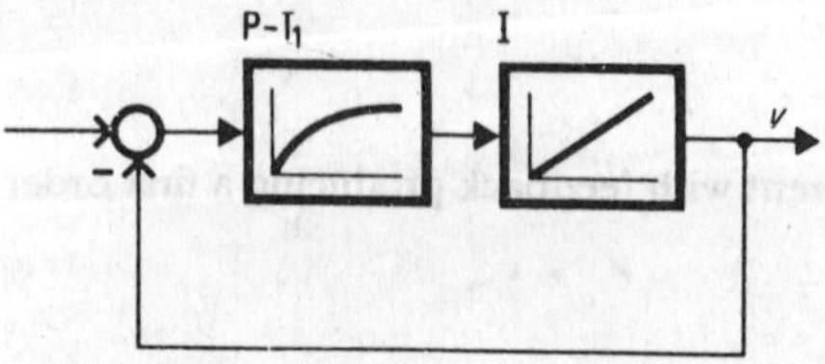

Fig. 5.23
Feedback circuit with a delay element and integrating element in series

A second order delay is obtained, the amplification being less than 1. The transient performance can be either aperiodic or periodic, since the damping factor

$$\zeta = \frac{1}{2}\sqrt{\frac{T_1}{T_2} + 2 + \frac{T_2}{T_1}}\sqrt{\frac{A_{S1}A_{S2}}{A_{S1}A_{S2}+1}}$$

can be either greater or less than 1.

Figure 5.23 can be used to represent the performance of a d.c. machine, where the delay element represents the armature circuit and the integrating element represents the mechanical performance. It is assumed that the flux is equal to the rated value. The transfer function for this circuit is

$$F(s) = \frac{\frac{A_S}{1+sT_1}\frac{1}{sT_i}}{1+\frac{A_S}{1+sT_1}\frac{1}{sT_i}} = \frac{1}{1+s\frac{T_i}{A_S}+s^2\frac{T_iT_1}{A_S}}. \tag{5.33}$$

This is a second order delay with a damping factor

$$\zeta = \frac{1}{2}\sqrt{\frac{T_i}{A_S T_1}}.$$

If the integration time constant T_i is less than $4A_S T_1$, periodic response is obtained. However, undamped oscillation is not possible.

If two integrating elements are connected in series with direct feedback (Fig. 5.24) the transfer function obtained is

$$\frac{\frac{1}{sT_{i1}}\frac{1}{sT_{i2}}}{1+\frac{1}{sT_{i1}}\frac{1}{sT_{i2}}} = \frac{1}{1+s^2T_{i1}T_{i2}}. \tag{5.34}$$

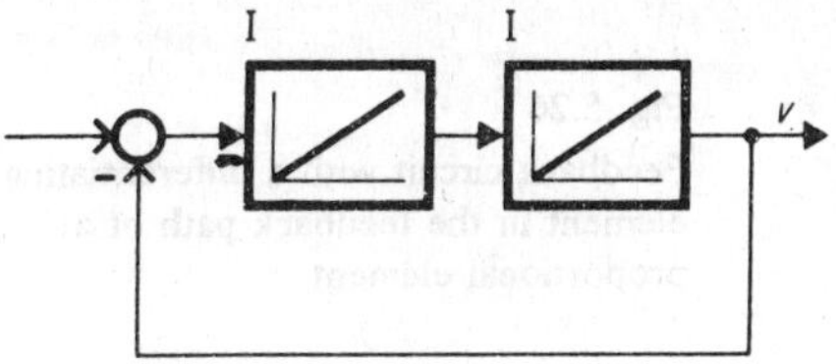

Fig. 5.24.
Direct feedback circuit with two series integrating elements

It will be seen that there is no s term in the denominator. Thus the damping factor is zero. An undamped oscillation occurs without the need for an external stimulus.

5.4.4. Examples of feedback with a second element in the feedback circuit

If the forward path of the circuit contains a proportional element and the feedback path contains an integrating element (Fig. 5.25), the following

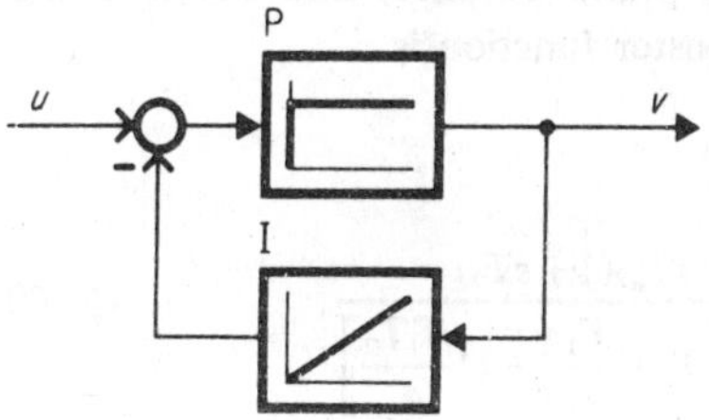

Fig. 5.25
Feedback circuit with an integrating element in the feedback path of a proportional element

equation for the transfer function is obtained:

$$F(s) = \frac{A_S}{1 + \dfrac{A_S}{sT_i}} = \frac{sT_i}{1 + s\dfrac{T_i}{A_S}} . \tag{5.35}$$

This is a practical differentiating circuit. If the amplification A_S is very large, the result is clearly a differentiating element with differentiation time constant T_i.

If the integrating element is replaced by a differentiating element (Fig. 5.26) the transfer function becomes:

$$\frac{A_S}{1 + sA_S T_d} = \frac{1}{\dfrac{1}{A_S} + sT_d} . \tag{5.36}$$

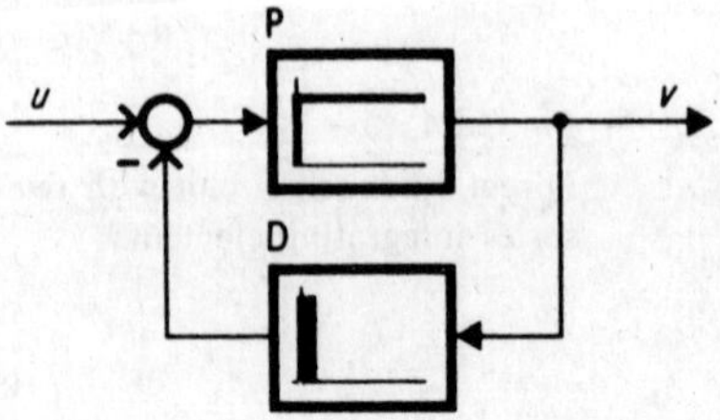

Fig. 5.26
Feedback circuit with a differentiating element in the feedback path of a proportional element

This is a first order delay but becomes an integrating element with integration time constant T_d if the proportional amplification A_S is very large.

It is clear from both examples that the denominator term of the feedback always appears in the numerator of the overall transfer function.

A delay in the feedback results in a phase advance in the overall behaviour. This is demonstrated in the example of Fig. 5.27 in which the PI element is in the forward branch (therefore already a phase advance) and the feedback branch contains a delay element. The transfer function is

$$F(s)=\frac{\dfrac{1+sT_n}{sT_i}}{1+\dfrac{1+sT_n}{sT_i}\,\dfrac{A_S}{1+sT_2}}=\frac{(1+sT_n)(1+sT_2)}{A_S\left[1+s\left(T_n+\dfrac{T_1}{A_S}\right)+s^2\dfrac{T_iT_2}{A_S}\right]}. \tag{5.37}$$

As expected, two phase advances occur. In other respects, the initial transient is dependent on the damping factor of the second order delay:

$$\zeta=\frac{1}{2}\sqrt{\frac{1}{T_2}\left(\frac{T_1}{A_S}+2T_n+T_n^2\frac{A_S}{T_i}\right)}.$$

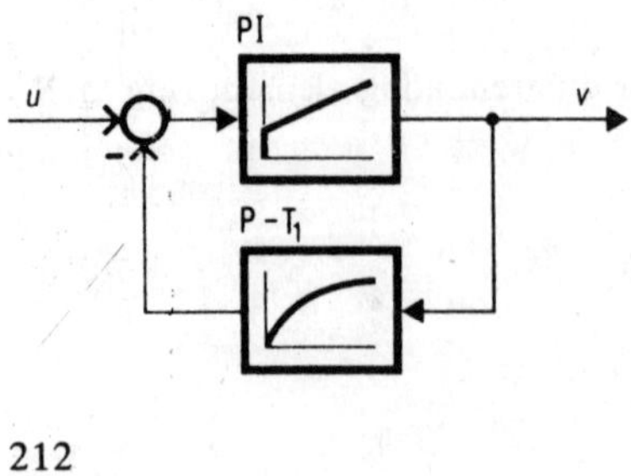

Fig. 5.27
Feedback circuit with a delay element in the feedback path of a PI element

5.5. Transformation of Branches and Additions

It is advantageous in many cases to transform existing combinations of system elements in order to make them more easily understandable, or by transformation to achieve a more favourable realization of a required function.

5.5.1. Transformation of branches

Figure 5.28 shows a system in which the output from a system element branches into two parallel branches. The following equations can be written:

$$\begin{aligned} v_1(s) &= u(s)F(s) \\ v_2(s) &= u(s)F(s). \end{aligned} \tag{5.38}$$

It will be observed that the circuit can be redrawn as shown with the element of transfer function F inserted in both parallel branches.

By considering Eqns (5.39), it can be seen that the two systems shown in Fig. 5.29 are equivalent:

$$\begin{aligned} v_1(s) &= u(s)F(s) \\ v_2(s) &= u(s)F(s)[F(s)]^{-1}. \end{aligned} \tag{5.39}$$

Figure 5.30 shows some examples of this.

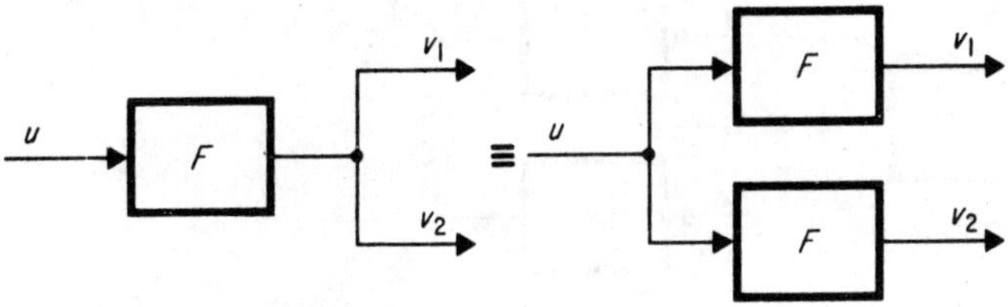

Fig. 5.28 Transformation of a control circuit I

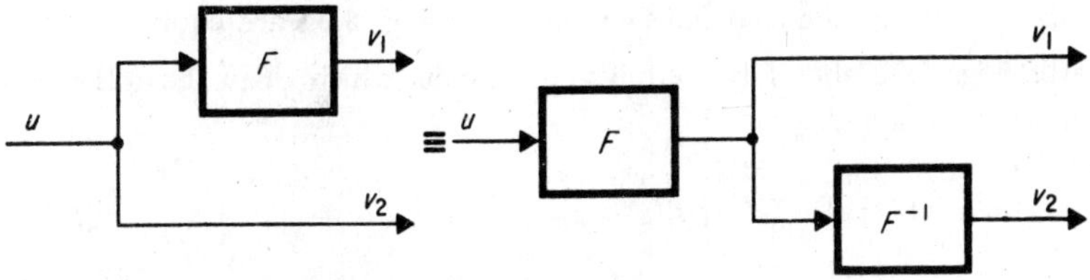

Fig. 5.29 Transformation of a control circuit II

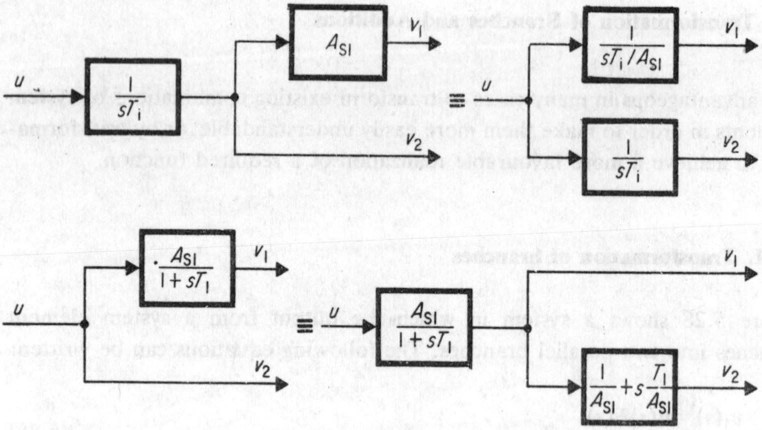

Fig. 5.30 Examples of transformation of circuits

5.5.2. Transformation of circuits with additions

Figure 5.31 shows a system in which two parallel branches meet at a summing junction at the input to a system element F. The following equations can be written:

$$v(s) = [u_1(s) + u_2(s)]F(s) = u_1(s)F(s) + u_2(s)F(s). \tag{5.40}$$

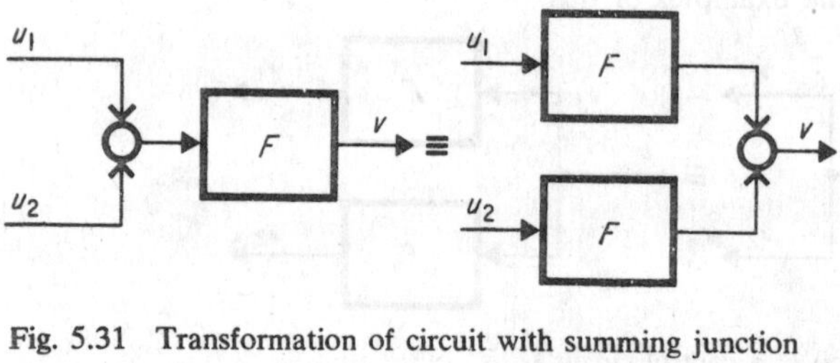

Fig. 5.31 Transformation of circuit with summing junction

From this it can be seen that the two circuits in Fig. 5.31 are equivalent. Similarly, Fig. 5.32 shows two equivalent circuits which obey the following equations:

$$v(s) = u_1(s)F(s) + u_2(s) = [u_1(s) + u_2(s)[F(s)]^{-1}]F(s). \tag{5.41}$$

Fig. 5.33 shows further examples.

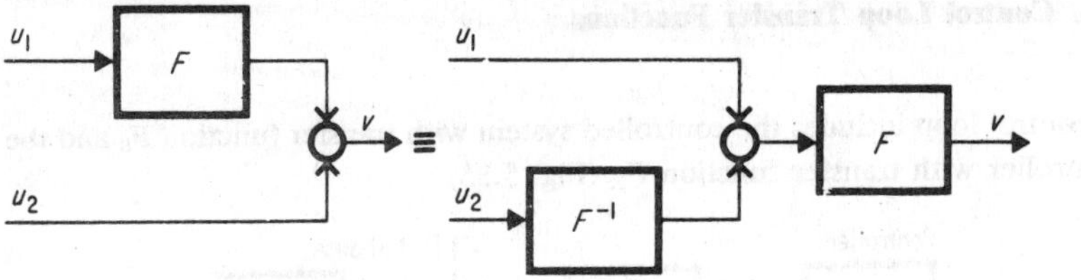

Fig. 5.32 Transformation of circuit with summing junction II

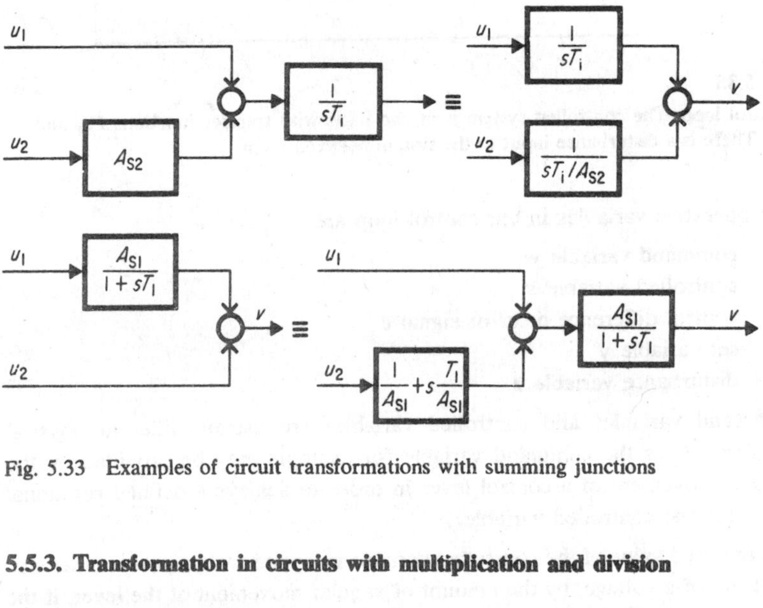

Fig. 5.33 Examples of circuit transformations with summing junctions

5.5.3. Transformation in circuits with multiplication and division

It is not possible to perform transformations in multiplication and division circuits by means of transposed transfer functions. However, a multiplication may, of course, be cancelled by a subsequent division by the same factor (Fig. 5.34).

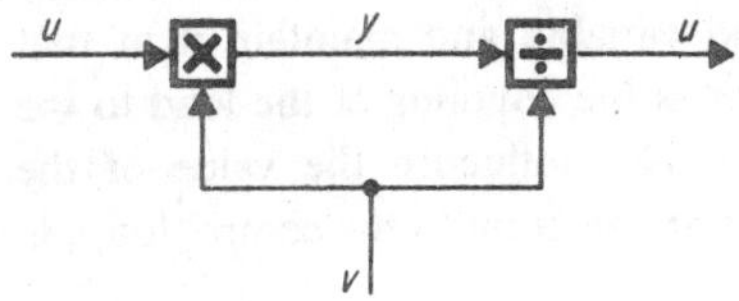

Fig. 5.34 Multiplication and division by the factor v

$$u(t)v(t) = y(t)$$

$$\frac{y(t)}{v(t)} = u(t)$$

5.6. Control Loop Transfer Functions

A control loop includes the controlled system with transfer function F_S and the controller with transfer function F_R (Fig. 5.35).

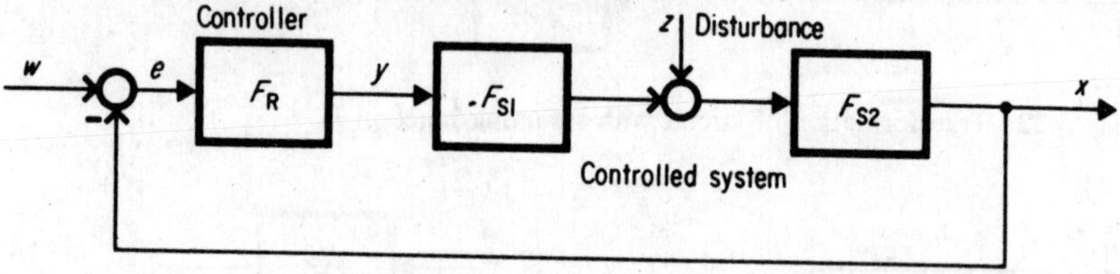

Fig. 5.35
Control loop. The controlled system is in two parts with transfer functions F_{S1} and F_{S2}. There is a disturbance input to the system between them.

The operative variables in the control loop are:

command variable w
controlled variable x
control difference or error signal e
set variable y
disturbance variable z.

Command variables and controlled variables are usually different physical variables. Thus the command variable for example may be provided by the angular movement of a control lever in order to achieve a defined rotational speed for the controlled variable.

The required value of the controlled variable is tapped from a potentiometer in the form of a voltage, by the amount of angular movement of the lever, if the actual value of the controlled variable is represented by a voltage. In the case of voltage parameters, currents arise in the command variable channel and the controlled variable channel, the difference between them being e, the parameter for the error signal. The set variable obtained from the error signal intervenes in the controlled system. Its effect is to bring the controlled variable to a value corresponding to the command variable and maintain it at that value. However, disturbance variables, such as the coupling of the load to the motor or a change in the supply voltage, also influence the value of the controlled variable. Their effects can appear at any point in the control loop, in the controlled system or in the controller.

In theoretical considerations of control loops, such as those dealt with in the following sections, dimensionless variables are employed, since this simplifies the calculations if the input variable of a system is a rotational speed, for example, and the output variable is a voltage. The values are always referred to nominal values, e.g. rotational speed x is

$$x = \frac{\text{instantaneous rotational speed}}{\text{nominal rotational speed}}. \tag{5.42}$$

Often, only perturbations of these variables are considered, e.g.

$$z = \frac{\text{load at time } t_1 - \text{load at time } t_0}{\text{nominal load}}. \tag{5.43}$$

It is useful to distinguish these normalized values by writing them as lower case letters.

5.6.1. Open loop control

An open control loop is considered first (Fig. 5.36). The loop is assumed to be open circuited in the feedback channel. If changes of disturbance variable z are zero then

$$w(s)F_R(s)F_{S1}(s)F_{S2}(s) = x(s).$$

The transfer function $F_0(s)$ for the open loop is

$$F_0(s) = \left.\frac{x(s)}{w(s)}\right|_{\text{open loop}} = F_R(s)F_{S1}(s)F_{S2}(s). \tag{5.44}$$

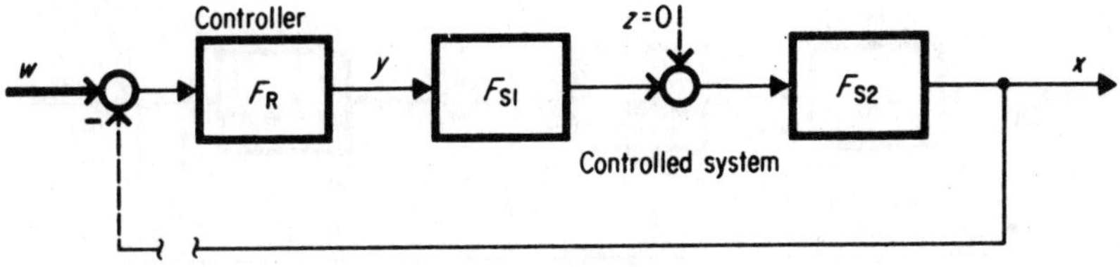

Fig. 5.36
Open control loop, feedback circuit open circuited. Interference variables are zero or unchanging, $z = 0$ or $dz/dt = 0$

By multiplying together the transfer functions of the three elements, the transfer function of the open loop system is obtained. This does not include the command variable elements (see Fig. 1.3).

For convenience when considering the closed loop system, the transfer function for the open loop $F_0(s)$ is written as follows:

$$F_0(s) = \frac{Z_0(s)}{N_0(s)}. \tag{5.45}$$

5.6.2. Closed loop control dependent on command variable

The feedback loop is now closed but all disturbance variables are unchanged ($z = 0$). It is seen from Fig. 5.37 that the summing junction at the input of the controller produces the difference between the command variable w and the controlled variable x. Thus the equation is

$$[w(s) - x(s)]F_R(s)F_{S1}(s)F_{S2}(s) = x(s)$$

or, using Eqn (5.44)

$$[w(s) - x(s)]F_0(s) = x(s)$$

or

$$x(s)[1 + F_0(s)] = w(s)F_0(s).$$

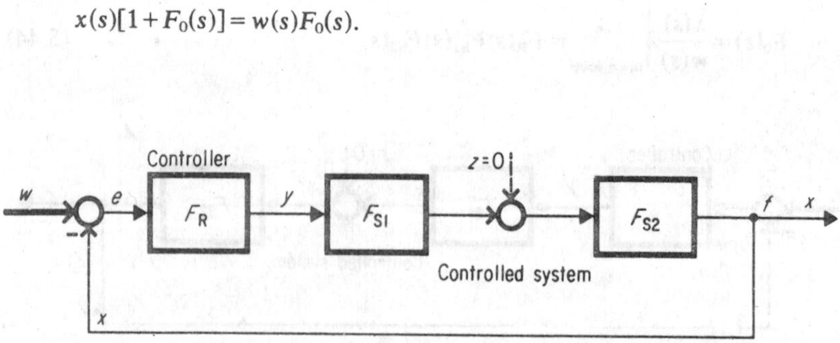

Fig. 5.37
Closed loop control, dependent on the command variable. The feedback loop is closed. The interference variables are zero or unchanged: $z = 0$ or $dz/dt = 0$

We see that the transfer function of the closed loop system is given as follows:

$$F_{\omega}(s)=\left.\frac{x(s)}{w(s)}\right|_{\text{closed loop}}=\frac{F_0(s)}{1+F_0(s)}$$
$$=\frac{1}{1+[F_0(s)]^{-1}}. \tag{5.46}$$

Using Eqn (5.45), Eqn (5.46) can be written as

$$F_{\omega}(s)=\frac{1}{1+[N_0/Z_0](s)}=\frac{Z_0(s)}{Z_0(s)+N_0(s)}. \tag{5.47}$$

Thus we see that the transfer function for the closed loop system can be obtained very simply from the transfer of the open loop.

The ratio of error signal to command variable can be obtained from Eqns (5.46) and (5.47):

$$\frac{e(s)}{w(s)}=\frac{w(s)-x(s)}{w(s)}=1-\frac{x(s)}{w(s)}=1-F_w(s)$$
$$=1-\frac{F_0(s)}{1+F_0(s)}=\frac{1}{1+F_0(s)} \tag{5.48}$$
$$=\frac{N_0(s)}{Z_0(s)+N_0(s)}.$$

According to whether the complex frequency s is used as a variable or as a fixed zero value (Eqn (1.5)), the dynamic, transient or steady state offset error can be determined. The absolute error signal can be obtained from

$$e(s)=\frac{w(s)}{1+F_0(s)}=w(s)\frac{N_0(s)}{Z_0(s)+N_0(s)}. \tag{5.49}$$

5.6.3. Closed loop control dependent on the disturbance variable

Since the purpose of control equipment is to counteract the effect of disturbances, this discussion is of special significance.

In the investigation of the influence of disturbance variables on the controlled variable, the command variable remains constant. This corresponds to a desired value change of zero ($w=0$). Only the negatively fed back controlled

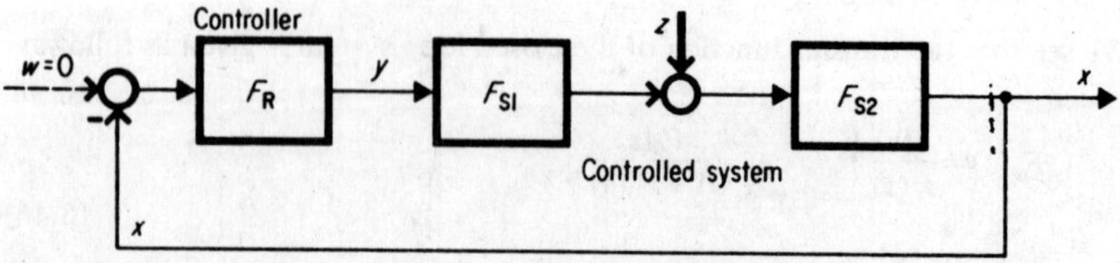

Fig. 5.38
Closed loop control, dependent on a disturbance variable. The feedback loop is closed. The command variable has a fixed value or does not vary, $w=0$ or $dw/dt=0$

variable acts at the controller input. As shown in Fig. 5.38, a disturbance variable z acts on the system. The following equation can be written:

$$[\{-x(s)F_R(s)F_{S1}(s)\}+z(s)]F_{S2}(s)=x(s)$$

or by rearrangement and using Eqn (5.44)

$$x(s)[1+F_0(s)]=z(s)F_{S2}(s).$$

From this we obtain the transfer function of the control loop with respect to a disturbance variable:

$$\begin{aligned} F_z(s)=\frac{x(s)}{z(s)}&=\frac{F_{S2}(s)}{1+F_0(s)}=\frac{1}{F_R(s)F_{S1}(s)+[F_{S2}(s)]^{-1}} \\ &=\frac{F_0(s)}{1+F_0(s)}\frac{1}{F_R(s)F_{S1}(s)} \\ &=F_w(s)\frac{1}{F_R(s)F_{S1}(s)}. \end{aligned} \tag{5.50}$$

The individual transfer functions can be written as follows:

$$F_0(s)=\frac{Z_0(s)}{N_0(s)} \qquad F_R(s)=\frac{Z_R(s)}{N_R(s)}$$

$$F_{S1}(s)=\frac{Z_{S1}(s)}{N_{S1}(s)} \qquad F_{S2}(s)=\frac{Z_{S2}(s)}{N_{S2}(s)}$$

Using these expressions, Eqns (5.50) can be written as follows:

$$F_z(s) = \frac{1}{\dfrac{Z_R(s)}{N_R(s)}\dfrac{Z_{S1}(s)}{N_{S1}(s)} + \dfrac{N_{S2}(s)}{Z_{S2}(s)}} = \frac{N_R(s)N_{S1}(s)Z_{S2}(S)}{Z_0(s)+N_0(s)}. \tag{5.51}$$

If the effect of the disturbance occurs at the input to the controlled system, then the function F_{S1} becomes equal to 1 and thus the transfer function becomes

$$F_z(s) = F_w(s)\frac{1}{F_R(s)} = \frac{Z_0(s)}{Z_0(s)+N_0(s)}\frac{N_R(s)}{Z_R(s)}. \tag{5.52}$$

We then see that a phase advance in the controller $[Z_R(s)]$ becomes a delay $[1/Z_R(s)]$ for the effect of smoothing out a disturbance.

5.6.4. Consideration of the influence of command and disturbance variables

If changes of the command variable w and disturbance variable z act simultaneously upon the control loop, it can be shown that

$$\{[(w(s)-x(s))F_R(s)F_{S1}(s)]+z(s)\}F_{S2}(s) = x(s)$$

or

$$w(s)F_0(s) - x(s)F_0(s) + z(s)F_{S2}(s) = x(s)$$

and thus

$$\begin{aligned} x(s) &= w(s)\frac{F_0(s)}{1+F_0(s)} + z(s)\frac{F_{S2}(s)}{1+F_0(s)} \\ &= w(s)F_w(s) + z(s)F_z(s) \\ &= F_w(s)\left[w(s) + \frac{z(s)}{F_R(s)F_{S1}(s)}\right] \\ &= F_z(s)[w(s)F_R(s)F_{S1}(s) + z(s)]. \end{aligned} \tag{5.53}$$

6 Optimum Adjustment of Control Systems

It is the task of the control engineer to design the control system in such a way that it produces a set variable y which will bring the controlled variable x to its required value as rapidly and as accurately as possible and as free from oscillation as possible, after a disturbance z or a change in the command variable, w (Fig. 6.1).

The ideal performance would therefore be attained if the control system could react so quickly that the controlled variable x remained unaffected by the occurrence of a disturbance z. Also, the controlled variable x would follow a change in the command variable w without delay and without any tendency to oscillation.

However, the delaying effect of the control equipment prevents this ideal performance. Therefore it is desirable to determine and apply the most favourable controller with the best possible transient response in order to minimize the delaying action of the controller. This process is known as optimization.

The investigation of a control loop with reproducible disturbances is not possible in practice. Therefore it is usual to examine the behaviour of a control loop from its response to a step change of command variable, even if one is primarily concerned with the behaviour during the occurrence of disturbances, for this information gives a good indication of the general behaviour of the system, and enables optimization to be obtained.

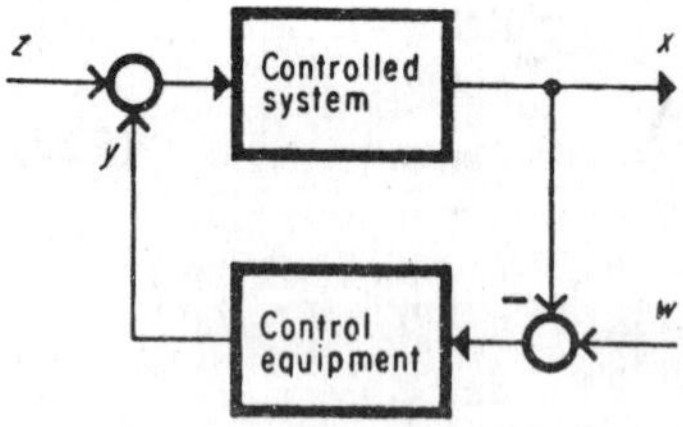

Fig. 6.1 Diagrammatic sketch of a control loop

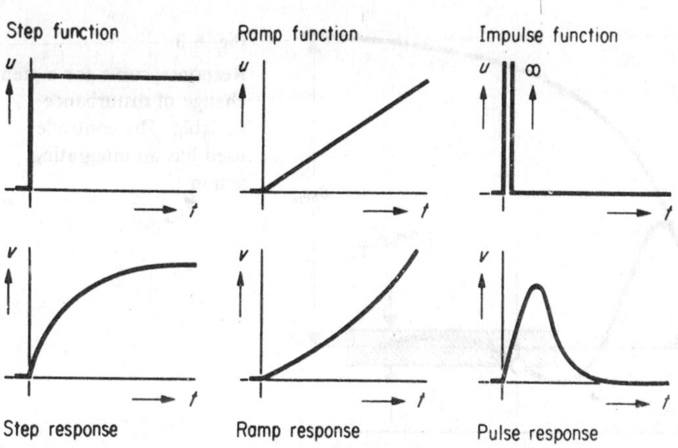

Fig. 6.2 Transient response for various standard test signals

6.1. Evaluation of the Step Response of the Controlled Variable

In order to determine whether a control system produces the desired action, one of the standard functions is applied to the control loop. These standard functions (Fig. 6.2) are the step function, the ramp function and the impulse or spike function.

The step function is preferable because it is easy to generate with a 'battery box' (Fig. 1.6). If it is required to compare the resultant step responses, resultant transient functions which are easily measurable must be chosen.

6.1.1. Response to a step disturbance variable

Even if disturbances are not step changes, consideration of a step response is comparable to consideration of a step response of command variable.

Consider a step change of disturbance variable and a control system without feedback. The deviation of the controlled variable from its original value is measured and the value of this deviation is designated as 100%.

If the step change is applied once again to the closed loop system, a step response similar to that of Fig. 6.3 results.

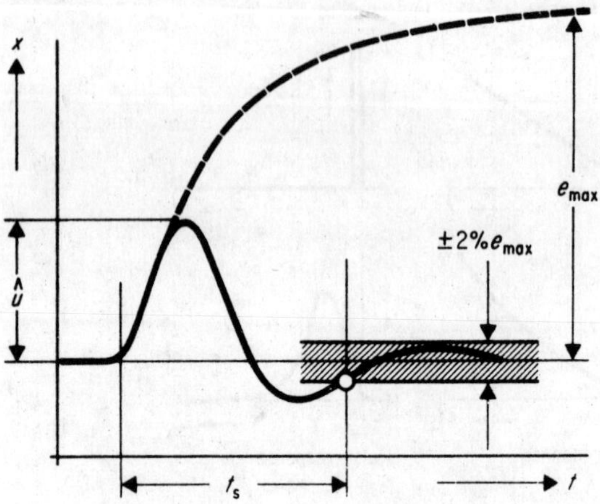

Fig. 6.3
Response curve for a step change of disturbance variable. The controller used has an integrating action

The maximum value of the first overshoot $\hat{u}$ is quoted as a percentage of the quantity e_{max}. Owing to the action of the controller, the controlled variable x follows approximately an exponential function back to its original value. The regulation or settling time t_s is defined as the time from the application of the step until a value within a certain tolerance of the final value, say ±2% of e_{max}, is obtained. The two values, overshoot $\hat{u}$ and settling time t_s give an indication of the system performance.

The performance shown in Fig. 6.3 only occurs if the controller has an integrating action. Later considerations will show that if the controller does not have an integrating action, a residual error signal e_{st} will occur (Fig. 6.4).

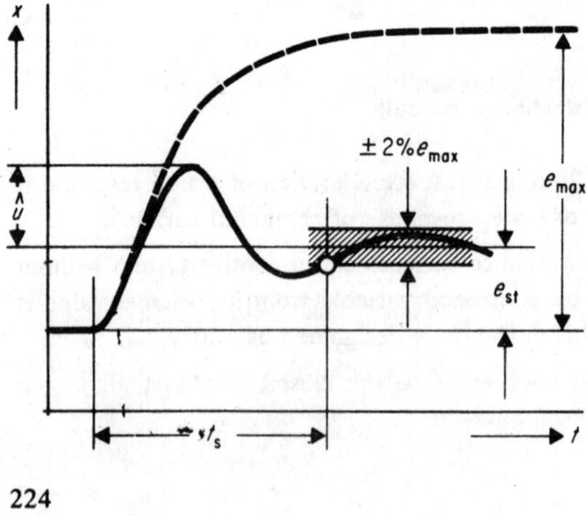

Fig. 6.4
Response to a step change of disturbance variable using a controller without integrating action. The offset error signal e_{st} is still present after the steady state is reached

6.1.2. Response to a step change of command variable

A step change of command variable produces a transient response similar to that shown in Fig. 6.5. The following variables are used to describe the performance.

Rise time t_r: this is the time taken to reach the required value before the first overshoot.

Settling time t_s: this is the time from the application of the step to a point beyond which the variation from the required value is no more than a given specified tolerance. It is necessary to define a finite tolerance since the decay is exponential. The tolerance is defined as a percentage of the command variable step and is usually ±2% of w.

The first overshoot $\hat{u}$ above the final steady state is also referred to as the maximum transient deviation of the required value during the transition from one state to another.

These definitions are not identical with those of DIN 19226 but they are simpler.

The rise time t_r, settling time t_s and overshoot peak $\hat{u}$ should be as small as possible. However, if a very small rise time is obtained by using a large proportional amplification, a large overshoot and a large settling time will be

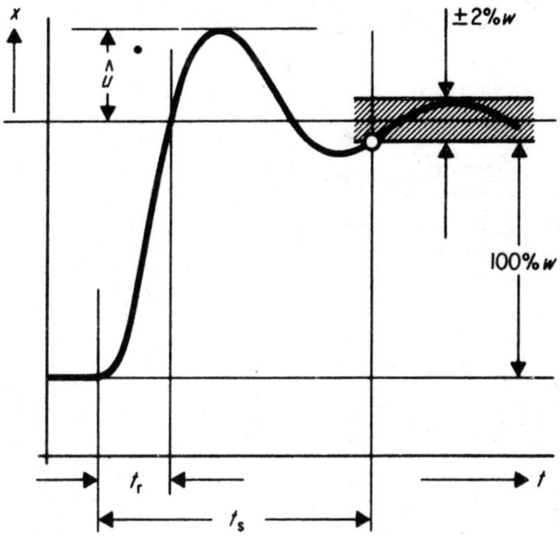

Fig. 6.5

Transient response to a step change of command variable, using a controller with integrating action

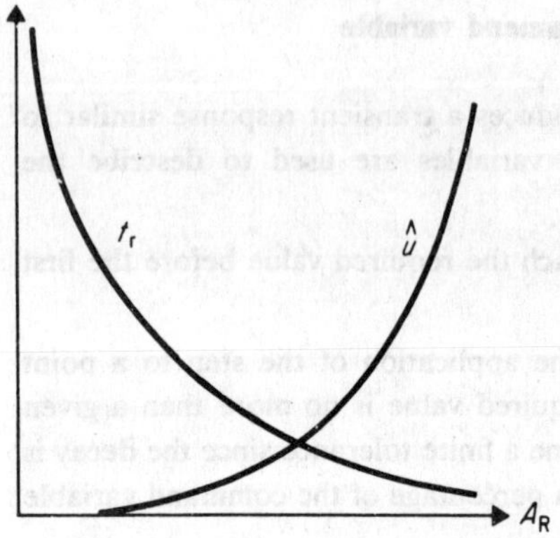

Fig. 6.6
Behaviour of rise time t_r and overshoot $\hat{u}$ with respect to controller amplification

produced because of the oscillatory nature of the transient response. A zero overshoot, i.e. an aperiodic response, gives a rise time and settling time which are identical and relatively large. Optimum behaviour of course lies somewhere between the two extreme cases described (Fig. 6.6).

As already mentioned, a regulator without integrating action cannot perform without a residual error signal e_{st}. In this case a step response as shown in Fig. 6.7 is obtained.

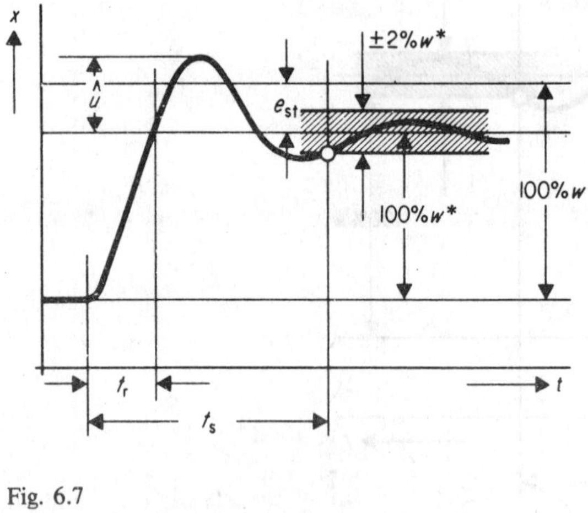

Fig. 6.7
Response to a step change of command variable using a controller without integrating action. The error signal is still present after the steady state is reached. The 2% tolerance limit here refers to 2% of w^* where $w^* = w - e_{st}$

6.2. Compensation

An important element of control systems is the first order delay with the transfer function

$$F(s) = A_S \frac{1}{1+sT_1}. \tag{6.1}$$

This delays the effect of the set variable on the controlled varible x more and more as the time constant T_1 increases. Therefore some compensation must be provided for the delay effect. For this purpose, a control element with a phase advance is required, containing a term $(1+sT)$ in the numerator of its transfer function.

If the time constant T of the phase advance is made equal to the time constant T_1, then the $(1+sT)$ terms in the numerator and denominator cancel out:

$$\frac{1+sT}{1+sT_1} = 1. \tag{6.2}$$

This is termed compensation of a first delay. This compensation is often essential in the optimization of the performance.

6.2.1. Compensation with a PD controller

Consider a PD controller with the transfer functon as follows (as in Eqn (4.71)):

$$F_R(s) = A_R(1+sT_v). \tag{6.3}$$

Let this be connected in series with a first order delay as shown in Fig. 6.8.

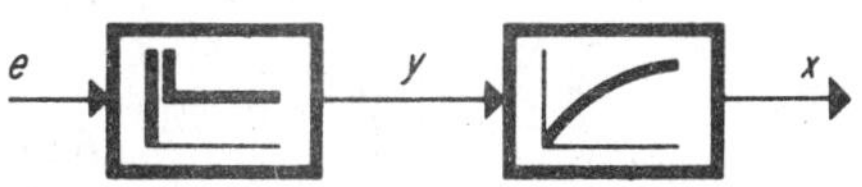

Fig. 6.8
Series connection of a first order delay and a PD controller

The overall transfer function is as follows

$$F_{ov}(s)=\frac{x(s)}{e(s)}=A_R(1+sT_v)A_S\frac{1}{1+sT_1}$$
$$=A_RA_S\frac{1+sT_v}{1+sT_1}. \tag{6.4}$$

By making the phase advance time constant T_v of the PD controller identical to the value of the delay time constant T_1, the overall transfer function becomes

$$F_{ov}(s)=A_RA_S. \tag{6.5}$$

The delay effect has disappeared and a proportional response is obtained However, if it is recalled that a PD controller can only be realized with a parasitic time constant t_d which produces a delay with a smaller time constant, it will be realized that even with exact equalization of the two time constants T_v and T_1, a delay effect is still obtained but with possibly negligible effect.

In many cases the time constant T_1 of the first order delay is dependent on the drive level and often it cannot be determined accurately. Therefore it is important to know the step response of the series circuit of PD controller and delay element with an erroneous determination of the phase advance time constant T_v. Therefore we consider the transfer function (6.4) and observe that at the instant of the step change, we have

$$F_{ov}(s)\,|_{s\to\infty}=A_RA_S\frac{T_v}{T_1}. \tag{6.6}$$

As for the steady state we have

$$F(s)\,|_{s\to 0}=A_RA_S. \tag{6.7}$$

Thus we see that at time $t=0$, with a step e_{step} at the input, a step is produced at the output which is greater or smaller than the amplitude of the steady-state value according to the ratio T_v/T_1

$$\underset{t\to 0}{x(t)}=e_{step}A_RA_S\frac{T_v}{T_1} \tag{6.8}$$

$$\underset{t\to\infty}{x(t)}=e_{step}A_RA_S. \tag{6.9}$$

The transition from one state to the other is defined by the equation

$$\underset{0<t<\infty}{f_{ov}(t)} = e_{step} A_R A_S \left[1 - e^{-t/T_1}\left(1 - \frac{T_v}{T_1}\right)\right]. \tag{6.10}$$

The exponential function is dependent on the delay time constant T_1 which is to be compensated. Figure 6.9 shows the possible step response, according to whether the phase advance time constant T_v is too small, correct or too large. By use of the 63% method the delay time constant T_1 can be defined as undercompensated (case a) or overcompensated (case c). It is also possible to find from the quotient of the initial step amplitude ($A_R A_S T_v/T_1$) divided by the amplitude in the steady state ($A_R A_S$), the percentage value of the mismatched phase advance time constant T_v with respect to the delay time constant T_1 which is to be compensated.

A PD controller is always accompanied by a parasitic delay. Therefore a slight overcompensation can be an advantage.

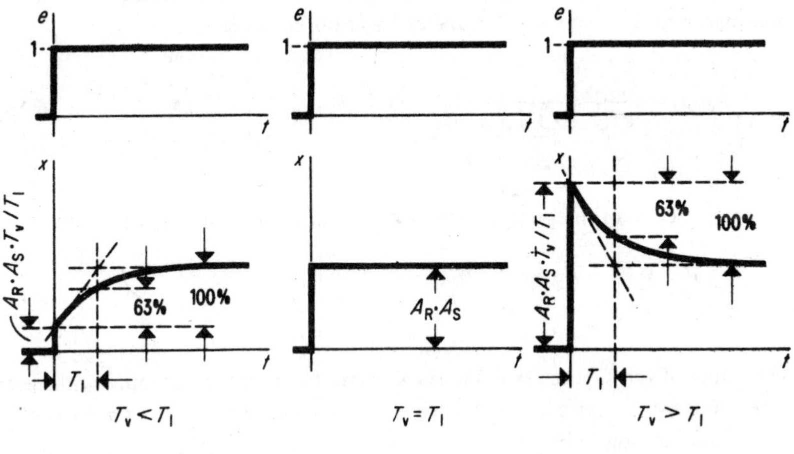

a) Phase advance time constant too small (under compensation)

b) Phase advance time constant (correct)

c) Phase advance time constant too large (over compensation)

Fig. 6.9
Compensation of a first order delay element with a PD controller: (input step of value 1)

6.2.2. Compensation with a PI controller

Consider a PI controller with a transfer function as given in Eqn (4.54):

$$F_R(s) = A_R \frac{1+sT_n}{sT_n}. \tag{6.11}$$

This also has a phase advance which is suitable for the compensation of a delay element (Fig. 6.10).

For the series connection of the two elements, the following overall transfer function is obtained:

$$F_{ov}(s) = \frac{x(s)}{e(s)} = A_R \frac{1+sT_n}{sT_n} A_S \frac{1}{1+sT_1}$$

$$= \frac{A_R A_S}{sT_n} \frac{1+sT_n}{1+sT_1}. \tag{6.12}$$

If the reset time constant T_n of the PI controller is made identical to the delay time constant T_1, the overall transfer function becomes

$$F_{ov}(s) = \frac{A_R A_S}{sT_n} = \frac{1}{s\dfrac{T_n}{A_R A_S}}. \tag{6.13}$$

This represents an integrating element with an integrating time constant

$$T_1^* = \frac{T_n}{A_R A_S}. \tag{6.14}$$

The effect of the first order delay is cancelled by the phase advance with reset time constant T_n (also termed a proportional phase advance) producing an overall integrating behaviour.

It is not always possible to make the reset time constant T_n exactly equal to the time constant T_1 of the first order delay. To estimate the error arising, the step response of the series circuit is investigated.

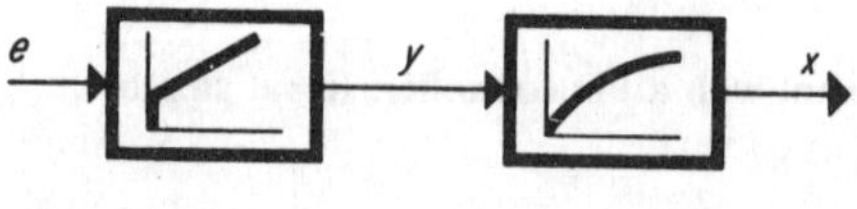

Fig. 6.10.
Series connection of a first order delay and a PI element

At the instant of application of the step input, the transfer function (6.12) gives

$$F_{ov}(s)\,|_{s\to\infty}=\frac{1}{s\dfrac{T_1}{A_R A_S}}\,.$$

This is an integrating behaviour whatever the value of the reset time constant.

In the steady-state condition ($s \to 0$) the step response appears to be infinite. The integrator is overdriven. However, this does not indicate the behaviour during the transient period.

Therefore, consider a time $t \geqslant 5T_1$ at which the phase advance $(1+sT_n)$ of the controller is almost negligible. Only the integration time constant T_1^* is significant. Thus we now have

$$\underset{t>5T_1}{F_{ov}(s)}=\frac{x(s)}{e(s)}=\frac{1}{s\dfrac{T_n}{A_R A_S}}$$

and in the time domain (Fig. 6.11)

$$\underset{t<5T_1}{x(t)}=e_{step}\frac{t}{\dfrac{T_n}{A_R A_S}}\,. \tag{6.15}$$

According to whether the reset time constant T_n is larger or smaller than T_1, the new integration time constant will be greater or smaller than the initial integration time constant. In between there is a transition from one slope to the other.

6.2.3. Compensation with a PID controller

If a control system contains two large delays, one of which with time constant T_1 is somewhat larger than the other with time constant T_2, a PID controller will be used for the compensation (Fig. 6.12). Its transfer function indicates two phase advances:

$$F_R(s)=A_R\frac{(1+sT_n)(1+sT_v)}{sT_n}\,. \tag{6.16}$$

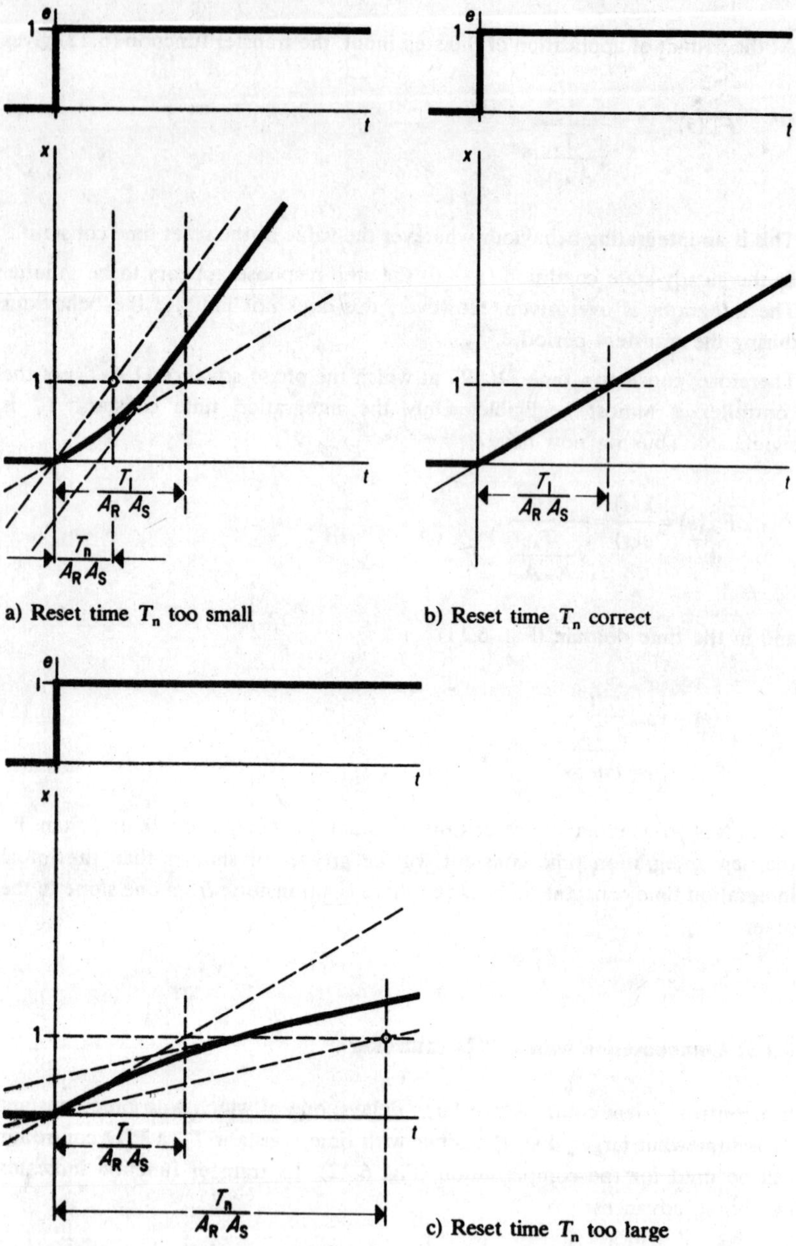

a) Reset time T_n too small

b) Reset time T_n correct

c) Reset time T_n too large

Fig. 6.11
Compensation of a first order delay with a PI controller (input step magnitude of 1)

Fig. 6.12 Series connection of a PID controller with two first order delays

A PID controller in series with two first order delays gives an overall transfer function as follows:

$$F_{ov}(s)=\frac{x(s)}{e(s)}=A_R\frac{(1+sT_n)(1+sT_v)}{sT_n}A_S\frac{1}{1+sT_1}\frac{1}{1+sT_2}$$
$$=\frac{A_RA_S}{sT_n}\frac{1+sT_n}{1+sT_1}\frac{1+sT_v}{1+sT_2}. \tag{6.17}$$

The PID controller is designed so that the reset time constant T_n is made identical to the larger delay time constant T_1 and the phase advance time constant T_v identical to the smaller delay time constant T_2, i.e. $T_n=T_1$ and $T_v=T_2$.

The transfer function (6.17) with full compensation thus becomes

$$F_{ov}(s)=\frac{A_RA_S}{sT_n}=\frac{1}{s\dfrac{T_n}{A_RA_S}} \tag{6.18}$$

This is the same result as Eqn (6.13). After each compensation by a controller with integrating action, a simple integral term remains.

If the initial slope is considered, a controller mismatch is evident:

$$F_{ov}(s)\,|_{s\to\infty}=\frac{1}{s\dfrac{T_1}{A_RA_S}\left(\dfrac{T_2}{T_v}\right)}$$

Further effects of mismatch are similar to those occurring with a PI controller.

6.3. Sum of Small Time Constants

Sometimes a series of first order delays occurs in a system. Only one, or at most two, large delays or an integrating action can be compensated with an integrating controller (PI or PID). This is because these controllers have only one or two phase advance terms. For a simple calculation, all residual smaller delays are treated on the assumption that only a single delay is present. The assumptions under which this is acceptable without appreciable errors will now be considered.

If an integrating controller is connected in series with a number of first order delays (Fig. 6.13), a transfer function of the following form is obtained:

$$F_{ov}(s) = \frac{x(s)}{e(s)} = \frac{1}{sT_I}\,\frac{1}{1+st_1}\,\frac{1}{1+st_2}\,\frac{1}{1+st_3}\cdots \tag{6.19}$$

This can also be written as follows:

$$F_{ov}(s) = \frac{1}{sT_I[1+s(t_1+t_2+t_3+\cdots)+s^2(t_1t_2+t_1t_3+\cdots)+s^3(t_1t_2t_3+\cdots)+\cdots]}\,. \tag{6.20}$$

If the time constants t_1, t_2, t_3 etc. are small with respect to the integration time constant T_I, the higher order products of the small time constants do not materially contribute to the overall behaviour. Therefore it is possible to neglect terms of a higher order of s than s^1 in the denominator of Eqn (6.20) without causing appreciable error. The transfer function then becomes

$$F^*_{ov}(s) = \frac{1}{sT_I[1+s(t_1+t_2+t_3+\cdots)]}\,. \tag{6.21}$$

Thus the series connection of a number of first order delays can be replaced by an equivalent delay with a time constant of

$$t_1+t_2+t_3+\cdots.$$

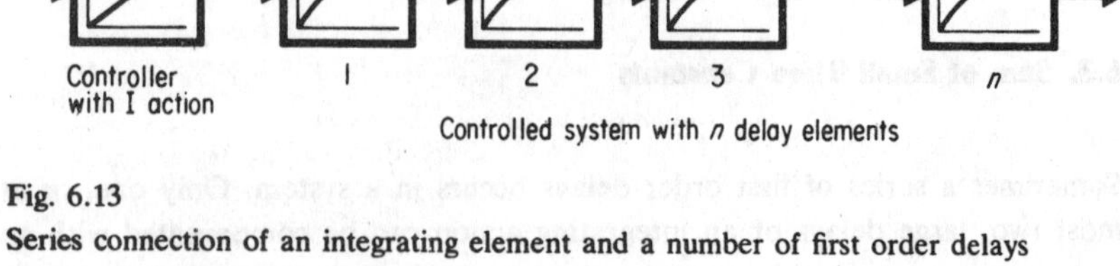

Fig. 6.13
Series connection of an integrating element and a number of first order delays

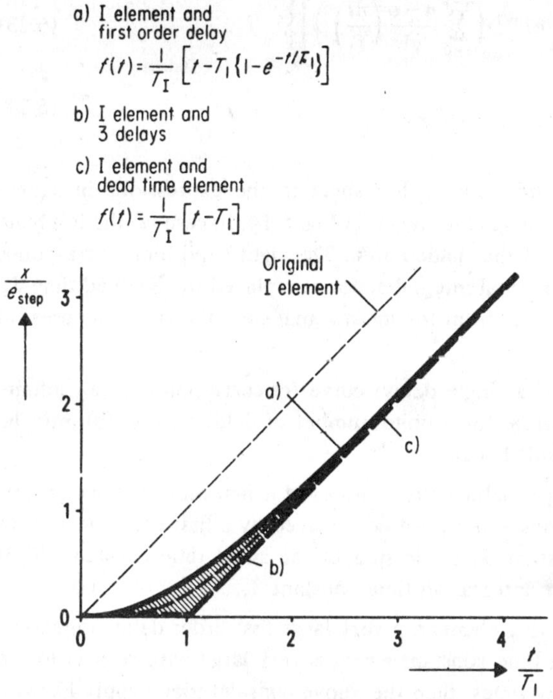

Fig. 6.14
Transient response for the series connection of an integrating element and different numbers of delay elements with $T_1=\sum t_v=T_t$

The transient behaviour confirms the validity of the above assumption (Fig. 6.14). Let an integrating element be connected in series with:

a) a single first order delay with time constant T_1,

b) a number n of first order delay elements with time constants

$$t_1+t_2+t_3+\cdots=T_1,$$

c) a dead time element with a dead time $T_t=T_1$.

The transient functions for the above are:

$$\text{a)}\quad f(t)=\frac{1}{T_I}\{t-T_1[1-e^{-t/T_1}]\}; \tag{6.22}$$

b) $f(t)=\frac{1}{T_I}\left\{t-T_I\left[n-\frac{1}{n}e^{-nt/T_I}\left(\sum_{v=0}^{n-1}\frac{n-v}{v!}\left(\frac{nt}{T_I}\right)^v\right)\right]\right\}$; (6.23)

c) $f(t)=\frac{1}{T_I}[t-T_I]$. (6.24)

These step responses differ only with respect to the expressions in square brackets. The associated curves are shown in Fig. 6.14. In case (a) the left hand curve becomes the limit of the shaded area. The right hand limit corresponds to case (c) in which the original integral action is replaced by the dead time T_t. After a sufficiently long time from the input signal step, the two responses (a) and (c) are the same.

Curve (a) corresponds to a single delay; curve (c) corresponds to an infinite number of delays. Therefore for a finite number of delays, curve (b) must lie intermediately in the shaded region.

Accordingly, without appreciable error, a series of n first order delay elements with a total of n time constants t_v, can be replaced by a first order delay with an equivalent time constant T_e if the sum of the small time constants T_e is small with respect to the integration time constant T_I.

If, instead of the integrating element, a very large first order delay appears in the series circuit, with a time constant which is very large with respect to the sum of the residual delay times, then the above considerations apply likewise to the sum of the small time constants. A dead time which is small compared with the integration time or with a very large delay time is added to the total of small time constants.

6.4. Simple Control Loop

As an example of a very simple control system, let us consider a first order delay with a delay time constant T_1 and amplification of 1, preceded by a proportional element with amplification A_S. The transfer function is

$$F_S(s)=\frac{x(s)}{y(s)}=A_S\frac{1}{1+sT_1}. \quad (6.25)$$

Let a disturbance occur between the two elements. The system is to be controlled (a) by a proportional controller and (b) by an integrating controller. The resultant performance will be investigated.

6.4.1. Control with a proportional controller

The transfer function of the open loop of Fig. 6.15 with a proportional controller is

$$F_0(s) = A_R A_S \frac{1}{1+sT_1}. \tag{6.26}$$

The transfer function of the closed loop is

$$F_w(s) = \frac{x(s)}{w(s)} = \frac{1}{1+\dfrac{1}{A_R A_S}+s\dfrac{T_1}{A_R A_S}}. \tag{6.27}$$

For the steady-state condition ($t \to \infty$), the operator s becomes zero and then

$$\left.\frac{e}{w}\right|_{s=0} = \frac{1}{1+A_R A_S}. \tag{6.28}$$

An offset error signal results which becomes smaller as the term $A_R A_S$ becomes larger.

The response of the loop with an introduction of a change in the disturbance variable, $z(s)$ is defined by

$$F_z(s) = \frac{x(s)}{z(s)} = \frac{1}{1+A_R A_S+sT_1}. \tag{6.29}$$

The steady state is described by

$$\left.\frac{x}{z}\right|_{s=0} = \frac{1}{1+A_R A_S}. \tag{6.30}$$

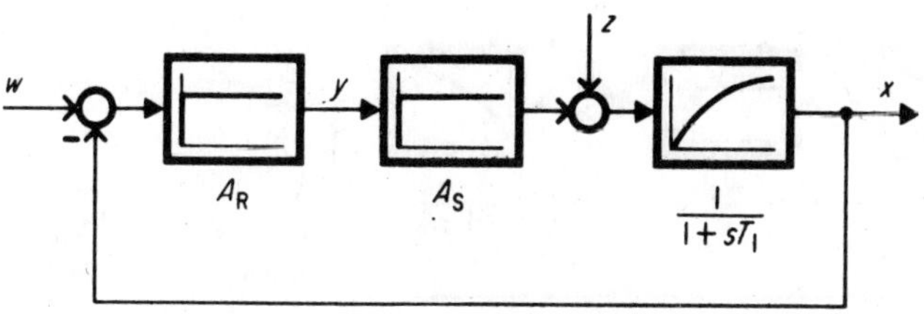

Fig. 6.15 Control with a proportional controller

Thus the loop controlled by a proportional controller also produces an offset error when the disturbance variable z is not equal to zero. Therefore it is only useful if the term $A_R A_S$, i.e. the loop amplification A_0, is sufficiently large.

The proportional speed controller represents a special case. At its output is produced the demand for the necessary acceleration of the drive. If the error signal here is zero, the drive runs with the prescribed speed. It does not need to be accelerated or decelerated.

6.4.2. Control with an integrating controller

The transfer function for the open loop of Fig. 6.16 with an integrating controller is

$$F_0(s) = \frac{1}{sT_I} A_S \frac{1}{1+sT_1}. \tag{6.31}$$

The transfer function of the closed loop, dependent on the command variable, is

$$F_w(s) = \frac{x(s)}{w(s)} = \frac{1}{1+s\dfrac{T_I}{A_S}+s^2\dfrac{T_I}{A_S}T_1}. \tag{6.32}$$

In the steady state ($t \to \infty$) the error signal is

$$\left.\frac{e}{w}\right|_{s=0} = 0. \tag{6.33}$$

Thus the integrating controller performs in such a way that the error between the command variable and the controlled variable is zero.

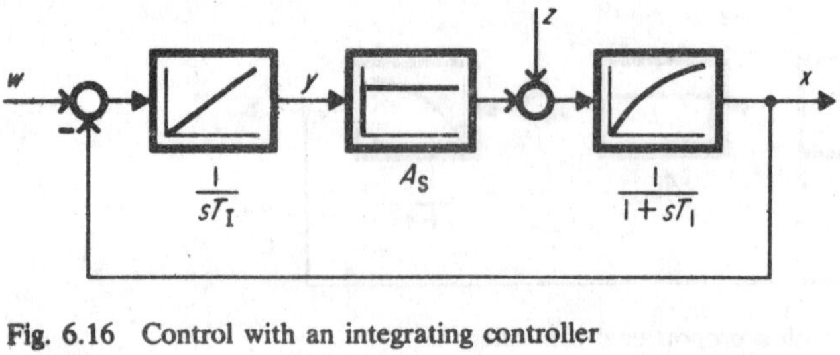

Fig. 6.16 Control with an integrating controller

The effect of a disturbance z is given by

$$F_z(s)=\frac{x(s)}{z(s)}=\frac{s\dfrac{T_I}{A_S}}{1+s\dfrac{T_I}{A_S}+s^2\dfrac{T_I}{A_S}T_1}. \tag{6.34}$$

For the steady state

$$\left.\frac{x}{z}\right|_{s=0}=0. \tag{6.35}$$

The integrating controller in the steady state always brings the controlled variable x to the value prescribed by the command variable w with no offset error.

Therefore, in most cases a controller with an integrating action should be used in order to achieve control as precisely as possible.

6.5. General Considerations for Optimization

For the optimization of a control loop (Fig. 6.17), we begin by considering the transfer function of the closed loop. This function, dependent on the command variable, is

$$\begin{aligned}F_w(s)&=\frac{x(s)}{w(s)}=\frac{F_0(s)}{1+F_0(s)}=\frac{Z_0(s)}{Z_0(s)+N_0(s)}\\&=\frac{Z_R(s)Z_{S1}(s)Z_{S2}(s)}{Z_R(s)Z_{S1}(s)Z_{S2}(s)+N_R(s)N_{S1}(s)N_{S2}(s)}.\end{aligned} \tag{6.36}$$

This cannot be equal to 1 while the input function is ongoing. This applies whatever the choice of controller parameters. The controller must have only one integrating component. To consider this further, it is useful to consider the associated frequency characteristic $F_w(j\omega)$ in place of the transfer function $F_w(s)$.

The dynamic performance of a control system is good if the controlled variable very rapidly reaches the value required by the command variable. In terms of the frequency characteristic, this means a frequency range as wide as possible

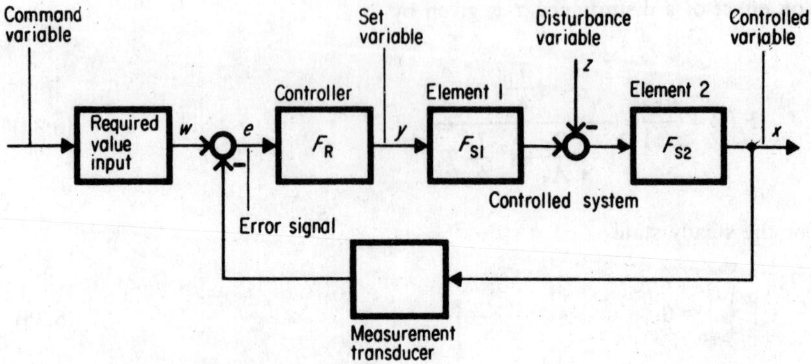

Fig. 6.17 Control loop for optimization

over which the modulus lies very near to 1 i.e. a wide bandwidth. At the instant of the input step, the controlled variable cannot correspond to the command variable, but very rapidly after, when lower frequencies come into effect, the modulus of the frequency characteristic comes very close to 1. Then the error between the command variable and the controlled variable rapidly becomes zero.

Optimization aims at bringing the modulus of the frequency characteristic as close as possible to the value 1 over a wide frequency range. This is termed modulus hugging or frequency response magnitude shaping. Further considerations for optimization are considered from the point of view of modulus hugging. The results are always control loops which give stable operation. Investigations into the stability of the control loops which have been set up according to modulus hugging are therefore not necessary.

Modulus hugging is characterized (Fig. 6.18) by the fact that the curve for the modulus plotting against frequency takes the value very close to 1 over a wide

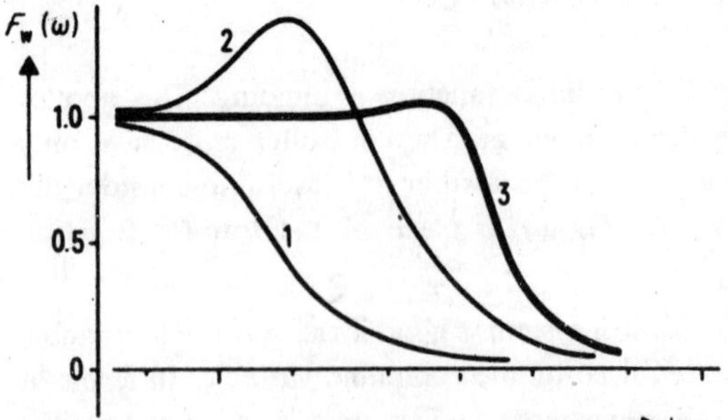

Fig. 6.18

Characteristic for modulus against frequency for a controller with integrating action

1) Rapid fall off
2) Overshoot
3) Modulus hugging

frequency range from zero upwards. At very high frequencies the curve may fall significantly.

The task is to find a controller which behaves in such a way that the modulus of Eqn (6.36) is very close to 1 over a wide frequency range.

The transfer function for the closed control loop relative to the command variable shows two characteristics. In terms of frequency response, they are

$$F_w(j\omega)=\frac{x(j\omega)}{w(j\omega)}=\frac{b_0}{a_0+j\omega a_1+(j\omega)^2a_2}, \tag{6.37}$$

$$F_w(j\omega)=\frac{x(j\omega)}{w(j\omega)}=\frac{b_0+j\omega b_1}{a_0+j\omega a_1+(j\omega)^2a_2+(j\omega)^3a_3}. \tag{6.38}$$

The two equations follows from the transfer functions for the open loop. Thus we have:

In Eqn (6.37)

$$b_0=a_0$$

In Eqn (6.38)

$$b_0=a_0$$

$$b_1=a_1.$$

Real and imaginary parts can be obtained from Eqn (6.37) and then the modulus is obtained as follows

$$|F_w(\omega)|=\sqrt{\frac{a_0^2}{a_0^2+\omega^2(a_1^2-2a_0a_2)+\omega^4a_2^2}} \tag{6.39}$$

If this modulus is to approach 1 at low frequency, the term in parentheses must become zero:

$$a_1^2-2a_0a_2=0.$$

This gives the first optimization equation for the design of the controller:

$$a_1^2=2a_0a_2. \tag{6.40}$$

Similarly, the modulus for Eqn (6.38) is obtained as

$$|F_w(\omega)| = \sqrt{\frac{a_0^2+\omega^2 a_1^2}{a_0^2+\omega^2(a_1^2-2a_0a_2)+\omega^4(a_2^2-2a_1a_3)+\omega^6 a_3^2}}. \tag{6.41}$$

For modulus hugging, the expressions in parentheses in the denominator must be zero. Thus the following two equations are obtained:

$$\begin{aligned} a_1^2 &= 2a_0a_2 \\ a_2^2 &= 2a_1a_3. \end{aligned} \tag{6.42}$$

If Eqns (6.40) and (6.42) are satisfied, then Eqn (6.37) becomes

$$|F_w(\omega)|_{opt} = \sqrt{\frac{1}{1+\omega^4(a_2/a_0)^2}} \tag{6.43}$$

and Eqn (6.38) becomes

$$|F_w(\omega)|_{opt} = \sqrt{\frac{1+\omega^2(a_1/a_0)^2}{1+\omega^6(a_3/a_0)^2}}. \tag{6.44}$$

These two equations for the modulus of the optimized system give a value of 1 only if the frequency ω is equal to zero. However, for frequencies greater than zero, the modulus remains close to 1 since these higher frequencies appear in the denominators of both expressions with the fourth and sixth powers, respectively. This modulus hugging behaviour is made clear in Fig. 6.19 by curve (a) for Eqn (6.43) and by curve (b) for Eqn (6.44). Thus curve (b) always shows an overshoot.

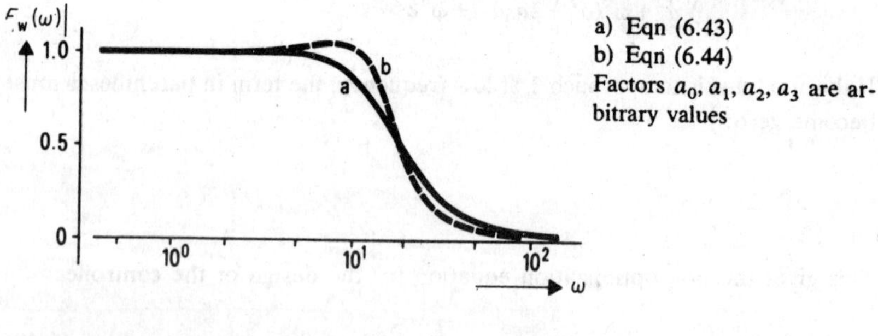

Fig. 6.19 Frequency characteristic (modulus) for conditions of optimization

6.6. Method of Optimization by Modulus Hugging

Using Eqns (6.40) and (6.42) and the discussion of compensation and the creation of an equivalent delay from Sections 6.2 and 6.3, we determine the controller parameters in order to achieve optimum working of the control system.

Firstly, assume that there is no integrating effect in the control system. In this case, use can be made of the optimization formula for the optimum modulus. The designation optimum modulus is obtained from the hugging of the modulus to the value 1 for as large a frequency range as possible.

6.6.1. System with many small first order delays

If the controlled system consists of numerous small delays connected in series, an integrating controller is used (Fig. 6.20). The many small delays are replaced as in Section 6.3 by one equivalent delay with an equivalent time constant T_e. The transfer function of the open loop is then

$$F_0(s) = \frac{1}{sT_I}\,\frac{A_S}{1+sT_e}\,. \tag{6.45}$$

The transfer function of the closed loop, dependent on the command variable, is

$$F_w(s) = \frac{x(s)}{w(s)} = \frac{A_S}{A_S + sT_I + s^2 T_I T_e}\,. \tag{6.46}$$

This transfer function has the form of Eqn (6.37). From the optimization Eqn (6.40), we have

$$a_1^2 = 2a_0a_2$$

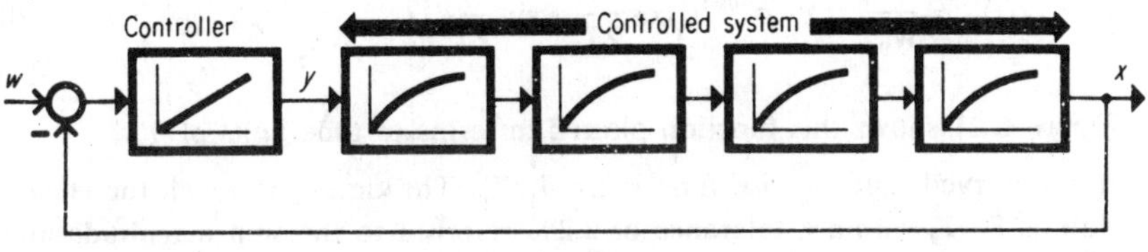

Fig. 6.20 Controlled system with many first order delays

and with

$$a_0 = A_S, \qquad a_1 = T_I, \qquad a_2 = T_I T_e,$$

the optimization equation for the integrating controller is obtained as

$$T_I^2 = 2A_S T_I T_e.$$

Hence the optimization formula for the integration time constant is

$$T_I = 2A_S T_e. \tag{6.47}$$

If this value is inserted in Eqn (6.46), the transfer function for the optimized loop is obtained:

$$F_w(s)_{opt} = \frac{x(s)}{w(s)} = \frac{1}{1 + s2T_e + s^2 2T_e^2}. \tag{6.48}$$

The transfer function of the optimized loop is dependent only on the sum of the small time constants. Since the polynomial in the denominator corresponds to the homogeneous differential equation describing the transient variations, the following equation can be written:

$$w(t) = x(t) + 2T_e \frac{dx(t)}{dt} + 2T_e^2 \frac{d_2x(t)}{dt^2}. \tag{6.49}$$

By comparison of coefficients with Eqn (2.32), the time constant T and the damping factor ζ are obtained for this second order delay:

$$T = T_e\sqrt{2}, \qquad \zeta = 1/\sqrt{2}.$$

Since ζ is less than 1, the step response Eqn (2.39) becomes effective for the application of a step command variable w_{step} to the optimized control loop

$$f(t)_{opt} = \frac{x(t)}{w_{step}} = 1 - e^{-t/2T_e}\left(\cos\frac{t}{2T_e} + \sin\frac{t}{2T_e}\right). \tag{6.50}$$

Figure 6.21 shows this function plotted in terms of time units of T_e.

It is observed that the rise time is $t_r = 4.7T_e$. The time t_s to reach the steady state is $8.4T_e$ within a tolerance of ±2% referred to the step magnitude and the overshoot $\hat{u}$ is 4.3% referred to the step magnitude.

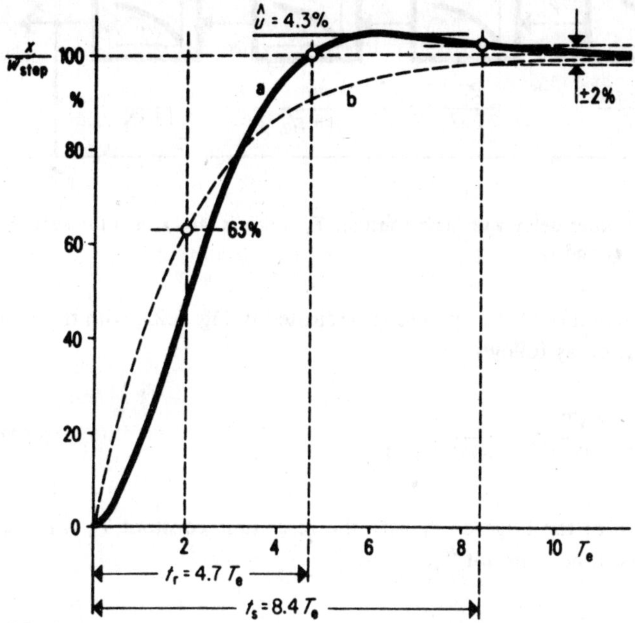

Fig. 6.21

a) **Step response of modulus optimized control loop**

b) **Equivalent function for modulus optimized control loop (first order delay with time constant $2T_e$)**

Equations (6.48) and (6.50) are typical for the optimum modulus. They are typical of an optimized control loop. Also the typical step response is as shown in Fig. 6.21. Only the time scale with units of T_e is changed with the magnitude of the equivalent time constant.

6.6.2. System with large and small first order delays

If one delay element among a number in a control system shows a greater time constant than the sum of the remainder, then this large time constant will have to be compensated; otherwise it would have to be added to the sum of the small time constants and would make the control response slow.

Since the requirement is to work with practically no steady state offset error, the controller must have an integrating characteristic. To achieve compensation of the large delay by means of the integrating controller, an additional proportional response is necessary. Therefore a PI controller is necessary.

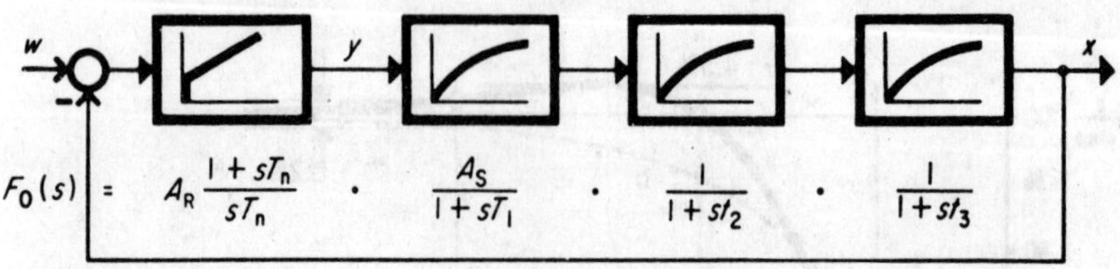

Fig. 6.22
System with a first order delay with time constant T_1 which is larger than the sum of the time constants t_2 and t_3

Let the transfer function of the open loop, indicated in Fig. 6.22, with the sum time constant T_e, be as follows:

$$F_0(s) = A_R \frac{1+sT_n}{sT_n} A_S \frac{1}{1+sT_1} \frac{1}{1+sT_e}. \tag{6.51}$$

For compensation of the large delay with the reset time constant T_n is made equal to the large time constant T_1:

$$T_n = T_1. \tag{6.52}$$

This is the first optimization formula for the PI controller. The application of the optimum value of modulus is also termed the compensation method. After compensation, the transfer function of the open loop is

$$F_0^*(s) = \frac{A_R A_S}{sT_1(1+sT_e)}. \tag{6.53}$$

Consequently, the transfer function for the closed loop system is

$$F_w(s) = \frac{x(s)}{w(s)} = \frac{A_R A_S}{A_R A_S + sT_1 + s^2 T_1 T_e}. \tag{6.54}$$

This equation is similar to Eqn (6.37). Therefore Eqn (6.40) again applies for optimization.

With

$$a_0 = A_R A_S, \quad a_1 = T_1, \quad \text{and} \quad a_2 = T_1 T_e$$

the second optimization formula is obtained for the PI controller:

$$A_R = \frac{T_1}{2A_S T_e}. \tag{6.55}$$

From this equation it can be observed that, in applying the optimum value of modulus, the loop amplification or all-round amplification is dependent on the ratio of the time constants of the system:

$$A_R A_S = A_0 = \frac{T_1}{2T_e}. \tag{6.56}$$

With optimization of the controller parameters, the transfer function becomes

$$F_w(s)_{opt} = \frac{x(s)}{w(s)} = \frac{1}{1 + s2T_e + s^2 2T_e^2}.$$

Consequently, this control loop has the transient response of Fig. 6.21.

If not one but two large delays appear in the series of first order delays which comprise the system, the controller should contain two phase advances for the compensation. A PID controller is advantageous in this case. Consider Fig. (6.23).

The equivalent time constant T_e is the sum of all time constants which are smaller than T_1 and T_2, the time constant T_1 being itself larger than the time constant T_2.

The denominator terms $(1+sT_1)$ and $(1+sT_2)$ which mathematically represent the two large delays, can be compensated by two phase advances $(1+sT_n)$ and $(1+sT_v)$ in the numerator of the expression for the controller. Then, using the

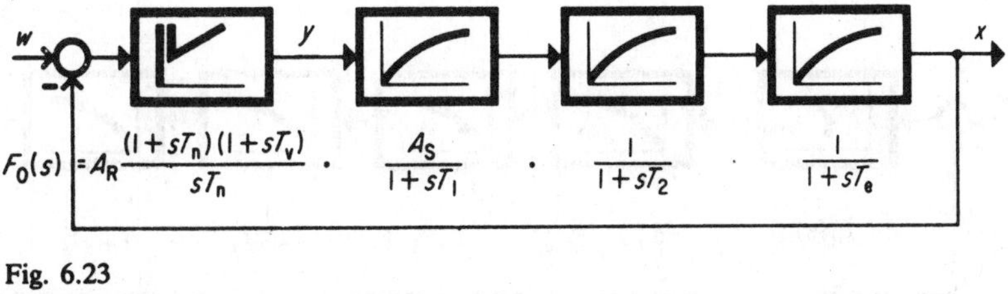

Fig. 6.23
System containing two delay elements with time constants T_1 and T_2 which are greater than the equivalent time constant T

first two formulae for optimization,

$$T_n = T_1, \tag{6.57}$$

$$T_v = T_2. \tag{6.58}$$

From the original transfer function of the open loop (Fig. 6.23), we now obtain

$$F_0^*(s) = \frac{A_R A_S}{sT_1(1+sT_e)}.$$

This is the same function as Eqn (6.53). Therefore for the third parameter of the PID controller, the optimization formula from Eqn (6.55) is used

$$A_R = \frac{T_1}{2A_S T_e}.$$

Then the transfer function is

$$F_w(s)_{opt} = \frac{x(s)}{w(s)} = \frac{1}{1+s2T_e+s^2 2T_e^2}.$$

6.6.3. Comparison of the effect of I, PI and PID controllers

Consider a system with four delay elements (Fig. 6.24) having time constants $T_1 = 400$ ms, $T_2 = 80$ ms, $T_3 = 15$ ms and $T_4 = 5$ ms. The control of this system will be considered in a number of ways.

Case 1. Firstly a controller with an integrating action will be considered. This means that all delays are regarded as small. The integrating controller can only

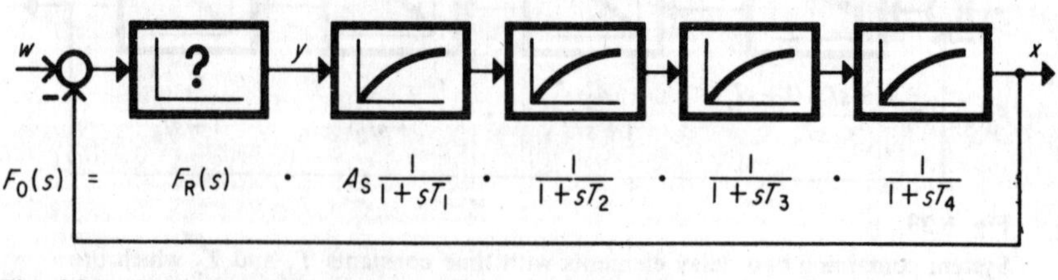

Fig. 6.24 Control system with four different delay elements

be adjusted in respect of its integration time constant:

$$T_I = 2A_S T_a.$$

The equivalent time constant is

$$T_a = T_1 + T_2 + T_3 + T_4 = 500 \text{ ms}.$$

Thus the rise time is

$$t_r - 4.7T_a = 2350 \text{ ms}.$$

Case 2. To improve the behaviour, the largest of the delays is compensated. A PI controller is used having a reset time of T_n equal to the delay time constant T_1.

The sum of the small time constants is now

$$T_b = T_2 + T_3 + T_4 = 100 \text{ ms}.$$

The proportional amplification of the controller is given by

$$A_R = \frac{T_1}{2A_S T_b}.$$

The rise time t_r is then only one fifth of that in the first example:

$$t_r = 4.7T_b = 470 \text{ ms}.$$

Case 3. Even this rise time can be considerably improved if it is possible to eliminate another of the small time constants by compensation with a differentiating phase advance. This is done by the second phase advance of a PID controller, whose reset time constant T_n is made equal to the largest time constant and whose phase advance time constant T_v is made equal to the second largest time constant:

$$T_n = T_1, \qquad T_v = T_2.$$

The equivalent time constant is now

$$T_c = T_3 + T_4 = 20 \text{ ms}.$$

Table 6.1: Summary of three examples of control behaviour

Controller	Controller time constant (ms)	Sum of small time constants T_e (ms)	Proportional amplification A_R	Rise time $4.7T_e$ (ms)
I	$T_1 = 1000A_S$	$T_1+T_2+T_3+T_4=500$	—	2350
PI	$T_n=400$	$T_2+T_3+T_4=100$	$2/A_S$	470
PID	$T_n=400$ $T_v=80$	$T_3+T_4=20$	$10/A_S$	94

The proportional amplification is now

$$A_R = \frac{T_1}{2A_S T_c}.$$

The amplification A_R is thus five times as great as in the preceding example and the rise time is one fifth

$$t_r = 4.7T_c = 94 \text{ ms}.$$

It is not feasible to compensate the third time constant to make the control action even faster. It would necessitate a controller with an integrating behaviour and two differentiating actions. Even with very low harmonic content in the controlled variable, the double differentiation would cause so much disturbance in the loop that it would be almost impossible to achieve stable control.

The results of these three examples are summarized in Table 6.1.

6.6.4. Controlled system with one very large and several small first order delays

Consider a system which contains a delay whose time constant is more than, say, twenty times the sum of the small time constants. We shall consider whether a proportional controller can be used for this system. For a super-imposed control loop, this would have the advantage that the subordinate loop in question can be set up in accordance with the optimum modulus and thus its equivalent time constant (see Fig. 6.21) may be fixed at $2T_e$. Otherwise, a PI controller would have to be used and set up in accordance with the symmetry

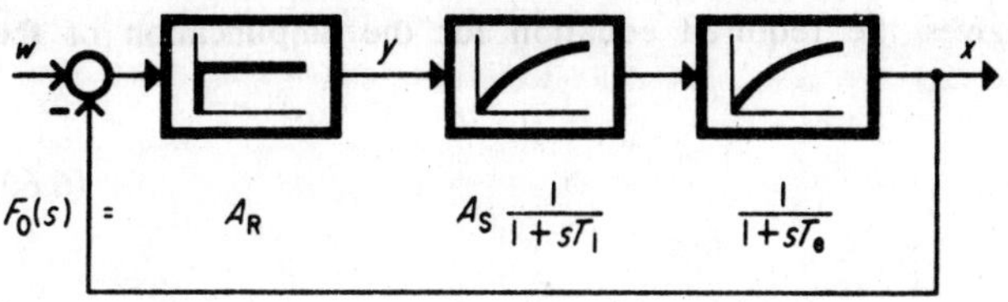

Fig. 6.25
System with one very large first order delay with time constant $T_1 \gg T_e$

optimum (see Eqn (6.74)) so that the equivalent time constant here would appear in the superimposed control loop as $4T_e$ and therefore cause the latter to become slower in action.

Figure 6.25 shows such a control loop with a proportional controller. The open circuit transfer function cannot be compensated. Therefore, the closed loop transfer function is obtained from the overall transfer function of the open loop

$$F_w(s) = \frac{x(s)}{w(s)} = \frac{A_R A_S}{A_R A_S + 1 + s(T_1 + T_e) + s^2 T_1 T_e}. \tag{6.59}$$

This expression is similar to Eqn (6.37). For modulus hugging, the optimization Eqn (6.40) applies, thus

$$a_0 = A_R A_S + 1, \qquad a_1 = T_1 + T_e, \qquad a_2 = T_1 T_e.$$

From $a_1^2 = 2a_0 a_2$, we get

$$(T_1 + T_e)^2 = 2(A_R A_S + 1) T_1 T_e$$

i.e.

$$T_1^2 + T_e^2 + 2T_1 T_e = 2T_1 T_e + 2A_R A_S T_1 T_e$$

$$T_1^2 + T_e^2 = 2A_R A_S T_1 T_e.$$

If T_1 is twenty times as large as T_e, then T_e^2 is sufficiently small to be neglected with respect to T_1^2:

$$T_1^2 = 2A_R A_S T_1 T_e.$$

Once again this gives the required equation for the amplification of the controller:

$$A_R = \frac{T_1}{2A_S T_e}. \tag{6.60}$$

The equation for the proportional amplification of a proportional controller is thus the same as for a PI or a PID controller.

If the calculated value is inserted in Eqn (6.59), a transfer function F_w is obtained which is similar to Eqn (6.48)

$$F_w(s)_{opt} = \frac{x(s)}{w(s)}$$

$$= \left(1 - \frac{2T_e}{T_1 + 2T_e}\right) \frac{1}{1 + s2T_e\left(1 - \frac{T_e}{T_1 + 2T_e}\right) + s^2 2T_e^2\left(1 - \frac{T_e}{T_1 + 2T_e}\right)} \tag{6.61}$$

In this equation, all expressions in parentheses are only a little less than 1:

$$\frac{T_e}{T_1 + 2T_e} \ll 1 \quad \text{since} \quad T_1 \gg T_e.$$

From Eqn (6.61), it can be seen that in the steady state, an offset error occurs, of magnitude

$$-\frac{2T_e}{T_1 + 2T_e}$$

in relation to the value $x/w = 1$.

In Section 6.1, the offset error signal e_{st} has already been pointed out (Fig. 6.7). The controlled variables does not reach the value prescribed by the command variable. If this is known and the percentage error is known, it is possible to eliminate this error by a suitable change of the command value.

The transient curve showing the manner in which the controlled variable reaches the new value is practically the same as in the control loop with an integrating controller.

The step response shown in Fig. 6.21 also applies up to the steady state for a control loop with a proportional controller. Therefore we see that the control loop is to be adjusted in accordance with the optimum modulus requirement.

Since the proportional controller always has a steady-state error, it is necessary to establish the magnitude of this error, for this will determine whether the P controller can be used at all. According to Eqn (5.49), the error relative to the command variable is

$$e(s) = w(s)\frac{1+s(T_1+T_e)+s^2T_1T_e}{A_RA_S+1+s(T_1+T_e)+s^2T_1T_e}. \tag{6.62}$$

In the steady state, the operator s becomes zero. Thus for $t \to \infty$

$$e(s)|_{s=0} = \frac{1}{1+A_RA_S}\,w(s)|_{s=0}. \tag{6.63}$$

This is the same result as Eqn (6.28). It gives the steady-state error signal:

$$e_{st}|_{t\to\infty} = \frac{2T_e}{T_1+2T_e}\,w|_{t\to\infty} \simeq 2\frac{T_e}{T_1}\,w|_{t\to\infty}. \tag{6.64}$$

If the proportional controller is adjusted in accordance with the optimum modulus, then the control error relative to the command variable is only dependent on the time constant ratio of the system.

With the assumption that a significant disturbance variable z affects the controlled system, the control error relative to the disturbance variable is defined according to Eqn (5.52)

$$\Delta x(s) = z(s)\frac{A_S}{A_RA_S+1+s(T_1+T_e)+s^2T_1T_e}. \tag{6.65}$$

Putting the operator s equal to zero for the steady state gives

$$\Delta x(s)|_{s=0} = \frac{A_S}{1+A_RA_S}\,z(s)|_{s=0}. \tag{6.66}$$

A similar result is indicated by Eqn (6.30).

A proportional controller always produces a steady-state error in the controlled variable:

$$\Delta x_{st}|_{t\to\infty} = A_S\frac{2T_e}{T_1+2T_e}\,z|_{t\to\infty} \simeq 2A_S\frac{T_e}{T_1}\,z|_{t\to\infty}. \tag{6.67}$$

The offset error caused by a disturbance variable is larger by a factor A_S (the amplification of the system) than the error which is produced by the command variable.

If Eqns (6.64) and (6.67) are considered, the total stationary error e_{ts} can be obtained:

$$w - x|_{t\to\infty} = e_{ts} = w - e_{st} - \Delta x_{st}$$

$$= w\left(1 - \frac{2T_e}{T_1 + 2T_e}\right) - z\left(\frac{2A_S T_e}{T_1 + 2T_e}\right). \tag{6.68}$$

The possible errors indicated by Eqns (6.64) and (6.67) will be examined by means of a number of examples. Consider a system with the following variables:

a) $T_1 = 400$ ms b) $T_1 = 2000$ ms.

$T_e = 20$ ms

1. $A_S = 0.2$, 2. $A_S = 1$, 3. $A_S = 5$.

The controller amplification A_R is calculated according to the optimization formula (6.60). The results of the calculations are given in Table 6.2. The steady state errors which occur are quoted as a percentage of the input variable. The error is the controlled variable relative to the command variable depends only on the time constants of the system. It is less than 5% for a time constant ratio T_1/T_e less than 38, and less than 2% for a ratio less than 98.

The non-controllable error due to a disturbance variable, however, depends on the amplification of the system. Amplifications less than 1 lead to a reduction in the error and amplifications greater than 1 lead to an increase in the error.

Only the amplification along the path from the disturbance action to the controlled variable is relevant. Therefore it is possible that with a P controller, although it appears suitable in regard to the error related to the command

Table 6.2: Results obtained by application of Eqns (6.64) and (6.67)

T_1	$400\text{ ms} = 20T_e$			$2000\text{ ms} = 100T_e$		
A_S	0.2	1	5	0.2	1	5
A_R	50	10	2	250	50	10
e_{st}/w	9.1%	9.1%	9.1%	1.96%	1.96%	1.96%
$\Delta x_{st}/z$	1.8%	9.1%	45.5%	0.39%	1.96%	9.8%

variable, it is not suitable with respect to error produced by a disturbance variable because the system amplification is too large.

Conversely, the proportional amplification A_R is a measure of the error in the controlled variable caused by a disturbance. Thus for an amplification $A_R = 50$, there is an error of a little less than 2%. For $A_R = 20$, less than 5%, and for $A_R = 10$, a little less than 10%.

How large the maximum permissible error may be can only be defined from the individual application. If the error for a P controller is too large for a particular application, a PI controller should be used instead. The method of optimization is discussed in Section 6.62 since compensation of the-large first order delay would make the smoothing of a disturbance unnecessarily slow because of the large reset time of the controller.

If it is established that the system contains a second large delay in addition to the very large first order delay, it will be compensated by a phase advance as discussed in Section 6.2. In compensating the second largest time constant of the system, the ratio of the largest time constant to the sum of the remaining time constants may justify the application of a P controller. Hence a PD controller should be used (Fig. 6.26).

In general, the second largest time constant T_2 is compensated by the phase advance T_v of the PD controller. Thus a sufficiently large difference must exist between the sum of time constants T_e and the constant T_1 if a controller without an integration action is to be used.

With compensation, the transfer function of the open loop becomes

$$F_0^*(s) = A_R A_S \frac{1}{1+sT_1} \frac{1}{1+sT_e}.$$

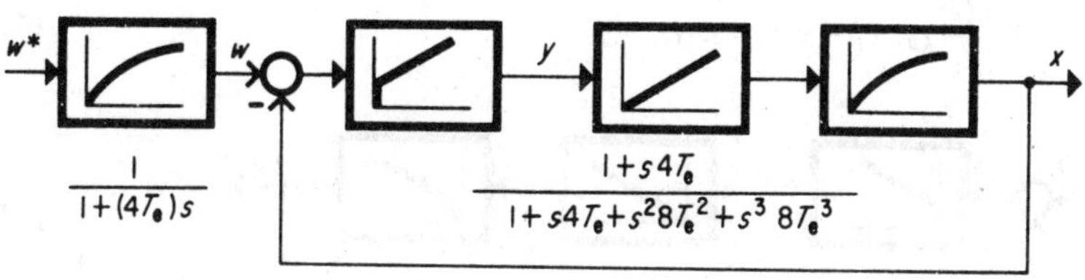

Fig. 6.26

Control system for an application where there is a first order delay whose time constant T_1 is very large in comparison to the equivalent delay for several small delays and also a second large delay whose time constant T_2 is smaller than the time constant T_1

This is the same equation as that already given for the control loop shown in Fig. 6.25. Consequently, the same considerations apply as for the control loop with the P controller.

6.7. Symmetrical Optimum

Systems which require automatic control do not only contain delay elements, proportional elements and dead time elements. Integrating elements also occur which cannot be governed by optimum modulus control. In this case compensation is not possible, for the integration of the controller would compound the integration of the controlled device and would lead to oscillation of the controlled variable. Consider the control loop shown in Fig. 6.27.

If it is desired to compensate the delay $1/(1+sT_1)$ in the transfer function of the open loop by means of the phase advance $(1+sT_n)$ in the PI controller, then the following transfer function is obtained:

$$F_0^*(s)=\frac{A_R\,A_S}{sT_n\,sT_0}=\frac{1}{s\dfrac{T_n}{A_R}}\,\frac{1}{s\dfrac{T_0}{A_S}}=\frac{1}{s^2T_1T_i}\,.$$

The transfer function for the closed loop is

$$F_w(s)=\frac{x(s)}{w(s)}=\frac{1}{1+s^2T_1T_i}\,. \tag{6.69}$$

The corresponding differential equation is

$$\frac{d^2x(t)}{dt^2}(T_1T_i)+x(t)=w(t). \tag{6.70}$$

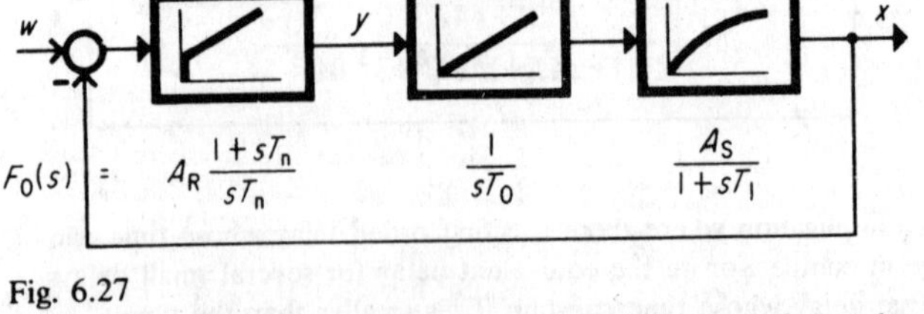

Fig. 6.27
Control of a system represented by an I element and a first order delay

If this differential equation is solved using the substitution

$$x(t) = e^{kt}$$

and the characteristic equation

$$k^2 T_1 T_i + 1 = 0$$

then the following two roots are obtained:

$$k_1 = +j/\sqrt{T_1 T_i}$$

$$k_2 = -j/\sqrt{T_1 T_i}.$$

The solution is

$$x(t) = e^{k_1 t} + e^{k_2 t} = e^{j(t/\sqrt{T_1 T_i})} + e^{-j(t/\sqrt{T_1 T_i})}. \tag{6.71}$$

This represents a continuous oscillation.

This result is to be expected since in the transfer function (6.69) the term in s^1 is missing. Therefore the damping factor is zero and consequently the oscillation in the control loop is undamped.

Therefore the optimization in this case is undertaken from a different point of view. However, it is again necessary to achieve modulus hugging.

6.7.1. Control of a system represented by an integrating element and many small first order delays

If a system to be controlled can be represented by an integrating element and a number of first order delays connected in series, whose time constants can be represented by a time constant T_e equal to their sum, the associated controller will need to be a PI controller (Fig. 6.28).

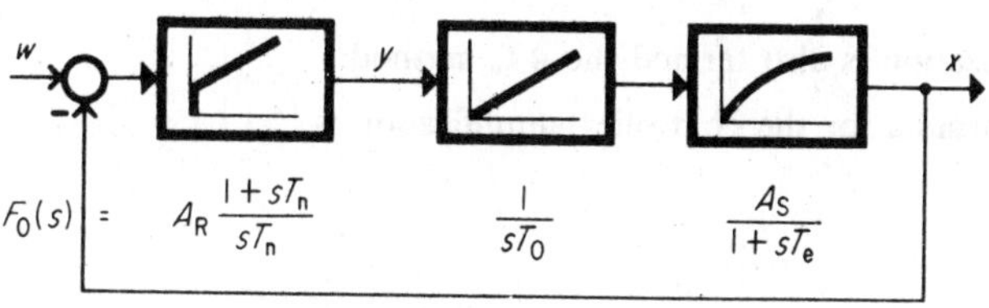

Fig. 6.28

Control loop with an I element and equivalent element for a series of first order delays

From the open loop transfer function

$$F_0(s) = A_R \frac{1+sT_n}{sT_n} \frac{1}{sT_0} \frac{A_S}{1+sT_e} \tag{6.72}$$

the transfer function for the closed loop is obtained as in Eqn (5.47), since compensation[1]) is not possible:

$$F_w(s) = \frac{x(s)}{w(s)} = \frac{A_R A_S(1+sT_n)}{A_R A_S + sA_R A_S T_n + s^2 T_n T_0 + s^3 T_n T_0 T_e} . \tag{6.73}$$

Since all terms from s^0 to s^3 are present in the denominator, it is possible to achieve a damped response.

The transfer function (6.73) of the closed loop is in the form of Eqn (6.38). Therefore the optimization Eqn (6.42) must be used if modulus hugging is to be achieved:

1. $a_1^2 = 2a_0 a_2$,
2. $a_2^2 = 2a_1 a_3$.

With

$$a_0 = A_R A_S, \qquad a_1 = A_R A_S T_n, \qquad a_2 = T_n T_0, \qquad a_3 = T_n T_0 T_e$$

this gives the optimization equations for the PI controller:

1. $(A_R A_S T_n)^2 = 2A_R A_S T_n T_0$,
2. $T_n^2 T_0^2 = 2A_R A_S T_n^2 T_0 T_e$.

Consequently, the optimization formula for the reset time constant is

$$T_n = 4T_e . \tag{6.74}$$

This form of optimization is also termed the $4T_e$ method.

The optimization formula for the controller amplification is

$$A_R = T_0 / 2A_S T_e .$$

---

[1]) It may be pointed out that it is not feasible to compensate the equivalent delay T_e by means of a phase advance controller.

This is practically the same formula as that for the controller amplification for the optimum modulus. In practice it is not possible to measure an integration time constant for an element which is removed from its environment. It will always appear with the amplification A_S. Therefore, only the integration time constant

$$T_i = T_0/A_S \tag{6.75}$$

will be used. The optimization formula for the controller amplification then becomes

$$A_R = T_i/2T_e. \tag{6.76}$$

If the optimization formula is inserted in the transfer function (6.73), the standard equation for the symmetrical optimum is obtained

$$F_w(s)_{opt} = \frac{x(s)}{w(s)} = \frac{1+s4T_e}{1+s4T_e+s^2 8T_e^2+s^3 8T_e^3}. \tag{6.77}$$

All control loops which are designed according to the symmetrical optimum show this form of transfer function.

It is now possible to clarify the concept of symmetrical optimum. Figure 6.29 shows the frequency characteristics of the individual system elements in the loop and the resultant open loop frequency responses. This polygon trace for the modulus of the transfer function F_0 shows symmetry of the corner points $1/4T_e$ and $1/T_e$ with respect to the gain crossover frequency $1/2T_e$ on the 0 dB line.

If the control loop is adjusted in accordance with the symmetrical optimum, the behaviour is dependent on the sum T_e of the time constants of the small delays in the control loop.

Conversion to the time domain gives

$$(4T_e)\frac{dw(t)}{dt} + w(t)$$

$$= x(t) + 4T_e\frac{dx(t)}{dt} + 8T_e^2\frac{d^2x(t)}{dt^2} + 8T_e^3\frac{d^3x(t)}{dt^3} \tag{6.78}$$

If this third order differential equation is solved with the assumption that the command variable makes a step of amplitude 1, the transient response

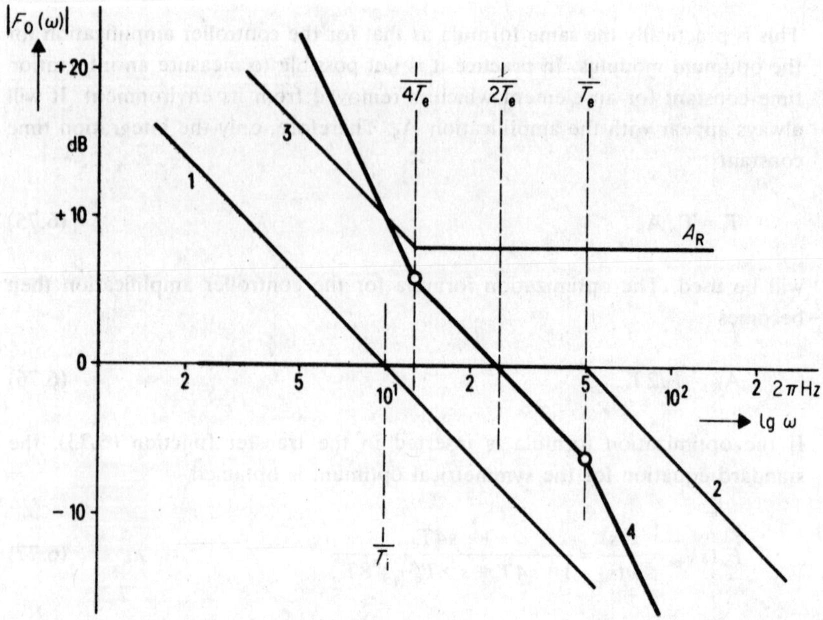

Fig. 6.29
Bode diagram of the control loop shown in Fig. 6.28. The following frequency characteristics are shown:
1. Integrating element ($T_i = 100$ ms)
2. Equivalent delay ($T_e = 20$ ms)
3. PI controller ($A_R = 2.5 \simeq 8$ dB and $T_n = 4T_e = 80$ ms)
4. Modulus open loop frequency response of the transfer function F_0

obtained is as follows:

$$f(t)_{opt} = \frac{x(t)}{w_{step}} = 1 + e^{-t/2T_e} - 2e^{-t/4T_e} \cos\frac{\sqrt{3}\,t}{4T_e}. \tag{6.79}$$

If this response is plotted with the time scale in units of T_e, the curve shown in Fig. 6.30 is obtained. From the transient response of the symmetrically optimized control loop, it can be deduced that the rise time t_r is $3.1T_e$, the first overshoot is 43.4% above the final steady-state value and the time to reach the steady state within ±2% (settling time) is $16.5T_e$.

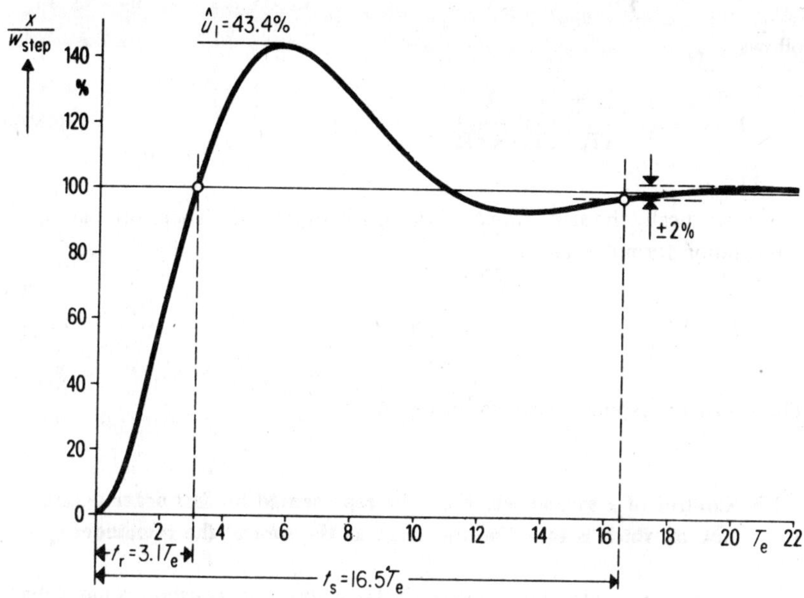

Fig. 6.30 Step response of a symmetrically optimized control loop

6.7.2. Control of a system which can be represented by an integrating element with one large and several small first order delays

Suppose that in the previous example there is, among the number of nominally small delays, one in which the time constant exceeds the others. In these circumstances, the delay will be compensated in order to accelerate the control process.

In this case the controller must have two phase advances. One is necessary for overcoming the integrating element and the other for compensating the large delay. Therefore the controller must have a PID characteristic. For the control loop of Fig. 6.31, this gives an open loop transfer function (with $T_v = T_2$) as

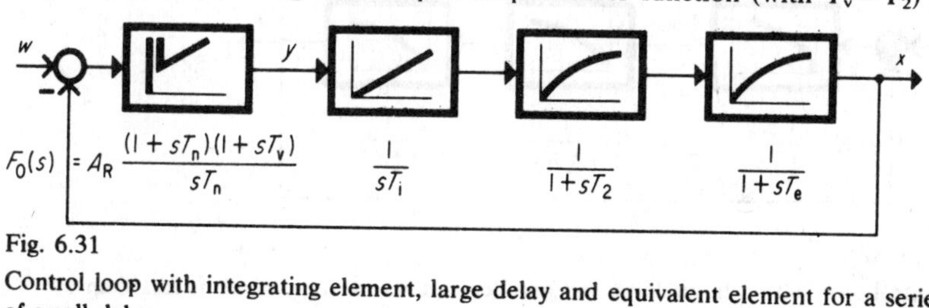

Fig. 6.31
Control loop with integrating element, large delay and equivalent element for a series of small delays

follows:

$$F_0^*(s) = A_R \frac{1+sT_n}{sT_n} \frac{1}{sT_i} \frac{1}{1+sT_e}. \tag{6.80}$$

This is practically the same transfer function as Eqn (6.72). Therefore the three optimization formulae apply:

$$T_n = 4T_e, \qquad T_v = T_2, \qquad A_R = T_i/2T_e. \tag{6.81}$$

The transient response is shown in Fig. 6.30.

6.7.3. Control of a system which can be represented by first order delays, one of which is four times as large as the sum of the remainder

If a system to be controlled includes a delay whose time constant is more than four times as large as the sum of the time constants of the remaining delays, then the large delay acts, as a first approximation, like an integrator.

With this assumption, it is permissible for the controller for the system described (Fig. 6.32) to be designed in accordance, with the symmetrical optimum. The $4T_e$ method of adjustment is applicable.

The transfer function of the closed loop is obtained from the transfer function of the open loop without compensation:

$$F_w(s) = \frac{x(s)}{w(s)} = \frac{A_R A_S (1+sT_n)}{A_R A_S + sT_n(A_R A_S + 1) + s^2 T_n (T_1 + T_e) + s^3 T_n T_1 T_e}. \tag{6.82}$$

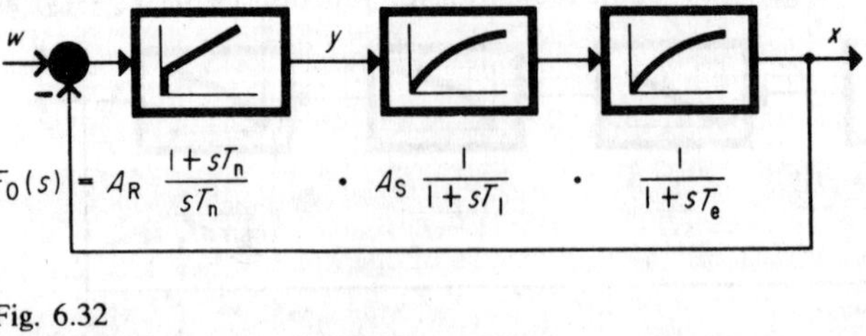

Fig. 6.32
Control loop with a large delay and another equivalent delay which is less than a quarter as large, i.e. $4T_e < T_1$

If $4T_e$ is substituted for T_n and $T_1/(2A_ST_e)$ for A_R, then the transfer function for the optimized control loop is obtained as follows:

$$F_w(s)_{opt} = \frac{x(s)}{w(s)} = \frac{1+s4T_e}{1+s4T_e\left(1+\frac{2T_e}{T_1}\right)+s^2 8T_e^2\left(1+\frac{T_e}{T_1}\right)+s^3 8T_e^3}. \tag{6.83}$$

There is no material difference compared with the standard Eqn (6.77) for symmetrical optimum, since with $T_1 > 4T_e$, the expressions in parentheses in Eqn (6.83) are only slightly larger than 1.

The frequency response of Fig. 6.30 is only valid for the symmetrical optimum if the system being controlled contains an integrating function. If on the other hand only first order delays are present, with a symmetrically optimized control loop the rise time becomes larger and the overshoot smaller. The deviation of the transient response of the symmetrical optimum in the direction of the optimum modulus is more marked, the closer the time constant ratio $T_1/4T_e$ approaches 1.

If $T_1 = 4T_e$, the transient response corresponding to the optimum modulus is obtained. If the ratio $T_1/4T_e$ becomes less than 1, it is no longer reasonable to use the formulae for the symmetrical optimum. The design should be based on the optimum modulus method.

If the controlled system contains two particularly large first order delays, a PID controller can be used. The time constant of the second largest delay will be compensated in the usual way with the D action. If the time constant of the largest delay is again more than four times as large as the sum of the remainder, the formulae for the symmetrical optimum are used in the design of the controller.

If it is of importance to make the control action as rapid as possible, the controller of the control loop shown in Fig. 6.32 can be more conveniently designed. The transfer function (6.82)

$$F_w(s) = \frac{1+sT_n}{1+sT_n\left(1+\frac{1}{A_SA_R}\right)+s^2T_n\frac{T_1+T_e}{A_RA_S}+s^3T_n\frac{T_1T_e}{A_RA_S}} \tag{6.84}$$

is compared with the standard transfer function (6.77) for the symmetrical optimum. It is convenient to write β in place of T_e

$$F_w(s)_{opt} = \frac{1+s4\beta}{1+s4\beta+s^2 8\beta^2+s^3 8\beta^3}. \tag{6.85}$$

Comparison of the coefficients of the two Eqns (6.84) and (6.85) gives the following:

1. $T_n\left(1+\frac{1}{A_R A_S}\right)=4\beta,$

2. $T_n\frac{T_1+T_e}{A_R A_S}=8\beta^2,$

3. $T_n\frac{T_1 T_e}{A_R A_S}=8\beta^3.$

This results in the following expressions:

1. $\beta_1=\frac{T_n}{4}\left(1+\frac{1}{A_R A_S}\right),$

2.÷1. $\beta_2=\frac{1}{2}\frac{T_1+T_e}{1+A_R A_S},$

3.÷2. $\beta_3=\frac{T_1 T_e}{T_1+T_e}.$

With $\beta_2=\beta_3$ the proportional amplification is

$$A_R=\frac{T_1}{2A_S T_e}\left(1+\frac{T_e^2}{T_1^2}\right). \tag{6.86}$$

With $\beta_1=\beta_2$ the reset time constant of the controller is

$$T_n=4T_e\frac{1+\frac{T_e^2}{T_1^2}}{(1+T_e/T_1)^3}. \tag{6.87}$$

If the values obtained by means of Eqns (6.86) and (6.87) are substituted in the transfer function (6.84), the following result is obtained:

$$F_w(s)_{opt}=\frac{1+4T_e\left\{\frac{1+T_e^2/T_1^2}{(1+T_e/T_1)^3}\right\}}{1+s\left\{\frac{4T_e}{1+T_e/T_1}\right\}+s^2\left\{\frac{8T_e^2}{(1+T_e/T_1)^2}\right\}+s^3\left\{\frac{8T_e^3}{(1+T_e/T_1)^3}\right\}} \tag{6.88}$$

The integration time constant of the controller is

$$T_{\mathrm{I}}=\frac{T_{\mathrm{n}}}{A_{\mathrm{R}}}=8A_{\mathrm{S}}\frac{T_{\mathrm{e}}^{2}}{T_{1}}\frac{1}{(1+T_{\mathrm{e}}/T_{1})^{3}}. \tag{6.89}$$

At this point, the following points may be anticipated for the optimum adjustment of the controller:

a) *Required value smoothing* (see also Section 6.7.4). Since this must be equal to the phase advance in the transfer function (6.88), the required smoothing time constant t_{sm} is

$$t_{\mathrm{sm}}=4T_{\mathrm{e}}\frac{1+T_{\mathrm{e}}^{2}/T_{1}^{2}}{(1+T_{\mathrm{e}}/T_{1})^{3}} \tag{6.90}$$

since the overshoot for a step change of command variable is as large as if there were an integral action involved.

b) *Equivalent time constant* (see Eqns (6.20) and (6.21)). The equivalent time constant t_{e} of the optimized control ,loop is always equal to the factor associated with the s^{1} term in the denominator of the function. In Eqn (6.88), this is

$$t_{\mathrm{e}}=\frac{4T_{\mathrm{e}}}{1+T_{\mathrm{e}}/T_{1}}. \tag{6.91}$$

The correction factors relative to the originally calculated values are given by the curves of Fig. 6.33. The smaller the ratio T_{e}/T_{1}, the less they deviate from 1.

Since the square of the ratio of the time constants is much less than 1, i.e.

$$T_{\mathrm{e}}^{2}/T_{1}^{2}\ll 1$$

it can usually be omitted. The following approximation can also be made:

$$(1+T_{\mathrm{e}}/T_{1})^{3}\simeq 1+3\frac{T_{\mathrm{e}}}{T_{1}}.$$

Consequently, the approximate values obtained for the behaviour of the effective symmetrical optimum are

$$A_{\mathrm{R}}\simeq\frac{T_{1}}{2A_{\mathrm{S}}T_{\mathrm{e}}},\qquad T_{\mathrm{n}}\simeq 4T_{\mathrm{e}}\frac{T_{1}}{T_{1}+3T_{\mathrm{e}}},\qquad T_{\mathrm{I}}\simeq 8A_{\mathrm{S}}\frac{T_{\mathrm{e}}^{2}}{T_{1}}\frac{T_{1}}{T_{1}+3T_{\mathrm{e}}}. \tag{6.92}$$

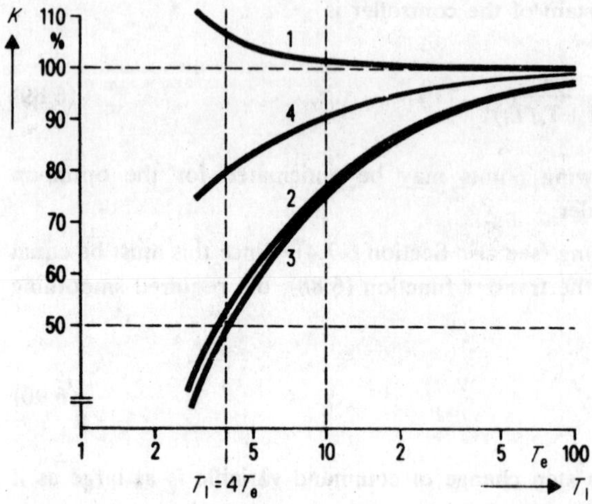

Fig. 6.33
Correction factors K to achieve symmetrically optimized behaviour in a control loop with only a first order delay in the system

1. Correction factor $1+(T_e/T_I)^2$ for the proportional amplification of the controller
2. Correction factor $[1+(T_e/T_I)^2]/(1+T_e)^3$ for the reset time constant T_n and the smoothing time constant t_{sm}
3. Correction factor $1/(1+T_e/T_I)^3$ for the integration time constant T_I
4. Correction factor $1/(1+T_e/T_I)$ for the equivalent time constant t_e

6.7.4. Required value smoothing

The step response of a control loop designed in accordance with the symmetrical optimum shows quite a considerable overshoot of the controlled variable, amounting to as much as 43.4%. Such a severe overshoot of the controlled variable is permissible only occasionally, during violent changes or sudden steps in the command variable. Therefore steps must be taken to prevent it.

If the transfer function (6.77) for the symmetrically optimized closed loop, i.e.

$$F_w(s)_{opt} = \frac{1+s4T_e}{1+s4T_e+s^2 8T_e^2+s^3 8T_e^3}$$

is compared with the function (6.48) for the optimized modulus control loop

$$F_w(s)_{opt} = \frac{1}{1+s2T_e+s^2 2T_e^2}$$

which exhibits only a 4% overshoot in the step response (6.50), it may be observed that the large overshoot for the symmetrically optimized loop is characterized in the transfer function by the numerator term $(1+4T_e s)$, which represents a phase advance.

It was shown in Section 6.2 how a phase advance in the controller compensates for a delay in the controlled system which retards the control action. Conversely, it is possible to compensate a phase advance by means of a delay or smoothing action. Since the sharp change of command variable is the cause of the overshoot, the required value smoothing must be located in the required value channel of the controller. Its transfer function is

$$F_{sm}(s) = \frac{w(s)}{w^*(s)} = \frac{1}{1+s4T_e}. \tag{6.93}$$

Usually a passive smoothing element, as in Fig. 4.61, is used. Its smoothing time constant is

$$t_{sm} = 4T_e = \frac{R_{s1}R_{s2}}{R_{s1}+R_{s2}} C_s \tag{6.94}$$

with the two resistances R_{s1} and R_{s2} in the series branch and the capacitance C_s in the transverse branch of the required value channel.

For the series connection (Fig. 6.34) of the smoothing element and the optimized control loop, the overall transfer function, referred to the command variable w^* is

$$F_w(s)_{opt} = F_{sm}(s)F_w(s)_{opt} = \frac{x(s)}{w^*(s)}$$

$$= \frac{1}{1+s4T_e} \frac{1+s4T_e}{1+s4T_e+s^2 8T_e^2+s^3 8T_e^3}$$

$$= \frac{1}{1+s4T_e+s^2 8T_e^2+s^3 8T_e^3}. \tag{6.95}$$

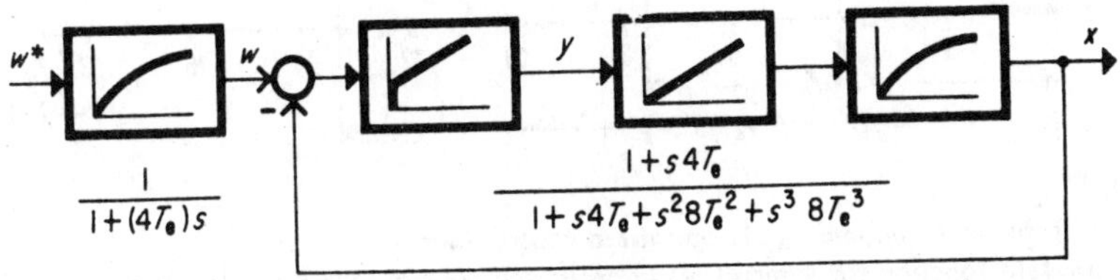

Fig. 6.34 Symmetrically optimized control loop with required value smoothing

Owing to the disappearance of the phase advance element, i.e. to the smoothing of severe changes of the required value, the overshoot is strongly damped. However, a significantly longer rise time results.

The associated differential equation

$$w^*(t) = x(t) + 4T_e \frac{dx(t)}{dt} + 8T_e^2 \frac{d^2x(t)}{dt^2} + 8T_e^3 \frac{d^3x(t)}{dt^3} \tag{6.96}$$

with a step input signal w^*_{step} leads to the transient response

$$f(t)_{opt} = \frac{x(t)}{w^*_{step}} = 1 - e^{-t/2T_e} - \frac{2}{\sqrt{3}} e^{-t/4T_e} \sin \frac{\sqrt{3}}{4T_e} t \tag{6.97}$$

which is shown in Fig. 6.35. The rise time t_r is $7.6T_e$. The settling time t_s is $13.3T_e$ to within ±2% and the overshoot is 8.1% relative to the steady-state value.

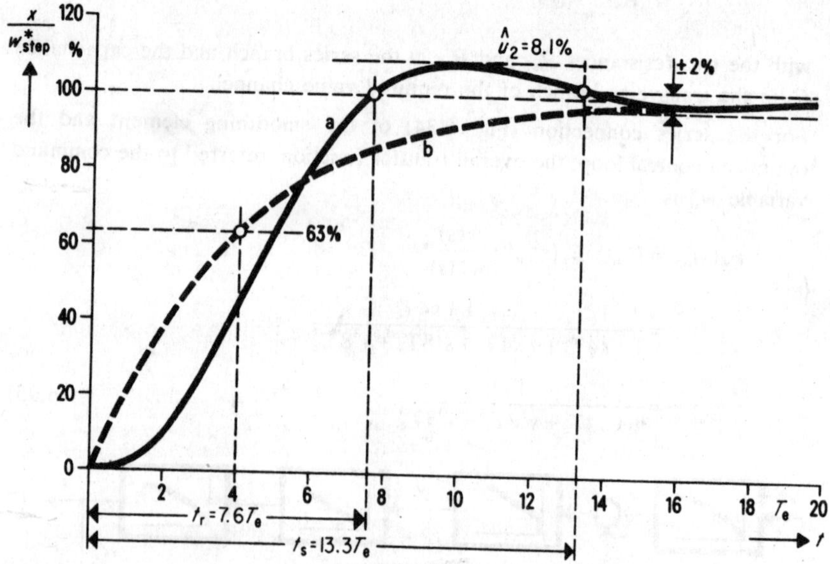

Fig. 6.35

a) Step response of symmetrically optimized control loop

b) Equivalent function for symmetrically optimized control loop with required value smoothing (first order delay, time constant $4T_e$)

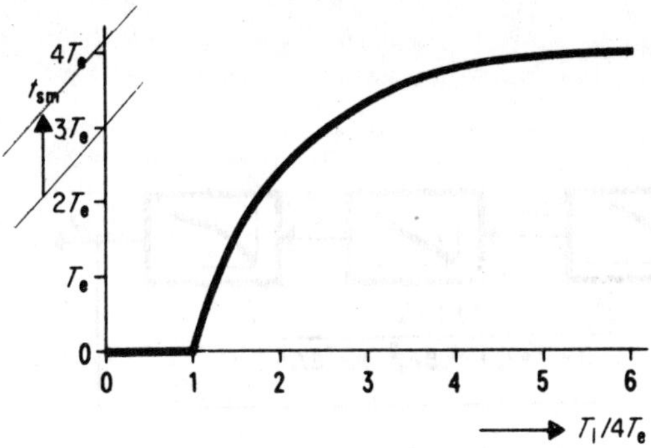

Fig. 6.36
Smoothing necessary for the required value in a symmetrically optimized control loop with one large delay and a number of small delays

If the controlled system contains only first order delays and the ratio of the time constants $T_1/4T_e$ is greater than 1, as in Section 6.7.3, the symmetrical optimum can be used. In the previous section it was seen that the overshoot of the controlled variable no longer amounts to 43%. It approaches the overshoot with modulus optimization (4%) the closer the ratio of time constants $T_1/4T_e$ approaches 1. Consequently, the necessary smoothing in the required values channel is again dependent on the ratio $T_1/4T_e$. The following equation applies (Fig. 6.36):

$$t = 4T_e(1 - e^{-((T_1/4T_e)-1)}). \tag{6.98}$$

If the overshoot of the controlled variable associated with a step signal change in the required value channel is to vanish completely, a more effective smoothing of the required value, with $t_{sm} = 6T_e$, can be inserted before the symmetrically optimized control loop containing only first order delays. The control loop consequently operates even more slowly for the command variable. In a control loop with an integrating element, an increase in required value smoothing is, however, not advisable, because this produces a substantial lag in the output time response

If the disadvantage of retarded control action caused by smoothing the required value is to be avoided and a fast rise time must be achieved, the smoothing element in the required value channel of the controller can be bridged by a differentiating element.

Figure 6.37 shows this circuit in which the behaviour for proportional feedback is described using Eqn (4.100). For a PI controller then

$$F(s) = \frac{y(s)}{w^{**}(s)} = \frac{1 + st_{sm2}(1+v) + s^2 t_{sm1} t_{sm2} v}{(1+st_{sm1})(1+st_{sm2})} A_R \frac{1+sT_n}{sT_n} \tag{6.99}$$

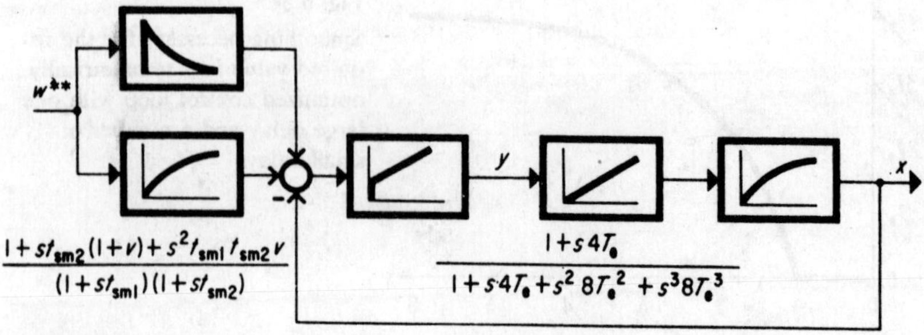

Fig. 6.37
Symmetrically optimized control loop with smoothing and differentiation of the required value

relative to the command variable channel with the required value w^{**} and

$$F(s)=\frac{y(s)}{x(s)}=A_R\frac{1+sT_n}{sT_n} \tag{6.100}$$

relative to the controlled variable with actual value x.

Only the effect of Eqn (6.100) contributes to the standard transfer function of the symmetrically optimized control loop. However, for the case in question, owing to the elements in the command variable channel (Fig. 6.37), the overall transfer function becomes

$$F_w(s)_{opt}=\frac{x(s)}{w^{**}(s)}$$

$$=\frac{1+st_{sm2}(1+v)+s^2 t_{sm1} t_{sm2} v}{(1+st_{sm1})(1+st_{sm2})}\,\frac{1+s4T_e}{(1+s2T_e)(1+s2T_e+s^2 4T_e^2)}. \tag{6.101}$$

The optimum values for t_{sm1}, t_{sm2} and v are now to be defined.

The original required value smoothing with the time constant t_{sm} appear as t_{sm1}. Accordingly

$$t_{sm1}=t_{sm}=4T_e.$$

The denominator term

$$1+s2T_e+s^2 4T_e^2$$

from the standard transfer function of the optimized loop is to be compensated by the numerator term

$$1+st_{sm2}(1+v)+s^2t_{sm1}t_{sm2}v.$$

By comparison of the coefficients

$$2T_e=t_{sm2}(1+v)$$
$$4T_e^2=t_{sm1}t_{sm2}v=4T_et_{sm2}v$$

which gives

$$t_{sm2}=T_e, \qquad v=1.$$

With these values for t_{sm1}, t_{sm2} and v the new equation is derived from Eqn (6.101)

$$F_w^*(s)_{opt}=\frac{x(s)}{w^{**}(s)}=\frac{1}{1+s3T_e+s^22T_e^2}. \tag{6.102}$$

For an arbitrary command variable, this gives the differential equation

$$w^{**}(t)=x(t)+3T_e\frac{dx(t)}{dt}+2T_e^2\frac{d^2x(t)}{dt^2} \tag{6.103}$$

and for a step change w^{**}_{step} in the command variable, the unit step response

$$f(t)_{opt}=\frac{x(t)}{w^{**}_{step}}=1+e^{-t/T_e}-2e^{-t/2T_e}. \tag{6.104}$$

This is shown in Fig. 6.38.

If the function (6.104) is compared with Eqn (6.97), it can be observed that the system response is appreciably faster owing to the additional differentiation of the command variable. According to Eqn (6.97), the 63% point is only reached at $4.93T_e$ compared with $3.16T_e$ with Eqn (6.104). No rise time can be quoted for the curve in Fig. 6.38, since the final value is reached asymptotically, but the settling time, within a tolerance of 2%, t_s is $9.2T_e$. This is less than that of Fig. 6.35 in which the settling time is quoted as $13.3T_e$.

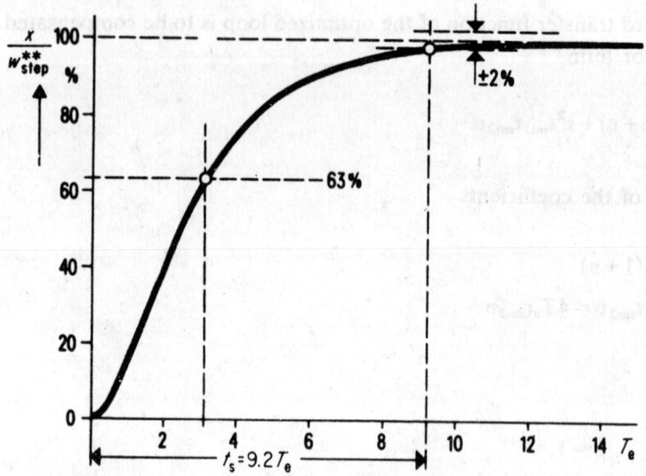

Fig. 6.38
Transient function of the symmetrically optimized control loop with smoothing and differentiation of the required value

6.8. Comparison of the Modulus Optimum and the Symmetrical Optimum Design Methods

Modulus optimum and symmetrical optimum design are both cases of optimization by modulus hugging. It is to be expected therefore that two control loops, one being modulus optimized and the other symmetrically optimized behave in a similar manner. This will be shown and also it will be shown how far it is possible to depart from the optimum adjustment without causing the loop behaviour to deviate materially from the desired optimum behaviour. Also consideration will be given to how an optimally adjusted control loop within a superimposed control loop should be dealt with.

6.8.1. Variations of the controller parameters

A difficulty which may arise in adjusting a control loop for optimum performance is that it is not always possible to obtain the characteristics of the apparatus being controlled. Most devices are non-linear and their characteristics change with the level of the drive. This can lead to an erroneous adjustment of the controller in the non-linear region.

The response of the controlled variable to a step change of the command variable will demonstrate the error. In the following discussion, a modulus optimized control loop and a symmetrically optimized control loop (see Figs. 6.22 and 6.28), each provided with a correctly adjusted PI controller, will be maladjusted both in the proportional amplification and the reset time constant by a factor of 2 and the resulting step response will be examined (Figs. 6.40 and 6.41). In the case of non-linearity or the impossibility of determining the characteristics of the equipment, it is then possible to deduce from the trend of the deviation of the transient response from that of the optimized loop, the direction in which the erroneous setting should be altered. From the step response of the control loop, obtained by means of a recorder, the necessary changes of controller parameters for optimum adjustment can be found.

Thus the aim will be to set the upper and lower extremes of value of non-linearity so that they will be as far as possible equally distant from the optimum adjustment (Fig. 6.39).

The correct adjustment of the differentiating phase advance in a PD controller will not be examined in more detail here since the controller connected as a PD element is set to the correct phase advance in the compensation procedure.

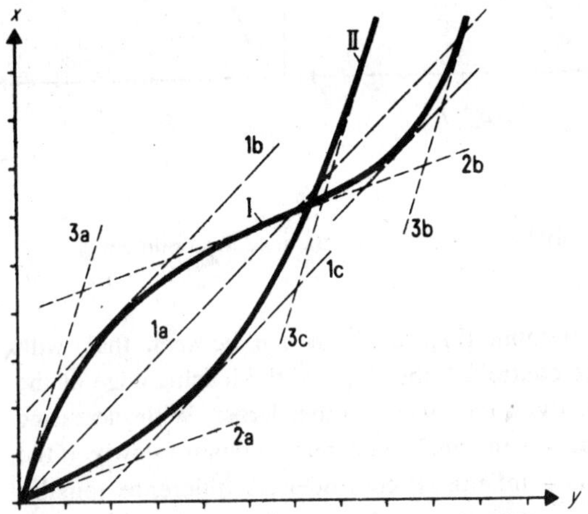

Fig. 6.39
Static characteristics of non-linear control systems. The tangents 2a and 2b are one third and tangents 3a, 3b and 3c are three times as steep as tangents 1a, 1b and 1c on the characteristics I and II. Therefore these non-linear characteristics in the extreme cases have an amplification at the points of minimum slope which is one third of the mean value of the proportional amplification but is three times larger at the steepest points. The mean value is given by the slopes of the straight lines 1a, 1b and 1c. The amplification A_S is given by dx/dy

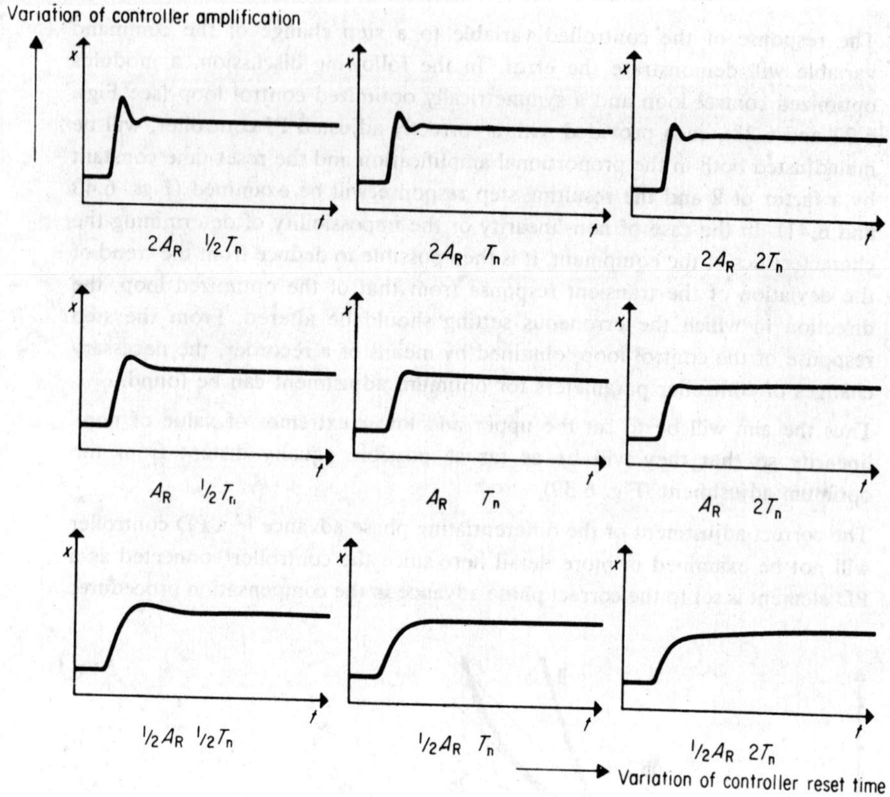

Fig. 6.40

Step response of the controlled variable at and close to the modulus optimum

Summarizing the modulus optimum (Fig. 6.40), it can be seen that, with increasing amplification of the controller, the slope of the leading edge of the response increases so that the overshoot also becomes larger. With increasing reset time, the response approaches the final value more and more slowly. If the integration capacitance becomes infinite (P controller), a difference remains between the command and controlled variables, i.e. the lag is extended infinitely and causes an offset error. On the other hand, if the reset time is smaller than the optimum value, the control loop tends to oscillate more and more with decreasing integration time constant, i.e. it approaches the symmetrical optimum.

If the proportional amplification in the controller is reduced by a factor of 2, but the reset time is correctly chosen in accordance with the modulus optimum, this setting corresponds to the linear optimum. This is the adjustment of the control loop to the aperiodic limit case, which was described in Section 2.3. In the simplest case its transfer function is

$$F_w(s)_{opt} = \frac{x(s)}{w(s)} = \frac{1}{1 + s4T_e + s^2 4T_e^2}$$

$$= \frac{1}{(1+s2T_e)^2} \tag{6.105}$$

and the associated unit step response is

$$f(t)_{opt} = \frac{x(t)}{w_{step}} = 1 - e^{-t/2T_e} - \frac{t}{2T_e} e^{-t/2T_e}. \tag{6.106}$$

If it is required that any arbitrary control loop shows no overshoot during a step response, so that it is adjusted according to the linear optimum, we begin with the general transfer function of the closed loop

$$F_w(s) = \frac{x(s)}{w(s)} = \frac{1}{a_0 + sa_1 + s^2 a_2 + s^3 a_3 + \cdots} \tag{6.107}$$

and make use of the optimization formula

$$a_v^2 \geqslant \left(1 + \frac{1}{v}\right)\left(1 + \frac{1}{n-v}\right) a_{v-1} a_{v+1} \tag{6.108}$$

where n is the degree of the denominator and the numerical value of v lies between 1 and $(n-1)$, i.e.

$$1 \leqslant v \leqslant (n-1).$$

Taking the control loop of Fig. 6.28 as an example, this optimization formula according to the transfer function (6.73) gives a controller amplification $A_R = T_i/3T_e$ and a reset time $T_n = 9T_e$ as the optimum.

Overall, Fig. 6.40 makes it clear that, with the modulus optimum, a maladjustment of the controller by a factor of 2 or $\frac{1}{2}$ with respect to the proportional amplification and the reset time, leads to errors which are insignificant in most cases.

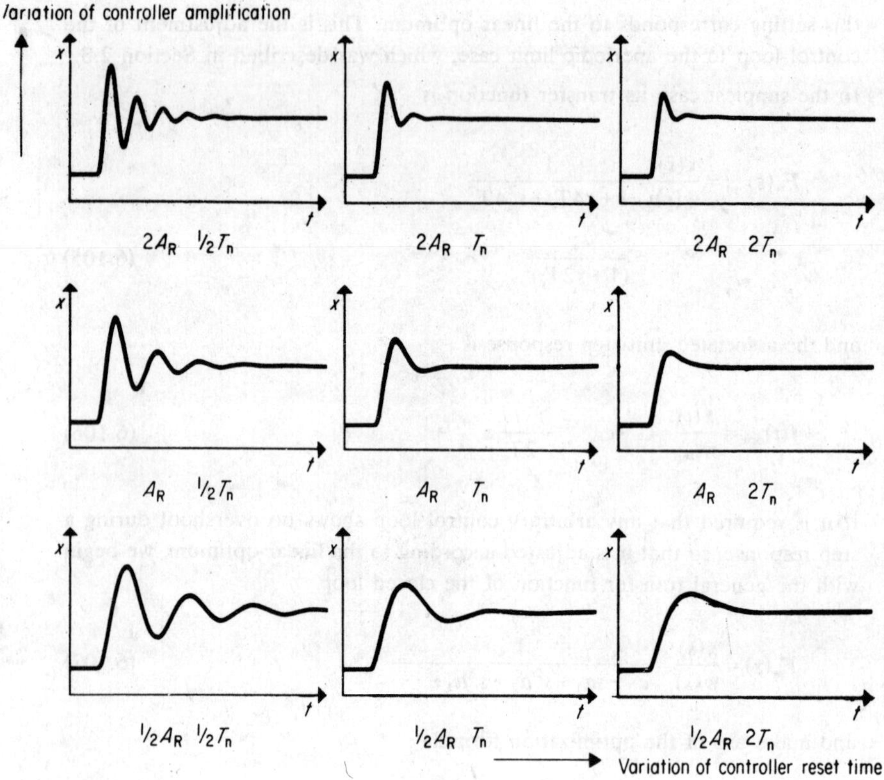

Fig. 6.41
Step response of the controlled variable at and in the vicinity of the symmetrical optimum setting

The transient response (Fig. 6.41) in the proximity of the symmetrical optimum shows similar tendencies to those of the modulus optimum. The larger the proportional amplification of the controller the steeper the rise time. Too large a proportional amplification leads to greater ringing of the controlled variable as does too small a reset time. If the reset time is too large, this causes a positive smoothing, but only in the immediate vicinity of the correct proportional amplification. If the latter is too large or too small, the overshoot increases and with too small a reset time, significant ringing occurs with all values of the proportional amplification. Its frequency rises with amplification.

It may be observed from the step response that the symmetrical optimum shows a higher sensitivity to maladjustment. If with this adjustment, the frequency characteristic of the phase response were to be superimposed on the frequency characteristic of the modulus (Fig. 6.29), it would be seen that by displacing the characteristic, a deterioration must occur, no matter whether the displacement results from a positive or a negative movement of the amplification. Moreover, with the symmetrical optimum the phase disparity for critical positive coupling is from the outset, smaller than with the modulus optimum. Therefore, while the modulus optimized control loop can be smoothed more and more by reducing the amplification, this is only possible in the symmetrically optimized loop by increasing the reset time, the correct amplification being maintained.

These considerations of an incorrectly adjusted reset time, however, are usually of secondary importance, since with the symmetrical optimum, the reset time ($T_n = 4T_e$) is dependent only on the sum of the small time constants and this sum normally remains constant throughout the overall control range. Thus in Fig. 6.41 only the variation of the amplification A_R is of interest.

When being driven, non-linear control systems often show the same tendency for variation of the amplification A_S and the most significant time constant T_1.

Under these circumstances, adjustment in accordance with the symmetrical optimum is chosen instead of the compensation method, even if the large time constant T_1 is not more than four times the sum of the time constants T_e. Of course, if greater changes of A_S and T_1 arise due to non-linearity, but the quotient T_1/A_S, which defines the controller amplification, remains virtually constant, the proportional amplification can be adjusted without error. In this respect, refer to Section 3.8.

Figure 6.42 shows how the control loop of Fig. 6.32 can be adjusted to optimum by experiment with the aid of the step responses of Figs. 6.40 and 6.41.

All that is known of the controlled system is that it comprises one large and several small delays and adjustment in conformity with the symmetrical optimum must be favourable. For this purpose, the controller must have a PI action.

However, in the first instance the integration capacitor is bridged over so that it is effectively a P controller. Steps are applied to the command variable input without smoothing. Transient responses appear which correspond with the middle column of Fig. 6.40, since without an integrating action the control loop works according to the modulus optimum (Fig. 6.42a) If the proportional action is adjusted to the optimum (see solid curve), the integration capacitor in the controller feedback is put into the circuit again and its capacitance selected according to the middle line of Fig. 6.41 so that an overshoot of approximately 40% is obtained (Fig. 6.42b). Again this is the solid trace. Another required

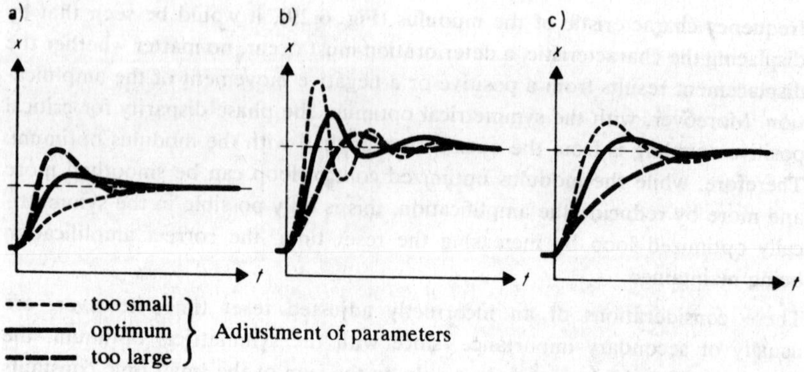

Fig. 6.42

Experimental adjustment of a control loop to the symmetrical optimum using a PI controller

a) Step response of control loop with a P controller. Owing to the offset error, the controlled variable does not reach the value prescribed by the command variable in the steady state

b) Step response of control loop with a PI controller which is adjusted for symmetrical optimum

c) Step response for a symmetrically optimized control loop with required value smoothing

value smoothing is now needed. Instead of connecting the command variable step directly to the required value channel, a smoothing element is used. The smoothing capacitance is adjusted until the result is as for trace (a) in Fig. 6.35. In this way the control loop is set to the optimum (Fig. 6.42c).

6.8.2. Equivalent time constant of an optimized control loop

Control systems often contain not only one or two system elements with significant time constants (delay or integration time constants), but several of them. If it is desired that these system elements, which significantly slow down the system response, are to be controlled by a single controller, this must contain as many phase advances as there are significant system elements in the system. However, it is not advisable in practice to use a controller with more than two phase advances. Therefore all the remaining time constants of the system which cannot be compensated by the controller phase advance must be added to the sum of small time constants defining the control times and a slow system response has to be accepted.

However, if the achievement of a fast system response is required for a system with more than two significant elements it is necessary to divide the system into separate sections each containing one or two large time constants and to compensate each of these time constants with a separate controller (Fig. 6.43). The separate sections will be selected so that each disturbance variable will be dealt with by a separate controller.

If for example the rotational speed in main control loop I is the main control variable, then the auxiliary variable, acceleration, can be controlled in the first subordinate control loop II and the machine torque in a further subordinate control loop III. Then the drive will be precisely under control.

For the auxiliary control loop III, control loop II is a superimposed control loop. Likewise, the main control loop I is superimposed on the auxiliary control loop II. This is also termed cascade control. For the superimposed loop, an optimized subordinate control loop is part of the controlled system. If the subordinate control loop is adjusted in conformity with the modulus optimum, then its action is a second order delay according to Eqn (6.48). On the other hand, if it is designed in accordance with symmetrical optimum and provided with required value smoothing, then Eqn (6.95) applies, exhibiting a third order delay action. However, to simplify the overall behaviour of the

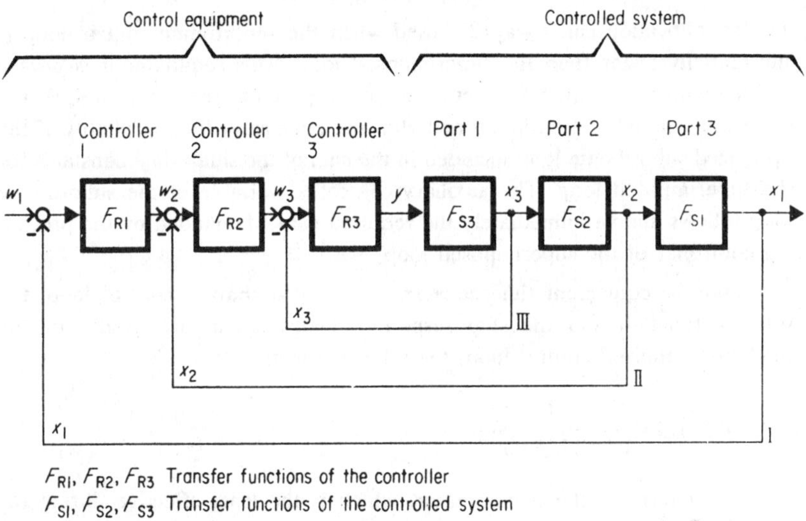

Fig. 6.43
Cascade control with subordinate control loops. I is main control loop, II and III are auxiliary control loops.

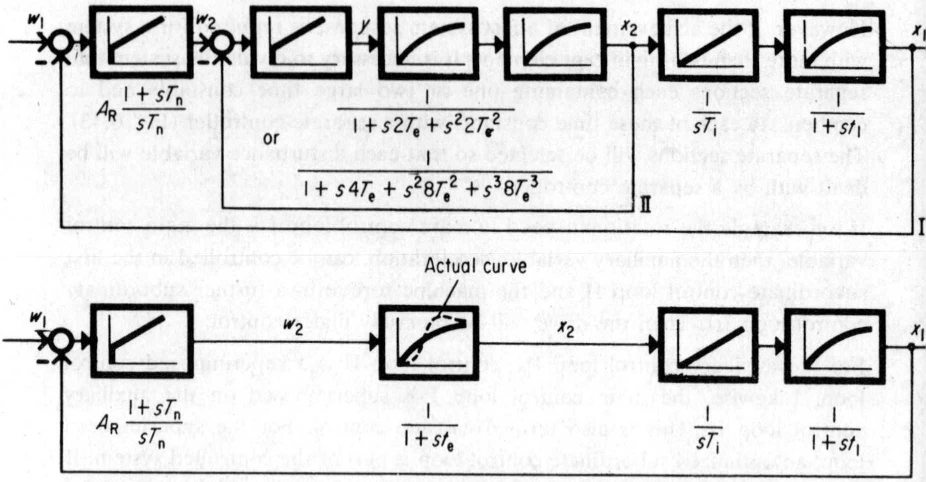

Fig. 6.44
Replacement of the subordinate control loop II by a first order delay in the overall control loop I

controlled system relevant to the superimposed loop, the subordinate control loop is replaced by a first order delay (Fig. 6.44).

This simplification can always be used when the subordinate control loop is substantially faster than the superimposed loop. This requirement is always fulfilled with the superimposed control loop adjusted to the modulus optimum or to the symmetrical optimum and with the equivalent time constants of the optimized subordinate loop included in the sum of the small time constants for the superimposed loop. The auxiliary controlled variable of the subordinate loop follows almost immediately the required value demanded by the preceding controller of the superimposed loop.

To define to equivalent time constant t_e of the optimized control loop, the transfer function and the step response of this circuit are used. For the modulus optimized control loop, the transfer function (6.48) is

$$F_w(s)_{opt} = \frac{1}{1+s2T_e+s^2 2T_e^2}.$$

If the last term in the denominator, which is the least effective during the transient period, is deleted, the following is obtained:

$$F(s)_{opt} = \frac{1}{1+s2T_e}. \tag{6.109}$$

If this equivalent delay is compared (curve b, Fig. 6.21) with the actual step response (curve a), a positive and a negative difference area appear, which are equal in magnitude. This indicates that a superimposed control action which is slow in relation to the control action of the subordinate loop, shows practically no difference whether a behaviour according to curve a) or according to curve b) is relevant. The equivalent time constant for the modulus optimized control loop is thus

$$t_e = 2T_e. \tag{6.110}$$

For the symmetrically optimized control loop which is provided with required value smoothing, the transfer function (6.95) applies

$$F_w(s)_{opt} = \frac{1}{1 + s4T_e + s^2 8T_e^2 + s^3 8T_e^3}.$$

If the denominator terms in s^2 and s^3 are ignored, the following is obtained:

$$F(s) = \frac{1}{1 + s4T_e}. \tag{6.111}$$

This is a first order delay, the step response for which is shown in Fig. 6.35, curve b). The actual step response for the optimized control loop with required value smoothing is then curve a). In this case also, there are positive and negative difference areas between the two curves, which are equal in magnitude. With a slower superimposed control action, both transient responses lead to practically the same transient response.

It is also permitted in the case of the symmetrical optimum to use the first order delay as an equivalent function with the equivalent time constant

$$t_e = 4T_e. \tag{6.112}$$

A subordinate loop which contains first order delays but no integrating action can likewise be set up in accordance with the symmetrical optimum. This system does not respond to a step in the command variable with an overshoot of 43% even when there is no required value smoothing. Thus the smoothing in this case may be smaller and in magnitude may follow the curve in Fig. 6.36. The equivalent time constant t_e of the optimized control loop with required value smoothing is not $4T_e$. To a good approximation, it is defined by the equation[1])

$$t_e = 2T_e + \tfrac{1}{2}t_{sm}$$
$$= 2T_e(2 - e^{-((T_1/4T_e)-1)}). \tag{6.113}$$

For a subordinate control loop which contains only first order delays and is adjusted in conformity with Eqn (6.92), the equivalent time constant is to be used, with

$$t_e = 4T_e \frac{T_1}{T_1 + T_e}. \tag{6.114}$$

A symmetrically optimized control loop which includes a smoothing element with a bridging differentiating element in the command variable channel of the controller, works in accordance with the transfer function (6.102)

$$F_w^*(s)_{opt} = \frac{1}{1 + s3T_e + s^2 2T_e^2}.$$

If the last term in the denominator is neglected, a first order delay is left

$$F(s) = \frac{1}{1 + s3T_e}. \tag{6.115}$$

Following the previous considerations, the equivalent time constant of such a control loop is

$$t_e = 3T_e. \tag{6.116}$$

6.8.3. Regulation of disturbances

It was shown in Section 1.1 that automatic control is used primarily to eliminate disturbances. However, since the behaviour of the controlled variable cannot usually be investigated during changes of disturbance variable in a reproducible and comparable manner, it is necessary to determine from

[1]) The latter equation is only valid if $\frac{T_1}{4T_e} \geq 1$.

calculation and modelling how the controlled variable will behave, with a defined controller adjustment, in response to a disturbance.

The transfer function (5.50) indicates how the control loop (Fig. 5.38) reacts to a disturbance

$$F_z(s) = \frac{x(s)}{z(s)} = \frac{F_w(s)}{F_R(s)F_{S1}(s)}$$

$$= \frac{N_R(s)N_{S1}(s)Z_{S2}(s)}{Z_0(s)+N_0(s)}$$

Accordingly, this control loop can be transformed as shown in Fig. 6.45. Instead of the command variable, whose change will be zero, the disturbance variable is applied to the closed loop via the two reciprocal elements.

The following considerations are somewhat simplified if it is assumed that the disturbance variable enters at the input of the controlled system and not at any optional point in the control loop. Thus the transfer function of the first part of the controlled system is

$$F_{S1}(s) = 1$$

and the transfer function of the control loop, relative to the disturbance affecting the input to the controlled system is

$$F_z^*(s) = \frac{x(s)}{z(s)} = \frac{F_w(s)}{F_R(s)}. \tag{6.117}$$

This simplification gives a good approximation if only unimportant parts of the controlled system, especially those with small time constants, are to be found in advance of the point in the plant at which the disturbance acts.

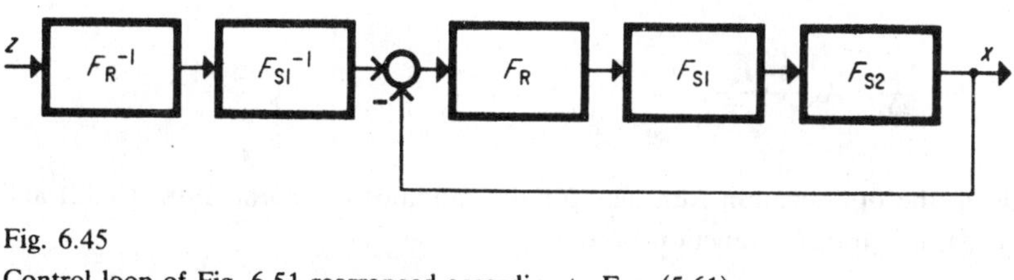

Fig. 6.45
Control loop of Fig. 6.51 rearranged according to Eqn (5.61)
F_R Transfer function of controller
F_{S1} Transfer function of section 1
F_{S2} Transfer function of section 2

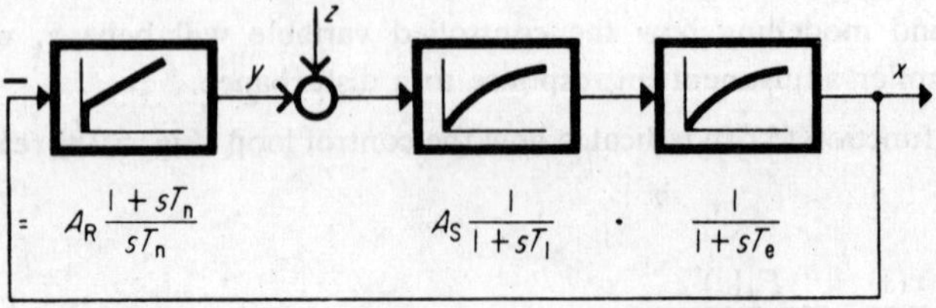

Fig. 6.46 Control loop to be investigated during a disturbance

For a qualitative investigation, let it be assumed that that controlled system shows a large first order delay and a series of smaller delays, the time constants of which are gathered into an equivalent time constant T_e (Fig. 6.46).

In this case a PI controller is used. If the time constant T_1 of the large delay is several times larger than the equivalent time constant T_e, symmetrical optimization is usually used and only rarely modulus optimization or linear optimization because the latter are too slow in controlling a disturbance.

The transfer function of a PI controller is

$$F_R(s) = A_R \frac{1+sT_n}{sT_n}.$$

Therefore the reciprocal is

$$\frac{1}{F_R(s)} = \frac{sT_n}{A_R(1+sT_n)}.$$

If it is desired to use the optimization formula for linear optimization, Eqn (6.108), the reciprocal of the transfer function of the PI controller becomes

$$\frac{1}{F_R(s)} = A_S \frac{s4T_e}{1+sT_1}.$$

Using the optimization formulae for the modulus optimum, Eqns (6.52) and (6.55), this transfer function becomes

$$\frac{1}{F_R(s)} = A_S \frac{s2T_e}{1+sT_1}.$$

If the optimization formulae for the symmetrical optimum, Eqn (6.83), are used, the transfer function becomes

$$\frac{1}{F_R(s)} = A_R \frac{T_e}{T_1} \frac{s8T_e}{1+s4T_e}.$$

For the case where an integrating element appears in the controlled system instead of the large delay, the reciprocal value according to Eqns (6.74) and (6.76) is

$$\frac{1}{F_R(s)} = \frac{T_e}{T_i} \frac{s8T_e}{1+s4T_e}.$$

These four transfer functions for the reciprocal behaviour of the PI controller are of the form of a practical differentiating element. They make it clear that at the instant of the step input variable, a step response occurs, for the linear optimum, of

$$H = A_S \frac{4T_e}{T_1} u_{step}$$

and for the modulus optimum and the symmetrical optimum, a response of half the amplitude,

$$H = A_S \frac{2T_e}{T_1} u_{step}.$$

Long after the input signal change, the step responses are zero once more. In between lies a transient with a delayed behaviour. The delay time, with the linear optimum and the modulus optimum is

$$T = T_1$$

and with adjustment according to the symmetrical optimum, it is

$$T = 4T_e.$$

The transfer function for the linear optimized control loop, Eqn (6.105), is

$$F_w(s)_{opt} = \frac{1}{1+s4T_e+s^2 4T_e^2}.$$

The function for the modulus optimized control loop, Eqn (6.48), is

$$F_w(s)_{opt} = \frac{1}{1+s2T_e+s^2 2T_e^2}$$

and the function for the symmetrically optimized control loop, Eqn (6.77), is

$$F_w(s)_{opt} = \frac{1+s4T_e}{1+s4T_e+s^2 8T_e^2+s^3 8T_e^3}.$$

The transfer function for the symmetrically optimized control loop, which has only first order delays and no integrating element, is

$$F_w(s)_{opt} = \frac{1+s4T_e}{1+s4T_e\left(1+\frac{2T_e}{T_1}\right)+s^2 8T_e^2\left(1+\frac{T_e}{T_1}\right)+s^3 8T_e^3}$$

Assuming that $T_1 \gg 4T_e$ so that $2T_e/T_1$ and T_e/T_1 are much less than 1, the penultimate equation can often be used.

For the control loop of Fig. 6.46, all transfer functions for the various optimization possibilities are now brought together for consideration according to Eqn (6.117). Therefore the associated transfer functions F_z for the closed control loop can be defined in relation to the disturbance at the input of the controlled system.

Application of the linear optimum gives

$$F_z(s)_{opt} = \frac{x(s)}{z(s)} = \frac{2A_S}{1+sT_1}\,\frac{s2T_e}{1+s4T_e+s^2 4T_e^2} \tag{6.118}$$

and for the modulus optimum

$$F_z(s)_{opt} = \frac{x(s)}{z(s)} = \frac{A_S}{1+ST_1}\,\frac{s2T_e}{1+s2T_e+s^2 2T_e^2} \tag{6.119}$$

The symmetrical optimum is thus

$$F_z(s)_{opt} = \frac{x(s)}{z(s)} = \frac{A_S}{1+s2T_e}\,\frac{4T_e}{T_1}\,\frac{s2T_e}{1+s2T_e+s^2 4T_e^2}. \tag{6.120}$$

The simplified form of F_w is used here in the representation of the transfer function F_z for the symmetrical optimum.

These three transfer functions F_z, adjusted in accordance with the three different optimization formulae, make it clear that the second part of the equations are always almost the same. However, material differences are caused by the first part, which characterizes the varied regulation of a disturbance. Thus, in linear optimization the first overshoot is twice as large as in modulus optimization. In both optimization methods, however, the control response is of the same duration, for in both cases the delay time is equal to the large delay time T_1. If the symmetrical optimum is used, the delay time is still only twice the sum of the small time constants. With the assumption that T_1 is large compared with $4T_e$, this delay time must be very small and in every case significantly less than T_1. Thus evidence is provided that control of a disturbance by adjustment of the control loop according to the symmetrical optimum is appreciably faster than by adjustment according to the modulus optimum or the linear optimum. Moreover, the first overshoot of the controlled variable during a disturbance is smaller if the control action is designed according to the symmetrical optimum rather than the modulus optimum.

The preceding mathematical considerations are demonstrated in Fig. 6.47. First the step responses for the reciprocally acting controller and for the optimized control loop are represented for the modulus optimum and for the

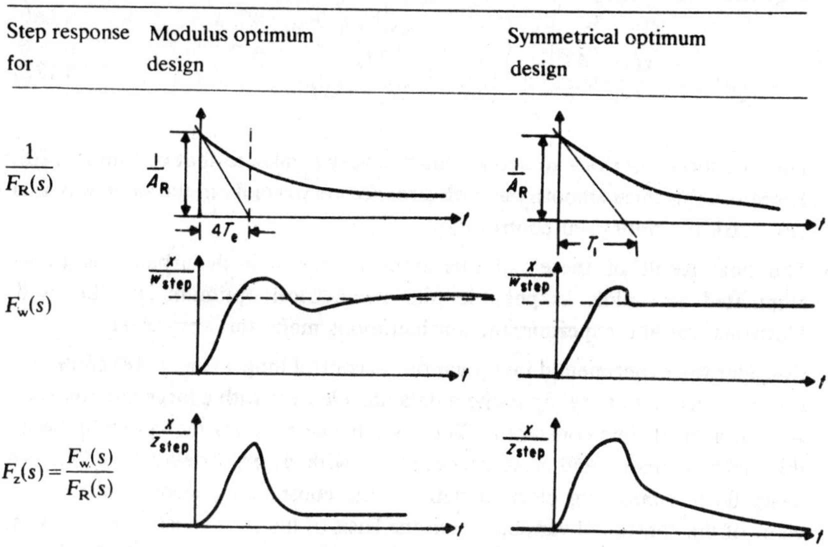

Fig. 6.47
Qualitative study of the control variable x in the control loop of Fig. 6.46 during a step input of the disturbance variable

symmetrical optimum. Because of the step response of the optimized control loop, the step response of the reciprocal controller is rounded off, so that by this means the qualitative step response for the optimized control loop during disturbances is generated.

From the doubled amplitude of the step response of the reciprocally acting controller and also from the doubled amplitude of the step response of the controlled variable during the regulation of a disturbance, the qualitative representations for the linear optimum are seen to be the same as for the modulus optimum. The linear optimum is therefore not included in Fig. 6.47.

Equation (6.120), to be precise, should be

$$F_z(s)_{opt} = A_S \frac{4T_e}{T_1} \frac{s2T_e}{1+s4T_e\left(1+\dfrac{2T_e}{T_1}\right)+s^2 8T_e^2\left(1+\dfrac{T_e}{T_1}\right)+s^3 8T_e^3}. \tag{6.121}$$

From Eqn (6.121), however, the qualitative picture of the behaviour during the smoothing of a disturbance is by no means clear.

If the controlled system happens to exhibit an integrating action instead of the large first order delay, the transfer function is

$$F_z(s)_{opt} = \frac{x(s)}{z(s)} = \frac{4T_e}{T_i} \frac{1}{1+s2T_e} \frac{s2T_e}{1+s2T_e+s^2 4T_e^2}. \tag{6.122}$$

This equation describes an action which is very similar to that of Eqn (6.120). Therefore this must smooth out a disturbance very rapidly in the same way as a symmetrically optimized control loop.

The final result of these considerations is that if a disturbance is to be eliminated as rapidly as possible, the symmetrical optimum is to be used. Mathematical and experimental considerations make this very clear.

Consider the experimental investigation. A control loop[1] (Fig. 6.48) controls a system which has at the input end a delaying element with a large amplification A_S and a small time constant t_2. The disturbance z enters the system between this delay element and a succeeding one with a large delay time T_1. An insignificant smoothing element with a time constant t_{sm} leads to the actual value of the controlled variable x. On the basis of the time constant ratio given, $T_1 \gg 4T_e$, the PI controller can be adjusted to the three optimization formulae: linear optimum (LO), modulus optimum (MO) and symmetrical optimum (SO).

[1]) For example, the control loop could be the armature current control loop of a speed controlled d.c. machine.

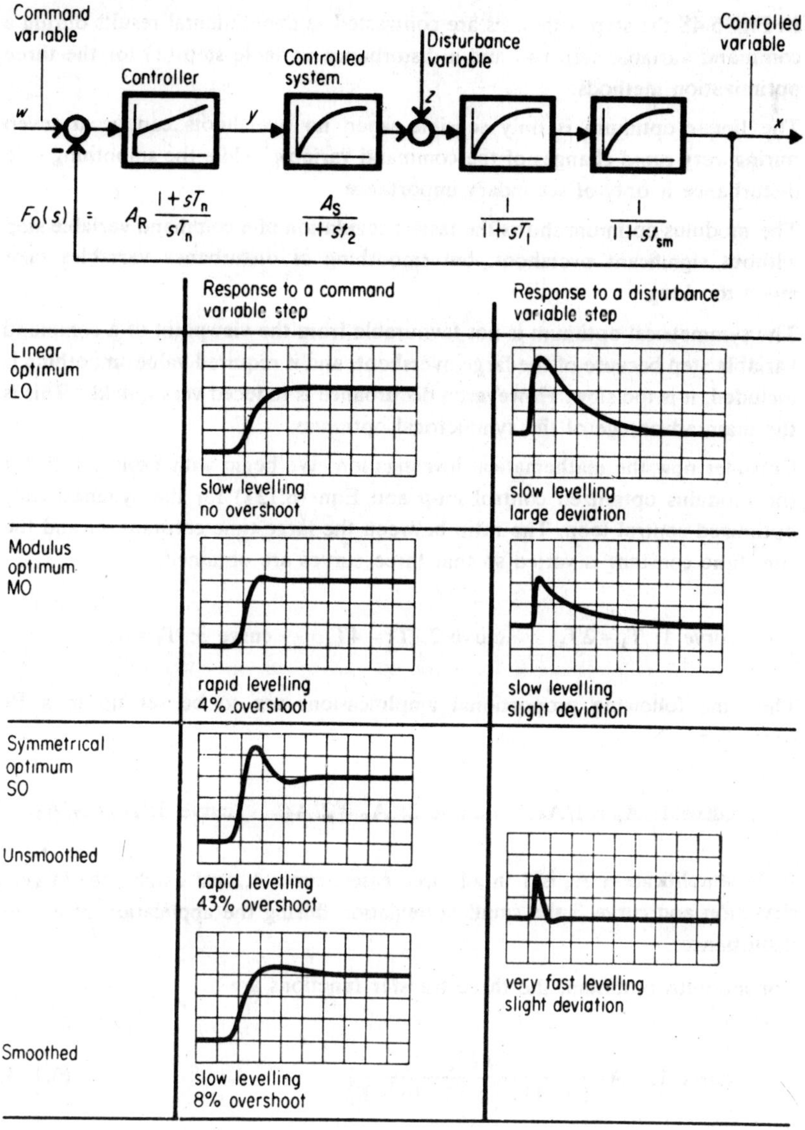

Fig. 6.48

Transient behaviour of the controlled variable for step inputs of command variable and disturbance variable

In Fig. 6.48 the step responses are contrasted as experimental results during a command variable step (w) and a disturbance variable step (z) for the three optimization methods.

The linear optimum is only sensible when no overshoots can occur, even during very rapid changes of the command variable, while the smoothing of a disturbance is only of secondary importance.

The modulus optimum shows the fastest regulation of a command variable step without significant overshoot. but smoothing of disturbance variables take much too long.

The symmetrical optimum is not favourable from the viewpoint of a command variable step because of the large overshoot, and if required value smoothing is included, it is too slow. However, a disturbance is reduced very quickly. This is the main advantage of the symmetrical optimum.

Consider now the mathematical investigation. We begin with Eqn (6.119) for the modulus optimized control loop and Eqn (6.121) for the symmetrically optimized control loop. The ratio between the large time constant T_1 and the sum time constant is varied so that three curves are obtained:

curve 1: $T_1 = 2T_e$, curve 2: $T_1 = 4T_e$, curve 3: $T_1 = 8T_e$.

Then the following proportional amplifications are to be set up in a PI controller:

curve 1: $A_R = 1/A_S$, curve 2: $A_R = 2/A_S$, curve 3: $A_R = 4/A_S$.

If the amplification A_S is 1 in all three cases, curve 1 must exhibit the largest deviation and curve 3 the smallest deviation during the application of a step disturbance.

For modulus optimum, the three transfer functions are

$$\text{curve 1:} \quad A_S \frac{s2T_e}{1 + s4T_e + s^2 6T_e^2 + s^3 4T_e^3} \tag{6.123}$$

$$\text{curve 2:} \quad A_S \frac{s2T_e}{1 + s6T_e + s^2 10T_e^2 + s^3 8T_e^3} \tag{6.124}$$

$$\text{curve 3:} \quad A_S \frac{s2T_e}{1 + s10T_e + s^2 18T_e^2 + s^3 16T_e^3}. \tag{6.125}$$

If the same control loop is designed according to the symmetrical optimum, the following transfer functions appear:

$$\text{curve 1:}\quad A_S \frac{s4T_e}{1+s8T_e+s^2 12T_e^2+s^3 8T_e^3} \tag{6.126}$$

$$\text{curve 2:}\quad A_S \frac{s2T_e}{1+s6T_e+s^2 10T_e^2+s^3 8T_e^3} \tag{6.127}$$

$$\text{curve 3:}\quad A_S \frac{sT_e}{1+s5T_e+s^2 9T_e^2+s^3 8T_e^3}\,. \tag{6.128}$$

In the case of the modulus optimum, the second term of the denominator is smallest ($4T_e$) for Eqn (6.123), i.e. curve 1. For symmetrical optimum, the second term of the denominator is smallest ($5T_e$) for Eqn (6.128), i.e. curve 3. Thus these curves must represent the shortest time to reach the steady state. Therefore, because of the faster smoothing of a disturbance, the symmetrical optimum is always advantageous, if the delay time T_1 is larger than four times the sum of the small time constants T_e. If it is not, the modulus optimum is more favourable.

Curve 2 is the same in both cases. With $T_1 = 4T_e$, the limit lies between modulus optimum and symmetrical optimum.

The mathematical transformation of Eqns (6.123) to (6.125) for the modulus optimized control loop gives the transient responses shown in Fig. 6.49. The

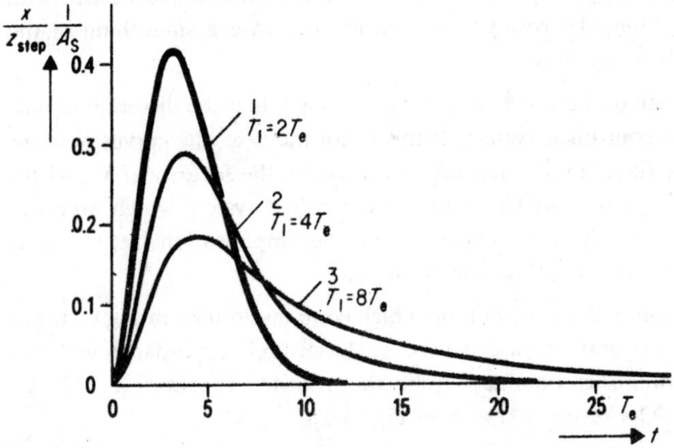

Fig. 6.49
Transient responses of the controlled variable during a step change of disturbance variable in a control loop as shown in Fig. 6.46 which is designed according to the modulus optimum

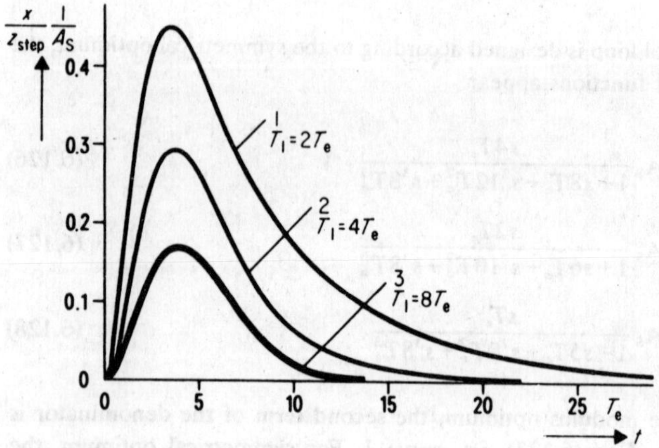

Fig. 6.50
Transient responses of the controlled variable for a step change of disturbance variable in a control loop as shown in Fig. 6.46, designed according to the symmetrical optimum

transformation of Eqns (6.126) to (6.129) similarly gives the transient responses shown in Fig. 6.50 for the symmetrically optimized loop. Curve 1 of Fig. 6.49 and curve 3 of Fig. 6.50 emphasize the optimum use of the adjustment formulae as they show the shortest smoothing time. If the control loop with a time constant ratio $T_1/4T_e$ less than 1 were to be adjusted in accordance with the symmetrical optimum or if the control loop, with a time constant ratio $T_1/4T_e$ greater than 1 were to be adjusted in accordance with the modulus optimum, the result would be in each case a smoothing of the disturbance which is too slow.

It is assumed in each of the transient responses shown that the disturbance acts at the input of the controlled system. If this is not the case, the curves must be multiplied, not by the amplification factor A_S but by the factor A_S/A_{S1} where A_{S1} is the amplification of that part of the controlled system which precedes the point of action of the disturbance. Often the amplification factor A_{S1} is greater than the overall amplification factor A_S.

The transient response of a control loop which contains an integrating factor in the controlled system and which is consequently set up in accordance with the symmetrical optimum, is obtained from the transfer function (6.122) by retransformation. The result is shown in Fig. 6.51.

The first overshoot in Fig. 6.51 appears quite large, for the factor is taken as 1. The curve should be multiplied by the specific factor of the control loop in question. This factor is usually very small.

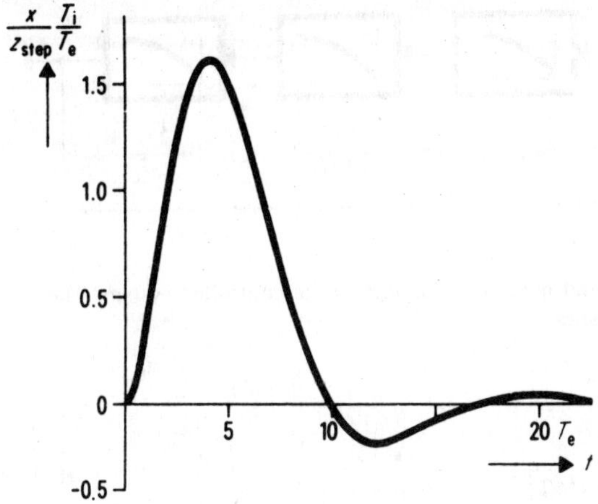

Fig. 6.51
Transient response of the controlled variable for a step change of disturbance variable in a control loop which has an integrating factor in the controlled system similar to Fig. 6.46 and is designed according to the symmetrical optimum

From Figs. 6.49 and 6.51 an estimate can be made of how much overshoot and smoothing time must be allowed for.

During the smoothing of disturbances with PI controllers, all loops considered appear as third order system elements, irrespective of whether the formulae for linear, modulus or symmetrical optimum are used. This control loop smooths all disturbances virtually to zero. The s term in the numerator of the transfer function $F_z(s)$ makes this clear. Obviously there always remain the errors of the operational amplifier, the measurement transducer and the required value adjuster, even though these are usually small.

The control loop with an I or PID controller must behave similarly. For these it may always be assumed that the disturbance variable acts at the input to the controlled system.

An I controller is used when there is no significant delay and no integrating action in the controlled system (Fig. 6.52). This control loop can only be adjusted to the linear optimum or the modulus optimum. When the loop is set up according to the linear optimum it reacts to a disturbance according to the

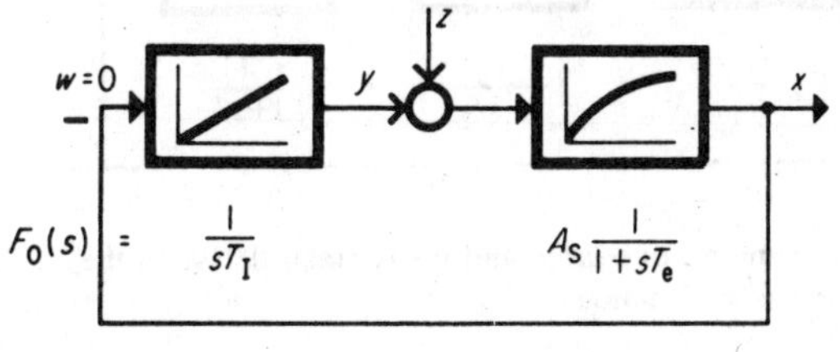

Fig. 6.52
Control loop with an I controller

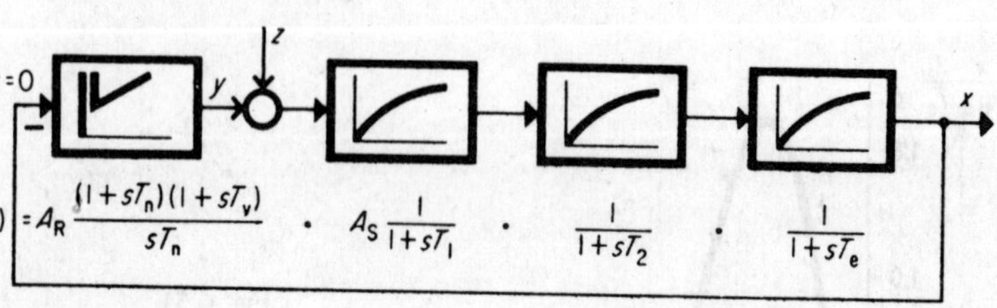

Fig. 6.53
Control loop with two large and many small delays in the controlled system. The controller has PID characteristics

following transfer function:

$$F_z(s) = A_S \frac{s4T_e}{1 + s4T_e + s^2 4T_e^2}. \tag{6.129}$$

When set up according to the modulus optimum, it reacts according to the following function:

$$F_z(s) = A_S \frac{s2T_e}{1 + s2T_e + s^2 2T_e^2}. \tag{6.130}$$

This control loop is described by a second order system element.

A PID controller is used if the controlled system contains two significant time constants. A distinction is made as to whether the system contains only first order delays or an integrating element. If, besides small first order delays, there are only two large ones, the ratio of the time constants $T_1/4T_e$ determines whether the control loop is to be set up in accordance with the modulus optimum or the symmetrical optimum. If besides the small delays there is only one large one and also an integrating element, the symmetrical optimum (Fig. 6.54) must be used.

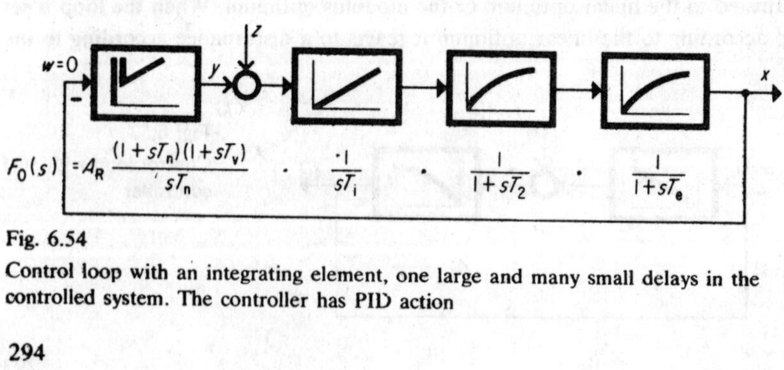

Fig. 6.54
Control loop with an integrating element, one large and many small delays in the controlled system. The controller has PID action

The following transfer functions are obtained from Fig. 6.53:

a) the modulus optimized control loop $T_1 < 4T_e$

$$F_z(s) = \frac{A_S}{1+sT_1} \frac{1}{1+sT_n} \frac{s2T_e}{1+s2T_e+s^2 2T_e^2}; \tag{6.131}$$

b) the symmetrically optimized control loop $T_1 > 4T_e$

$$F_z(s) = A_s \frac{1}{1+sT_2} \frac{s2T_e}{1+s4T_e\left(1+\frac{2T_e}{T_1}\right)+s^2 8T_e^2\left(1+\frac{T_e}{T_1}\right)+s^3 8T_e^3}; \tag{6.132}$$

c) the case of linear optimum

$$F_z(s) = \frac{A_S}{1+sT_i} \frac{1}{1+sT_2} \frac{s4T_e}{1+s4T_e+s^2 4T_e^2}. \tag{6.133}$$

All of these functions are fourth order system elements.

If an integrating element occurs in the controlled system, as in Fig. 6.54, the transfer functions are:

a) for the symmetrically optimized loop

$$F_z(s) = \frac{4T_e}{T_i} \frac{1}{1+sT_2} \frac{1}{1+s2T_e} \frac{s2T_e}{1+s2T_e+s^2 4T_e^2}; \tag{6.134}$$

b) for the case of linear optimum

$$F_z(s) = \frac{9T_e}{T_i} \frac{1}{1+sT_2} \frac{1}{1+s3T_e} \frac{s3T_e}{1+s6T_e+s^2 9T_e^2}. \tag{6.135}$$

Again, fourth order transfer functions are obtained.

If the transfer functions (6.131) to (6.135) for smoothing out a disturbance by a PID controller are compared with the control loop functions (6.118) to (6.122) which have a PI controller, it can be seen that with a PID controller, a delay term always occurs in the function $F_z(s)$. This is

$$\frac{1}{1+sT_2}.$$

While a command variable change is controlled more rapidly with a PID controller than with a PI controller, this is not the case in the smoothing of a disturbance which acts at the input to the controlled system. However, if the disturbance acts after the delay element with delay time T_2, the delay caused by the phase advance time $T_v = T_2$ disappears, in consequence of Eqn (5.50), owing to the reciprocal delay element which acts as a phase advance. With these assumptions the PID controller smooths out a disturbance significantly faster than the PI controller.

According to the foregoing equations, the control loop, during a disturbance acts as

a second system element with an I controller;
a third order system element with a PI controller,
a fourth order element with a PID controller.

A control loop, whose controller contains no integrating element behaves differently under the influence of a disturbance from the control loop described above. Whether it is a P controller or a PD controller, the transfer function $F_z(s)$ contains no numerator term.

The disturbance is not smoothed out to a zero error signal. An offset error is always present.

For the system with a very large delay time T_1 and a very small sum of delay times T_e, a modulus optimized P controller is used (Fig. 6.55).

The transfer function which describes the behaviour during a disturbance is

$$F_z(s) = A_S\left(1 - \frac{T_1}{1+2T_e}\right)\frac{1}{1+s2T_e\left(1-\frac{T_e}{T_1+2T_e}\right)+s^2 2T_e^2\left(1-\frac{2T_e}{T_1+2T_e}\right)}. \tag{6.136}$$

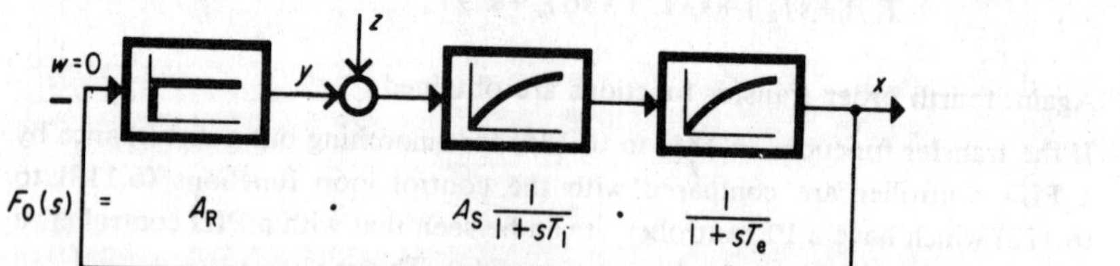

Fig. 6.55
Control loop with one very large delay and a number of very small delays in the controlled system. The controller has a P action

This shows a second order delay characteristic. The transient response is similar to the same control loop during a change of command variable and described by Eqn (6.61). It can only be compared with the transient response (6.130) of the control loop of Fig. 6.52, where an I controller is used. However, while the I controller does not permit an offset error, the offset error already indicated by Fig. 6.14 occurs here, in accordance with the following equation:

$$F_z(s)|_{s=0} = A_S\left(1-\frac{T_1}{T_1+2T_e}\right) = A_S\frac{2T_e}{T_1+2T_e}. \tag{6.137}$$

Since the P controller is usually used only when the large delay time T_1 is at least twenty times larger than the sum time constant T_e then an offset error of less than $\Delta x = 0.091 A_S\,\Delta z$ appears.

Since the smoothing of a step disturbance takes place with practically the same response as the control of a command variable step with the modulus optimum, a rise time of approximately $4.7T_e$ appears, and an overshoot of about 4%. The damping factor of this second order system element is

$$\zeta = \frac{1}{\sqrt{2}}\sqrt{1+\frac{T_e^2/T_1}{T_1+2T_e}}.$$

The expression under the square root sign is only slightly greater than 1. For a time constant ratio of $T_1/4T_e \geq 5$, it is 1.001 14.

If the sum time constant T_e of the system discussed contains another large delay time T_2, which is to be compensated, then a PD controller should be used (Fig. 6.56). When adjusted to the modulus optimum, the transfer function is

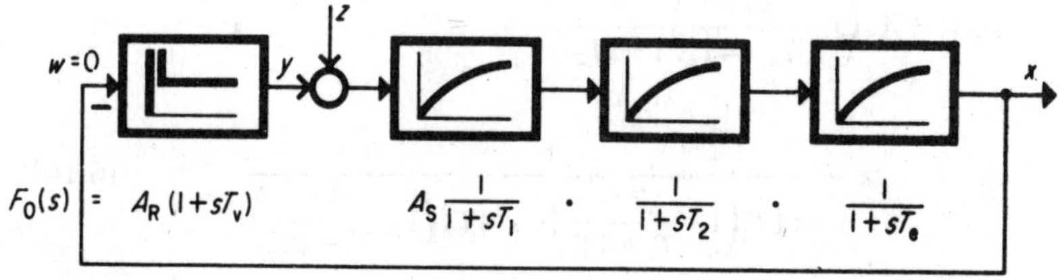

Fig. 6.56
Control loop with two very large delays and a number of very small delays in the controlled system. The controller has a PD action

$$F_r(s) = A_S\left(1 - \frac{T_1}{T_1 + 2T_e}\right)\frac{1}{1 + sT_2}$$

$$\times \frac{1}{1 + s2T_e\left(1 - \dfrac{T_e}{T_1 + 2T_e}\right) + s^2 2T_e^2\left(1 - \dfrac{2T_e}{T_1 + 2T_e}\right)}. \tag{6.138}$$

The smoothing action is the same as the control loop previously considered (Fig. 6.55). However, the sum time constant T_e which defined the transient response is now smaller by the large time T_2. A delay with a time constant of T_2 is therefore also effective. However, if the disturbance does not enter the loop at the input to the controlled system, but acts after the element with delay of time constant T_2, the smoothing action is rapid because the factor $1/(1 + sT_2)$ disappears.

If the two control loops of Figs. 6.55 and 6.56 are to be set up according to the linear optimum, the following transfer functions then arise for the loop controlled by the P controller

$$F_z(s) = A_S\left(1 - \frac{T_1}{T_1 + 4T_e}\right)$$

$$\times \frac{1}{1 + s4T_e\left(1 - \dfrac{3T_e}{T_1 + 4T_e}\right) + s^2 4T_e^2\left(1 - \dfrac{4T_e}{T_1 + 4T_e}\right)} \tag{6.139}$$

and for the loop controlled by the PD controller,

$$F_z(s) = A_S\left(1 - \frac{T_1}{T_1 + 4T_e}\right)\frac{1}{1 + sT_2}$$

$$\times \frac{1}{1 + s4T_e\left(1 - \dfrac{3T_e}{T_1 + 4T_e}\right) + s^2 4T_e^2\left(1 - \dfrac{4T_e}{T_1 + 4T_e}\right)} \tag{6.140}$$

Similarities can be seen to Eqns (6.129) and (6.133).

6.9. The Avoidance of Overshoots of the Controlled Variable in Overdriven Controllers

The preceding considerations about the optimization of control loops rest on the assumption that none of the controllers are overdriven. For small command variable changes, this can be seen to be usually the case. However, for large and fast changes of the command variable, the controlled variable is unable to follow rapidly enough and overdriving of the controller occurs. Consequently, the set variable at the output of the controller does not show the magnitude and transient behaviour required on the basis of the difference between the command variable and the controlled variable and according to the design of the controller. As a result of this, during the transient period, the controlled variable assumes values other than those which the calculated transient response would anticipate. Since the set variable cannot reach the necessary amplitude, a much slower change of the controlled variable is produced.

Usually, the controller contains an integrating action. If an integrator is overdriven, it can only leave this state if the input variable reverses in sign. This means that the difference between the command variable and the controlled variable must reverse its sign. This leads to a vigorous overshoot of the controlled variable. This overshoot is then necessary to bring the controller back to the steady-state condition.

This undesirable overshoot during large changes of the command variable can be prevented in three ways:

1. by a run up controller or required value integrator,
2. by a special controller for the change of the command variable,
3. by a phase advance in the controlled variable channel of the controller.

Consider a simple speed control system for a d.c. machine (Fig. 6.57).

Owing to an almost instantaneous application of a speed command variable at the input of the speed controller, the latter goes into the overdriven state. This is because the moment of inertia of the drive is large and the torque produced by the motor is insufficient to accelerate the drive rapidly enough. The motor can only draw the permitted maximum current in accordance with the current limiting facility, so that the torque is limited. Accelerated by the maximum torque, the machine runs up to the speed required by the command variable and overshoots significantly as the accelerating torque cannot be reduced fast enough.

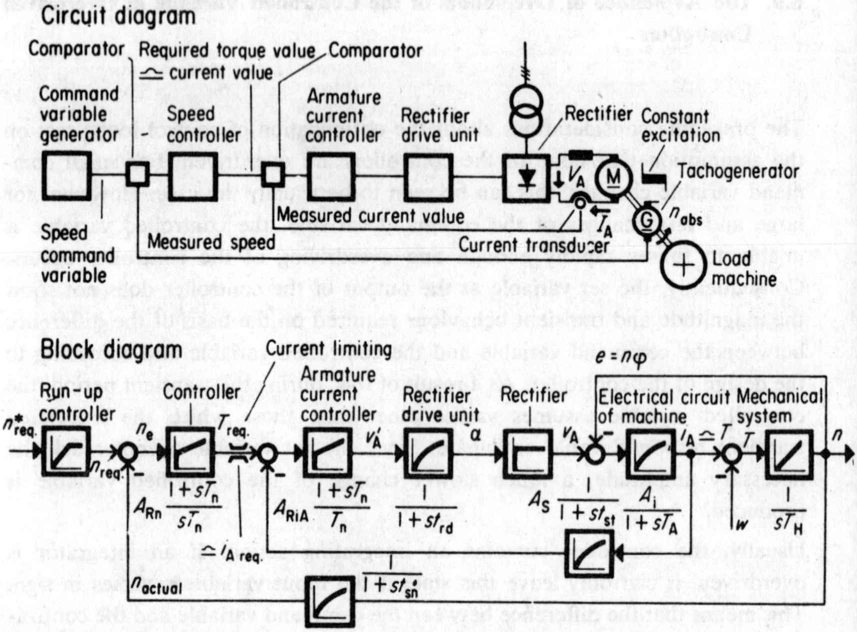

Fig. 6.57 Speed control for a d.c. drive

6.9.1. Run up controller

To prevent overshooting of the controlled variable during vigorous changes of the command variable, a run up controller or required value integrator is often used. In the example referred to it is often called an acceleration limiter. An integrator will convert rapid changes of the command variable into a ramp function. The slope of the ramp should not be so large as to cause the rate controller to go into the overdriven state (Fig. 6.58). The rate of change of speed is now just large enough for the drive with its maximum permissible torque to be able to follow the required speed correctly.

The run up controller (Fig. 6.59) consists of a non-inverting amplifier of very high amplification (flip–flop or two state element) and an integrating element with very large integrating time constant. The input voltage of the integrator is adjusted by means of a potentiometer. At the input of the non-inverting amplifier the voltage of the command variable is compared with the output voltage of the integrator. At the instant when these two voltages at the input of the non-inverting amplifier deviate only very slightly from each other, the amplifier goes into the overdriven state and its output is integrated by the

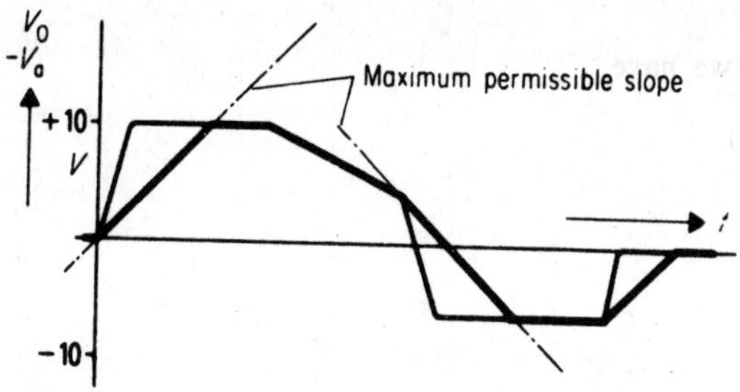

Fig. 6.58
Action of a run up controller
Unlimited rate of change of command variable ———— V_0
Maximum permissible rate of change of command variable ———— $-V_a$

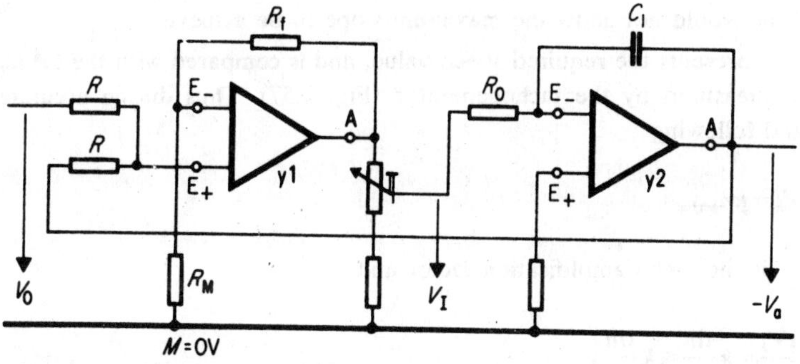

Fig. 6.59
Circuit diagram of a run up controller. The input voltage V_1 tapped off from the potentiometer is always the same even for quite small voltage differences between V_0 and $-V_a$, because the amplification of the amplifier y1 (ratio $R_f/R_M > 100$) is very large

integrator, according to the tapping point on the potentiometer. The integration stops only when the output and input voltages are of equal magnitude in absolute values, within the unavoidable errors of the amplifier.

Let the permissible rate of change of speed for the drive with maximum load on the motor be

$$\left.\frac{dn}{dt}\right|_{\text{max load}}$$

Considering the integrator we have

$$-V_a = \frac{1}{T_1}\int_0^t V_1(t)\,dt$$

and thus

$$\frac{dV_a}{dt} = \frac{|V_1|}{T_1}$$

Hence

$$T_1 = \frac{|V_1|}{|dV_a/dt|_{max}}$$

since a smaller value would allow of too high a slope of V_a (Fig. 6.58) and a large value would not allow the maximum slope to be achieved.

Now V_a represents the required speed value, and is compared with the actual value n measured by the tachogenerator (Fig. 6.57). Thus during accurate command following

$$V_a = kn_{actual}$$

where k is the tacho amplification factor and

$$\frac{dV_a}{dt} = k\frac{dn}{dt} \leqslant k\frac{dn}{dt}\bigg|_{max\ load}$$

since dn/dt must be less than the maximum acceleration.

Combining the above statements, we then have

$$\frac{dV_a}{dt}\bigg|_{max} = k\frac{dn}{dt}\bigg|_{max\ load}$$

and therefore

$$T_1 = \frac{1}{k}\frac{V_1}{|dn/dt|_{max\ load}}. \tag{6.141}$$

All the quantities on the right-hand side of Eqn (6.141) are known from the specification of the motor, the flip–flop and the tachogenerator.

V_1 is the flip–flop voltage and having fixed $C_1 = T_1/R_0$ from Eqn (6.141) some adjustment can be made to the run up control by varying the potentiometer of Fig. 6.59.

6.9.2. Acceleration controller

Instead of the run up controller connected before the speed controller, an acceleration controller connected after it can be used. The argument of the individual controllers is shown in Fig. 6.60, together with their additional circuits.

A proportional speed controller is used in this case instead of the more usual PI controller.

When the required value and the actual value of the speed are unequal, acceleration or deceleration is necessary. The output variable of the speed controller represents the acceleration demand. It is zero when the required and actual values of the speed are the same. The output voltage of the speed controller is limited to the maximum permitted acceleration or deceleration.

The acceleration controller conforms in basic design to the circuit of Fig. 4.68. The differentiating capacitor C_0 in the controlled variable channel produces the actual value of acceleration, for it enables the change of the actual value of the speed to be determined. The capacitor displacement current I_v during maximum permissible acceleration must have the same value but opposite sign

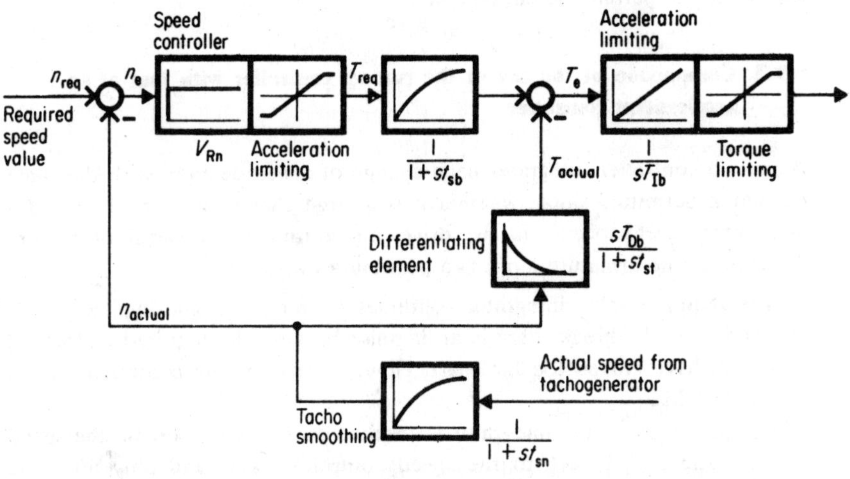

Fig: 6.60 Block diagram for a speed controller with acceleration controller

as the current in the command variable channel with the maximum required acceleration value $V_{b\,req}$.

The choice of this capacitance depends on the permissible run up time T_h of the drive, within which the machine runs up with the maximum permitted constant acceleration from the stationary state to the nominal speed:

$$C_0 = \frac{I_v}{V_{b\,req}} T_h. \tag{6.142}$$

In series with capacitor C_0 is the decoupling resistance R_0. For the actual acceleration value l_{act}, a delay occurs with time constant t_{sb}. The resistance R_0 is normally chosen so that the time constant is not larger than

$$R_0 C_0 = t_{sb} \approx 5 \text{ ms}.$$

In order to achieve the same delay time t_{sb} and the necessary phase reversal for the required acceleration value in the path of the proportional speed controller which itself causes a reversal of phase, an active delay element as shown in Fig. 4.63 is provided in the command variable channel. The integration time constant T_{Ib} of the acceleration controller can easily be matched to the behaviour of the controlled system by the modulus optimization method using the circuit of Fig. 4.38. A buffer amplifier must be used for the comparison of the required and actual values, with the capacitor C_0 in the actual value channel so that the input impedance of the integrator can be made high with respect to the parallel potentiometer.

6.9.3. Comparison of the use of the run up controller with that of an acceleration controller

A run up controller integrates each change of speed demand with the same maximum permitted slope, whether it is a large change or a small one. If a momentary break occurs in the drive, e.g. during the reversal of current direction in the armature loop, two possibilities arise:

1. The required value integrator continues to integrate, ignoring the break. Then after the break there is an impulse because the required and actual speeds have moved too far apart. However, the run up controller should prevent this.
2. By special action the integrator is checked during such a break, the speed command is fed back to the speed control variable and only after the momentary break is the integration continued.

The necessity of such an action is certainly a disadvantage. An advantage of the run up controller is that the acceleration is always the maximum permitted, independent of the magnitude of the speed error signal. The acceleration is under control.

This is not the case with the acceleration controller. If the speed error signal is small, the speed controller does not go into action and a smaller acceleration value than the maximum permitted is demanded. The controlled removal of the speed difference proceeds more slowly than is permissible, and only larger error signals are controlled with the maximum possible torque. This is the disadvantage of the acceleration controller. On the other hand, it is an advantage that the actual acceleration value is measured and therefore the acceleration controller remains in operation even during a momentary break. The drive is continually commanded by the acceleration controller. Additional actions in the controller are not necessary in this case.

6.9.4. Controlled variable channel with proportional/differential action

A third possibility (seldom used, however) to avoid controlled variable overshoot during large changes of the command variable is by comparing the command variable w with both the controlled variable x and the rate of change of x, i.e. dx/dt.

The error signal is

$$e(t) = w(t) - \left[x(t) + \frac{dx(t)}{dt} \right]. \tag{6.143}$$

A controller using this principle senses that the command and the controlled variables are equal at a time when the latter is still approaching the command value. If the controller has an integrating action which leaves the overdriven state only when the error signal changes sign, the discharge of the feedback capacitor begins at a time when the controlled variable is still rising towards the command variable value. This reversal slows the rise of the controlled variable and ensures no overshoot.

Figure 6.61 shows the controlled variable x which responds to a step function of the command variable w, together with its differential dx/dt and the sum of the two quantities, in one case without the controller being overdriven, and in the other, with an overdriven controller.

In the speed control system shown in Fig. 6.57 the speed controller must have a PI characteristic and must be set up in conformity with the symmetrical

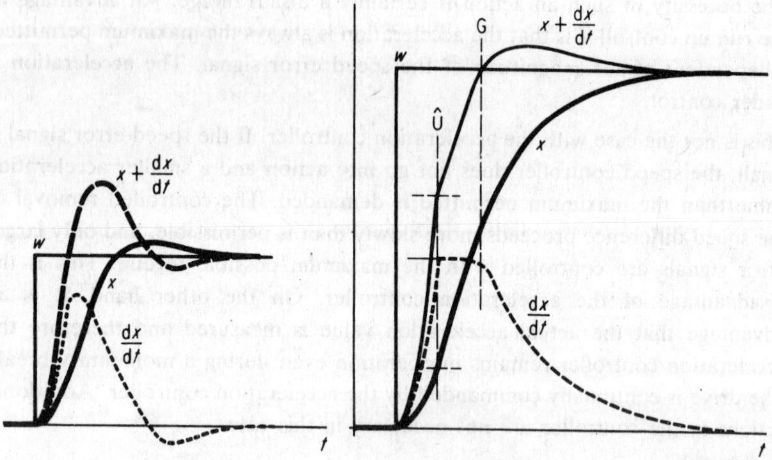

a) Controller does not go into the overdriven state

b) At point Û the controller goes into the overdriven state. At point G, the required and actual values are equal. From point G the controller integrates in the reverse direction

Fig. 6.61
Curves showing the behaviour of a controlled variable x in a control loop in which the controlled variable and its rate of change are combined in the actual value channel

optimum. This is because in the controlled system, besides a series of small delays (the subordinate optimized current control loop is equivalent to such delays), there is an integrating element with integration time constant T_i. According to the formula for the symmetrical optimum, the required value smoothing in the command variable channel is to be designed with the time constant t_{sm} as the reset time T_n of the PI controller:

$$T_n = t_{sm} = 4T_e.$$

If it is remembered that a PI controller can be made up of a PD element in series with an I element (Fig. 5.15), the PI controller can be transformed so that the actual value is processed proportionally and differentiated in the controlled variable channel of an I controller. Figure 6.62 shows the individual steps of this transformation. A new control loop arises as shown in Fig. 6.63.

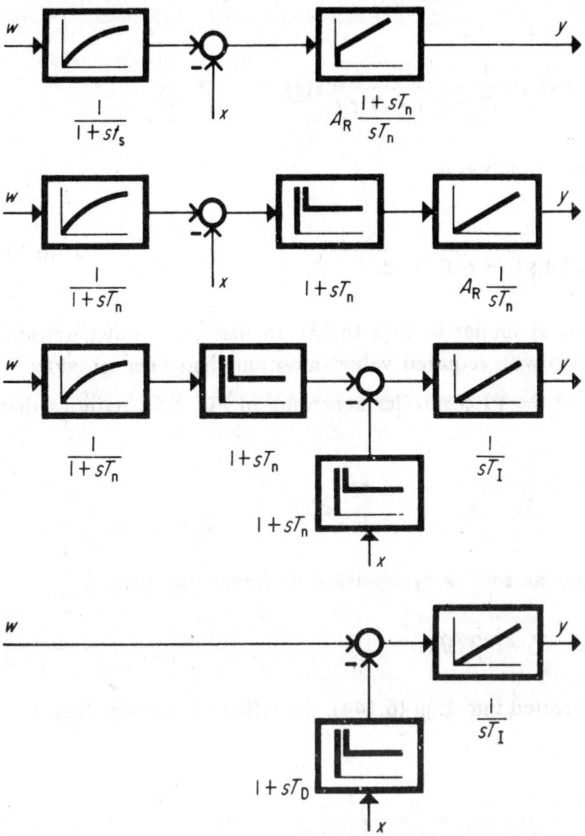

Fig. 6.62

Transformation of a PI controller with required value smoothing into an I controller with a PD element in the actual value channel

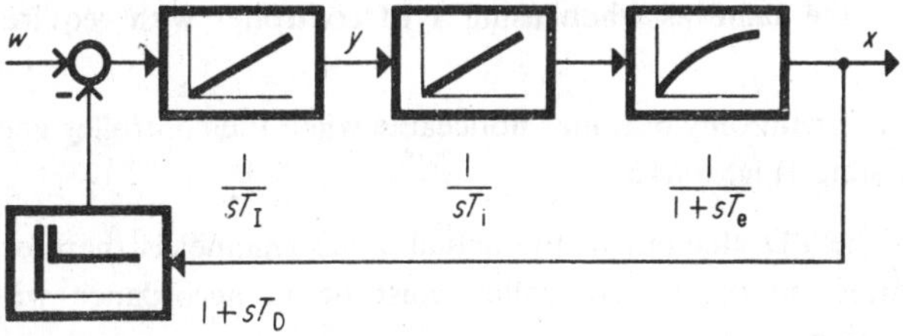

Fig. 6.63

Control loop with an integrating element and an equivalent delay in the controlled system, in which the PI controller is split into a PD element in the actual value channel and an I controller

For this control loop

$$[w(s)-x(s)(1+sT_D)]\frac{1}{sT_I}\frac{1}{sT_i(1+sT_e)}=x(s).$$

Therefore the transfer function is

$$F_w(s)=\frac{x(s)}{w(s)}=\frac{1}{1+sT_D+s^2T_IT_i+s^3T_IT_iT_e}. \quad (6.144)$$

This transfer function is similar to Eqn (6.95). In that case, a symmetrically optimized control loop with required value smoothing had been provided. The transformation of the PI controller according to Fig. 6.62 requires that

$$T_D=T_n, \qquad T_I=\frac{T_n}{A_R}=\frac{T_D}{A_R}.$$

With the design formulae for the symmetrical optimum, this gives

$$T_D=4T_e \quad \text{and} \quad T_I=(8T_e^2)/T_i.$$

If these values are inserted into Eqn (6.144), the following transfer function is obtained

$$F_w(s)_{opt}=\frac{x(s)}{w^*(s)}=\frac{1}{1+s4T_e+s^2 8T_e^2+s^3 8T_e^3}.$$

Provided that none of the elements in the control loop goes into the overdriven state, especially the controller, the transient behaviour during a change of command variable is the same as when using a PI controller with required value smoothing.

The advantage of this circuit only becomes noticeable when the controller goes into the overdriven state (Fig. 6.61b).

The controller with the PD element in the actual value channel is therefore used when the setting up of the controller must be in accordance with symmetrical optimization.

This also applies when the controlled system contains no integrating element but a large delay with a time constant T_1 which is more than four times the sum time constant T_e. For the PD element in the actual value channel and for the I controller, the relevant optimization formulae are

$$T_D = 4T_e\left(\frac{T_1}{T_1+3T_e}\right) \quad \text{and} \quad T_1 = A_S\frac{8T_e^2}{T_1}.$$

The circuit of the I controller with the PD element in the actual value channel of Fig. 6.62 is made up from a PD element (Fig. 4.54) and an I controller (Fig. 4.38) so that the two parts do not influence each other and the adjustment of the controller parameters can be undertaken with complete freedom.

The circuit shown in Fig. 4.69 has the same effect. However, it does not permit independent adjustment.

6.10. Optimum Adjustment of Controllers Using Tables

In this section is demonstrated the design of a controller using tables and diagrams and the effect on the controlled variable.

Using Table 6.3, the control loop is established with respect to the type of optimization appropriate to the ratio of the time constants of the controlled system, and the characteristics of the controller are defined. Consideration is given to large time constants, integration time constant T_0 and the largest delay time T_1, and if necessary the less significant delay time T_2, and to the ratio between the large time constant and the sum time constant T_e (Section 6.3). Depending on the number of significant constants in the controlled system

T_0 or T_1; T_2; T_e

the controller provided has one, two or three parameters:

I controller; PI controller; PID controller.

The modulus optimum (MO) or symmetrical optimum (SO) is used, depending on the time constants or on the time constant ratio, respectively.

If the ratio between the time constants is very large, the integrating part in the controller can be omitted and the controller can be set up according to the modulus optimum.

It must always be remembered, however, that an offset error arises when a P controller or a PD controller is used. The decision on whether the control error

Table 6.3: Selection of controller

Controlled system: Large time constants[1] — Integration time constant T_0	Delay time constant T_1	T_2	Ratio[2] between large time constant and small time constants $T/4T_e$: <1	>1	≫1	Required controller: controller action	optimisation method	smoothing time constant (required value) t_{sm}	equivalent time constant t_e
	3		X	X	X	I	BO		$2T_e$
	X		X			PI	BO		$2T_e$
	X			X		PI	SO	$0 \cdots 4T_e$	$2 \cdots 4T_e$
	X				X	P	BO		$2T_e$
	X	X	X			PID	BO		$2T_e$
	X	X		X		PID	SO	$0 \cdots 4T_e$	$2 \cdots 4T_e$
	X	X			X	PD	BO		$2T_e$
X			X	X		PI	SO	$4T_e$	$4T_e$
X					X	P	BO		$2T_e$
X		X	X	X		PID	SO	$4T_e$	$4T_e$
X		X			X	PD	BO		$2T_e$

[1] Only one integration time T_0 or one delay time T_1 can be effective.
[2] The ratio between the large time constant T and the equivalent time constant T_e is referred to either the time constant T_1 of the largest first order delay or to the integration time constant T_0.
[3] An absence of delay in the controlled system indicates that it is to be treated as large.

arising from Eqns (6.28), (6.68) or (6.137) is acceptable for this control method can only be made in relation to the type of application.

Required value smoothing, as in Section 6.7.4, is necessary when adjustment to the symmetrical optimum is used. For the case when only first order delays are present in the controlled system, and symmetrically optimized adjustment is to be undertaken on the basis of the time constant ratio according to Eqn (6.98), the minimum necessary smoothing time constant t_{sm} in the range 0 to $4T_e$ of the curve in Fig. 6.64 will be specified.

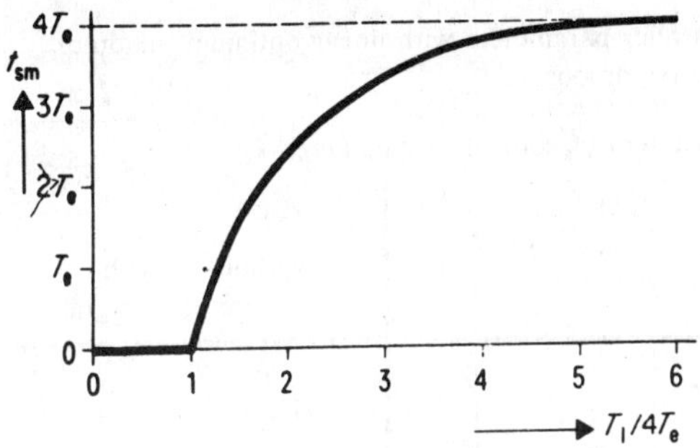

Fig. 6.64
Minimum required value smoothing t_{sm} necessary in the application the symmetrical optimum, when only first order delays are present in the controlled system

Finally the time constant t_e for the optimized control loop is given in Table 6.3. This is described in Section 6.8.2 and is always needed when the optimized control loop appears as a subordinate control loop which is part of the overall loop. Its simplest definition follows Eqn (6.113), i.e.

$$t_e = 2T_e + \tfrac{1}{2}t_{sm}.$$

The linear optimum which responds to a command variable step without overshoot does not appear in Table 6.3. This is because the linear optimum does not depend on the particular controlled system but on the way in which it is used.

When it has been established, using Table 6.3, which controller and which optimization method is to be used, Table 6.4 gives the necessary controller parameters for linear optimum, modulus optimum and symmetrical optimum conditions. The adjustment follows on the basis of the time constants of the controlled system and the amplification A_S.

When adjusting according to the symmetrical optimum, it is necessary to decide from the controller amplification whether an integral of time constant $T_i = T_0/A_S$ is to be included or not. If it is present, the correction factor $T_1/(T_1 + 3T_e)$ as in Eqn (6.92) is often used for the reset time T_n.

A PI controller or a PID controller must always be used for the application of the symmetrical optimum. If a PD controller is used for a controlled system with an integration time constant T_i, the proportional amplification should be

$$A_R = T_i/2T_e \quad \text{or} \quad T_i/4T_e$$

according to whether a modulus optimized or linear optimized action is required.

Table 6.4:
Optimization formulae for the controller parameters with linear optimum, modulus optimum and symmetrical optimum conditions

Optimization method	Adjustment of controlled parameters T_1	T_n	T_v	A_R without system	A_R with integral
LO Linear optimum	$4A_ST_e$	T_1	T_2	$\frac{T_1}{4A_ST_e}$	
MO Modulus optimum	$2A_ST_e$	T_1	T_2	$\frac{T_1}{2A_ST_e}$	
SO Symmetrical optimum without system integral		$\frac{T_1}{T_1+3T_e}$	T_2	$\frac{T_1}{2A_ST_e}$	
SO Symmetrical optimum with system integral		$4T_e$	T_2		$\frac{T_i}{2T_e}$
Controller action	I	PI PID	PD PID	P PD	PI PID

For the symmetrical optimum without system integral the data in Fig. 6.33 and possibly Eqn (6.92) are applicable

Table 6.5 gives the characteristic values described in Fig. 6.5 for the three optima, for a controlled variable response to a command variable step, namely: the rise time t_r, the settling time t_s and the extent of overswing $\hat{u}$.

If the mode of optimization, the controller action and the magnitudes of the controller parameters are established on the basis of the data for the controlled system, Table 6.6 gives the diagrammatic representation of the transient response, the mathematical transfer function and reference to where the controller is described, for the various types of controller action. This reference is necessary because the forms of realization for one and the same controller characteristic can be very different. Table 6.7 shows the fundamental circuit and the controller parameters for the simplest form of controller with a single inverting amplifier. The necessary second input channel for a controller is not shown.

If the parameters of a given system are known, it is possible to determine from Tables 6.3 to 6.7 and Fig. 6.64 the appropriate controller for simple cases as well as its adjustment and circuit.

Table 6.5:
Characteristic values for the transient response of the controlled variable in response to a step change of command variable

Optimization method	Controller response to required value step		
	Rise time t_r	Time to steady state t_s	Overshoot $\hat{u}$
LO Linear optimum	[1]	$12T_e$	0
BO Modulus optimum	$4.7T_e$ [2]	$8.4T_e$	4.3%
without smoothing	$3.1T_e$ ↓	$16.5T_e$ ↓	43.4% [3] ↓
SO Symmetrical optimum	$4.7T_e$	$8.4T_e$	4.3%
with smoothing	↑ $7.6T_e$	↑ $13.3T_e$	↑ 8.1% [4]

[1] Because of the asymptotic approach to the new value, no rise time can be quoted for the linear optimum.
[2] The rise time is $4.7T_e$ for the modulus optimum if the sum time constant T_e stands for only a single time constant. It is reduced to $3.8T_e$ if the equivalent time constant T_e represents an infinite number of time constants.
[3] The values in this line apply for unsmoothed command variable step and an integrating element in the system. They tend towards the values for the modulus optimum if a large first order delay occurs in the system instead of the integrating element. They approach these values more closely the more the ratio $T_1/4T_e$ approaches 1.
[4] The values of the lower line apply for smoothed command variable step and an integrating element in the controlled system. They tend towards values for the modulus optimum if a large first order delay occurs in the system instead of the integrating element, and they approach these values more closely the nearer the ratio $T/4T_e$ approaches 1.

As an example, consider, the armature current controller for the control of speed as shown in Fig. 6.57. The controlled system (Fig. 6.65) contains the armature loop of the d.c. machine as the largest delay with the armature loop time constant T_A as in Eqn (3.15). Above the discontinuous current limit, suppose that a value of $T_A = L_A/R_A = 31$ ms has been measured by the 63% method (Fig. 3.12). From the point by point non-linear characteristic recorded (cf Fig. 3.39) for the controlled system, i.e. output voltage $V_{iA\,act}$ of the measurement converter (for armature current I_A) against the drive voltage V_{st} at the input of the rectifier drive unit while the machine is held stationary, a system amplification A_{SiA} may be determined at the steepest part of the curve

Table 6.6: Response of controllers

Controller action	Step response	Transfer function $F(s)=\frac{-y(s)}{e(s)}$	See section
P	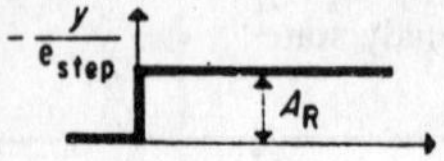	$\frac{-y(s)}{e(s)}=A_R$	3.1 4.3.1
I	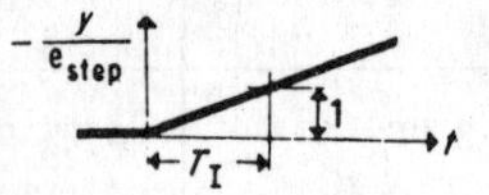	$\frac{-y(s)}{e(s)}=\frac{1}{sT_i}$	3.2 4.3.2
PI	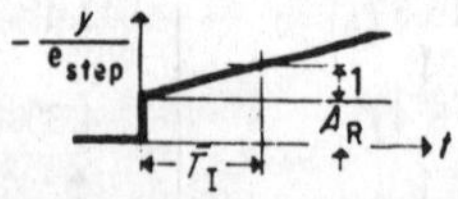	$\frac{-y(s)}{e(s)}=A_R\frac{1+sT_n}{sT_n}$	4.3.4
PD	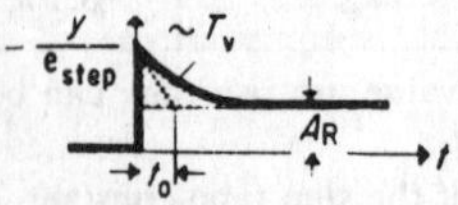	$\frac{-y(s)}{e(s)}=A_R\frac{1+sT_v}{1+st_d}$	4.3.6
PID	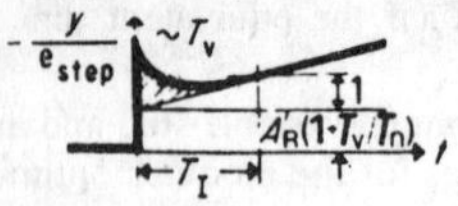	$\frac{-y(s)}{e(s)}=A_R\frac{(1+sT_n)(1+sT_v)}{sT_n(1+st_d)}$	4.3.7

e, error signal ($e=w-x$)
e_{step}, step change of error signal
y set variable at controller output

above the discontinuous current limit of

$$A_{SiA}=\frac{\Delta V_{iA\,act}}{\Delta V_{st}}=12.8$$

The input amplifier of the drive unit is provided with a delay to prevent the input signal changing too rapidly. The delay time is

$$t_{rd}=2.5\text{ ms}.$$

The feedback channel for the controlled variable, armature current, is provided with smoothing, since the current from the rectifier includes a ripple corresponding to the number of impulses in one period of mains voltage. The

Table 6.7: Circuit arrangements of the inverting amplifier

Controller action	Basic circuit	Proportional amplification	Time constants
P	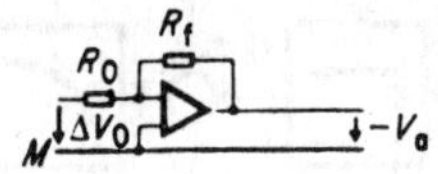	$V_R = \frac{R_f}{R_0}$	
I	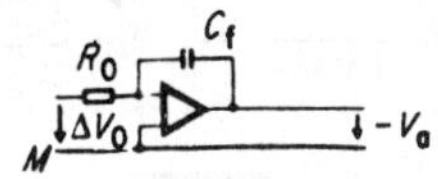		$T_I = R_0 C_I$
PI	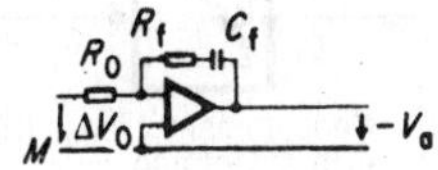	$V_R = \frac{R_f}{R_0}$	$T_n = R_f C_f$ $T_I = R_0 C_f = \frac{T_n}{V_R}$
PD	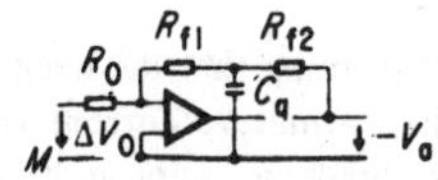	$V_R = \frac{R_{f1} + R_{f2}}{R_0}$	$T_v = \frac{R_{f1} \cdot R_{f2}}{R_{f1} + R_{f2}} C_q$ $t_d = \frac{V_R}{V_u}\left[1 + \frac{R_0}{R_{f1}} + \frac{R_0}{R_e}\right] T_v$
PID	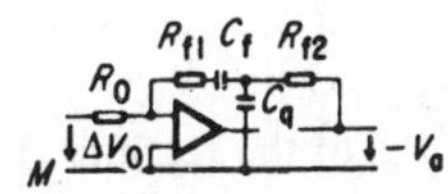	$V_R = \frac{R_{f1} + R_{f2}}{R_0}$	$T_n = [R_{f1} + R_{f2}] C_f$ $T_v = \frac{R_{f1} \cdot R_{f2}}{R_{f1} + R_{f2}} C_q$
	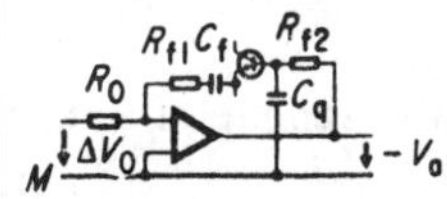	$V_R = \frac{R_f}{R_0}$	$T_n = R_{f1} C_f$ $T_v = R_{f2} C_q$

T_I Integration time constant
T_v Phase advance time constant
t_d Damping time constant
T_n Reset time constant

smoothing of the actual value should have a time constant

$$t_{si} \leq \frac{1}{2} \frac{\text{mains period}}{\text{number of pulses}}$$

which is about 1.5 ms for a full wave, six pulse, three-phase bridge circuit. Since the sum time of these two small delays

$$T_{iA} = t_{rd} + t_{Si} = 4 \text{ ms}$$

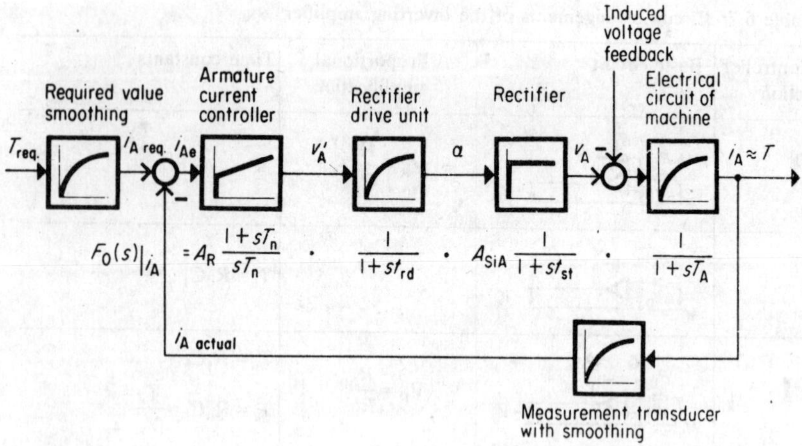

Fig. 6.65
Block diagram of an armature current control loop. Assuming that the excitation is constant, the required torque value and the required armature current value are identical. The feedback of the induced voltage of the machine is the most significant disturbance variable

is larger than the average statistical dead time T_{SR} of the rectifier (Eqn (3.53)), the dead time can be neglected on the basis of the integrating character of the current controller.

Thus the data for the controlled system in this example of armature current control are known

$$T_A = 31 \text{ ms}, \qquad T_{iA} = 4 \text{ ms}, \qquad A_{SiA} = 12.8.$$

With the aid of Table 6.3, since

$$\frac{T_A}{4T_{iA}} = \frac{31 \text{ ms}}{4.4 \text{ ms}} = 1.94 > 1$$

it is seen that a PI controller is to be used and is to be adjusted according to the symmetrical optimum.

For this case, Fig. 6.64 indicates that required value smoothing is to be provided with a time constant t_{sm} which is approximately $2.4 T_{iA}$.

It can be deduced from Table 6.4 that for the PI controller the reset time is[1])

$$T_n = 4T_{iA}\frac{T_A}{T_A+3T_{iA}} = 4\times 4\text{ ms}\frac{31\text{ ms}}{31\text{ ms}+3\times 4\text{ ms}} = 11\text{ ms}$$

and the proportional amplification is

$$A_{RiA} = \frac{T_A}{2A_{SiA}T_{iA}} = \frac{31\text{ ms}}{2\times 12.8\times 4\text{ ms}} = 0.303.$$

Table 6.6 indicates the characteristic values for the transient state of the armature current as a response to a step in the command variable. Therefore, for the data chosen for the symmetrically optimized control loop without required value smoothing, a rise time t_r of about 12 ms must be set up.

For the PI controller, Table 6.6 also shows the transient response and indicates that the various circuits in use are to be found in Section 4.3.4. The transfer function

$$F_{RiA}(s) = A_{RiA}\frac{1+sT_n}{sT_n}$$

is obtained for the armature current controller with a PI characteristic.

For the simplest case of realization of the PI controller (Fig. 4.41), it can be seen from Table 6.7 what values of resistance and capacitance are to be used to obtain the controller parameters which were obtained by calculation, i.e. the proportional amplification and the reset time.

With a resistance $R_s = 22\text{ k}\Omega + 22\text{ k}\Omega$ and a maximum possible command variable voltage $V_{iA\,req} = 10\text{ V}$ for the maximum armature current in the machine, a maximum current I_v (numerator comparison current) of 0.227 mA results in the command variable channel of the controller (Fig. 4.21). In the case where this maximum armature current is represented by the measurement transducer with a voltage $V_{iA\,act} = 8.65\text{ V}$[2]) the resistance R_i in the controlled variable channel must be $19.03\text{ k}\Omega + 19.03\text{ k}\Omega$ for the same comparison current $I_v = 0.227$ mA.

[1]) Since the correction value $T_A/(T_A+3T_{iA})$ reduces the reset time T_n so that a behaviour like that of a genuine symmetrical optimum occurs, the required value smoothing t_{sm} must now equal $T_n = 11$ ms.

[2]) The measurement transducer in fact would indicate 10 V with a current of 1000 A but the maximum armature current in the example given is only 865 A.

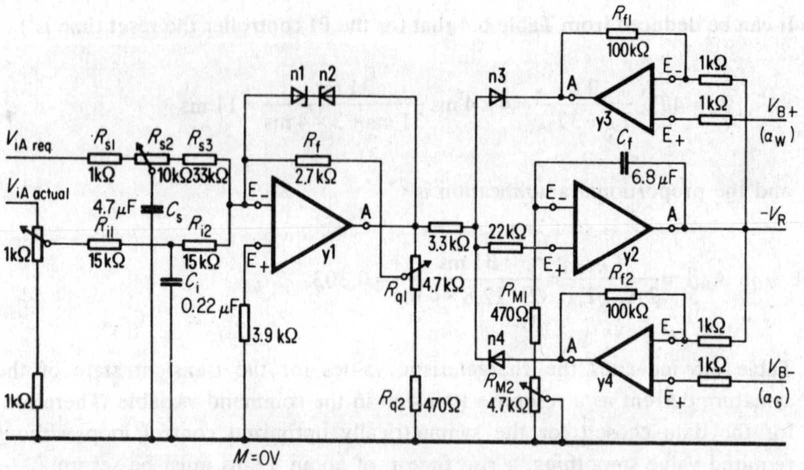

Fig. 6.66
Circuit diagram of an armature current controller (PI characteristic) with input matching and output limiting

This resistance is not normally available and to adjust it to this value would be too costly. It is preferable to use a potential divider, for the measurement transducer can usually be loaded with a sufficiently large current. Thus in the circuit of Fig. 6.66, the tapping point (here at 6.82 V) is adjusted so that the calculated comparison current I_v of 0.227 mA flows in the controlled variable channel via the resistance R_i, which is, for example 15 kΩ+15 kΩ.

In the controlled variable channel, the actual value smoothing should be adjusted for a time constant $t_{si} = 1.5$ ms. From Fig. 4.61, we see that this requires a capacitance

$$C_i = t_{si}\,\frac{R_{i1}+R_{i2}}{R_{i1}R_{i2}} \quad \text{(see Eqn (4.93))}.$$

With $R_{i1} = R_{i2} = 15$ kΩ, this gives $C_i = 0.2\ \mu$F.

A commonly available capacitance value is 0.22 µF. If this is used, the time constant becomes 1.65 ms.

Required value smoothing with the calculated time constant $t_{sm} = 11$ ms is to be provided in the command variable channel. This is achieved by a parallel capacitance which must have a value

$$C_s = t_{sm} \frac{R_{s1} + R_{s2}}{R_{s1} R_{s2}}.$$

For $R_{s1} = R_{s2} = 22\ \mathrm{k}\Omega$ this gives $C_s = 1\ \mu\mathrm{F}$. This is a value which is readily available.

From Table 6.7, the feedback resistance R_f is to be adjusted to give the required controller amplification $A_{RiA} = 0.303$, i.e.[1])

$$R_f = A_{RiA} R_i = 9.09\ \mathrm{k}\Omega.$$

The reset time, according to Table 6.4, should be $T_n = 11$ ms. Therefore the capacitance required in the feedback is

$$C_f = T_n / R_f = 1.21\ \mu\mathrm{F}.$$

The required values for R_f and C_f are not normally available. Therefore, in the first instance, the circuit of Fig. 4.43 is suggested. This has an inverting amplifier and a potentiometer adjustment each for the controller amplification and the reset time.

However, it is preferable to make use of the circuit of Fig. 4.45 for the armature circuit controller. The calculations for the command variable and controlled variable channels can then be undertaken. Thus a feedback resistance can be chosen according to the equation

$$R_f = \tfrac{1}{3} A_{RiA} R_i = 3.03\ \mathrm{k}\Omega$$

to achieve the proportional amplification A_{RiA} with the first amplifier, using the adjustable parallel potentiometer R_q of $4.7\ \mathrm{k}\Omega + 470\ \Omega$.

The factor $\frac{1}{3}$ appears so that with the potentiometer it is possible to reduce the proportional amplification down as far as one third of the calculated value. For the feedback resistance R_f, the nearest available value to the calculated value is used, i.e. $2.7\ \mathrm{k}\Omega$, and the potentiometer tapping point α is set at about 0.43.

Realization of the reset time constant $T_n = 11$ ms takes place with the non-inverting amplifier. If the adjustable resistance R_M is $4.7\ \mathrm{k}\Omega + 470\ \Omega$ the feedback capacitor is calculated as

$$C_f = 3 T_n / R_M = 6.38\ \mu\mathrm{F}.$$

---

[1]) Only the resistance R_i of the controlled variable channel is located in the control loop (Fig. 1.3).

With an available value of 6.8 μF a resistance of

$$\beta R_M = T_n / C_f = 1.62\ \text{k}\Omega$$

is used or the tapping point adjusted to $\beta = 0.313$. The circuit design chosen permits the realization of the reset time T_n in the range 3.2 to 35 ms.
The circuit of the armature current controller discussed above is shown in Fig. 6.66. Use is made here of the possibility of adjusting the required value smoothing in the command variable channel by means of a potentiometer. Moreover the inverting amplifier shown in Fig. 4.75 is limited to an output voltage of ±10 V with two zener diodes n1 and n2 connected back to back. Thus no voltage beyond the standard range is possible at the output of the controller.
The armature current controller is to drive the drive unit of the rectifier which regulates the armature voltage of the d.c. machine.

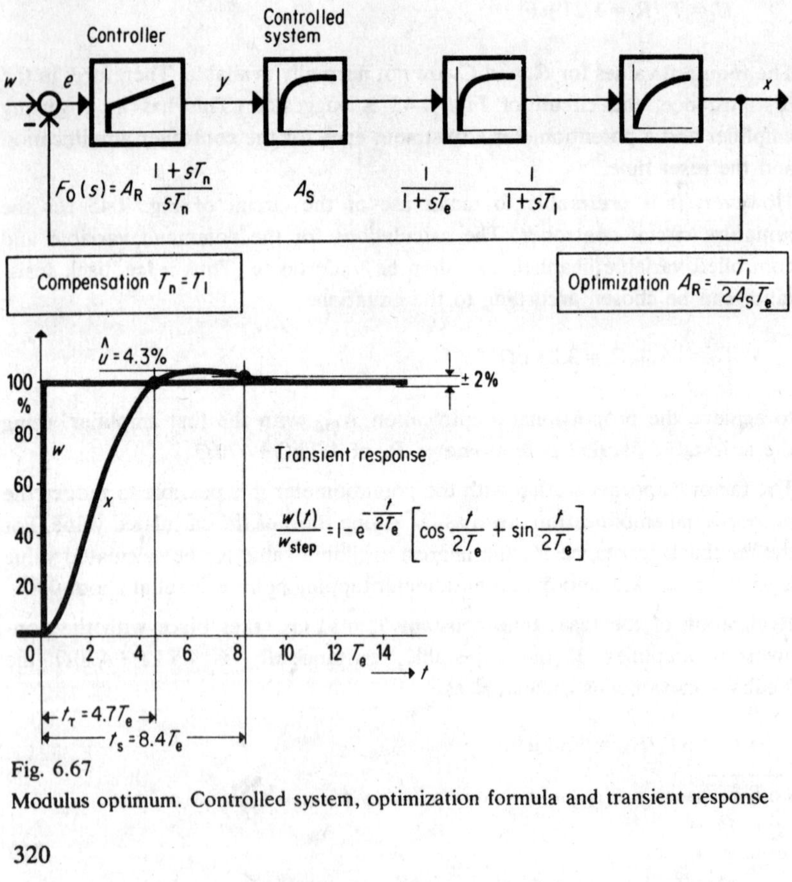

Fig. 6.67
Modulus optimum. Controlled system, optimization formula and transient response

It is customary for a drive unit to respond to an input voltage change in the negative direction with a reduction of the triggering angle (Fig. 3.41). This causes a voltage change in the armature loop of the machine which leads to a greater driving current in the armature. However, since the armature voltage V_A on the commutator must not exceed a certain specified value, the voltage must be limited to this value by limiting on the negative side of the controller output (triggering angle α_G). A similar arrangement applies on the positive side of the controller output. The triggering angle α must be far enough away from the 180 limit to prevent a flashover in the inverter range of the rectifier. This is termed the inverter limit α_w. In order not to exceed it the controller output voltage is positive limited. Active limiting as in Fig. 4.77 will be used for both limits.

In conclusion, the action of the modulus optimum is contrasted again with that of the symmetrical optimum in Figs 6.67 and 6.68, assuming that the command

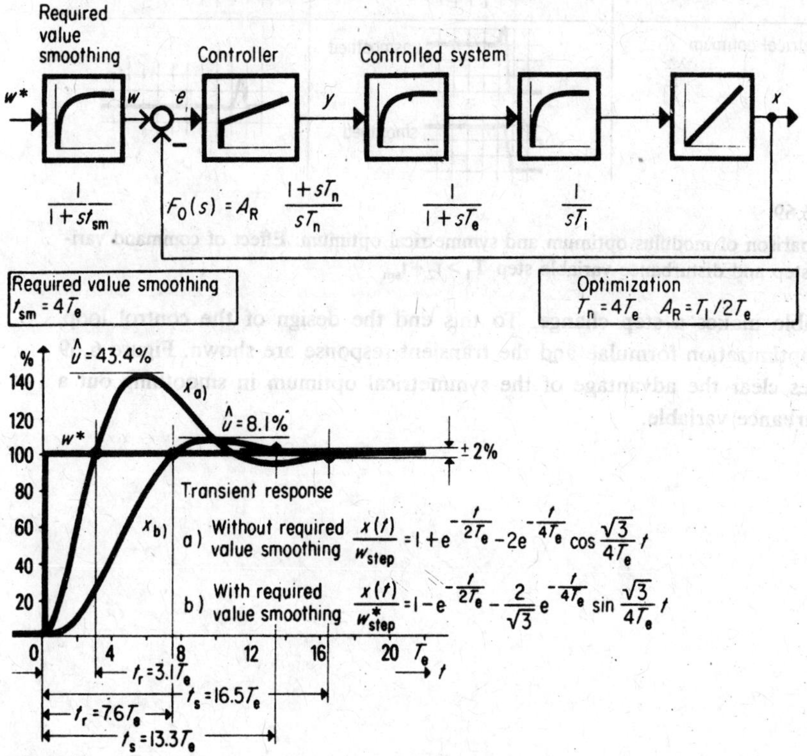

Fig. 6.68
Symmetrical optimum. Controlled system, optimization formulae and transient response

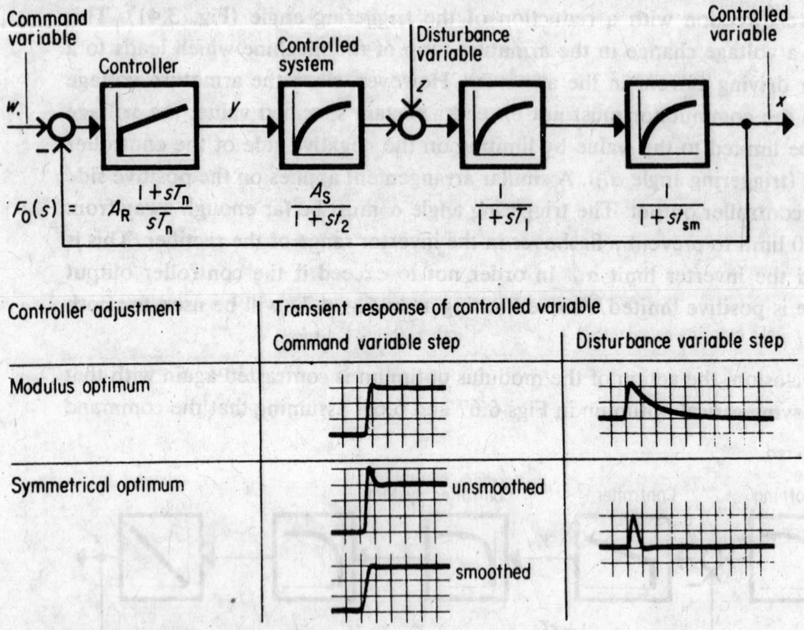

Fig. 6.69

Comparison of modulus optimum and symmetrical optimum. Effect of command variable step and disturbance variable step $T_1 > t_2 + t_{sm}$

variable makes a step change. To this end the design of the control loop, the optimization formulae and the transient response are shown. Figure 6.69 makes clear the advantage of the symmetrical optimum in smoothing out a disturbance variable.

7. Appendix

7.1. Notation and Symbols

A	Amplitude of a square wave
A_g	Amplifier common mode amplification
A_n	Amplitude of *n*th harmonic
A_u	Amplification or gain of amplifier
A_S, A_R	Amplification of amplifier
$A_{R\alpha}$	Adjustable amplification factor
A_0	Loop amplification
C	Capacitance
C_f	Feedback capacitance
C_q, C_0	Differentiating capacitance
dB	Decibels
e	Error signal
e_{st}	Residual error signal
e_{ts}	Total stationary error
e_{step}	Step change of e
E	Generated e.m.f. of electrical machine
E_{GM}	Generated voltage of d.c. machine
E_Q	Controlled voltage source
E_R	Rated value of generated e.m.f. of electrical machine
$E+$	Non inverting input of amplifier
$E-$	Inverting input of amplifier
f	Frequency
f_c, f_d	Break frequencies of Bode diagram
f_D	Phase advance area
$f(t)$	Transient function
F	Transfer function
F_e	Input element of a control system
F_f	Feedback element of a control system
F_R	Transfer function of controller
F_S	Transfer function of controlled system
F_V	Operational amplifier
F_{eiA}	Transfer function for armature current controller
$F(s)$	Transfer function
$F_o(s)$	Open loop transfer function

$F_{ov}(s)$	Overall transfer function
$F_w(s)$	Closed loop transfer function
$F_w(s)_{opt}$	Transfer function of optimized system
$F_z(s)$	Transfer function for disturbance
$F(\omega)$	Frequency response
$\|F(\omega)\|$	Modulus of frequency response
F_1, F_2	System elements
G	Any parameter
G_N	Nominal value at rated temperature and supply voltage of a parameter G
i, I	Current
i_E	Emitter current
I, i	Current
I_a	Amplified output current
I_e	Amplified differential input current
I_{e0}	Amplified impressed current
I_{e1}, I_{e2}	Input currents to difference amplifier
I_f	Feedback current
I_A	Armature current of electrical machine
I_{AR}	Normal or rated current of electrical machine
I_F	Field current of electrical machine
I_L	Load current
I_{LN}	Rated amplifier output current
I_O	Input current
I_O	Difference current
I_{SC}	Short circuit current of electrical machine
I_{St}	Hall effect control current
I_V	Capacitor displacement current
Im	Imaginary part of a complex number
J	Moment of inertia
k	Amplification
k	Roots of a characteristic equation
k_g	Amplifier common mode suppression
k_i	Integration factor
k_p	Proportionality factor, amplification or gain
k_{sc}	Current amplification factor of electrical machine
k_H	Hall effect factor
$k\alpha$	Correction factor
L	Inductance
L_A	Armature inductance of electrical machine
L_F	Field winding inductance of electrical machine

M	Reference potential (0 volt)
n	Shaft speed revs min^{-1}
n_R	Unloaded or rated speed
R	Resistance
R_a	Amplifier output impedance
R_d	Damping resistance
R_e	Amplifier input impedance
R_f	Feedback resistance
R_i	Source impedance of voltage source
R_u	Amplifier transfer impedance
R_v	Input resistance
R_A	Armature resistance of electrical machine
R_F	Field winding resistance of electrical machine
R_L	Load resistance
R_{Lmin}	Minimum value of load impedance
R_W	Eddy current equivalent resistance
R_0	Input resistance
Re	Real part of a complex number
s	Laplace operator
S_G, S_M	Conductance of feedback network
t	Time, time constant
T_d	Decay time constant, damping time constant
t_e, T_e	Equivalent time constant
t_r	Rise time
t_s	Settling time
t_{sm}	Smoothing time constant
t_R	Run up time of a machine
t_ε	Infinitely short time period
T	Time constant
T_a	Accelerating torque
T_d, T_D	Differentiation time constant
T_e	Torque produced by electrical machine
T_e, t_e	Equivalent time constant
T_f	Torque due to friction
T_g	Decay time constant
T_h	Permissible run up time
T_i	Integration time constant
T_n	Reset time constant
$T_{n\beta}$	Adjustable reset time constant
T_t	Dead time constant
T_v	Phase advance constant

$T_{v\gamma}$	Adjustable phase advance time constant
T_A	Armature circuit time constant of electrical machine
T_D, T_d	Differentiation time constant
T_F	Field circuit time constant of electrical machine
T_{Ib}	Integration time constant of acceleration controller
T_M	Mechanical time constant
T_R	Rated troque
T_{SR}	Statistical dead time of a rectifier
T_W	Eddy current or damping time constant
T_1, T_2	Delay time constant, decay time constant
u	Input variable
u_{step}	Input step function
$\hat{u}$	Maximum value of first overshoot
v	Output variable
v, V	Voltage
v_{e1}, v_{e2}	Input voltages to difference amplifier
V, v	Voltage
V	Voltage source at amplifier output
V_a	Amplifier output voltage
V_{a0}	Initial value of V_a
$V_{a\infty}$	Steady state output voltage
$V_{a\,max}$	Maximum permisible value of output voltage
$V_{d\alpha}$	Rectified output voltage
V_e	Differential input voltage of amplifier
V_{e0}	Amplifier input offset voltage
V_g	Amplifier common mode input
V_h	Auxiliary voltage
V_i	Actual value of controlled variable
V_{iAact}	Actual value of transducer voltage measuring armature current
V_s	Command variable desired value
V_{st}	Drive voltage at input of rectifier unit
V_x, V_y	Input values of a multiplier circuit
V_A	Armature voltage of electrical machine
V_{AR}	Rated armature voltage of electrical machine
V_{B+}, V_{B-}	Limiting voltages
V_E	Common input potential
V_F	Field circuit voltage of electrical machine
V_H	Hall effect voltage
V_R	Controller output voltage
V_R	Rectifier control voltage

V_T	Tachogenerator voltage
V_{ref}	Stabilized reference voltage
V_0	Input voltage
ΔV_0	Input error signal to amplifier
ΔV_{0step}	Step value of ΔV_0
w	Command of input variable
w_{step}	Step change of w
x	Controlled variable
x^*	Voltage representations of controlled variable
x_a	Output variable of a system element
x_e	Input variable of a system element
y	Set variable
y^*	Representation of set variable
z	Disturbance variable
z_a	Complex output impedance of amplifier
z_e	Complex input impedance of amplifier
z_f	Feedback impedance
z_i	Internal impedance of input·voltage source
z_i	Impedance of control variable channel
z_s	Impedance of command variable channel
z_u	Transfer impedance of amplifier
z_0	Impedance of amplifier input channel
α	Feedback ratio
α	Rectifier triggering angle
δ	Decay coefficient
Δ	Small change of a variable
θ	Temperature
μ	Permeability of magnetic material
ξ	Damping factor
ϕ	Phase angle
ϕ	Flux of electrical machine
ϕ_R	Rated flux of electrical machine
ω	Angular frequency ($\omega = 2\pi f$)
ω	Rotational speed (rad s^{-1})
ω_g	Corner frequency in Bode plot
ω_R	Resonant frequency
$\omega_0, \omega_1, \omega_2$	Crossover frequencies in Bode plot
Ω	Normalized frequency
Ω_R	Frequency referrred to resonant frequency

7.2. Abbreviations

A	Output of amplifier
B−, B+	Limiting connections of amplifier
D	Differentiating
$D-T_1$	Second order delay
E−	Inverting input of amplifier
E+	Non inverting input of amplifier
I	Integrating
LO	Linear optimum
M	Reference potential (0 volt)
MO	Modulus optimum
N	Negative supply potential
P	Proportional
P	Positive supply potential
PD	Proportional—differentiating behaviour (phase advance)
PI	Proportional—integrating behaviour
$P-T_1$	First order delay
$P-T_2$	Second order delay
$P-T_t$	Dead time
SO	Symmetrical optimum

7.3. List of Transfer Functions and Corresponding Transient Functions

No.	Transfer function	Transient response
1.	A	A
2.	s	Unit impulse function
3.	$\frac{1}{s}$	1
4.	sT	Impulse function
5.	$\frac{1}{sT}$	$\frac{t}{T}$
6.	$1+sT$	1+impulse function
7.	$\frac{1}{1+sT}$	$1-e^{-t/T}$
8.	$\frac{1+sT}{sT}$	$1+\frac{t}{T}$
9.	$\frac{sT}{1+sT}$	$e^{-t/T}$

No.	Transfer function	Transient response
10.	$\dfrac{1+sT_a}{sT_1}$	$\dfrac{T_a}{T_1}+\dfrac{t}{T_1}$
11.	$\dfrac{sT_a}{1+sT_1}$	$\dfrac{T_a}{T_1}\,e^{-t/T_1}$
12.	$\dfrac{1+sT_a}{1+sT_1}$	$1-e^{-t/T_1}+\dfrac{T_a}{T_1}\,e^{-t/T_1}$
13.	$\dfrac{1}{1+s2\zeta T+s^2T^2}$	
	$0<\zeta<1$:	$1-\dfrac{1}{\sqrt{1-\zeta^2}}\,e^{-\zeta t/T}\sin\left(\dfrac{\sqrt{1-\zeta^2}}{T}\,t+\arccos\zeta\right)$
		$=1-e^{-\zeta t/T}\left(\cos\omega t+\dfrac{\zeta}{\omega T}\sin\omega t\right)$
		with $\omega=\dfrac{\sqrt{1-\zeta^2}}{T}$
	$\zeta=1$:	$1-\dfrac{T+t}{T}\,e^{-t/T}$
13a.	$\zeta>1$:	
	$\dfrac{1}{1+s2\zeta T+s^2T^2}$	$1-\dfrac{T_1}{T_1-T_2}\,e^{-t/T_1}-\dfrac{T_2}{T_2-T_1}\,e^{-t/T_2}$
	$=\dfrac{1}{(1+sT_1)(1+sT_2)}$	with $T_1=\dfrac{T}{\zeta-\sqrt{\zeta^2-1}}$,
	with $\zeta=\dfrac{1}{2}\sqrt{\dfrac{T_1}{T_2}+2+\dfrac{T_2}{T_1}}$	$T_2=\dfrac{T}{\zeta+\sqrt{\zeta^2-1}}$
14.	$\dfrac{1}{1+s2T+s^22T^2}$	$1-e^{-t/(2T)}\left(\cos\dfrac{t}{2T}+\sin\dfrac{t}{2T}\right)$
15.	$\dfrac{1}{1+s3T+s^22T^2}$	$1+e^{-t/T}-2e^{-t/(2T)}$
16.	$\dfrac{1}{1+s4T+s^24T^2}$	$1-e^{-t/(2T)}-\dfrac{t}{2T}\,e^{-t/(2T)}$
17.	$\dfrac{1}{1+s^2T^2}$	$1-\sin\left(\dfrac{t}{T}+\dfrac{\pi}{2}\right)$
18.	$\dfrac{1}{1+s4T+s^28T^2+s^38T^3}$	$1-e^{-t/(2T)}-\dfrac{2}{\sqrt{3}}\,e^{-t/(4T)}\sin\dfrac{\sqrt{3}}{4T}\,t$
19.	$\dfrac{1+s4T}{1+s4T+s^28T^2+s^38T^3}$	$1+e^{-t/(2T)}-2e^{-t/(4T)}\cos\dfrac{\sqrt{3}}{4T}\,t$
20.	$\dfrac{1}{sT_1(1+sT_1)}$	$\dfrac{1}{T_1}[t-T_1\{1-e^{-t/T_1}\}]$

No.	Transfer function	Transient response
21.	$\frac{1}{T_I} \cdot \frac{1}{(1+sT/n)(1+sT/n) \cdots}$	$\frac{1}{T_I}\left[t - T\left\{n - \frac{1}{n} e^{-nt/T}\left(\sum_{\nu=0}^{n-1} \frac{n-\nu}{\nu!}\left(\frac{nt}{T}\right)^{\nu}\right)\right\}\right]$
22.	$\frac{(1+sT_a)(1+sT_b)}{sT_I(1+sT_1)}$	$\frac{t}{T_I} + \frac{T_a + T_b}{T_I} + \frac{T_a T_b}{T_I T_1} e^{-t/T_1}$
23.	e^{-sT_t}	$\frac{X_e(t-T_t)}{X_e}$
24.	$\frac{1}{T_I} e^{-sT_t}$	$\frac{1}{T_I}[t - T_t]$

8. Bibliography

German sources: books

F. H. Effertz and F. Kolberg, *Einführung in die Dynamik selbständiger Regelungssysteme.* VDI-Verlag, Düsseldorf.

D. Ernst and D. Ströle, *Industrieelektronik, Grundlagen–Methoden–Anwendungen.* Springer-Verlag, Berlin, Heidelberg and New York (1973).

O. Föllinger, *Regelungstechnik, Einführung in die Methoden und ihre Anwendung,* 3rd Edn. Elitera-Verlag, Berlin (1980).

F. Fröhr and F. Orttenburger, *Technische Regelstrecken bei Gleichstromantrieben.* Siemens AG, Berlin and Munich (1971).

A. Hoffmann and K. Stocker, *Thyristor-Handbuch,* 4th Edn. Siemens AG, Berlin and Munich (1976).

A. Leonhard, *Die selbsttätige Regelung.* Springer-Verlag, Berlin, Heidelberg and New York.

W. Leonhard, *Einführung in die Regelungstechnik.* Friedr. Vieweg, Braunschweig (1969).

G. Möltgen, *Netzgeführte Stromrichter mit Thyristoren,* 2nd Edn. Siemens AG, Berlin and Munich (1971).

R. C. Oldenbourg and H. Sartorius, *Dynamik selbsttätiger Regelungen,* Vol. 1. R. Oldenbourg Verlag, Vienna and Munich.

W. Oppelt, *Kleines Handbuch technischer Regelvorgänge,* 5th Edn. Verlag Chemie, Weinheim (1972).

E. Pestel and E. Kollmann, *Regelungstechnik in Einzeldarstellungen,* Vol. 1: *Grundlagen der Regelungstechnik,* 3rd Edn. Verlag Franz Vieweg & Sohn, Wiesbaden (1979).

J. G. Truxal, *Entwurf automatischer Regelsysteme.* R. Oldenbourg Verlag, Vienna and Munich.

E. Samal, *Grundriß der praktischen Regelungstechnik,* Vol. 2. R. Oldenbourg Verlag, Vienna and Munich (1970).

VDE-Buchreihe, Vol. 2: *Energieelektronik und geregelte elektrische Antriebe.* VDE-Verlag, Berlin (1966).

German sources: journals

K. Böhm and F. Wesselak, Drehzahlregelbare Drehstromantriebe mit Umrichterspeisung. *Siemens Z.* **45,** 753 (1971).

D. Eichmann and I. Neuffer, Zur Anwendung integrierter Schaltungen in der Analogtechnik. *Siemens-Z.* **42,** 723 (1968).

N. Ettner, Berechnung und Auslegung von Regel-Einrichtungen. *Elektro-Anzeiger* 181 (1968).

N. Ettner, H. Gäde and W. Geyer, Projektieren von Regelanlagen mit Bausteinen des Systems TRANSIDYN B. *Siemens Z.* **39,** 860 (1965).

R. Fischer and P. Möller-Nehring, Kommandostufe für Antriebe mit Stromrichtern in kreisstromfreier Gegenparallelschaltung. *Siemens-Z.* **45,** 183 (1971).

F. Fröhr, Optimierung von Regelkreisen nach dem Betragsoptimum und symmetrischen Optimum. *Automatik* **12,** 9 (1967).

F. Fröhr, Drehzahlregelung von Gleichstrom-Antrieben. *Automatik* **13,** 126, 164 (1968).

W. Geyer and D. Ströle, Entwicklungstendenzen bei geregelten elektrischen Antrieben. *Siemens Z.* **39,** 490 (1965).

H. Gröne and H. Prenzlau, Thyristorbausteine und Thyristorsätze. *Siemens Z.* **42,** 253 (1968).

E. Grünwald, Entwurf von Reglern and Rückführungen. *Regelungstechnik* **3** issues 6, 7 (1955).

C. Kessler, Über die Vorausberechnung optimal abgestimmter Regelkreise. *Regelungstechnik* **2,** 274 (1954); **3,** 16, 40 (1955).

C. Kessler, Ein Verfahren zur Vorausberechnung von Regelkreisen. *Siemens Z.* **31,** issues 10, 11 (1957).

C. Kessler, Das symmetrische Optimum. *Regelungstechnik* **6,** 395, 432 (1958).

C. Kessler, Ein Beitrag zur Theorie mehrschleifiger Regelsysteme. *Regelungstechnik* **8,** 261 (1960).

I. Kröger, G. Lönne and M. Richter, Potentialtrennende Analogwertgeber für Strom und Spannung. *Siemens Z.* **45,** 744 (1971).

W. Leonhard and H. Müller, Stetig wirkender digitaler Drehzahlregler. *Elektrotech. Z. Ausg.* A **83,** 381 (1962).

W. Leonhard, Regelkreise mit symmetrischer Übertragungsfunktion. *Regelungstechnik* **13,** 4 (1965).

I. Neuffer, Stromrichterantriebe mit Momentenumkehr. *Siemens Z.* **39,** 1079 (1965).

K. Palme, Regel- und Antriebsmodell für Demonstrationzwecke in der Antriebstechnik. *Siemens Z.* **45,** 214 (1971).

W. Reinhold and G. Schlosser, Aufbau von Reglern im Bausteinsystem TRANSIDYN B. *Siemens Z.* **39,** 855 (1965).

D. Ströle, Adaptivsystem der elektrischen Antriebstechnik. *Elektrotech. Z. Ausg.* A **88,** 182 (1967).

E. Zemlin, Das Frequenzkennlinienverfahren. *Zeitschrift für Messen·Steuern Regeln* **2,** issue 7 (1959).

English language sources

J. J. D'Azzo and C. Houpis, *Linear Control Systems Analysis and Design*, 2nd Edn. McGraw-Hill, New York (1981).

A. J. Diefenderfer, *Principles of Electronic Instrumentation.* W. B. Saunders Co., Philadelphia (1972).

Electrical Engineering Handbook. Siemens AG and Heyden, London (1976).

J. G. Graeme, *Application of Operational Amplifiers.* McGraw-Hill, New York (1973).

S. C. Gupta, *Fundamentals of Automatic Control.* Wiley, New York (1970).

C. D. Johnson, *Process Control Instrumentation Technology.* Wiley, New York (1977).

D. E. Johnson, J. R. Johnson and H. P. Moore, *A Handbook of Active Filters.* Prentice-Hall, New Jersey (1980).

G. B. Rutkowsski, *Handbook of Integrated Circuit Operational Amplifiers.* Prentice-Hall, New Jersey (1975).

F. G. Shinskey, *Process Control Systems: Application, Design, Adjustment,* 2nd Edn. McGraw-Hill, New York (1979).

J. I. Smith, *Modern Operational Circuit Design.* Wiley-Interscience, New York (1971).

J. G. Truxal, *Control Systems Synthesis.* McGraw-Hill, New York (1955).

T. W. Weber, *An Introduction to Process Dynamics and Control.* Wiley-Interscience, New York (1973).

Index